MORALISM AND THE MODEL HOME

DOMESTIC ARCHITECTURE AND CULTURAL CONFLICT IN CHICAGO

1873-1913

MORALISM AND THE MODEL HOME

GWENDOLYN WRIGHT

THE UNIVERSITY OF CHICAGO PRESS
CHICAGO AND LONDON

The University of Chicago Press, Chicago 60637
The University of Chicago Press, Ltd., London

 Published 1980
Paperback edition 1985
Printed in the United States of America
94 93 92 91 90 89 88 87 86 85 6 5 4 3 2

Library of Congress Cataloging in Publication Data

Wright, Gwendolyn.
Moralism and the model home.

Bibliography: p.
Includes index.
1. Architecture, Domestic—Illinois—Chicago—Social aspects. 2. Architecture—Illinois—Chicago—Human factors. 3. Architecture and society—Illinois—Chicago. I. Title.
NA7238.C4W74 728.3′01′03 79-25584
ISBN 0-226-90835-6 (cloth)
ISBN 0-226-90837-2 (paper)

CONTENTS

ACKNOWLEDGMENTS

The work of many other historians has been invaluable for my wandering research on this book, and I would like to acknowledge my debts to them. Mark Peisch's and Carl Condit's books on the Chicago school of architecture and H. Allen Brook's investigations of the midwestern Prairie school provided the background for my own explorations. Vincent Scully and William H. Jordy have explored the cultural contexts of numerous well-known American buildings. Sam Bass Warner opened a new avenue of urban history with his studies of housing. John Brinckerhoff Jackson has given provocative readings of almost every aspect of the American environment, moving between numerous disciplines. Dolores Hayden's thorough scholarship in architectural and social history is combined with a determination to ask questions about the politics and ideology of design. Robert N. Bellah has illuminated a long and diverse American tradition of texts which rely on symbolic themes to promote social or political goals. And Herbert G. Gutman has infused his prodigious scholarship with a moving awareness of how the lives of families, political goals, and working conditions fit together into a complex whole.

Many friends and colleagues have thoughtfully read and discussed parts or all of this book with me, some of them seeing it through several incarnations. Spiro Kostof, Norma Evenson, and J. B. Jackson of the Department of Architecture at the University of California at Berkeley have been fastidious critics. Robert Bellah, Jeremy Brecher, Mason Cooley, Ruth Schwartz Cowan, Samuel Haber, Dolores

Hayden, Brian Horrigan, William H. Jordy, Florence Ladd, Lawrence Levine, Peter Marris, Albert Tannler, Joanna Taylor, Susana Torre, and Virginia Yans-McLaughlin have given me unfailing encouragement, valuable suggestions, and the examples of their own work. Katherine Ingley helped with the final checking of sources. The staffs of the Regenstein Library of the University of Chicago, the Chicago Historical Society, the Burnham Library of the Chicago Art Institute, the Newberry Library, the Schlesinger Library of Radcliffe College, the New York Public Library, the Avery Library of Columbia University, and the libraries of the University of California at Berkeley, especially the Environmental Design Library staff, have been extremely helpful. The Woodrow Wilson Foundation provided much-appreciated financial support. And, through it all, my husband, Paul Rabinow, helped me to clarify my ideas, to curb some of the excesses of moralistic rhetoric, and finally to finish the book and to go on and share our home.

INTRODUCTION

There are several ways in which architecture reveals the designer's cultural biases and often those of the larger society as well. When something is built, the process documents underlying structures of work, technology, and economics. It also serves as a metaphor, suggesting and justifying social categories, values, and relations. Domestic architecture in particular illuminates norms concerning family life, sex roles, community relations, and social equality. Of course, architecture itself does not directly determine how people act or how they see themselves and others. Yet the associations a culture establishes at any particular time between a "model" or typical house and a notion of the model family do encourage certain roles and assumptions.

The many Americans who have designed such model houses—and the group includes architects, carpenters, housewives, feminists, social critics, and industrialists—have generally tried to promote ideas of social welfare and family stability through their designs. The dwellings suited what each designer considered to be the "average American family." A shared belief professed that the home environment could mold or "influence" (to use the favored nineteenth-century term) both inhabitants and passersby. Individuals, families, communities, and, by accumulation, the larger society would reap the benefits of a fortuitous design or, likewise, bear the burden of a poor one. The architect Calvert Vaux, for instance, writing shortly before the Civil War, was one of many authors who told the story of a boy who declined into a covetous, disagreeable man. "The single explanation," Vaux mused, "is all-sufficient: he never had a pleasant home."[1] This awesome power raised the design exercises of these many individuals to a plane of social and moral reform.

However, despite the frequent similarities in preferred forms, this belief in the molding power of architecture also implied conflicts, for different groups of designers had very different visions of the future they were trying to bring into being through architecture. Economic, technological, political, and social forces, as well as individual artistry, have had a decided effect on the images and on the closely associated expectations for model-home designs. Rivalry among architects, builders, building workers, and reform-minded individuals has certainly cast its shadow across the pages of home design.

Today, the word "model" evokes an abstract, artificial construction, following ideal laws, against which ambiguous and complex social situations are judged. The model, then, in all likelihood, becomes not just an intellectual construct but a rigid structure imposed on a social situation. The political implications of their models were not lost on the writers and designers I am concerned with in this study. They often envisioned their model homes as one means for bringing order and control to what seemed dangerously volatile social conditions. Some of them demanded better opportunities for women outside the home, others that the nuclear family be stabilized at all costs. Some worried about too rapid and arbitrary a social mobility, others about the political demands of those whose opportunities had not arrived. Controlling aesthetic disorder seemed one method for controlling the society.

John Wellborn Root was one late-nineteenth-century architect who contrasted a harmonious environment of anonymous, simple, model cottages for the majority of Americans with a select number of finer, more individualized, expensive dwellings he and his associates would design for powerful and well-to-do clients. In contrast, the Chicago builders Samuel Eberly Gross and Fred Hodgson hoped to equalize American society by providing almost every family with its own distinct, moderate-cost, model dwelling. Usually these more popular designers wanted to introduce individual variations into each dwelling, offsetting the uniformity of a model. They linked this aesthetic variety with a more democratic and participatory approach to politics. However, the image one discerns in their work is that of a diverse but only theoretically equal society, not that of a political system that guaranteęs truly democratic government. Thus, the ways in which these men and women envisioned using the model home reveal deep strains in the culture, then and now. For many model-home designers and promoters, the image of improvement supplanted the complex politics of achieving it.

I am presenting the models for American home and family that were dominant over the four decades between 1873 and 1913. During this period, the form of the ideal middle-class dwelling underwent a major transformation: from an exuberant, highly personalized display of irregular shapes, picturesque contrasts, and varieties of ornament, supposedly symbolizing the uniqueness of the family, to a restrained and simple dwelling, with interest focused on its scientifically arranged kitchen. The twentieth-century model house was more visibly like the others in a planned, homogeneous community.

Analogous formal changes were, of course, taking place in many kinds of architecture and in every European country, as well as in the United States. Architectural historians have often tended to compare the formally similar work of architects in different countries, pointing to the spread of new aesthetic formulas within this elite. While architects do follow the formal and technological innovations of others within their profession, they are also deeply rooted in their particular cities and cultures. Many people other than architects have been involved in defining and spreading architectural reform. This is particularly true with something as deeply meaningful as the home. Architects have exchanges with people outside their profession which undeniably affect their theories and designs. Furthermore, most building and even most discussion about residential architecture takes place outside the profession, especially in cultures like our own where the environment is a lively topic. While professional architects generally view this interest as an intrusion on their domain, they have to respond to current ideas. Changes in form seldom result simply from an architect's ideas, achieved in a hermetic world of purely aesthetic criteria, which then filter down to the rest of the society. It is the interaction between architects and nonarchitects, between groups that sometimes have a common purpose and often are in bitter conflict, that leads eventually to any widespread change in the way buildings look and how they are used.

To focus on such distinctions, I have taken the example of one American city: Chicago. Here population expansion and the accompanying increase in the building of houses and the production of goods for them were especially striking to nineteenth-century observers. The great fire of 1871 made the need for more and better houses especially acute, and the need did not abate. Experiments in architecture, construction, politics, labor unionization, literature, and education all broke new ground in the decades after the fire. Reform activities of all sorts abounded. Many Chicagoans saw the middle-class house as a critical architectural and social issue. For styles and theories, they often had to rely on information and ideas from books and magazines published on the East Coast (or occasionally from Europe). But local architects, builders, building workers, progressive reformers, educators, journalists, settlement house residents, and women's rights activists all promoted what they believed to be the right kind of homes for their own changing city.

The opening and closing dates of this study also reflect the range of influences that have affected or subtly colored these model-house images. In 1873, Chicago inaugurated a grand Inter-State Exposition. The massive structure built for the exposition was filled with displays of the latest technological wonders and artistic objects and also with diverse exhibits of fashionable items for house-building, home decoration, and "home culture." Four decades later, images of the model home were presented in a fundamentally different way. A prominent local progressive group, the Chicago City Club, organized a competition for an entire model suburb in which the individual dwelling "units" were considered less important than a rational, balanced plan for the whole. The persons who now seemed best suited to undertake that scale of planning were professionally trained experts—architects, social scientists, and political advisers—who worked in close cooperation.

In addition to such public displays, the formal prototypes and the trumpeted reform themes of nineteenth- and early twentieth-century model houses circulated through printed media of many sorts.[2] Journals and books disseminated house designs, advice on family matters, and tips on running the household. These publications helped promote an elaborate domestic architecture and an equally elaborate set of references for interpreting the forms. My research relies primarily on three kinds of media, each dealing with housing as form and as social setting, each written by and for a different group: architectural books and periodicals, or the professional press; builders' trade journals and pattern books of house designs, or the more resolutely practical press;

and domestic guides and home magazines for women, as well as other middle-class family literature, or the popular press.

I am not suggesting that everyone who read these texts, or even all of the authors and designers themselves, actually believed that their various systems of social order would be achieved through architectural models alone. The rhetoric was, of course, an elaborate construction, not an actual social code for behavior or an infallible statement of principles. But these statements did express deeply felt social concerns. Even when attitudes about the family or about art or democracy were vague, contradictory, or self-serving, they nonetheless constituted an important set of shared issues for Americans. These considerations influenced designers of every rank and therefore affected the kinds of houses that were built. They also helped set expectations for family harmony and mobility, for wifely efficiency and household sanitation, for neighborhood organization and social services. While such expectations are not the same as actual practices, they did become cultural norms.

If one considers the issue of class, for example, the confused but nonetheless potent influence of this literature on housing becomes somewhat clearer. An assumption of class differences and a desire to prevent conflict engendered by those differences are inextricably bound up in the campaigns for model houses. Most American designers of this period envisioned homes for a society that would be virtually entirely middle-class (although architects consistently separated out one elite class of wealthy, educated individuals who would be the patrons for their designs). In such an American middle-class family, the husband might have been a salesman, a clerk, an accountant, or a skilled craftsman, working for a fixed salary. Throughout most of the nineteenth century, at least, it was assumed that his wife would remain at home, tending to house and children. The dwelling itself, and what went on there, as well as the man's employment, was considered one of the principal ways in which middle-class status could be established. Even the workers in the building trades who became involved in housing controversies often proposed and designed inexpensive housing models in order, they claimed, that every American could own a home and move into the ranks of the middle class. Issues born of economic inequalities, of social pressures and political goals, have often led to conflict but also have helped to define shared images of middle-class homes and the very idea of "middle class" in America.[3]

This is not to put forth a crude formula for a social or economic determination of architecture. Rather, I am attempting to elucidate the context in which architects, builders, building workers, reformers, and the publics they addressed decided what was appropriate for American homes. Within this framework, one does not find strict causes, only complex interrelations. There is room for artistic creativity that is independent of these influences. There is also ample room for chicanery by advertisers and developers who manipulate the images of home and family. But we can only begin to understand the creativity, or the manipulation for that matter, by placing these images and words in the cultural context from which they first emerged.

PART ONE

THE VICTORIAN CULTURE OF DOMESTICITY

1873–1893

1 POPULIST VISIONS

American architecture must aim at the benefit of the million.

Fred T. Hodgson, "Domestic Architecture," *Builder and Woodworker* (1884)

The celebration of the family home as a stronghold of traditional values and a refuge from the frenzy of city life permeated American literature throughout the nineteenth century. From the 1830s, authors of popular novels, magazine articles, and domestic guides (a flourishing literary form addressed largely to middle-class women) capitalized on such sentiments. Just below the poetic surface of Lydia Maria Child's widely read domestic guide, *The Frugal Housewife,* or the Reverend Jonathan Stearns's moralistic treatise, *Female Influence,* or a short story by Fanny Forrester were messages declaring the home's formative influence in the larger social and political world. Home, to these authors, was much more than a retreat. In a society with this preoccupation, it is not surprising that a complementary literature of architectural specifications soon emerged alongside the ringing prose of the moralists. In the 1840s, descriptions of model domestic settings supplemented the familiar florid tales of the ideal or the wayward family, providing intricate drawings and practical advice about the dwellings themselves. Both kinds of authors carefully outlined the characteristics of homes that would encourage or discourage proper family life and, in large enough numbers, determine the course of American society.

The treatises on residential design were usually written by carpenters or physicians, ministers or educators, novelists or housewives, rather than professional architects. (However, many of the carpenters and builders nonetheless called themselves architects, even though they had no formal training.) These authors wrote for a general audience, not for specialists. "That damned mob of scribbling women" condemned so bitterly by Hawthorne for its large following and sentimental prose used architectural descriptions of homes to strengthen stories and advice. These writers suggested the calibre of a family by focusing on the quality and upkeep of a home.[1] In maintaining a clean, artistic, personalized setting for the family's activities, the good wife was guiding her husband and children, forming their characters through the "influence" of the home environment. Dark suggestions that the saloon, the club, the office, or the bright lights of the city might intrude made this domestic mission all the more critical.

Another new area was that of "pattern books," which juxtaposed drawings of picturesque villas or cottages with extensive texts that explained to readers the meaning of the forms.[2] Almost all of the early pattern-book writers lived and practiced in the cities and towns of the East Coast. (During these years, later metropolises like Chicago were only recently founded towns, and their citizens would have to rely on pattern books from the East for several decades to come.)

The most famous pattern-book writer was the Hudson River Valley landscape architect Andrew Jackson Downing. In his magazine editorials and his books, especially *Cottage Residences* (1842) and *The Architecture of Country Houses* (1850), Downing outlined the architecture, decoration, and landscaping he deemed fitting for American homes.[3] Good residential architecture, based on variations of English Gothic Revival cottage-styles, would, Downing claimed, keep alive the Jeffersonian ideal of the private home as the basis of a stable society. To provide such representative dwellings for all Americans was the highest duty of the architect. Yet, Downing complained, the "dry and barren manner in which architects have usually written on the real meaning and philosophy of their art" revealed their inadequacies for the task. Others must take up the mantle of the designer, calling themselves architects if they wished, in order to stress the significance of their projects. If builders designed "republican homes," comfortable and beautiful, yet never so ostentatious as to belittle the neighbors or aggrandize the children's manners, they were worthy of the title of architect. Every American dwelling could be "a home of the virtuous citizen"—if American builders accepted this challenge.[4]

If few professionally trained architects heeded Downing,[5] other

Americans certainly did. His books sold through numerous editions. Inspired by them, one Philadelphia publisher, Louis Antoine Godey, decided to promote an "own-your-own-home" campaign by featuring American villa, cottage, and farmhouse designs in his monthly fashion journal for women. Between 1846 and 1898, *Godey's Lady's Book* published some 450 model-house designs. At first the designs were drawn directly from the English models of J. C. Loudon's *Encyclopedia*. Yet there was a strong undercurrent of nationalism in the descriptions. After 1854, the editor, Sarah Josepha Hale, announced that all "*Lady's Book* Houses" would henceforth come from American designers. As in the early years of the republic, American men and women from all backgrounds explored the notion of a distinctly American dwelling. Godey's journal published drawings and descriptions from Downing's books and from other recent pattern books of house designs, such as Henry Cleaveland's *Village and Farm Cottages* (1854) and Calvert Vaux's *Villas and Cottages* (1857). The dwellings were usually Gothic Revival cottages in lush, fertile landscapes, or occasionally more rambling and esoteric shapes, including octagons and other polyhedrons. Readers, whether they were housewives or carpenters, had only to write the journal's office to receive a full set of drawings for any model house; from these, they could adapt their own designs. According to one report, *Godey's* provided the models for over four thousand American houses in the first decade of the project alone.[6]

As important as the actual plans and specifications were the ideas about house design in these mid-century guides. The books were intended for a population still largely rural. A balance between practicality and individual expression was the goal; these dwellings were simultaneously genteel suburban villas and utilitarian American farmhouses. The populist builders promised to balance their stylistic exuberance with higher moral purpose by symbolizing in their designs, and thereby strengthening, both the nuclear family and the values of American democratic society. Their nationalism was vehement. John Bullock's *The American Cottage Builder* (1854), Gervase Wheeler's *Homes for the People in Suburb and Country* (1855), Charles Dwyer's *The Economic Cottage Builder* (1855), intended for recent immigrants, or even Catharine Beecher and Harriet Beecher Stowe's later treatise, *The American Woman's Home* (1869), all pledged to do much more than provide examples of good taste and current fashion.[7] The authors' mission, as their titles suggest, was to create and spread model houses that were distinctly American.

Most explanations of this idea proclaimed that American houses would be simple and economical, eschewing the taste for luxury and expense associated with the wealthy and their architects. The Gothic Revival details of good democratic homes, the argument continued, proudly revealed the unpretentious construction materials (notably wood) and their occupants' devout Christian values. Furthermore, a democracy required the celebration of differences in the pursuit of a common goal, so there would be appropriate styles for different locations, regions, and classes. Within a single text might be houses intended for hillsides, lakesides, and bustling towns. There would be cottages costing twenty dollars and mansions estimated at twenty thousand dollars. Domestic architecture, these builder-theorists explained, should express the owner's occupation and background, as well as values held in common with other citizens. (The man of the household was always the reference in this iconography.) Downing catalogued three kinds of houses for three groups in the society: villas for "persons of competence," cottages for mechanics or working men, and farmhouses for farmers.[8] In sum, the homes built from these pattern-book models were supposed to reinforce both a democratic spirit of progress and an individual family's sense of privacy.

Despite the nationalistic fanfare, the primary source for much of this popular romantic theory about the home in the antebellum decade, and for a long time after the war's end, came from abroad. All over the country, people of every class, from the mechanic to the dowager, had become familiar with the aesthetic and social theories of John Ruskin. Books, articles, and lectures for every kind of audience cited him reverently. Ruskin's most important writings on architecture—*The Stones of Venice* and *The Seven Lamps of Architecture*—were first published in England between 1849 and 1854. American editions were immediately available, and continued to be popular for more than four decades, with over one hundred editions and issues of his works appearing before 1895.

With Ruskin, domestic architecture was a critical moral issue. He specified that moral principles should be central to the choice of a house design, not only for elegant country houses but for small cottages too. Ruskin emphasized that each dwelling should reveal something about the personal character and class, or "condition," of the occupant. But even more important, especially for smaller, less pretentious cottages, were the general domestic sentiments that should be symbolized, strongly and clearly, in the facade and the interior decor. Every residential design should emphasize certain architectural elements—prominent chimneys and fireplaces, wide overhanging roofs, and bay windows—which, according to Ruskin, evoked the revered domestic virtues of protection, security, trust, and traditional family bonds. The sight of these architectural details would then inspire anyone, passerby or resident, with recollections of home, and thereby reinforce the family-based strengths of Anglo-Saxon culture. All architecture, Ruskin claimed, was, "in some sort the embodiment of the Polity, Life, History, and Religious Faith of nations," but it was domestic architecture, above all, that possessed the power to uplift as well as reflect human development.[9]

The associations Ruskin drew between architectural details and domestic virtues encouraged many Americans to hope that house design could indeed strengthen middle-class home life. Several of Ruskin's other well-known texts, more sentimental and less architectural, raised this celebration of the home to a cult. A typical passage from *Sesame and Lilies* sets the tone:

> This is the true nature of home—it is the place of peace; the shelter, not only from all injury, but from all terror, doubt and division. In so far as it is not this, it is not home; so far as the anxieties of the outer life penetrate into it, and the inconsistently-minded, unloved, or hostile society of the outer world is allowed by either husband or wife to cross the threshold it ceases to be a home; it is then only a part of the outer world which you have roofed over and lighted fire in. But so far as it is a sacred place, a vestal temple, a temple of the hearth . . . it is a home.[10]

The true home kept a delicate balance, then. It had to feature prominently the architectural and decorative motifs which represented domestic virtues. And it had to appear as individual and independent, safe from the intrusions of others, as possible.

Authors of popular American domestic theory, whether they were builders offering guidelines on construction or women advising other women about house decor, drew extensively from Ruskin. In many ways, in fact, vernacular literature paralleled the professional architectural treatises of the time, citing the same sources and expressing similar attitudes about American culture. Yet both popular writers and professional architects claimed that they alone understood the true significance of Ruskin and the needs of the American people. Accordingly, each group chastized the other's presumptive statements about these matters.

The antagonisms involved issues of style, ability, and understanding. Thus, the builders' literature increasingly tended toward an effusive rhetoric and a tolerance for stylistic freedom of interpretation. Most contemporary architects scorned this literature. Many later social and architectural historians have, as a consequence, bypassed these writings and designs. Yet, the populist campaigns for an American domestic architecture constitute an important set of documents. From them it is possible to glean the common ideology of home and family, the most pervasive aesthetic ideas about architecture and furnishings, and the probable ways families might have used the various spaces in and around their homes. One can explore how popular ideas about family, health, and other such matters influenced architectural styles, and how fashions were passed down to the general public. In addition, the carpenters' and builders' hopes for social reform and their attempts to manipulate those hopes for personal profit become clearer. The first task in this exploration is to decipher the builders' philosophy.

The fact that they were designing for a large, often anonymous audience, attempting to reach as many people as possible, was significant to the nineteenth-century American builders. It signalled the principal difference distinguishing them from professional architects. The scope of their practice gave them the right to take over the term "architect," as Downing and others had suggested, because they were, in fact, the nation's true designers. Until the end of the century, no regulations prevented them from doing so. Even if a man, or occasionally a woman, lacked apprentice training in an architect's atelier and the thorough education in historical scholarship which supposedly characterized the professional architect, it was permissible for that person to call himself, or herself, an architect. And many did so, proud of their own calling.

George O. Garnsey, a self-proclaimed architect who practiced in Chicago and was editor of a magazine on house design, made the architect-builders' cause into a crusade. "Architectural journals there are in profusion," he wrote in the first editorial for the *National Builder* in 1885, "but they are too theoretical and aesthetic to meet the needs of practical men actually engaged in the erection of buildings.''[11] Several months later he taunted the professionals who were displeased with his practical journal which had so boldly announced its campaign to spread knowledge about construction and design.

> [In] educating the builder we educate the people, and in directing the minds of the proprietor in the right direction we materially assist the builder. Architects criticize this journal because we are giving information to the people broadcast, and free of cost, that we supply plans and specifications, details and estimates to the proprietor and builder alike at a ridiculously low price. . . .[12]

The builders' appropriation of the name ''architect,'' at a time when criticism of professional elitism was extensive, bespoke a sense of mission. The affrontery infuriated the professionals, who nonetheless, as we shall see, would have an increasingly difficult time explaining the differences between the two groups.

The Home and the Commercial World

In the decades following the Civil War, the antagonism between professional architects and builders intensified, fanned by a growing awareness of the potential market for new homes. Both groups recognized that styles of domestic architecture and furnishing were becoming more complicated and ornate as new fashions and products became available; each group wanted to direct the course of architectural planning. The builders' press, still located predominantly on the East Coast, but slowly moving into other regions by the 1880s, provided thousands of illustrations and pages of advice for would-be homeowners and enterprising builders. The professional architectural press tried to rise above this ordinary market with more esoteric writing and more expensive dwellings. Yet the architects still claimed to influence all residential design by their elegant examples. But, before we examine the formal and philosophical tenets of the builders' guides, and the differences between these guides and architects' treatises, it is worth considering the commercial situation which supplied the texts and the products both groups recommended.

Chicago was the bright star on the western horizon during these years, a town suddenly propelled into national stature. Its 1850 population of thirty thousand had grown to almost ten times that number two decades later. New industries brought commerce, capital, and workers. Refrigeration cars, invented in 1869, stimulated the local packing industry; grain elevators rose along the river to store the products of the midwestern fields, while the McCormick plant supplied agricultural implements to the thriving farms. A midcontinental junction with water and rail connections, the city had also recently become a center for lumber trade and for steel production. This sudden prominence altered the city's industrial area, and then every part of Chicago. Potter Palmer transformed a muddy, sleepy State Street into a thriving commercial district with a luxury hotel and two majestic department stores. The great fire of 1871 in effect fanned this already vigorous growth. Adopting the emblem of the phoenix rising from its own ashes, the city immediately began rebuilding its downtown business district in the image of a thriving,modern metropolis of skyscrapers.

Boosters' enthusiasm ran high. Among others, however, there was an undeniable sense of inferiority about Chicago's houses. While some observers insisted that no slums existed there, and that every worker could own his own small frame house (ungainly and unsanitary though the observer might have found it), other people worried about the crowded and unhealthy back-alley housing in which many immigrant families were forced to live. At the opposite end of the scale, wealthy families began to commission celebrated East Coast architects to design mansarded mansions along Michigan Avenue and then Prairie Avenue, hoping to be able to assure themselves of a solid image of taste, propriety, and fortune. Yet these monuments seemed inadequate symbols of domesticity for the city as a whole. As early as the 1870s, critics levelled charges that Chicago's domestic architecture lagged far behind its commercial and industrial architecture. The same indictments would echo again and again through the end of the century. Some people blamed the situation on transience, others on ignorance, others on the Chicagoan's consuming interest in making money, an interest that overshadowed more idealistic concerns. The hope seemed to lie in the new suburbs; as early as 1873, the *Chicago Times*, claiming nearly one hundred such settlements already existed, predicted that soon "what is now the prairie beyond will be gridironed."[13] In the suburbs, Chicagoans would find true homes: detached, tiny villas on bucolic lots, not far from the city itself.

Despite the charges that Chicago citizens did not care about their homes, most city dwellers and suburbanites were deeply involved in issues of house design and furnishings. Women saw in their homes their greatest opportunity to raise the family's status, inspire the children to future success, and demonstrate their own taste and talents. Their husbands were willing, if not always believing, accomplices in these schemes to improve the home. Moreover, many men's jobs were either directly or indirectly involved in the business of residential construction and home furnishing. The excitement aroused by Chicago's commercial activity and her business buildings certainly did not eradicate the general interest in homes, especially not during a period when "home influence" was considered so powerful a force.

In fact, the rapid commercial expansion in the years after the Civil War actually promoted this focus on the home. The large department stores eagerly provided the latest household goods for customers, ranging from inexpensive bric-a-brac, imitating European antiques, to American-manufactured wallpapers. Impressive fairs and exhibitions presented elaborate displays of the latest products for the home as well as the most recent industrial and agricultural advances, offering thousands of visitors the appealing vision of domestic splendor.

The most famous of these great spectacles, at least until the end of the century, was the Crystal Palace, which was erected in London in 1850–51. An American version, hosted by New York City, proved a financial failure. It was not until the expansive years after the Civil War that such expositions became popular and profitable. The first major American fair, a model for the Philadelphia Centennial of 1876, was Chicago's Inter-State Industrial Exposition. It was first held in 1873 and continued to be an annual event until the end of the century. The backers, mostly local politicians and businessmen like Potter Palmer and Marshall Field, saw the exposition as a way to sponsor the city's industrial and artistic achievements, displaying the latest goods for farm and factory, home and office, to thousands of marveling visitors.

Even if most of the attention was focused on technical means for providing beauty in the home and productivity in the workplace, the domestic setting was not excluded from the exposition. In an elegant structure designed by W. W. Boyington—a building 200 by 800 feet, of brick, stone, cast iron, and glass, lighted by massive glass domes and Gothic windows—cast-iron booths presented an array of the latest plumbing equipment and the most fashionable parlor furniture, alongside exhibits of farm produce, machinery, and crowd-pleasing exotic wonders like the stuffed polar bear. Manufacturers of goods for residential construction were also prominent, displaying an impressive variety of brick and stonework, saws and stencils, wood and terra-cotta detailing for inside and outside the dwelling. Entire model rooms were constructed by the department stores (the most lavish being those of Marshall Field's) and by the major local furniture companies. Here visitors could see a fashionable way of combining the latest furniture, mantels, wallpaper, and rugs, with their own handmade "personal" art objects.[14] As in the contemporary pattern-book descriptions, these arrangements emphasized a complicated combination of the personal and the universal, the expressive and the uplifting, the interesting and the instructive.

Exhibitions like Chicago's, as well as the ever more sumptuous department stores, attempted to be constantly innovative. The lavish new displays transformed the pattern-book components of an ideal house into three-dimensional objects to be seen and then purchased. The focus on the home is important, not only because it relates to the evolution of styles for home design, but also because of the quite straightforward connection between the home, a haven of personal life, and advances in American industrial production. Perhaps, as many critics observed, American art was dwarfed by the quality of European work. But "household art" seemed a national talent that would unite art and industry. William Dean Howells, visiting the Philadelphia Centennial, was one of many commentators who expressed the hope that American technology would help this country achieve the same artistic level as that reached by the English. He envisioned an American commitment to democratic art, bringing splendor into every home through mass production, although he cautiously recognized the danger of relying too absolutely on technology.[15]

The expression of such hopes for American domestic culture, like the products that supposedly embodied that culture, prompted an outpouring of popular treatises on the domestic environment. At the time of Chicago's exposition, hundreds of American builders and amateur designers were turning to the printed page to publicize their causes and their designs. As Clarence Cook, a prominent New York art critic, wrote in 1878, "There never was a time when so many books written for the purpose of bringing the subject of architecture—its history, its theory, its practice—down to the level of popular understanding were produced as in this time of ours."[16] In addition to those who built, there were now many men and women who simply wrote about domestic architecture with a donnish and moralistic intensity. This group, in the course of elevating certain styles and condemning others, gave fastidiously exacting instructions to housewives and home-buyers. They insisted that the recent diversity in products, the greater choice in styles, required expert advice, if one were to achieve the desired effect.

Middle-class Americans wanted morality with their art, especially in the home. These writers eagerly explained how the dwelling could be used as a didactic setting. The good homemaker could instill virtue in her family through careful choice of architectural detail and furnishing. Clarence Cook, for instance, in articles written for *Scribner's Monthly* in 1876, collected and reprinted two years later as *The House Beautiful*, explained how a house filled with "interesting and instructive" objects could become "an important agent in the education of life."[17] While he paid his respects to American carpenters, with their robust endorsement of personal expression in domestic architecture, Cook stressed the need to combine such expression with more refined "high art." The housewife could, in effect, buy a virtuous home. He demonstrated how the principles of honesty, simplicity, and economy—evoked by educated Gothic Revivalist architects and American vernacular builders alike—could be parlayed into lavish mixes of styles in a single room. He showed illustrations (fig. 1) which featured rich tapestries, upholstery, drapery, and pillows to soften the "art groupings" of inspiring objects, both purchased and handmade. But the woman's passivity in Cook's portrait suggests that she is no longer making as much finery for her home.

According to many such domestic guides, education in the home was no longer primarily a social activity in which the mother talked with her children; it was the passive contemplation of universally acclaimed objects of beauty. The art-minded homemaker no longer made all the pieces of inspiration for her parlor. Her own taste and ability were not necessarily refined and aesthetic. She now personalized rooms in a different way: by filling them with mass-produced art objects, then arranging these in a manner that was fashionable, educational, and individualistic.

The women who gave advice on homemaking continued to emphasize the moral influence of the domestic environment, too. However, like Cook, they were well aware of the recent increases in factory production of art objects, furnishings, and architectural detailing for

Figure 1. Interior study depicting "Much in Little Space." (From Clarence Cook's *The House Beautiful,* 1878.)

the middle-class American home. Interior decorators provided by major department stores in the 1880s helped clients buy "truly artistic" furniture and bric-a-brac. Women who wrote about the home tended to balance their enthusiasm for the varieties of new merchandise with a more traditional reverence for personalized interiors and handmade decor. A few even insisted that simple arrangements produced the best home environments. Ella Rodman Church, for instance, writing in 1881, declared that "Art does not exact costly things, but it requires sincere things."[18] Yet even her opposition to extravagance suggests the extent to which commercialization had entered the domestic sphere. By the 1880s, most women who handed out decorating advice combined a rhetoric of idealism with a strong endorsement of the many kinds of household furnishings on the market. Quantity would increase the effect of "home-training," they promised. As Harriet Spofford explained, "Provided there is space to move about, without knocking over the furniture, there is hardly likely to be too much in the room."[19]

There was strong opposition to the commercialization of the home, and to the general reliance on technology in late-nineteenth-century American life. Yet it seemed to many people that the abundance of objects now available for their homes would, in fact, help define the home as a place of beauty, comfort, and individuality. Small builders, who relied on magazines and catalogues for new images and materials, were caught in much the same quandary as the women who extolled the idealized home. They both recognized their mutual dependence on industrial production and advertising, as well as on the pervasive interest in domestic life. But it was easier to downplay the fact of the commercialized home, and instead claim to be protecting ideals.

The Builders' Program

By the 1870s, American builders had established a well-defined and widely circulated literature for spreading their popular domestic advice. In addition to pattern books and domestic guides, numerous journals provided builders and other interested readers with up-to-date models for homes and a running commentary on the designs. The *American Builder and Journal of Art,* published under various titles in New York and Chicago between 1868 and 1895, was the best known. In its pages could be found a surprising variety of viewpoints about architecture in general and houses in particular. There were learned articles on the major English theorists; designs by trained architects such as William Woollett, Solon S. Beman, and Margaret Hicks (the builders' press was consistently favorable toward women in all architectural fields); models from pattern-book designers, notably from E. G. W. Dietrich and George Palliser of New York and D. S. Hopkins of Grand Rapids; practical advice on home sanitation from Catharine Beecher; and specifications from the manufacturers of prefabricated dwellings, woodworking machinery, and plumbing equipment.[20]

When Congress lowered the postage rates for magazines in 1879, the number of journals and their circulation jumped ahead. *Carpentry and Building* was founded in New York. *The Carpenter,* organ of the United Brotherhood of Carpenters, was established in Philadelphia in 1881 by the union's founder, the socialist Peter McGuire. *Scientific American* began its architects' and builders' edition, entitled *Building Monthly,* which gave special notice to the latest equipment for construction and sanitation. In New York, William T. Comstock, a well-known publisher of architectural books, founded the weekly *Building* magazine, and Robert W. Shoppell, director of the Co-Operative Building Plan Association, later began a quarterly publication, *Shoppell's Modern Houses.* By the end of the 1880s, Chicago had joined in and soon became the nation's third-largest publishing center, the base for scores of journals connected with the building and decoration of homes. These included publications with titles like *National Builder, American Furniture Gazette, Careful Builders, Sanitary News, Domestic Engineering, American Artisan,* and *Art Review.* The range was great, covering domestic architecture as art form, national culture, commercial market, and sanitary problems.

In these journals, despite their seeming diversity, one can find clear, consistent statements about values, both for architecture and for society. The themes of providing for the private family, advancing democracy, and opposing the architectural profession were intricately woven together. In a long American tradition, the editors, authors, and designers for these journals must be considered "populists," given their strong attacks against elite privilege and special interests, and their fervent defense of ordinary citizens' rights, in this case, to solid homes and good design.

Editors of most of the late-nineteenth-century American builders' journals, as well as their readers, were quite suspicious of European precedent, which was considered the special province of the trained architect. The theme of luxury as the great corrupter, the favorite tool of despots, had been a pervasive one since the eighteenth century.

Many Americans both feared and resented the evidence of idle pleasure among the wealthy, and European art seemed especially decadent.[21] Shoppell emphasized the originality of the American carpenter and the variety of the simple, indigenous house-forms that made up his heritage. David Williams, editor of *Carpentry and Building*, condemned those who relied on the houses of the well-to-do for inspiration, charging that these were aristocratic efforts to make the inhabitants appear more prestigious than their neighbors. Most mansions, he claimed, were "pedantic" attempts to copy European, and especially French Beaux-Arts, forms. American architects and their clients, he charged, did not dare exercise their own imaginations.[22]

There was, all the same, some sympathy for English forms. Even Williams showed examples of brickwork and terra-cotta ornament, clearly and carefully derived from English High Gothic sources. The *American Builder* often featured illustrations of English gate lodges and praised their picturesque lines. But most of these writers and builders insisted that there had to be a peculiarly American response to these English forms. It was the spirit of inventiveness, in aesthetics as in technology, and the drive for economy of materials, labor, and upkeep, that they saw as typically American.

Even the tone of the builders' pattern books and journals was distinct from the formality of the architectural press. These populist writers addressed their readers with comradely sympathy and respect. Gilbert Croff, in *Progressive American Architecture*, paid his courtesies to "the art-loving and mechanical public." He promised them his best and most diligent work, "very elaborate, but cheaply constructed designs" of all shapes and sizes.[23] This abundant creativity was, above all, the mark of the American builder.

Stylistic accuracy, or even stylistic consistency in a single dwelling, did not matter. The aim was visual delight. Tudor mullioned windows, Corinthian columns, delicate Adamesque relief, and heavy neo-Gothic balustrades might be applied to the same facade. According to popular design theory, the choices would reflect the individuality of the occupants and the vigor of the national creative spirit. Illustrations were often lively sketches of interior scenes, suggesting how rooms might be used and enjoyed rather than how the detailing had been refined. In every builder's guide, intimate spaces were considered more fitting than grand architectural ones, since the aim was expressly to describe an average family at home (fig. 2). Authors often mentioned

Figure 2. Interior study of a library. (From the *National Builder Album of Beautiful Homes,* published in Chicago by George O. Garnsey, 1891. Courtesy of the Art Institute of Chicago.)

a bay window for a vase of roses, a niche for the well-used piano, a mantel for hand-painted porcelain, hunting trophies, or other personal treasures. Sometimes, even the names selected for rooms in pattern-book stories supposedly reflected personal or family priorities—the "growlery" for the husband's retreat from domestic fuss, the "family room" for evening togetherness.

Most popular builders of the 1870s and 1880s began to invent and publicize new interpretations of existing fashions. The Palliser brothers, two builders from Bridgeport, Connecticut, authors of a dozen widely read pattern books, wrote in one preface that "present styles, while bearing many characteristics of their prototypes, do not adhere strictly to any of them." Eleven years later, in 1887, they claimed that "American Homes of to-day [are] not, however, of any well-defined style of Architecture, except what may be termed our National style,"[24] by which they seem to have meant eclecticism or stylistic invention. They had successfully replaced the artificial "regulations" of academic foreign transplants and the monotony of the Greek Revival (characterized by the Pallisers as a "vulgar, meaningless, square-box or barnesque style") with a seemingly unlimited profusion of vigorous hybrids. Their "popular teachings," the Pallisers contended, echoing other builders, had improved the public taste and given new expression to the American way of life.[25] Architects, in contrast, were bound to the traditions of Europe and the beck-and-call of the wealthy.

The material carried in the builders' journals did in fact excite many Americans, who saw technical improvements, united with moral purpose, as the way to social progress. Daniel Coit Gilman, president of Johns Hopkins University, an advocate of functional rather than fashionable institutional buildings, praised the advantages technology could bring to the home. Machinery "brings to every cottage of our day," he declared, "comforts and adornments which in the days of Queen Bess . . . were not known outside of the palace."[26] A. J. Bicknell & Co. received a special award from the Philadelphia Centennial for "the Cheapness and Value of sundry Architectural Publications."[27] The spread of information about domestic architecture, as well as the multiplication of actual goods—both art objects and mechanical equipment—for more homes, seemed the sign of democratic progress.

Editors of builders' journals, authors of pattern books, and writers of domestic advice all claimed that they were leading a crucial national reform by focusing on the housing needs of middle-class Americans. Yet their program for democracy through residential design, like their opposition to the architectural profession as an aristocratic institution, was, for the most part, inchoate. The appeals for diversity fostered designs that were at times awkward and fussy, if at others delightfully imaginative. The profuse ornament could often become expensive as well as flamboyant, especially since most builders concentrated on the individual dwelling rather than on the block or the neighborhood. Not with a theoretical stand but with euphoric rhetoric, these popular authors dodged one of the principal issues perplexing professional architects, that of uniformity. They simply insisted that it was possible to have an infinite amount of variation on any theme.

In fact, beneath the profuse ornament of late-nineteenth-century houses, standardization was a reality. Certainly even the builders knew this, despite their appeals for individualized architecture. Simple economics dictated building from similar floor plans, so that carpenters and masons would be familiar with the arrangement and so that materials could be ordered with greater accuracy. Lot sizes in most subdevelopments were standard rectangular sections of a grid plan. Equally important was the need to have a clear code of meaning in these homes. If the essence of a Victorian middle-class home was its symbolic values, its messages and reminders to family and neighbors, then a common set of meanings for architectural details was necessary. The home had to be based upon a readily understood language of these symbols, a precise vocabulary of forms, so that it could be easily read and understood.

Certain themes were especially important to all late-nineteenth-century writers on the home. Invariably, suburban architecture of the period referred to these ideals in certain specific ways. For instance, in popular iconography, closeness to nature was paramount. The natural environment in which the dwelling was set was to be an inspiration for the individual, a reminder to the family members of their place in the God-given order of the universe, and a miniature vision of the nation's vast bounty. Planners of earlier exclusive suburbs of Chicago like Lake Forest and Riverside had emphasized the picturesque qualities of the site, with curving roads and lush landscaping. However, the site chosen for a late-nineteenth-century moderate-income subdivision was often rather barren and flat; for economy, the developers preferred to lay out gridiron streets and undertake as little improvement as possible. Despite names like Forest Glen, Halcyon Heights, and Galewood—three developments of the mid-1870s on the outskirts of Chicago—few of the new suburbs were arcadian joys. Nonetheless, the architecture of the houses could assert almost as much naturalism as the landscape itself.

The work of the Chicago architect-builder George Garnsey illustrates the techniques vividly (fig. 3). The irregular shape of each house was intended as a sign of natural complexity, as well as an expression

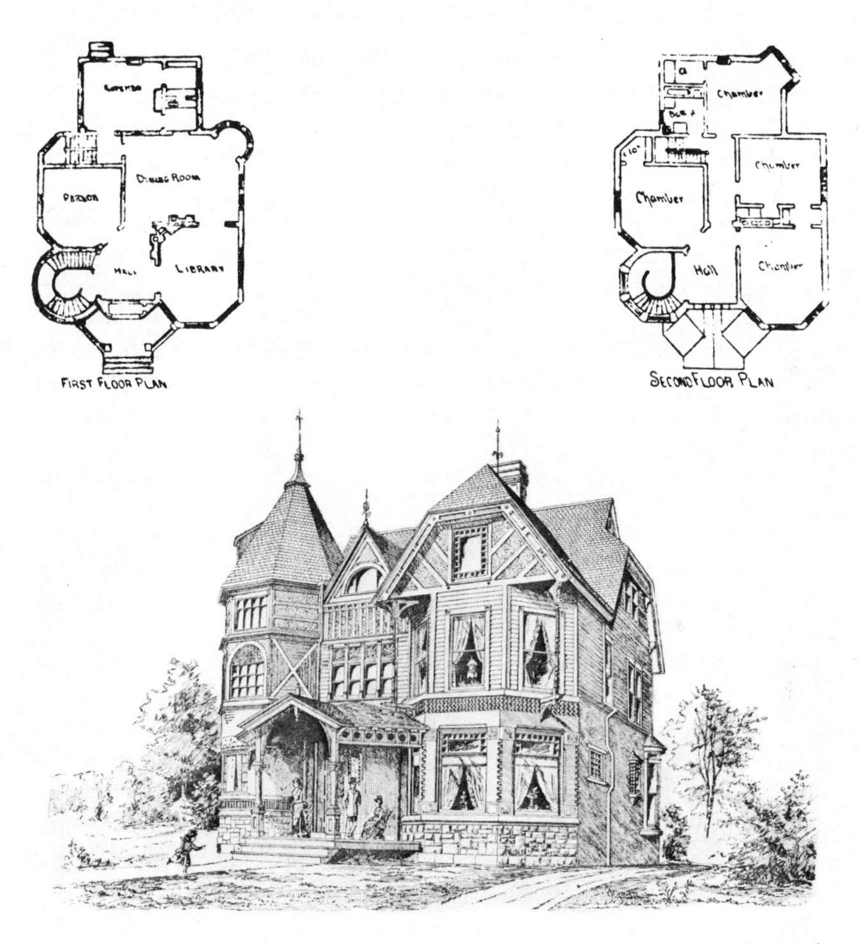

Figure 3. Model house design by Chicago's George O. Garnsey. (From the *National Builder,* 1886.)

of the particular family's daily domestic activities. In a series entitled "How To Build a House," published in the *National Builder,* Garnsey encouraged readers to be imaginative, to avoid the "dry-goods box" look of a plain square house. "Don't be afraid to introduce breaks, jogs and angles, the more the better," he counseled, for "an irregular plan breaks the sky line at the roof and lends picturesque beauty to the exterior corners, [while it] costs comparatively nothing."[28]

Furthermore, the natural home was to have the appearance of

having grown up out of the earth's rugged and varied materials. Materials for the facade were chosen and put together in a way that was, in theory, imitative of nature's complex juxtaposition of color and texture. Rough limestone, cedar shingles, moss-green patina on slate tiles, all on a single facade, gave the look of venerable age to a new house. Sometimes the wood was left unfinished to achieve the slow silver-gray of time. But it was faster, and therefore more common, to simulate the hues of nature with mineral paints and stains in the deep reds and greens of leaves or mosses, the soft browns and grays of weathered wood. Even the lines of the house drew it down close to the ground. The deeply sloping irregular roof, with overhanging eaves and decorated barge boards or brackets beneath each gable, emphasized the horizontal ground plane. So too did the use of different materials for the first and second stories (usually clapboards or brick, or perhaps more expensive "nature's stone" below, with shingles above). All of these principles were laid out in the best-known pattern books, beginning with Calvert Vaux's, who had told his readers to trust their "instinctive good taste" in the choice of a minimum of four colors for the facade of a house.[29]

The fashionable Victorian home opened wide to the out-of-doors. Designs emphasized openness between interior and exterior, between the built environment and the natural. Houses usually had large bay windows, with wide panes of glass to let in sunlight and fresh air, while offering residents a pleasant view. The porch, too, was being handled in a different way. In the last quarter of the nineteenth century, spacious porches of varied shapes and sizes appeared all around the house. There were entrance porticoes and simple back service porches, open verandas (galleries along the side of a building), piazzas (an Americanism for the veranda), upper-floor balconies and porte cocheres for carriages. These porches often had specific uses: resting, dining, or doing household chores, watching the afternoon sun or relaxing in the evening breezes of summer. Their ornamentation also became more elaborate by the 1880s; support posts were rounded rather than squared-off, and were heavy with detailing.

The widespread interest in presenting the house as a part of a well-ordered natural system even came into the parlor. By the late 1870s, popular decorations included pine-cone frames and gray southern moss draped over a molding, leaves pinned up to make a cornice or suspended with thread over an entrance as if they were falling. Bay window conservatories of potted plants were found in many homes. Just as the house now opened more to the outdoors through windows and bays and porches, women in particular were eager to bring nature into the home and cultivate it. The ideal was to show the changing seasons, the varied forms, the luxuriant richness of nature. But underlying even this fashionable display was the desire to control that world, to impose upon it a clearly human organization, to allay fears of death and decay by domesticating and preserving the smallest twigs and flowers. In all of the many ways in which the Victorian builder and housewife attempted to evoke natural bounty, they clearly sought to contain it as well.

The yard figured prominently in almost every pattern-book illustration of the period, whether the house was large or small (fig. 4). Often people were shown playing some newly popular outdoor game, or watching the activity from an open turret balcony or a spacious porch. The yards in these illustrations—with their badminton or croquet matches, frolicking children and leisurely observers—were uncommonly commodious. The intent seems to have been to stress the autonomy of each estate, and through it the independence of each family.

The proper site, however, like so many of these architectural symbols of model domestic life, was also a practical matter. In those days when summer camps, national parks, and resort hotels caught the fancy of the middle class, the pleasures of outdoor life were widely touted. Fresh air and exercise were considered healthy, and good health was a major promotion theme for suburban life. Disease, and especially the epidemics which still struck the large cities, seemed frightening and mysterious matters to most people. Fraught with anxiety, they turned to experts for advice about protecting their families (although many people were also suspicious of the new techniques in treatment). In the 1870s, several English physicians' texts on household sanitation reached the American public. B. W. Richardson's utopian vision and Henry Hartshorne's practical report both warned that industrialization had destroyed the natural balance; now it was necessary to rely on elaborate technological precautions—better systems of heating, ventilation, and draining—in order to prevent massive epidemics.[30] Soon American doctors and sanitarians were publishing their own treatises on household sanitation. In terms of epidemiology, some of these analyses were correct and others were not. Professor William H.

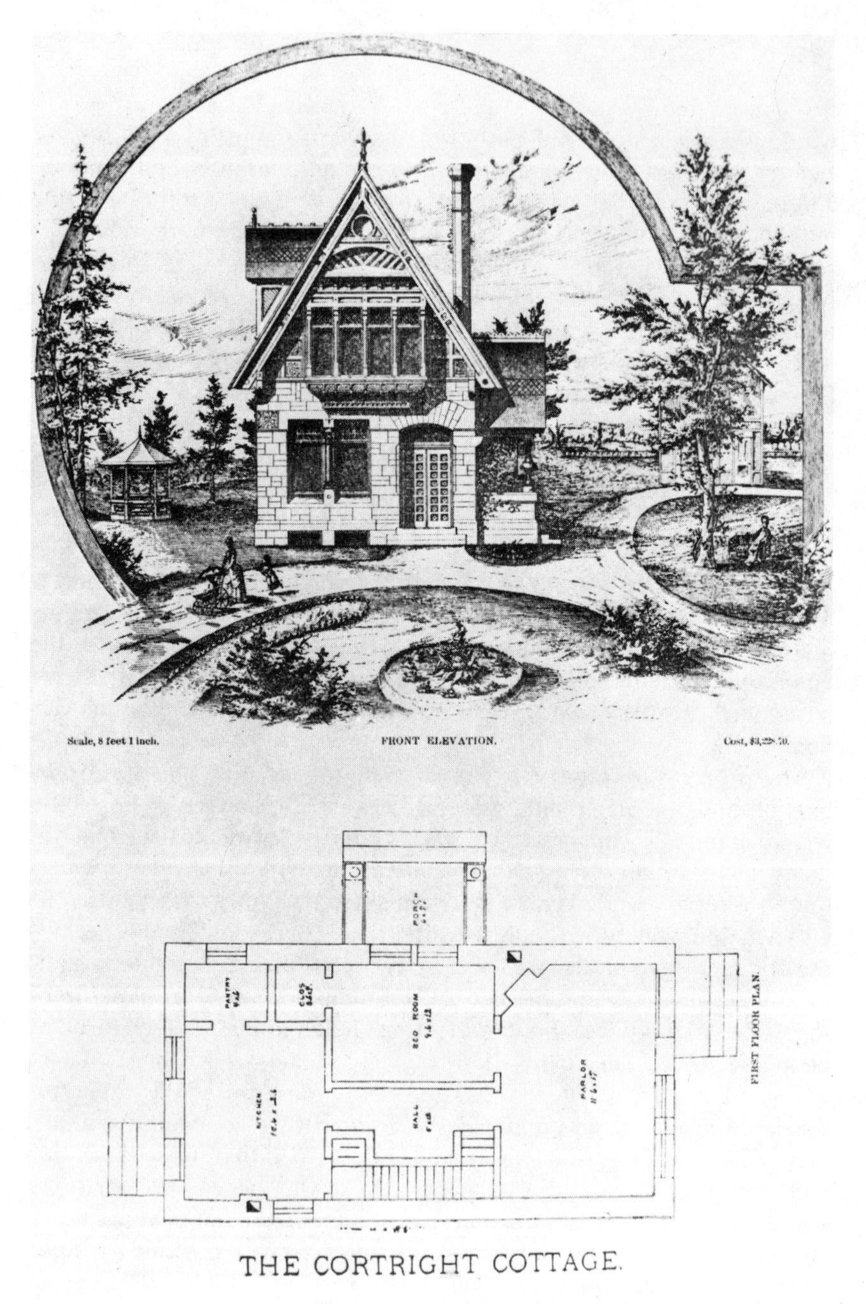

Figure 4. "Cortright Cottage" model house design. (From the *National Builder Album of Beautiful Homes*. Courtesy of the Art Institute of Chicago.)

Cornfield and the sanitary engineer George Preston Brown, editor of Chicago's *Sanitary News,* warned of the dangers of "sewer gas" escaping from poorly installed plumbing fixtures, becoming trapped by poor household ventilation, and infecting the residents with deadly diseases.[31] Since, in theory, sewer gas was heavier than air, houses were often raised up off the ground, especially in swampy climates like Chicago, to keep the frame dry and allow poisonous gases to escape beneath.

The understanding of disease was still primitive in these accounts. The germ theory was first published in this country in 1883, by Dr. Henry Gradle of Chicago Medical College, and even then there were many skeptics.[32] Yet, it was generally accepted that cleanliness in the home, as well as virtuous moral character, was related to good health. Most American physicians, ministers, social reformers, and builders argued that the foundation for public health had to be laid in private homes, especially those outside the cities, although city engineers of these same decades busily campaigned for municipal regulations as the more effective solution.

To most people the individual home seemed easier to regulate than the crowded city. The responsibility for family health lay with the builder and the housewife. As one Chicago builder baldly put it, his houses were outside the city limits, "away from the streets leading to the cemeteries."[33] Mrs. H. M. Plunkett, editor of the Sanitary Department of the *New York Independent,* published a morality tale about a woman whose inadequate care of her basement led to her husband's untimely death. She then went on to explain in detail what women should look for in terms of pipes, cisterns, and water tables when they bought or built a house. These matters, she admonished the fashion-conscious, would prove far more important than parlor furnishings.[34] Both women and men had to learn what kinds of windows, floors, ceiling heights, and sewer traps could help control "the dread sewer gas." This individual responsibility would continue to dominate household reform movements through the 1890s, when the pendulum would begin to swing in the other direction toward standards formulated by experts and enforced by legislation.

The second major theme of popular builders was the independence and protective quality of each home. A visual reference here, again drawn from Ruskin, was the fireplace. It had an even clearer symbolic meaning than other architectural details of the time, for the widespread use of furnaces and stoves made fireplaces unnecessary for warmth. The appeal, then, was not functional but evocative. The image of the family gathered around the hearth was the most common way to call up the ideal of the home as a place of protection and communality. Clarence Cook even contended that the symbolic power of the domestic fireplace could counter the "social science" of the "Spencer-Youmans theory of life."[35] By this, Cook was claiming that the hearth evoked the memory of the nuclear family as an eternal form of human social life. Therefore, the sight of the hearth could drive out any spurious evolutionary schemes which might suggest that there had been other kinds of human living patterns. Locked into the architecture was the collective memory of the nuclear family as God's will.

Such suggestions of the hearth and chimney as deeply rooted reminders of family stability stirred a vogue for large central fireplaces. Their use by fashionable English and American architects ensured their great popularity. In 1881, John Pickering Putnam, a Boston architect, published a historical survey of the fireplace which stressed the social function of the hearth as a gathering place for the family. He described the great variety of furnaces, mantels, grates, and cleaning equipment to supplement and adorn fireplaces that was now available on the market.[36] Given this range, it is not surprising that there soon appeared, in middle-class houses, more than one way to present the fireplace. The parlor or sitting room, wherever the family came together for the evening, remained the first choice and the most majestic. But there were also cozy, tiled fireplaces for the mother's bedroom, to welcome her children into her special affectionate realm. Other builders began to imitate the wealthy family who placed the staircase and fireplace in a formal living hall (fig. 5), so that its message would be visible to every visitor. The focus of many a family temple was the elaborately carved wood mantel, perhaps with a portrait of a child at the center, or a blessing carved into the surface. Other, more pretentious mantels might feature elegantly cut mirrors to reflect the happy scenes of family harmony. But the principle was always the same. The symbolic purpose of the prominent fireplace was to declare that the family was the focus here. Even simple illustrations of "chimney nooks" echoed the message. A fireplace might have imitation logs of asbestos, fired by gas, or a hidden furnace register, a mantel of marble or of wood painted to simulate expensive stone, but it gave the home its center. The living hall might be a pinched and restricted space in a small middle-class home, but with a fireplace it radiated security.

Figure 5. Chimney mantel and stairway. (From Robert W. Shoppell's *Modern Houses, Beautiful Homes,* 1887. Co-Operative Building Plan Association, New York.)

The fireplace was one of many architectural symbols that had to appear in every house; the rhetoric of diversity was modified by many such standard items. Similarly, although builders promoted individualized plans, there was actually a precise organization of rooms in every house. The plan was based upon a common cultural understanding of what should take place within the home, who should oversee it, and who should mix together. We tend to think of the Victorian home as a playful arrangement of irregularly shaped rooms, with a complex system of names for each volume. The builders themselves emphasized the supposed uniqueness of each plan. In truth, the complexity referred to the increased awareness of specialized functions within the home. There was a distinct pattern of rooms and layout. By the time of the Inter-State Exposition, most American houses had three distinct kinds of spaces: spaces for presenting the home ideal to guests and to the family, spaces for the production of domestic goods, and spaces for privacy. Even modest middle-class residences provided for a complex social life and work routine. The plan segregated the various groups that used the home—visitors and residents, women and men, adults and children, family and servants—in defined areas. Each area was a distinct zone. Each had its particular furnishings, materials, even shapes of rooms. In each space different activities took place, different people congregated, different aesthetics ruled. This functional division was also a symbolic matter, reinforcing divisions by sex within a home, strengthening the division between work and leisure.

The front presentation area was the most important space in the home, the principal focus of almost every pattern book and housewife's guide. Lavishly decorated, the place for entertaining guests and for bringing the family together, the parlor announced status and familial harmony. The most formal room in the house, it served as the repository for the most elegant and most artistic objects. Although a separate room, the dining room was considered integral to this presentation of refined good taste. Books and magazine articles encouraged housewives to spend money on the furnishings for these spaces where the family would gather and guests would form their opinions.

Through the 1870s, in part because of the depression which lasted from 1873 to 1878, middle-class housewives filled their presentation rooms with "household elegancies" or "ladies' fancy work" of their own making, as well as a few artistic objects they had purchased. Even architects and decorators praised the personal touch that hand-crocheted pillows and rustic furniture, knotted rugs and hand-painted screens, gilded rockers and laminated bric-a-brac stands could give to a room. Such pieces blessed the home, they wrote, with "sincere," "chaste" charm and personality.[37]

But, as noted earlier, when the effects of the depression began to wear off, fewer decorations for the fashionable middle-class parlor were handmade. Domestic guides and architectural treatises had less tolerance for the handcrafted touch. By the 1880s, American machine-made furniture had increased dramatically in quantity and quality over the products of the industry's origins in the 1850s.[38] Grand Rapids and Chicago had emerged as the centers of a thriving furniture industry. Factories produced elegant mahogany or cherry tables, simple rocking chairs, and inexpensive parlor sets in artificial ebonized wood. With the enthusiasm for Japanese and pseudo-Japanese work in the 1880s, delicate latticework emerged from these factories, too. Many new kinds of woodwork appeared inside houses now: close-set spindled screens were suspended to create a graceful partition within a room; thin moldings formed baseboards, chair rails, and borders for the panels of golden oak wainscotting which ran along the walls. The plate rail was invented to provide another continuous surface on which to display china. In the literature of the 1880s, parlors were sometimes described as "thickets," a word that evoked the variety and density of furnishings which filled these spaces.

An atmosphere of soft sensuality hung over the home, especially in the parlor and front presentation rooms. All of the objects for creating this mood, in particular the exotic imports, were obviously purchases, not things made by the housewife herself. Materials became more luxurious. Plush upholstery replaced the coarse, glossy horsehair on sofas, and velvet portieres hung to sweep the floor in front of an alcove. Soft pillows and throw rugs created a Moorish mood. Rugs replaced carpets now, as hardwood floors replaced the rough floorboards of a generation before. An American Axminster or an imported Oriental rug could be moved from the parlor out onto the doorstep or porch on sultry summer evenings.

Even colors became more opulent. The parlor and dining room walls were usually painted in rich colors—vermilion, russet, bottle green were popular, with gold trim or cream on the moldings. The sitting room was in "tender tones" of olive, maize, or peach blossom. Increasingly, the lower halves of walls would be covered rather than painted. Cloth was often used, usually a textured surface, such as burlap, muslin, or denim, perhaps even flat or patterned velvet in an especially pretentious home. The more elegant wallpapers were sold in sheets, and often a single surface would combine several different patterns. Against the walls would hang prints and portraits and display cabinets or shelves, all with ornate frames. Juxtapositions of colors, textures, and even styles were bountiful in these rooms. In the heart of the home, the place of refuge from the world, was vivid evidence of worldliness and materialism.

In contrast to this lavish and prominent display, the production area was relegated to the rear of the house. "Queen Anne in the front, and Mary Anne in the back" was the quip of the time, referring to a typical house plan. By this account, the lady of the house gave all her time and attention to the front parlor, where she reigned amidst her fashionable, English-inspired splendor, while her servant—a young, native-born farm girl—was hidden away in the back kitchen. There were several misconceptions in this simple formula. In Chicago, as in other urban areas, only about 20 to 25 percent of all households employed even a single servant in 1880, and this ratio was noticeably higher than the national average. Moreover, the Chicago servant was increasingly likely to be an immigrant woman, usually Irish, rather than native-born. The trend toward hiring married women meant that, by the end of the century, more of these Irish (and, by the early twentieth century, black) women would "live out."[39] Yet, it nevertheless was true that the kitchen area was planned as the hired woman's territory.

In the succeeding decades the number of servants remained fairly stable, while the population as a whole, and especially the number of financially secure but socially insecure middle-class families, increased conspicuously. Much talk ensued about the "servant problem." But this was, in fact, as much a matter of poor household planning and ambiguous social status as it was an acknowledgment of the fact that fewer women were willing to work as servants. In a sense, both the isolation of the production area in the back of a house and the inclusion of a "servant's bedroom" in so many house plans implied efforts to deny these changes. Attempts to imitate the wealthy, who did have several servants to tend to most household production and upkeep tasks, levied a heavy toll on the comfort and convenience of the middle-class housewife, who had to do more and more of the housework herself.

Even if the preparation area received short shrift in most nineteenth-century texts on domestic architecture and decoration, common sense kept it quite liveable. The female members of the average household did, after all, spend many hours there. E. C. Gardner called this the "housekeeper's headquarters" in one book,[40] since so much time-consuming women's work took place in the kitchen and pantry area. Even if there were a servant, the housewife and her daughters probably joined her for a good part of the day in an average middle-class home, for there was always more to do. Most women's and children's clothing was still made at home, and constant mending went on; cooking required tending to the stove every ten minutes, if there was to be constant heat; washing entailed boiling water on the stove, mixing up laundry soap or starch, and rubbing everything fiercely up and down a laundry board. And these were only a few of the household tasks that still took place in the home, much as they had for generations before.

Despite this demanding and repetitious work, few friends of the housewife discussed how to rationalize the tasks and the work-space of the kitchen. The most important book to do so was a domestic guide and home economics textbook, *The American Woman's Home,* first published in 1869 and widely used through the end of the century. Here Catharine Beecher and Harriet Beecher Stowe had featured revolutionary approaches to housework and layout, most notably a centralized core of mechanical services and efficient organization of every functional space, especially storage areas.[41] The two sisters believed that women should take control of their homes, and not rely on the help of servants or the advice of men. In order to strengthen the "woman's profession," it was necessary to plan the house to be totally under her control.

Although middle-class women did try to achieve Beecher and Stowe's ideal of the selfless, self-sufficient housewife, whether or not they had servants, builders did not follow through on the innovative architectural proposals of the two authors. During most of the nineteenth century, the average builder envisioned the kitchen as simply a large volume of space for work (fig. 6). Still, if the work was hidden, there was at least ample room for doing it. Frequently, even in a fairly unpretentious house, there would be 200 to 250 square feet devoted to food preparation, or about a quarter of the downstairs area. Most of this space was simply the open kitchen itself, but a considerable amount went to storage. A rear pantry was usually provided where all the goods put up by the household—canned fruits and vegetables, jellies and pickles—as well as the staple goods that had to be bought in bulk could be kept. An additional space was the cooler, either in a window or in the cellar, where perishables were kept, protected from insects by a screen. Sometimes there was even a special china pantry for cooking- and serving-ware. This area often had the additonal function of shielding the dining room from the sights, sounds, and smells of the kitchen. The various walk-in cupboards and storage areas of the Victorian kitchen indicate the amount of preparation that still took place in the home.

In its plain, spacious austerity, the kitchen, more than any other room, showed signs of the standardization and rational planning which

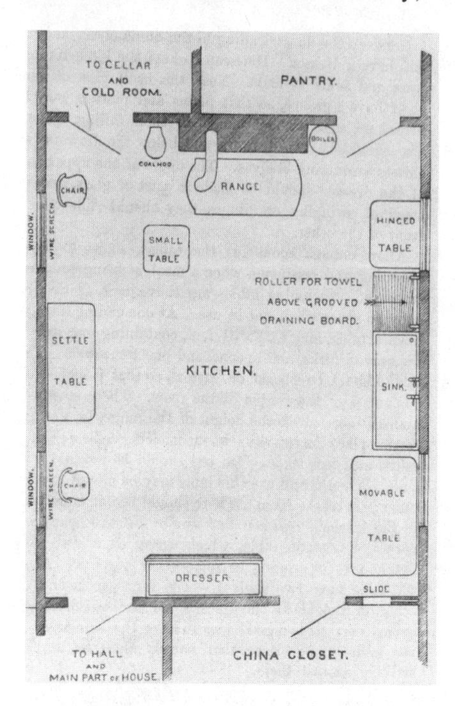

Figure 6. An Ideal Kitchen. (From Maria Parloa's *Miss Parloa's Kitchen Companion,* 1887.)

would come to the fore in domestic design at the end of the century. Or, more precisely, in planning the kitchen, the builder did not try to disguise practical, standardized layout. Almost every kitchen was simple in shape, either square or rectangular, without the protruding bays and bulges that distinguished other areas of the house. There was no ornamentation, except for the growing array of utensils, from the egg-beater and the aluminum cookware on wall hooks to the modern gas "fireless cooker" that stood against a wall. Shelves in the pantry were built-in, although the large appliances and tables in the kitchen were simply placed flush against a wall or, sometimes, squarely in the center of the room. Books of household advice seldom considered where these various pieces should be located. In general, plumbing was still primitive—a sink was the norm in most houses, perhaps connected to a hand-pump but usually without hot water—but there was time-honored attention to health and comfort. Windows were large and often placed for cross-ventilation as well as bright sunlight. Walls were usually painted light green or yellow, in shiny oil-based enamels so that they would be easy to clean. The smooth oak floors were simply varnished, and rugs were scattered about so there would be soft surfaces on which to stand. The simple decor and practical furnishings contrasted sharply with the ornate pieces the housewife purchased for her parlor. This clean and well-kept kitchen had its own aesthetic. It was essentially a standard, alike from house to house, a ballast in the shifting styles that kept changing the front of the house.

Places for privacy in a middle-class home were the smallest and least visible of spaces, but they were carefully defined and, in general, well situated. First there were bedrooms: one for the parents, several for the children (who could be divided according to sex, since most model houses featured at least four bedrooms). If at all possible, these rooms were upstairs, away from the indiscreet comings and goings of visitors. Guides to home decoration skipped the bedrooms with a slight blush, but modesty notwithstanding, general guidelines emerged. Bedrooms were usually large enough to serve as sitting rooms; in one of them a mother might spend the afternoon with her daughter, or a young woman with her girl friend, enjoying the quiet of these spacious, sunny rooms. Decoration was largely a personal matter, not an architectural concern. Mementoes and handmade objects would be displayed, generally in an artistic, stylized arrangement. Often the servant woman was allocated a room on the same floor with the other bedrooms, off a common hallway, instead of being assigned to the attic. The separateness of these private spaces for the family members, away from the social spaces, made such a close accommodation of the servant more acceptable. Besides, what was advertised as a servant's room, denoting social class, could always be used as a child's bedroom instead.

The most important private space in the home, the bathroom, was just coming to be accepted in middle-class American families during the last decades of the nineteenth century, although the acceptance was by no means universal. Still, it did become more common to unite in a single room the various pieces of equipment formerly found in separate niches or in individual bedrooms: a tub, a sink or washbowl, certainly the water closet, earth closet, or chamber pot.[42] The special room for these sanitary functions did not look too different from other rooms in terms of surface materials, size, or lighting; but it was luxuriously private.

Quite rapidly, a fascination with new technology and an interest in maintaining one's health and that of the family now combined to generate a host of new objects for the bathroom. Most of these, like the "Grecian Vase water closet," were quite ornate pieces of sculpture, testifying to the plumber's artistry and to some extent glorifying, while disguising, the functions for which they were intended. The appeal of the multiple-purpose object generated some extraordinarily ingenious appliances (fig. 7). Since standards for plumbing fixtures changed so quickly, they seemed novelty pieces. It was useful to buy a piece that would have another purpose when its sanitary function had been superseded by something more modern.

Equally important for privacy were the numerous small niches scattered through the house: the bay-window seats and inglenooks by the fireplace, alcoves and porches, attics and small side yards, all the intimate spaces we associate with the late Victorian dwelling. These provided opportunities for retreat, even in the very rooms that were supposed to foster family unity. In particular, the parlor and sitting room were provided wtih these private cubbyholes for seclusion. Here an individual could sit apart, while being with the family. Like the ideal of personal expression through industrialized building materials, this was a clever compromise. It was possible to have the image of a harmonious family and still provide for withdrawal from cloying togetherness. Delicate balances such as these characterized the Victorian builder's fiction of the model home.

Implementing the Vision

Of course, no quantity of books and expositions could alter American housing unless builders themselves accepted the models. Despite regional variations and the eccentricities of personal taste, they did so to a surprisingly unanimous degree. The rhetoric of individual expression and artistic inventiveness did not, in fact, generate flamboyant differences in middle-class houses of the period. These houses are still extremely easy to recognize, as they were then. The example of Samuel Eberly Gross, Chicago's foremost builder, proves the point.

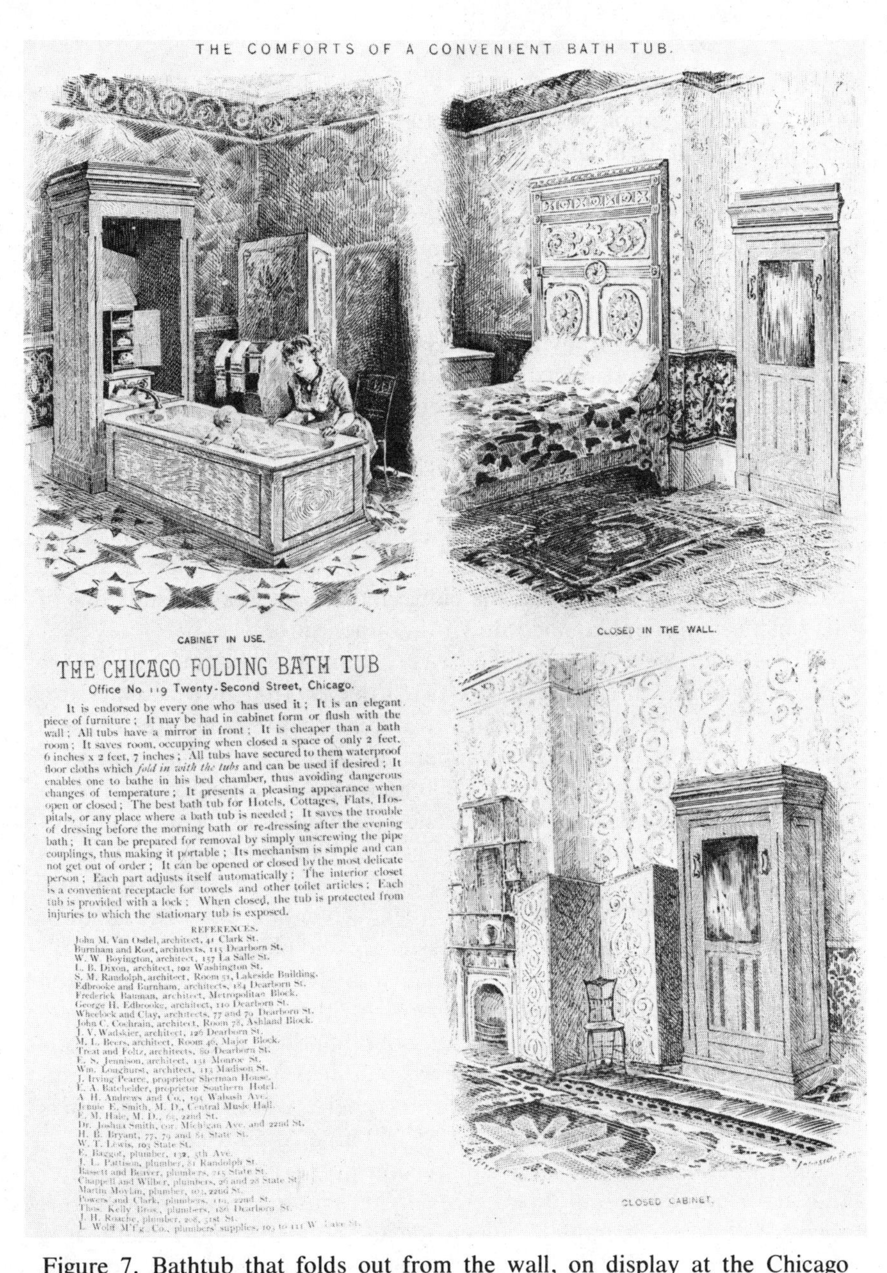

Figure 7. Bathtub that folds out from the wall, on display at the Chicago Inter-State Industrial Exhibition, 1883. (From *Sketch-Book of the Inter-State Exposition*. Courtesy of the Chicago Historical Society.)

Gross skillfully employed every subtlety of the builder's code, from an emphasis on individualized houses (actually constructed from standardized plans and with familiar symbolic details) to a proudly declared ethic of public service. His career clearly demonstrates the wide appeal of the builder's model for houses and profit.

Gross came to Chicago at the time of the Civil War. He lost his first real estate business in the depression of 1873 but came back in 1880, after a fling as an attorney and a playwright. A flair for drama certainly marked the advertisements he circulated in the decades of his greatest fame (fig. 8). He vividly limned the customary themes of harmony with nature, celebration of artisanal crafts in construction, and protection of the family in its suburban home. To these conventional themes, he added a strong personal pledge. It was, Gross claimed, the builder who provided all of these essential services for the worthy middle-class and working-class families of the metropolis. His portrait appears in the corner of one advertisement; his name and the impressive statistics of his business are emblazoned down the other side.

Gross's home designs and his "easy payment" system, with its remarkably liberal financing terms (as little as $100 down and $10 a month, with additional financing available to prevent foreclosures) made his fortune and his great popularity. By 1892, he had sold over 40,000 lots, built and sold over 7,000 houses, developed over 16 town and 150 subdivisions outside Chicago.[43] Among the most notable of his planned new towns were Gross Park, in 1882 (now the area west of Lincoln Park); Brookdale, 1886 (south of Jackson Park); Calumet Heights, 1887; and Grossdale, 1889 (near Riverside, now Brookfield). In each of these developments, Gross exercised close control. He built train depots and installed water, gas, and sewage lines. He donated trees and a grand, gaslighted boulevard to the major towns. He enforced rigid design guidelines and strict building ordinances in his communities. These practices assured a unified aesthetic, sound construction, and a strong residential atmosphere, whether the dwellings were $1,000 four-room cottages or $5,000 nine-room houses.

The brochures for Gross's subdivision properties illustrate a carefully delineated program. In cottages of 500 square feet or in the larger, relatively expensive models, the facade and plan are almost identical to those in countless pattern books of the time. Gross preached individualized design combined with functional planning in each house and in the overall plan. He openly played upon the dominant symbolic themes

Figure 8. Advertising broadside reproduced in an 1891 catalogue for S. E. Gross and Company, Chicago. (Courtesy of the Chicago Historical Society.)

that Victorian culture associated with the home and family. His success was spectacular, but it depended on more than his "own your own home" financing terms. Gross sold houses that almost everyone in Chicago could comprehend and admire. His remarkable rise as a builder and developer depended upon his ability to manipulate the popular domestic images of the time. His dwellings seemed indeed to be personalized designs which would make a family proud and secure. He was able to standardize these designs, to create an effective system, so that his houses were profitable to produce and appealing to buy.

Not only was Gross's financial success outstanding for a nineteenth-century real estate developer, he actually embodied the builder's role-model of the true democrat. In 1889, the Workingman's party nominated Gross for mayor, so impressed were its members with the thousands of inexpensive frame cottages he had made available on good terms for so many of the city's working-class families. Gross, although surely pleased with the acknowledgment, did not accept. But he continued to devote himself to furthering his ideal of the family home. After a trip to Europe in 1889, during which he toured new working-class and middle-class housing outside several capitals and visited the housing displays at the great Paris exposition, Gross explained his formula to the *Chicago Tribune*. Echoing a generation of American builders, he claimed that European houses lacked the grace and sentiment, the individuality and symbolic power of American dwellings. In the plainness of their construction and detailing, the European homes were concessions to the simple need for shelter. Moreover, landlords, industrialists, or even the state usually owned the property. And private ownership was a principle Gross cherished. His countrymen deserved more, he declared, and he would work with them to promote model homes for everyone in the city of Chicago. He tied the themes of citizenship and domesticity together again at the end of his statement. This builder paid his enthusiastic respect to "the most earnest and appreciative owners of what is in fact the noblest result of the civilization of the nineteenth century, the American home."[44]

Gross's words, part honest sentiment and part clever hyperbole, won him more than clients. Like other late-nineteenth-century builders who asserted that they were designing model homes for a great, diverse, egalitarian, and cultured American public, he had found an extraordinarily potent symbol. Americans of many ethnic backgrounds and economic strata, of divergent political views and social ambitions, found a commonality in the image of the home presented by these men. Pattern books and the advertisements for new subdivisions had a wide appeal. Not only were the porches and parlors pleasantly enticing. There was, in addition, a sense of cultural mission. These homes—that is, the images of the homes as well as the dwellings themselves—directly addressed each family's desire for stability and prestige, providing assurances of symbolic virtue on the one hand and fashion on the other.

The Victorian builders also went beyond these private hopes. They suggested a vision of American filled with independent, attractive homes, each economical enough to be owned by its occupants. That vision had been an integral part of the American dream for countless immigrants from many countries. It would continue its hold for future generations. The Victorian builders sensed the range and the power of this vision. The styles with which they experimented, like the themes of individuality and independence, were not in fact startlingly new. But they were given a heightened complexity, in both architectural and symbolic terms. Although the fanciful, intricate styles promoted by Victorian builders would not last into the next century, their awareness of the significance of the home as the primary symbol in many Americans' lives, as well as their ability to manipulate that symbol, would be transferred, with relative ease, to the simpler forms of the twentieth century. It was, after all, the *idea* of the American home, as well as the physical object of shelter, that counted to them and to their public.

2 PROFESSIONAL AMBITIONS

The architect alone can design a convenient and elegant house—that might pass as such under the close examination of a committee of experts.

William Le Baron Jenney, "Architecture," *Inland Architect* (1883)

The professional architect's attitudes toward design and social responsibility were radically different from those of the builder. Pattern-book writers made much of the distinction; self-styled crusaders, they presented themselves as being vigorously for the public and against the professional elite. A strongly egalitarian impulse surged up in America between 1830 and 1880, a period of great national expansion and industrial growth. Suspicious levelers of rank and class castigated anything that seemed to bespeak special privilege. Educated practitioners of medicine, law, and teaching in turn banded together in reaction to these assaults. Architects made a similar effort. In 1851 they established a small professional organization, the American Institute of Architects (AIA), hoping to provide themselves with "mutual protection" against populist attacks on their skill and integrity.[1] Yet the position of the architect was to remain far more ambiguous than that of the doctor or lawyer. With no legal sanction defining the profession until 1897 and only a minimal system of graduate education, architects were actually a self-declared elite, not a state-approved specialized profession. As a result, they were highly defensive about their professional qualifications and responsibilities.

Bitter Words and Noble Causes

American architects faced intense opposition as they attempted to solidify their ranks. Builders, journalists and citizens' groups in every city accused them of pandering to a wealthy elite, and of wasting public funds when they built civic structures. They were criticized as extravagant and arrogant, concerned only with ideal beauty, or with their own commissions, rather than with the functional issues of daily life and economy. Even the more sympathetic pattern books contained derisive descriptions of "professional follies" and impracticalities.

There was a certain truth to the accusations. Well-publicized instances of fixed competitions and payoffs, building failures and health or safety hazards, promoted suspicion. The most notorious examples concerned large public buildings. For instance, angry citizens were in an uproar over graft in the awarding of the Chicago Cook County Court House commission, and over the fact that the cornice later fell off the building onto the street. In another instance, a lawsuit was filed against several New York architects over municipal buildings which were virtually unventilated. The Chicago public effectively lobbied against architect J. J. Egan's proposal for a dome on their city hall, charging that it was an unnecessary expense, since the dome would be seen to its best advantage only from the suburbs. And a Chicago fence manufacturer was eventually censured for offering commissions to architects who used his products.[2]

The same problems were, of course, as common for domestic architecture as for public buildings. However, the most damaging of all the charges against the architectural profession, a charge made by the majority of critics, was that professionals did not know or care about building homes for the average citizen. George Ellwanger, for instance, in his autobiographical *The Story of My House,* testily asserted that "[i]f we leave the house to the architect, he builds merely for himself."

Well-regarded professional architects were indeed highly ambivalent about whether they should actually build or even design prototypes for moderate-cost housing. And it was true that journals like the *Inland Architect* of Chicago did carry statements which argued that the architect, as an artist, should be "removed from practicalities," leaving such matters to mere contractors, even though most Americans would never appreciate the need for this "higher state" of the art. Likewise, the New York architect, Henry Hudson Holly, writing on new residential styles in 1878, railed against the overly enthusiastic client who offered suggestions, thus "trammelling the professional man in producing the best arrangement and effects. These amateur designs should be taken as suggestions simply, nothing more."[3]

All the same, populist charges of misconduct and disdain were much too generalized. William Le Baron Jenney's lectures at the first University of Chicago (a Baptist college) in 1876 pleaded with architects to take their clients' particular needs and tastes into account. Most professional architects were keenly interested in the engineering and technical aspects of construction which, by necessity, included experimental structures. In fact, all of the American professional journals featured articles and letters about recent improvements and research in the fields of plumbing, ventilation, and construction. Information on pipes and foundations, electricity and fireproofing appeared alongside treatises on ideal beauty and historical styles.[4]

The members of the profession, particularly those who wrote books and articles on design theory or edited architectural journals, in turn blamed avaricious builders and poorly trained building workers for faulty construction and ugly design. They did seem at times to resent their clients' participation in design decisions. But they were especially hostile toward the upstart builders who designed model houses and published plans of them, often calling themselves architects in their publicity.

The *American Architect and Building News* (the first professional journal for architects to originate in the United States, published in Boston from 1876 to 1938) struck out repeatedly against such "Self-Made Architects."[5] The journal was vehemently opposed to the fact that these untrained, unscholarly builders could legally call themselves "architects" without any repercussions. The educated profession would stand its ground against this slander. The first editor of the *American Architect,* William P. P. Longfellow, declared that an exuberance of stylistic fantasy and the builder's claim to be the professional architect's equal were dangerous tendencies; he did not, however, clearly explain whether he saw this as a threat to the nation, to art, or to the profession. One thing he was clear about: whatever the function of the modern architect, it certainly was not the manufacture of styles; true architects, he insisted, were distinguished by their respect for and knowledge of tradition. The AIA memebers associated with his journal—including such eminent men as Richard Morris Hunt, John Wellborn Root, and Henry Van Brunt—were equally scornful of the ambitious builders who dared to call themselves architects without any scholarly training. William Rotch Ware, just after he opened the Department of Architecture at the Massachusetts Institute of Technology, lashed out against those who had usurped the title of architect, declaring angrily that "The profession is at present in the hands of mechanics," who might be capable of handling practical points in building yet were "ignorant of the higher branches of their calling."[6]

An ambiguity about the precise meaning of "the profession" clouds this and other, similar statements. By far the largest part of the building taking place in the United States consisted of moderate-cost houses, designed and often constructed by small builders. Ware did not believe that trained architects should take on this restricted and repetitious work, judging from the design problems he gave students. Yet he was harshly condescending toward those who did specialize in moderate-cost residential architecture, claiming that these "ignorant mechanics" could never elevate themselves to follow universal principles of beauty as true artists.

In 1878 the *American Architect* formalized its views of pattern books with a series entitled "American Vernacular Architecture." The articles were, for the most part, attacks on those who had "discovered a profitable field of enterprise in flattering and gently leading the tastes of the people." Occasionally there was praise for the model of a simple, unpretentious and unadorned dwelling, as in the work of E. C. Gardner or A. J. Bicknell and Co. But most of the designs, reviewers complained, were "commonplace," "vulgar," festooned ridiculously with decoration—bastard details, outrageous colors, everything cheap and machine-made. "The tendency of American architecture is to the fantastic," lamented one architect. The American public was being led astray by popular designers who audaciously claimed that originality was the basis for a national style; the people had been seduced with symbols of home and nation, with mechanical gimcracks and sensual, flamboyant ornament.[7]

This "heathen" condition, that reviewer hoped, would strengthen the determination of professional architects to "go forth like missionaries" and lead the country into the purity of educated ideals. He did not, however, mean that his colleagues should design model middle-class homes; rather, they should spread the enlightened example of their designs, erecting beautiful monuments far and wide.

Still, it is difficult to define precisely what these theorists saw as the distinguishing marks of their professional authority. One article in the *American Architect* insisted that "Skill comes by discipline, and discipline is maintained by precedent."[8] That is to say, it was essential to follow historical precedent, and attention to precision in style should override consideration of practical problems, which were more temporary matters. A call for discipline and restraint sounded again and again. According to the professional press, those qualities possessed only by trained architects were: "reserve and elegance of form which are the result of high training, the chastisement and self-denial which come from knowledge and discipline, the imagination which dares to venture upon new flights, the education which prevents these flights from repeating the disaster of Phaeton."[9] Neither the practical engineer, nor the simple mechanic, nor the socialistic workman, nor the exuberant and ambitious carpenter, nor even the individual client could ever create true architecture. Disciplined education and self-restriction to appropriate commissions should be the mark of the professional. These were also, more obliquely, the path toward purifying the national environment. "What is needed is not patriotic inspiration, not eagles or maize, not originality," Longfellow declared, "but agreement and skill."[10]

Professional architects did not entirely turn their backs on the American craftsman. Even the *American Architect* acknowledged a national vernacular tradition that was almost (but not quite) as legitimate as the medieval heritage of Europe. It was the legacy of small-town carpenters, especially those of New England, who were totally ignorant—or perhaps, they suggested, simply contemptuous—of the pattern-book designs. The romantic image of simple, unpretentious buildings, designed according to honored, unchanging folk traditions, of handicraft techniques for wood-frame construction preserved intact over generations, appealed to educated architects in a way that the creative feats of the carpenter-builders could never do. Their avid reading of Ruskin encouraged this sentimental conception of the simple, traditional carpenter, for Ruskin had idealized the craftsman as a contemporary worker who preserved the Gothic traditions of skill and creativity, strengthened by the worker's unquestioning acceptance of his place in the existing social order.

Given that image of the artisan, it was still possible to have kind words for "the worker" in general and to take pleasure in architectural details which celebrated his craft. Thus, James R. Osgood, the publisher of the *American Architect,* wanted the journal to reach builders and engineers as well as architects. A regular feature on "Building News" in the nations' larger cities covered a range of building types, including small cottages. Even Longfellow was occasionally somewhat romantic: he praised those American carpenters who still worked "without regard for precedent or rule . . . exactly as did the mediaeval builders."[11] This folk tradition, however, differed fundamentally from the lack of regard for precedent or rule of those who wanted to change residential architecture, to infuse it with new forms and meanings. Furthermore, it was distinctly separate from the unions' agitation for better working conditions, greater autonomy on the job, and increased political leverage. Parallels between the medieval craftsmen's guilds and contemporary building-trades unions were seldom part of this mythology.

The role of the professional architect, in this account, was to protect the naive American tradition, to refine it, to infuse the roughness with style and carefully applied ornament, and to halt dangerous libertarianism. Professional superiority in design was attributed to a rigorous education in architectural history which could only be acquired in a school or in the office of a trained architect. In theory, scholarship enabled the architect to handle revival idioms with grace and to apply them accurately to the new needs of the day. It also taught the architect to be concerned with ideal beauty rather than particular minor problems, to ascend from materialistic issues into the realm of the universally beautiful. This is not to say that the profession ignored matters of construction or technology. Nor were its members oblivious to the ways their work could improve and uplift society. However, their cause was, for the most part, conceived as a duty to set examples for others to emulate, rather than as a responsibility to take on commissions for small houses. The professional press asserted that a combination of specialized education, restricted entry to the profession, and reverence for stylistic accuracy would temper and control the prevailing boldness and flamboyance of all American architecture. Such claims suggest an inflated sense of the tiny profession's power to influence the larger American environment.

An interest in housing, if often an impatient and disdainful one, was nonetheless present in architectural publications of the 1870s. It was, in fact, during this decade, at least according to *Industrial Chicago*, that the American profession began to assert a stronger influence in residential design.[12] Of course, a few earlier American architects, such as Alexander Jackson Davis, had specialized in individual homes and even small suburban developments, albeit for the upper middle classes.

But these had been individual efforts, and not the concerns of the profession as a whole. And, even then, it was rare for an architect to be interested in the problem of housing, taken as a complex national social issue as well as an aesthetic problem.

Prior to this time, the few trained architects in this country—those who studied in England, attended a state-supported French or German school, or served as an apprentice to an architect with such a European background—had tended to leave domestic design, at least as a social and political issue, to others. Their special education, the architects' argument went, gave them the responsibility for the few elegant mansions of the new nation and its important public and ecclesiastical buildings. These structures gave them the opportunity to practice their art and present the country with dignified monuments. Most of the early American architects (all males and usually Europeans by birth) were anxious to establish the principles of architectural aesthetics, as they were understood in European academies, on American soil. (However, a few, to be sure, like Benjamin Latrobe and Samuel Sloan, experimented with an indigenous aesthetic based on organic forms native to America.) The majority of the young profession, from Charles Bulfinch in Boston to William Strickland in Philadelphia, or Robert Mills, who directed many of the federal buildings in Washington, devoted their talent to giving the country elegant neoclassical works of art.

Of course, most professional architects of any period have designed houses for specific clients. Yet the housing of a large, diverse national population has seldom been their stock-in-trade. Throughout the nineteenth century an occasional small cottage—a folly, a maisonette, a gate lodge, based on clearly French or English counterparts—might appear in an American architect's sketchbook or even a published folio of designs. But these were rare. They were romantic exercises, variations on the ideal dwelling set in nature. This ideal small house had been a favorite architectural topic abroad, at least since the Enlightenment, when Laugier had put forth his theories of the primitive house and the beginnings of architecture, when noblemen and noblewomen had commissioned fanciful rustic retreats.[13] The ideal cottage was thus either an essay in architectural principles or else a stylized appendage to a wealthy estate. Again, of course, one finds exceptions. The English architect Calvert Vaux had worked for Andrew Jackson Downing and, like him, published a pattern book of small-house designs. But, on the whole, professionally trained architects before the late 1870s did not conceive of their occasional cottage studies as prototypes for real moderate-cost houses, models for countless dwellings for anonymous families all over the country. Each architect's design was, in theory, a unique solution to an abstract design problem, and perhaps to a particularly demanding site. The design drew upon established historical precedent for continuity with the art of the past; as a piece of architecture, however, it was singular.

Thus, the interest in moderate-cost housing that was shown in American architectural journals of the 1870s and 1880s signalled a new course for the profession itself, a direction that only a few architects had hitherto followed. While the editors of the professional journals were certainly ambivalent about the quality of most builders' housing in this country, and troubled by the idea of an architect's design being duplicated (or bungled) without supervision, they cautiously undertook a campaign to consider the problem of the small house. This campaign entailed reviews of pattern books, plates of architect-designed cottages, occasional competitions for small houses, and numerous comments about the sorry state of housing in the United States. Professional journals and organizations vaguely endorsed the general principle of a simple, refined, rather traditional dwelling type that could become the prototype from which all small houses would be constructed. This process, to them, involved a reduction of the stylistic details that architects used for larger houses. Builders and carpenters should not try to experiment with style or even details on their own. Yet there were few attempts to explain how this simplified model would be circulated, or who should build the actual houses, or how the individual dwellings were to relate to one another.

Such silence was not limited to the professional journals' ambivalent coverage of middle-class or working-class housing. The editors of the journals were extremely cautious about laying down programs or rules for any of the subjects they considered. Except for drawings or photographs of historical monuments, they generally refrained from offering more than a few identifying lines about any of their illustrations, whether the subject was a cottage or a mansion. It is as if the editors were attempting to separate the discussions on style and philosophy—a discourse that ran through all the articles, book reviews, editorials, letters, and replies—from the material objects themselves. The representation of a given building was, therefore, not to be taken as an embodiment of the philosophical issues raised on the same page. The endorsement of a particular model could lead readers to attribute too much philosophical or social significance to that form; and this, to the editors, was the manipulative tactic favored by the builders' press. They would carefully refrain from expressing too much enthusiasm for a particular style or building, concentrating instead on general principles. The role of the architect, the nature of beauty, the value of discipline were all issues well worth discussing. But the suggestion that a certain piece of architecture (especially contemporary architecture) represented such abstractions assumed a closer fit between thoughts and things than these men wanted to accept.

Beauty in architecture, to them, was universal, an ideal that could not be easily captured and certainly not easily imitated. Furthermore, a formal model would overly restrict the architect's freedom (within the limits of academic discipline) as a designer. It would suggest a similarity with builders that the editors were determined to avoid. Standardization in particular was anathema to these architects, who considered themselves true artists. They designed individual buildings, works of art, not templates to be copied. Professional architects therefore evaded the touchy subject of standardization, in the sense of the repetition or duplication of houses based on a model, but not as the builders did, with effusive rhetoric calling for infinite variations on basic models. Instead, they spoke of "ideal types" that only trained architects could appreciate. These images were not at all meant as actual prototypes to be adapted and duplicated all over the country. Instead, they were studies, not prototypes, based on abstract ideals about how the house, and all forms of architecture for that matter, should function.

Both actual commissions for small houses or vacation houses and the less frequent uncommissioned explorations of the model cottage followed similar principles. In direct contrast to common builders' models, these architects' designs were demure, unshowy, often rather plain. These were academic explorations of the idea of simple, undemonstrative architecture, of the basic principles of shelter. By these accounts, "housing" simply provided a quiet backdrop to more interesting designs. In addition, the texts about the issue of the small house relied on a rather superior and esoteric language, for the authors were making the point that most people did not comprehend the principles of architecture, even in matters pertaining to the small house. Thus, while many architects professed a deep sense of outrage about the state of housing in this country and a strong desire to upgrade the environment, they effectively renounced any direct responsiblity for the larger built environment by opposing unauthorized repetition of any of their designs and condemning almost everything that the builder built.

A Common Grammar of Styles

Actually, the theoretical basis for the architect's understanding of how an artifact embodied or "reflected" a culture was quite similar to what it was for the builder. The principles of "associationism" dominated nineteenth-century aesthetic theory from the esoteric to the popular levels. According to this understanding, derived from late-eighteenth-century British essayists, but so popularized by the 1870s that it seemed self-evident, one's senses react to the sight of a natural or historical subject—or the reproduction of such a subject—by evoking memories and emotions associated with that image through one's earlier education. These evocations could then influence behavior as well as thought. The theorists of the Gothic Revival—Pugin, Ruskin, Viollet-le-Duc, and the Americans Henry Van Brunt and Leopold Eidlitz—derived their attitudes toward structural expression, natural materials, symbolic ornament, and historical precedent from this premise. But the general assumptions of associationist theory were also familiar to the builders who wrote pattern books and the women who published domestic guides. The belief that the environment influenced the individual buttressed countless egalitarian reforms, from public schools and charity organizations to housing models, from the late eighteenth century into the nineteenth.

Many kinds of people drew upon the idea that architectural elements were signifiers of social and moral laws. Through their version of the theory, professional architects sought an ideal world of harmony, history, and educated response, above the melee of participatory activity favored by the more populist builders. For the architect, only the cultivated few had the correct responses to their surroundings. It required a rigorous education to comprehend and be moved by true beauty. Builders, on the other hand, responding to the same sources, delighted in using the principles of associationism to promote personal expression, inventive details, and handicraft skills. Their favorite associations were with more everyday concerns, ranging from sturdy buildings to family stability, rather than with abstract concepts of beauty. Both groups relied on architectural associations to reveal what they called the "character" of a building. The architect meant by this "character" a combination of a clear "fitness of purpose" and a visible artistic ideal. The builder was more likely to be referring to the combined expression of the owner's personal taste and the craftsman's inventive skill.

Despite the purportedly different ways of understanding architecture, battle lines between the architect and the builder were not drawn as sharply on the construction site as in the books and articles written about residential architecture. Both groups still followed certain prevalent styles of the time, experimenting with or embellishing upon recognizable fashions. Even the Victorian Gothic houses shown in the professional journals were not necessarily so different from those in the builders' publications. Occasionally, as with the exuberant house that the builder George Palliser designed for P. T. Barnum, an architectural journal even printed the worker of an upstart builder.[14] Builders wrote insistently about imaginative combinations of details and about freedom from European precedent, but they followed the same fashions as did the architects. In turn, while the professional architectural journals inveighed against fanciful combinations of historical styles, the best architects did just that, and it was these stylistic inventions that the European journals chose to praise.

Particularly outside the major cities of the East Coast, at least until the 1880s, a residential design by an architect and one by a builder could often only be distinguished from each other by scale and quantity of ornament. Illustrations of currently fashionable neighborhoods around Chicago in 1874, taken from Everett Chamberlin's guidebook (fig. 9) still showed mostly Gothic and Italianate Revival residences, not far advanced from Downing's designs.[15]

But Chicago architects were by no means unaware of current styles, nor unmoved by the heated debates about style that were pitting architect against builder in the eastern journals. For example, during the late 1870s, an elaborate Venetian Gothic, much admired by John Ruskin and suddenly stylish, found adherents in this city. Drawings of W. L. B. Jenney's country house near Chicago, Burnham and Root's elegant dwelling on Drexel Avenue, and Peter B. Wight's study for a residence near the city, all illustrations in the *American Architect* of 1876, testify to the speed with which these local architects took up this

Ruskinian fashion of steeply gabled polychrome roofs, Italianate arches, delicate ornament, and complex massing.[16] (Wight, for one, had been an advocate of the style since the 1860s.)

Chicago architects were also certainly aware of the widespread enthusiasm for Ruskin's ideas about architecture, especially domestic architecture, that extended to builders and other kinds of popular writers. It was, perhaps, because of this popularity that the professional architectural press, in the Midwest as in the East, now generally avoided articles about Ruskinian theory, even during the height of his fame as a critic and his influence as an arbiter of style. The fact that builders and women writers were bombarding the public with Ruskin's name and quotations from his writings did not increase his prestige among the members of the profession. Many of them nonetheless followed Ruskin in believing that architecture represents the larger culture in which it is produced. They certainly agreed with his contention that architecture, as distinguished from mere building, was concerned with characteristics that were venerable or beautiful rather than utilitarian. However, Ruskin's ideas were then being used to buttress the legitimacy of ordinary carpenters and builders, and the professionals certainly disputed this. The architects' perspective was more likely to be that illumined by the "Lamp of Sacrifice"—Ruskin's claim that it was the duty of each family, but particularly of the wealthy family, to spend its money on houses, churches, and monuments of beauty from which others could learn and derive enjoyment.[17] Few architects shared the builders' fascination with the creative possibilities of inexpensive houses. And, to the trained professional, the "Lamp of Memory" also had a particular meaning, beyond the general cultural symbols of domesticity that the builders loved to evoke. By the light of a perfectly executed detail, this "lamp" revealed aspects of revered monuments from the past, but only to the educated observer.

Professionals were highly critical of the popular interpretations of Ruskin's mimetic theories. It seemed to many of them that he too easily encouraged architectural excess in the name of symbolic influence. His elaborate symbolic code for domesticity, which gave every roofline, every chimney and porch, a noble meaning, seemed a dubious invitation to architectural license on the part of the untutored. Moreover, was it not, the idealists wondered, looking back to discussions of the 1850s, simply a greater appeal to materialism to have buildings represent the values of nature, family, and humanity? And

Figure 9. Daniel Goodwin House (above) and Frank W. Palmer House (opposite), both at Lake, Ill. (From Everett Chamberlin's *Chicago and Its Suburbs* 1874.)

was not Ruskin overly vague and sentimental? asked those architects who wanted to find the scientific laws of cognitive associations.[18]

By the end of the 1870s, two other theorists were competing with Ruskin as expositors of the Gothic Revival. One was a rationalist and the other something of an idealist, or at least more of a romantic. Here again, in Chicago as in New York, their works were read by builders, architects, and the general public; and everyone again would interpret the ideas slightly differently.

Translations of works by Eugène-Emmanuel Viollet-le-Duc, the French medieval revivalist, appeared in the American builders' press as frequently as in the architectural media. His claim to a scientific approach to design had a broad appeal, especially since it focused on the planning of houses. *The Habitations of Man in All Ages* was first

published in the United States in 1876. Excerpts appeared in Chicago's *Inland Architect, National Builder,* and *Building Budget* soon after each journal commenced publication, as well as in numerous other American magazines.[19] Viollet-le-Duc claimed that architecture, construction, and social life of the past or present followed common, universal principles. A skilled observer could discern these laws. Once the system of relationships had been discovered, through the study of history, anthropology, and construction techniques, then it was possible to explain how architectural form had reflected the society, the family life, and the technological state of a given race. Most of Viollet-le-Duc's drawings, republished in numerous American journals of the time, showed the social habits that he linked to a particular kind of construction. Each culture had a "typical" home and household, a type that, to him, could be analyzed and catalogued. By compiling information on these other cultures, their architectural and social organization, he claimed that one could chart—and then determine fairly accurately—the course of their future development.

Even if the claims to objective observation were insubstantial, Viollet-le-Duc's detailed descriptions of cultural settings attracted a fascinated audience of readers. They saw in his writings the promise of a rational discipline which explained, at least in part, the evolution of culture. They also saw a strong assertion of universal laws beneath diverse types of architecture and social life. Architects, however, had a further interest in Viollet-le-Duc's work. The editors of professional architectural journals in the United States, and individual architects who translated his writings (including Nathan Ricker of the University of Illinois) saw themselves and their colleagues as the educated elite who could understand each of the necessary disciplines. They could unite the various arts and sciences and then direct the progression of architecture and society toward the next stage of human development. Accordingly, Viollet-le-Duc was among the European architects elected as honorary members of the American Institute of Architects. W. L. B. Jenney, publishing his lecture on the art and practice of architecture, delivered at the University of Chicago in 1882–83, used illustrations and quotations from *The Habitations* to make his point that "Architecture is the visible and lasting 'history of civilization.' . . . A knowledge of the architecture of a country at any epoch is a knowledge of the people."[20] Such a reading of Viollet-le-Duc says a great deal about the architectural profession in America. The architect considered the supervisory role important. The theoretical level was superior to the empirical. And he would serve humanity by seeking to understand rationally the complex, underlying principles of form.

The confusion over the so-called Eastlake style during these same years demonstrates the hold of an almost opposite rationale for an architectural aesthetic: the assertion that certain forms are inherently pure and moral. The term derived from the writings of Charles Locke Eastlake, a member of the Royal Institute of British Architects. Distressed by the decline in craftsmanship and the overly ornate quality of the machine-made products he saw in expositions and shops, Eastlake had published the tract *Hints on Household Taste, in Furniture, Upholstery and Other Details* in 1868. Seven American editions of the book appeared between 1872 and 1883, when interest began to ebb.

This was a philosophy of design (and, by implication only, of architecture), rich with associations about the inherent worth of particular forms. Eastlake's proposed reforms were based on the spirit (although not necessarily the exact methods) of Gothic furniture-making. He advocated simple, straight-line, foursquare shapes. The only ornamentation was based on the natural grain of the wood, structural pegging (no glue or nails were to be used), and the essential hardware. Or so he said. The illustrations showed heavy pieces of furniture, with massive iron hinges and handles, and deep, rectilinear carving. "Simplicity" was a word that could be used to describe many kinds of objects, and this left Eastlake's guidelines open to interpretation.

American manufacturers quickly began to turn out furniture in the "Eastlake style," and builders used the term for a house bedecked with weighty, squared-off, Gothic trim. Eastlake himself repudiated the quickly made "artistic" objects turned out in American factories, protesting that they debased his name and his reform motives into pure commercialism.[21] Despite his disclaimers, there was an enthusiastic American market for anything that could be termed "Eastlake." According to most popular art critics at the time, including Clarence Cook and Harriet Prescott Spofford, these objects, whether furniture or architectural ornament, represented a merger of fashion and morality, a combination they found irresistible.

Eastlake was destined to be an excuse for display, rather than a guide for control of it, in architecture as in home decorating. Never an actual style, but more a mood, an expression of complexity, irregularity, a play of light and shadow, a feeling for—rather than reliance on—historical precedent, "Eastlake" could be used to describe almost any type of wooden ornament, however fanciful or awkward, if it were rectilinear in form and looked vaguely structural in purpose. Once given this appellation, the piece had been elevated to the ethereal realm of moral art.

In effect, the term "Eastlake" gained such a sudden and widespread popularity because it did not entail significant alterations from the already fashionable American Gothic of builders, carpenters, and furniture manufacturers of the 1870s and 1880s. Already popular wooden ornament was simply incised in a more intricate manner; the lines were more resolutely rectilinear; the interest in structural or seemingly structural ornament now erupted into a complicated, interlocked puzzle of parts, sometimes playful, sometimes awkward and bizarre. What looked like braces for tables or balusters for stairways soon appeared in gables and around door or window openings. By the 1880s, the Eastlake had become the most widely used builder's term for cottage architecture in almost every American city and town. The practical editors of *Industrial Chicago* described it as one of the city's most popular styles, if usually poorly executed, for residences of every class.[22]

On the whole, the architectural journals insisted on defining the Eastlake as a furniture style. The *American Architect* ventured a few examples of Chicago furniture with this label; among these were a mantel designed for the Sheldon house by Boston's Household Art Company and individual room studies by W. L. B. Jenney (fig. 10).

Figure 10. Eastlake dining room furniture by W. L. B. Jenney of Chicago. (From *American Architect,* 1876.)

The sketch of a suburban cottage by Julius Huber of Chicago, which appeared in the *Inland Architect* in 1884, while not labeled as Eastlake, was a more unusual example of a professional journal showing an entire dwelling decorated in this intricate, flattened, woodworking manner.[23] Although the term was extremely fashionable—or perhaps because of this—the professional press avoided using it, except for furnishings that closely resembled Eastlake's own drawings. They did not care to define the Eastlake as a proper style, and certainly not for houses. They seldom even deigned to criticize the liberties taken with Eastlake's name by builders and furniture manufacturers. The explanation, when a discussion of this fashion did appear, was that Eastlake himself had put forth a philosophy rather than a set of templates.[24] Likewise, the American profession should be reserved and not present models for others to copy.

What was occurring was a transition from the clearly established historical revival styles, expounded by academic theorists, which had been the sure basis for architectural design before the Civil War. Now designers of all ranks could freely adapt these earlier styles and more recent fashions to create a looser, more interpretative range of stylistic motifs. Architects continued to claim that their profession had a special understanding of revival styles, a scholarly training in the historical precedent and aesthetic theory which were necessary to use those styles correctly. Yet this elaborate justification was difficult to sustain when the historical references had become so unclear and imprecise, except in the most rigid copying of an earlier monument. The factory production of intricate but seldom historically accurate ornament, and the widespread circulation of both academic and popular treatises on architectural design, made it impossible for the profession to establish a control over style, in any case. But even the profession was no longer certain about the true basis of architecture. The principles of design, whether the premises were scientific or romantic, were increasingly vague.

Yet another popular domestic style of the 1870s and 1880s, among architects and builders alike, reveals this quandary again. The Queen Anne Revival was the most common generic term, in England and the United States, to describe the eclectic houses or institutional buildings that featured any or all of the hodgepodge of materials and details which supposedly characterized a distinct historical style. Despite extensive discourse on the origins of the Queen Anne mode—in professional journals, builders' pattern books, popular monthly magazines, and even in *Industrial Chicago*—none of this discussion constituted a precise definition of a style. It was a matter of symbolic reference and inference, romantic inspiration and individualized interpretation, rather than prescribed rules, even among professional architects.

The first designers to use the term "Queen Anne," a group of young British architects led by Richard Norman Shaw, had been historically inaccurate from the start. They sought to revive traditions of skilled carpentry and masonry which they believed were commonly practiced during the reign of Queen Anne. In fact, the styles they revived were those of earlier Elizabethan artisans. In addition, these architects substituted the image of a wholesome manorial past, one with rich architectural details and expansive spaces, for the actual building skills and technology they supposedly revered. Thus, Queen Anne facades featured elegant combinations of stone and brickwork (although tiles or shingles could be substituted), half-timbering (usually tacked on at the end, rather than forming the structural support), walls of casement windows, and Tudor chimney groups to supplement furnaces. A similar complexity defined the interior spaces of such houses. A plan of irregularly shaped rooms was focused around a massive fireplace and handsome open staircase. These were often combined in a characteristic "living hall." Abundant numbers of bay windows, alcoves, and inglenooks further broke up the space.

Clearly, these design elements all combined quite easily with the dominant American vernacular tendencies of the time. Builders as well as architects, in Chicago as in Boston, quickly picked up the term and the varied components of the style. Interpretations of the Queen Anne began to appear in American architectural journals about 1876. Francis M. Whitehouse's 1878 sketch for a country residence near Chicago caught the extravagant intent of the style, but not the grace or historical references.[25] In any case, though, the Queen Anne house did not really have to be precise. As one architectural writer put it in 1876, the goal was a loose calling up of "historical reminiscences," and not references to specific buildings or epochs.[26] Within a few years, Chicago architects showed as much spirit and exuberance in their Queen Anne residences as the more celebrated East Coast resort architects. W. W. Boyington's Allen house at Des Moines, for instance, rather fitfully combined half-timbering, shingles, clapboards, stone, and delicately turned wooden spindles.[27] Closer to home, his Kirk house at Waukegan (fig. 11), also published in the *Inland Architect,* contrasted richly textured materials and juxtaposed a round, shingled turret with a triangular half-timbered gable (where the date of construction was proudly emblazoned).

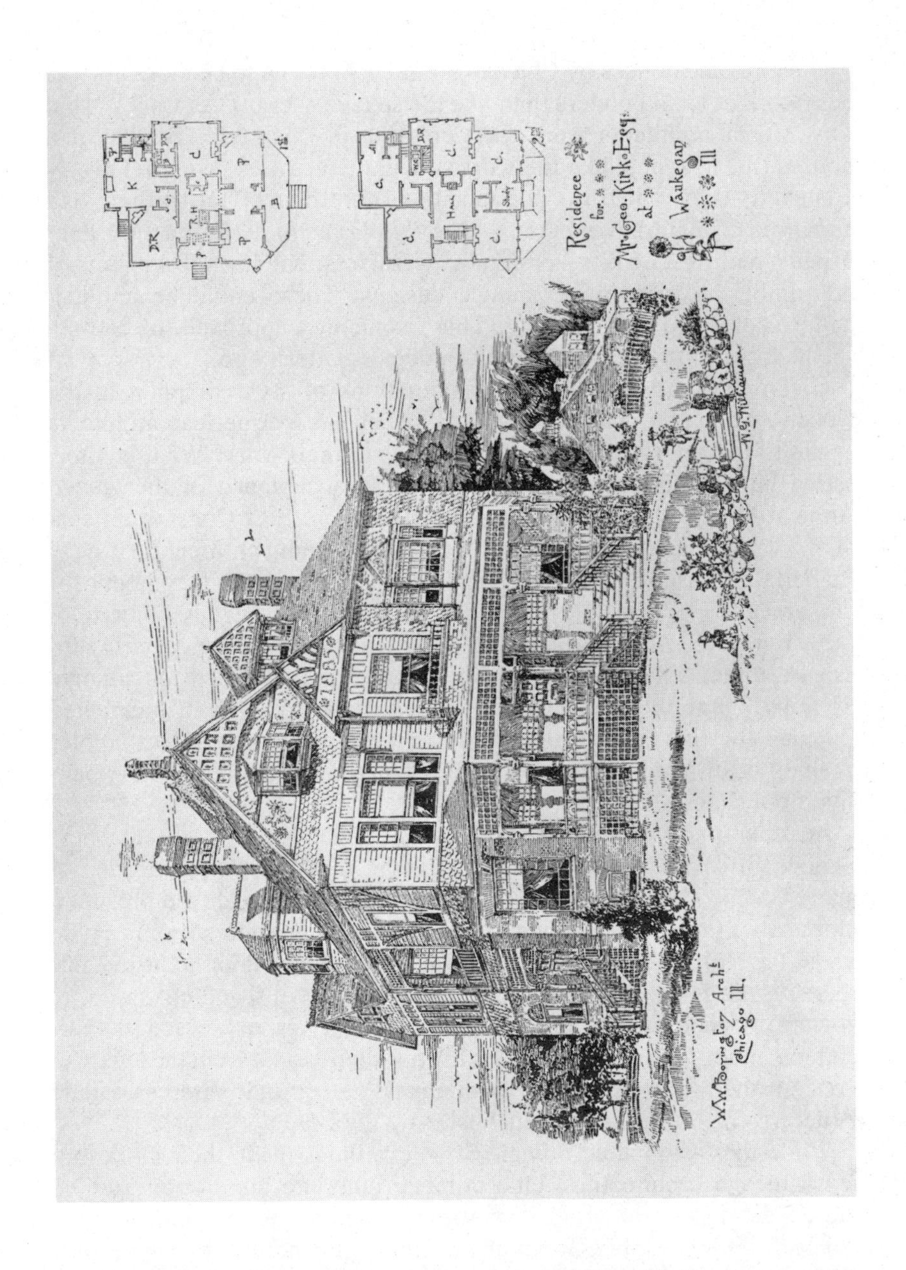

Figure 11. George Kirk House, Waukegan, by William W. Boyington. 1885. (From *Inland Architect*, 1886. Courtesy of the Art Institute of Chicago.)

Queen Anne houses by Chicago architects proved to be more like the best work of local builders than like the spacious resort "cottages" that East Coast architects were then erecting in this style. Boyington's houses, for instance, like the work of George Garnsey, were relatively compact. They relied on juxtapositions for their effect, rather than expanses of material and space. The *Inland Architect* frequently published "picturesque bits" of detailing—turrets, windows, fragments of half-timbering, decorative shingle designs. These could be applied, helter-skelter, to any dwelling. This fragmented approach, of course, seemed frightfully disorderly in a builder's pattern book.

Given the tendency toward combinations of styles implicit in the Queen Anne fad, it was not surprising when a few American architects began to incorporate still more variations in their work. What is interesting here, in contrast to the nationwide acceptance of the Queen Anne style, are the strong regional distinctions. East Coast architects of the 1880s began to mix seventeenth- and eighteenth-century New England architecture with the English importations. The argument for this practice claimed that the two precedents were roughly contemporary. Especially in the seaside resort towns and wealthy eastern suburbs, a distinct American hybrid emerged. Since labeled the Shingle Style by historian Vincent Scully, it relied on expanses of unfinished shingles for the facade (rather than mixtures of materials), simpler geometric forms to give a more refined composition, and open, expansive floor plans.[28]

In other parts of the country, the Colonial Revival and the new Shingle Style had little following. By the mid-1880s, the facades of many Chicago houses shown in the architectural journals did present a more sober face of restraint, it is true. The Zimmerman house in Hyde Park (fig. 12) is a case in point. But its compact floor plan did not recreate the flowing spaces of fashionable eastern dwellings. And its graceful arched porch and wood-shingled tower expressed the architects' admiration for Henry Hobson Richardson's Romanesque Revival, rather than an effort to duplicate the grand, impressionistic structures of Newport or Manchester-by-the-Sea.

While the fashionable Shingle Style dwellings made their mark in a few Chicago architectural club competitions and classroom studios, there was more local enthusiasm for the Romanesque.[29] Similarly, the vogue for the Colonial Revival received little notice in midwestern journals or in architects' offices until the 1890s (see figs. 36 and 45). In-

Figure 12. William Carbys Zimmerman House, Hyde Park, by Flanders and Zimmerman. 1887. (From *Inland Architect*, 1887.)

stead, the *Inland Architect* published architect W. A. Otis's translation of a scholarly French text on the Romanesque in 1889–90.[30] Photographs and drawings of row houses, cottages, and mansions in this style—some in massive limestone, others in wood shingle over frame—filled every local design journal well into the 1900s (see fig. 33).[31] It was not only the Chicago students of architecture and young draftsmen who had caught the fever for the Romanesque. As with the Queen Anne a decade earlier, builders shared the architects' ardor for the style, and also a solid appreciation of its simple beauty and economy. Fred Hodgson, editor of *Builder and Woodworker* and then of Chicago's *National Builder,* claimed that Henry Hobson Richardson exemplified the native American genius. Any observer could immediately recognize the quality of his buildings. Furthermore, Hodgson explained to his readers, Richardson's work glorified economy, but never cheapness, by celebrating "simpler means with less effort and cost."[32] The carpenter and mason could recognize a kindred soul.

Because this common taste existed, the Chicago architectural profession's interest in the problem of the small, moderate-cost house represented even more of a challenge to professional identity than the contemporary studies of this issue by East Coast architects. None of the Chicagoans published pattern books of designs, such as Alexander Oakey's *Building a House* (1881) or Arnold Brunner's *Cottages* (1884), produced while both young men were apprenticing in prestigious New York offices.[33] Nor did the *Inland Architect* sponsor competitions such as those organized by the *American Architect,* which in 1882 asked readers to submit proposals for a "Cheap Dwelling" to cost $3,000 and then for a less expensive "Mechanic's Dwelling." Instead, the Chicago journal simply published a number of sketches for inexpensive cottages in the mid-1880s.[34] Some of these were actual commissions and others were intended as exploratory models for inexpensive housing.

This is not to say, by any means, that the small house was a primary concern of this journal. But Robert McLean, its editor, seems to have recognized the public-relations aspect to the eastern journal's endeavors. The editor of the *American Architect,* in announcing the 1884 competition—its last competition for a small house for several decades—openly stated that the intention was "to justify, in the eyes of the people, the existence of the architectural profession and to show that its members can and will exert their talents for the poor as well as for the rich."[35]

The Regional Crusade

One way to resolve the growing awareness of America's urban problems was to concentrate on regional issues rather than on larger national problems. Such an emphasis on an area's or even a city's particular qualities, history, climate, and future became a strong current in literature, design, and politics throughout Europe and the United States during the 1880s.

Chicago was an ideal location for such a self-focus. Architecturally, it could never be an elegant, older East Coast city, certainly not a Newport, with stately colonial houses alongside expansive Shingle Style "cottages." The city needed its own forms. A burly metropolis, it had been growing at an extraordinary rate, only mildly set back by the depression of 1873 (which had cut back construction rates in most American cities for six years). Inexpensive frame houses from pattern books, luxurious mansions, modern apartment flats, huge factories and warehouses for the goods made in the city and shipped from it went up quickly in the construction boom of the late nineteenth century. Since the Great Fire of 1871, and increasingly thereafter, industrialists, financiers, architects from the East Coast, and ambitious midwesterners tired of rural life had been flocking to Chicago, looking to profit from the rebuilding and the rise to prominence of the "lightning city," the "City of Speed."[36] There was much talk of the distinct, new environment going up so quickly, and of the opportunities available for anyone with determination and a little luck.

The professional architects among these newcomers to Chicago were actually a small and self-protective group. There were only 126 listed in the census figures in 1883. Nonetheless, several among this number had been professionally trained on the East Coast or in Europe and were skilled designers. Daniel Burnham, John Wellborn Root, William W. Boyington, Peter Bonnett Wight, Henry Lord Gay, John Van Osdel, and the architect-engineers Dankmar Adler and William Le Baron Jenney were already well established. Each of these men designed houses for a few well-to-do clients in the city, and, occasionally, even moderate-sized dwellings. But their professional emphasis was and would continue to be overwhelmingly on larger monuments to civic and particularly commercial culture.

They were quite conscious of this preference for the monumental project. The writings of Peter B. Wight, for instance, make the point again and again. Born and educated in New York, he had come to

Chicago in the aftermath of the 1871 fire. He maintained his eastern ties though, and outlined the particularities of Chicago architecture for several East Coast art journals, including the *American Architect*. Chicago commercial architecture had great potential for combining engineering feats with innovative design, Wight declared. Residential architecture, however, was unworthy of the architect's attention. In fact, it was slightly disreputable because of the standards set by local builders.

> The dwelling-house architecture of Chicago has always been far behind that of her business buildings. It has been an admitted fact that Chicago has no homes. Her population has always been so transient, and the spirit of speculation has been such, that no one ever thought of living long in one house, or of making it a comfortable home. Every one was aspiring to a higher state; and no one felt warranted in building for permanence. The frame buildings which were the rule—stone or brick being the exceptions—were always built with heavy sills, so that they could be moved away. The best avenues were cluttered with mean, cheap frame houses. . . .[37]

Commercial architecture seemed to offer a more rewarding, as well as more profitable arena for the trained architect.

Like Wight, other local architects deplored the condition of Chicago housing. House-moving, they knew, was an old nineteenth-century tradition, but flexibility and movability did not seem appropriate criteria for real architecture. And the flamboyance these architects saw around them was not, they exclaimed, traditional practice. John Root was such a critic. He had studied at Oxford and apprenticed at James Renwick's office, before coming to Chicago in 1872. He worked briefly with Wight and then opened an office with Daniel Burnham. However, the Panic of 1873 made for hard times for the two young architects, and perhaps the memories of having to take on houses and barns, rather than grand commissions, left a residing bitterness. Root continued to lambaste the state of the city's residential architecture. His charge, simply put, was that this architecture had too much color, too much gaudiness, too much waste and pretense. The local builders' reliance on rapidly built frame construction promoted slipshod building practices. The builders' rhetoric of moral effect and individual expression stifled any respect for the more enduring principles of beauty.[38] In sum, the professional architects of Chicago saw themselves as a minority, on the defensive.

Despite such gloomy appraisals, commissions for anyone interested in residential building were on the rise. From the building notices in architectural and building magazines, it appears that many women as well as men practiced during the 1880s, designing moderate-cost cottages and row houses in small numbers all around the city. (Among the most frequently cited were Sophia Wixtrom, Agnes Irons, Barbara Titus, Mrs. E. S. Merriman, and Mrs. B. Naughton.) Chicago's population was growing faster than that of any other American city of the time, and the wealth of its inhabitants was increasing too. Houses were needed—and fashionable ones for many families, to testify to their owners' good taste and position in society. The editors of *Industrial Chicago* praised the 1882–91 decade, not only for the "new 'commercial' style" (exemplified, they said, by the Montauk Building), but also for the modern cottages being constructed in the southern suburbs and the platted land on the fringes of the city.[39] Given these opportunities, many of the young architects who arrived in Chicago during the 1880s—among them Joseph Lyman Silsbee, Solon S. Beman, and Frank Lloyd Wright—turned their attention toward housing.

The Chicago architectural profession, faced with several possible goals in the 1880s, tried to resolve them. These men claimed that they wanted to deal with the particular needs and aesthetic possibilities of their area. Many of them, from Louis Sullivan to William W. Boyington, insisted that the time and opportunity had come to make a decisive break from the styles of the past, from the formulas that limited European and East Coast architects. There was talk of a democratic architecture. Yet no one advocated a real break with the profession. Instead, Chicago architects sought to define a new course for the American profession. They spoke of that course in both aesthetic and social terms, although the considerations of aesthetics proved to be paramount.

A Chicago-based professional journal, the *Inland Architect and News Record,* began publication in February 1883. It openly stated the conflicts and prejudices of the midwestern architects. For the next decade, this journal provided a strong emphasis on technical as well as stylistic concerns, a bias toward German over English or French theoreticians, and a rhetoric of democratic values triumphing over aristocratic pretense. Early issues included the lectures that W. L. B. Jenney delivered at the first University of Chicago (his talks included many technical pointers on construction); the reminiscences of John Van Osdel on his career in the Midwest; John Root's articles on the theory of color and his translations of Gottfried Semper. Editorials endorsed women architects and praised the skillful plumber as a member of the team (overseen, to be sure, by the architect).[40] After a decade, the tone would change. But if the *American Architect* was crucial to the development of the East-Coast-dominated architectural profession, the *Inland Architect* was an important factor in organizing midwesterners around what they contended was an alternative approach. After its first year of publication, the Chicago journal could boast 4,000 subscribers, almost twice the number of its Boston competitor, although still far below the circulation of the major builders' journals.[41] Robert Craik McLean, the editor, encouraged publication of the writings as well as the drawings of local architects. He wanted to prove that Chicago was more libertarian—both architecturally and politically—than the East Coast.

The keen sense of a regional crusade—improving the general environment of the Midwest and rehabilitating the good name of the architect—led to the formation of the Western Association of Architects (WAA) in 1884. When McLean called the first organizational meeting to order, there were one hundred twenty-five people present, more than half of them from Chicago. An open antagonism toward the East Coast architect—labeled the "gentleman decorator"—marked the meetings and the transcripts reprinted in McLean's journal. Only a small number of midwestern architects had any use for the AIA; in fact, only one person from Chicago, W. L. B. Jenney, had attended the 1873 AIA convention at Newport.[42]

Yet there was hardly a unanimous stand on the midwestern definition of the professional architect. When the second annual WAA convention attempted a precise pronouncement, the language was surprisingly practical:

> An architect is a professional man [changed to "person"] whose sole ostensible occupation consists in supplying all data preliminary to the material, construction and completion of buildings, in exercising administrative control over the operations of contractors, supplying materials and labor incidental to the construction and completion of buildings, and in officiating as custodian and arbitrator of contracts, stipulating terms of obligation and fulfillment between proprietor and contractor.[43]

This was the group's consensus on the professional skills and responsibilities of its members. The architect (implicitly a man or a woman) was limited to practicing architecture (not taking too much of a hand in real estate or profits from contracting). He or she coordinated the various stages and people involved in a building's design and construction. There was not a word about the noble artistic ideals and classical training so touted in the eastern journals.

When it came to the issue of the architect's client, an even greater confusion arose. There was little desire to announce publicly the ties with the wealthy which in fact characterized the profession, here as elsewhere. The members of the Chicago contingent in particular felt a need to put themselves forward as democratic designers, interested in beautiful surroundings for all Americans and in their well-being. But they still felt a revulsion against most of what was being constructed and against those whom they held responsible for what seemed aesthetic chaos. At one WAA meeting, W. W. Boyington lamented the crudity of aesthetic taste among the lower and middle classes, and regretted that it was so easy for persons from these classes to become wealthy enough to commission a house, since of course it would reflect their innate bad taste. Dankmar Adler quickly took up the issue and insisted that, in America, class differences did not exist. Even the wealthy were middle class, or recently so, he contended. Therefore, everyone was equal in worth and in taste. Indeed, Adler later insisted that architects should respect "their clients, the American people." From such "equality" it was a short step to belief in a typical American. And Boyington seemingly realized that he should at least echo the sentiment that neither architects nor their clients were an elite. He declared, "We are all middle class in our own estimation." The argument that their clients were the same as all other citizens, if only a little richer, and that the architect was always therefore designing for a "typical American," would remain an important assertion for these self-declared "democratic architects."[44] As with the "democratic" builders, they made good use of rhetoric.

Despite the egalitarian statements, class resentment was not easily covered over and became an issue with increasing frequency. At a WAA banquet, John Root presented his audience with a caricature of the middle-class woman client who thought that she should be able to tell the architect how much she wanted to spend and how she wanted her house to look. Of course, in his story, these were wildly disparate goals. But the audience agreed in its laughter that the problem with the middle class was that they not only wanted a say about the design of their homes, but they did not have enough money to carry out their intentions. Within a few years, the WAA would also include "lazy, uneducated workers" as part of the problem it faced in trying to keep "the art divine."[45] The architects' antagonists were increasing in number: builders, moderate-income clients, reform-minded women, and building workers.

Consequently, although many individual architects concentrated on residential commissions, the midwestern profession as a whole, and the journal which represented it, still saw the focus for its aesthetic search not in housing, but in public buildings, particularly commercial ones. Here, the argument went, the architect could represent what he or she saw to be the spirit of the entire people. These were the designs—an office tower, a department store, a governmental building—that would eventually serve every citizen. This then was democratic architecture.[46]

No generalization is absolute, of course. Not only were Joseph Silsbee, Frank Lloyd Wright, W. Carbys Zimmerman, and numerous other Chicago architects concentrating on distinctive styles of domestic architecture during these years. In a few cases, architects considered the special problems of planning a group of houses in a suburban setting or a city block. One who in fact specialized in this scale of work was Solon S. Beman. After an apprenticeship with Richard Upjohn in New York, Beman was brought to Chicago in 1879 by George Pullman. He designed Pullman's house, an office building for the company, and then oversaw the construction of the entire model town of Pullman on the outskirts of Chicago. In addition to these projects, Beman undertook other houses on his own. These included, for instance, a row of three houses in Kenwood, which alternated Queen Anne gables and softer Shingle Style rounded turrets in order to emphasize the distinctiveness of each unit.[47]

Even more interesting an undertaking was the block of moderate-sized detached dwellings in Hyde Park known as Rosalie Villas. With Irving Pond as his foreman (who would later become well known as an architect of settlement houses and a resident of Hull House), Beman laid out most of the houses between 1883 and 1890.[48] This forty-house suburban development had the variety of a builder's vision and the restrained, geometric emphasis that came from a professional's training. (Beman designed most of the houses, although Pond and other architects filled in several.) Most important, Rosalie Villas was an attempt to design a number of similar houses as a group, rather than to consider each dwelling in isolation. Yet there was no single aesthetic imposed over the entire project (fig. 13). Some of the houses were adorned with flat Tudor or Eastlake-derived ornament; others featured graceful Richardsonian arched porches and balconies facing onto small, shared side yards. Even the larger houses resembled the builder's wood vernacular, although treated with considerable restraint.

Figure 13. Bird's-eye view of houses at Rosalie Villas, Hyde Park, ca. 1888, mostly by Solon S. Beman. (From *A Holiday at Rosalie Villas*. Courtesy of the Chicago Historical Society.)

The interiors, too (fig. 14), were purposefully different from one house to the next, emphasizing a flat Colonial Revival doorway detail in one home, a delicately turned Queen Anne stair balustrade in another.

Rosalie Villas was an experiment in residential planning. It also

Figure 14. Interior of the E. W. Heath House at Rosalie Villas by W. I. Beman, 1886. (From *A Holiday at Rosalie Villas*. Courtesy of the Chicago Historical Society.)

stands as a cautious exercise in an architect's idea of social reform: a middle-class neighborhood where each house was different from the others, yet a neighborhood which was to be a harmonious community. Like Beman's other, more famous project, the model town of Pullman, Rosalie Villas never appeared in the professional journals. Such ommissions are significant, for they reveal the profession's concern with the individual building over the planned community. Yet, like other architectural work of the time, Rosalie Villas and Pullman suggest that a few midwestern architects saw their designs in social as well as aesthetic terms. They too wanted to design models to encourage an orderly society as well as to provide a harmonious setting.

The idea of a small, planned, middle-class community of houses was a temperate reform indeed. But even this was not a prominent professional goal of the 1880s. Speculative planning, especially when it was carried out with such diverse styles, with a seeming lack of seriousness, was not acceptable—at least to the editors of professional architectural journals, the professors in architecture schools, and the leaders of the professional organizations. Architects, to them, were responsible for individual commissions and theoretical studies. Robert McLean and Henry Lord Gay soon declared that the Queen Anne style itself was too picturesque, too prone toward novelty and randomness to be classified as true architecture. Perhaps they had been stung by the ambiguous praise accorded the city by C. H. Blackall, writing for the *American Architect:*

> [H]owever disposed to magnitude the Chicagoan may be in business life, in the domestic world the rooms are always snug and small, cosy and convenient, but by no means of the size or style which would imply extended social life. In an architectural sense most of the private work in Chicago is questionable, but in personal feeling, the houses are thoroughly enjoyable.[49]

Criticism of moderate-size houses that were "cosy and convenient" was certainly the official stand on domestic architecture. Architects' work and builders' fancies had to be distinguished.

It is not that the profession, in Chicago or elsewhere in America, believed that social reform was unimportant. But architects had a narrow way of viewing reform. Even if individuals pursued their own courses, the official policy of the professional establishment was uncomfortable with the idea of housing, as opposed to detached houses. They could not accept the premise of the model house, for it meant an environment they had created only indirectly, without being assured of control over what was built.

In a sense, professional architects of this period were Mugwumps, in spirit if not affiliation. It was in 1884—the year Chicago families first moved into Rosalie Villas, the year Arnold Brunner published his pattern book of model cottages—that a group of radical Republicans who came to be known as Mugwumps bolted their party to support a presidential candidate whom they believed to be committed to civil service reform. The term, to men and women of the late nineteenth century, meant more than this single group of patrician reformers. It stood for a type: the well-educated, well-to-do person, generally a resident of an eastern or midwestern metropolis, who contended that it was the duty of the American upper middle classes, especially the professionals, to initiate improvements for the common good. In their own phrase, the Mugwumps were on the offensive against the "crass materialism" of their time, hostile to the values and ostentation of the newly rich, determined to preserve the stability of a society they saw changing much too quickly. They wanted efficient government, well-run cities, a good society, but they insisted that only the educated elite could oversee these reforms. As Richard Hofstadter has so ably shown, the Mugwumps were threatened by the "status revolution" taking place around them. They were the predecessors of the Progressives; conservative and established, they were firm in their belief that the nation and the community would benefit from a reassertion of ideals and the guidance of a concerned group of experts.[50]

Chicago architects of the time demonstrate this Mugwump mentality quite clearly. They wanted improvements—in their case, better cities and suburbs—but only on their own terms. Fearful of the builders below them, and of the builders' blustery language of democracy and exuberant displays of ornamental fancy, they were also subservient to the wealthy who commissioned their buildings. They were caught between these powerful groups. The official proposals for reform showed this compromised situation. Architects, as individuals, did, in many cases, want to use their skills for the common good. But the words they used to discuss this possibility were vague, abstract, theoretical and universal. They were seldom clear, much less certain, about how to improve the cities where they lived. And they were unwilling, for the most part, to propose working models for the houses in which most American families were going to live. The code of the American profession disapproved of such models as unartistic, uncontrollable, and unrefined.

3 THE STRUCTURE OF THE SUBURBS

Certain dangerous doctrines have been preached of late, which have not been duly limited and explained; such as the dignity of labor and the duty of self-reliance. Our lecturers enforce these as if they were of universal application; and forget to emphasize the fact that, in existing communities, masculine and feminine virtues still form two distinct classes.

Abba Gould Woolson, *Woman in American Society* (1873)

Builders' pattern books of the nineteenth century celebrated the eccentricities of middle-class American dwellings with great pride. Professional architectural journals and texts, with equal fervor, condemned the exuberant display and complex variety of the untrained builders. The disagreements were real enough, for the two groups had antagonistic aesthetic philosophies: one endorsed a free play of forms; the other, refined good taste. Moreover, they were directly competing for public recognition as America's true architects: the givers of form to the nation's built environment. The builders waged a campaign based on abundance—inexpensive advertising broadsides, readily available plans, luxuriantly symbolic ornamentation, promises of widespread social equality—with the aim of inspiring the general public. The professional architects, on the other hand, went on the opposite tack. They would elevate the nation's homes by providing elegant examples in their mansions and prominent public monuments; ordinary builders, they insisted, should recognize the superiority of the architect's training and respectfully follow his lead, rather than try to create independent styles.

The hostility between the two groups ignored several important facts. For one, both professional architects and self-trained builders drew their aesthetic and social theories from many of the same sources. There was even a great deal of similarity between actual residential commissions by architects and builders, if one disregards size and quality of materials. But this should not be taken as a sign that the builders were simply copying outright the work of professional architects. Rather, members of both groups were reading, or reading about, current English treatises on aesthetics, especially the works of Ruskin and Eastlake. Later, in the 1880s, they both sought to explore the possibility of an indigenous, democratic American architecture, although they would define their terms and goals differently. Builder and architect shared an intellectual world, therefore, but they interpreted that world in radically divergent ways.

Moreover, the two groups were both working within the same economic and social structure, even if their clients were of markedly different classes. Both architects and builders relied upon an increasingly well-organized system of industrial manufacture and commercial distribution of the many goods that had come to be considered necessary for residential construction and home decoration. And, as this system grew more complicated, the work that went into producing the goods and designing the houses became more specialized. Architectural offices, building-trades unions, and consortiums of builders grew into larger and more complex entities. As organized groups, they vied with one another for political power and for control of the rapidly expanding housing market.

The rapid growth of American industrial capitalism in the late nineteenth century generated not only more products but also a larger urban middle class with enough money and stability to invest in houses and in goods for homes. In fact, home ownership was, by and large, taken as a central part of a family's definition as "middle class"—a word just coming into the national vocabulary. Most of the members of this group could not afford the services of an architect to custom-design their homes. Yet they were extremely susceptible to current ideas about house design.

This widespread interest in residential architecture was one aspect of a more general focus on the home itself in the late nineteenth century. As Abba Gould Woolson sought to emphasize, the home was supposed to be a haven apart from the industrial and commercial world. Home was idealized as a retreat for men and a refuge for women. The late Victorian sentimentalization of womanhood—that is, middle-class womanhood—was intimately bound up with the highly expressive, supposedly organic architectural motifs which had come to be so popular for American homes. Moreover, as we shall see, the opening of the suburbs to middle-class families, a development made possible by the dramatic breakthroughs in public transportation of the 1880s and 1890s, would further intensify this cult of difference between men and women, work and home. But it was a tenuous distinction. Obviously, it relied upon advances in industrial technology—quite directly in fact. And it would not last.

The Industrialization of Home-Making

The ideology celebrating the ornamented, personalized home was facilitated by the increased availability of descriptions and images of model homes. Advances in printing technology, reproduction techniques for illustrations, and transportation services refined and disseminated ideas for the home. Improved papermaking in the 1880s yielded an inexpensive high-gloss paper. Even more important for cutting costs and printing time was the use of standardized type sizes and column widths, a practice that most larger publishing companies adopted during this decade and that led eventually to the linotype machine. Illustrations grew more numerous as they became easier and cheaper to produce. Zinc cuts replaced the earlier, crude wood blocks which had to be slowly cut by hand. In the mid-1880s, journals began to offer special inserts with heliograph reproductions of drawings and photographs, although there was initially an additional fee for these plates. Halftone photography introduced a less expensive process which closely simulated contours and depth through minute dots. The illustrations of houses in builders' guides and in professional architectural journals could now, as never before, emphasize details of texture and ornament as well as mood. Although the popular media certainly did not create the cult of the romantic home, these technological advances allowed that ideal to be intimately connected to specific symbolic details of architecture.

As these images crossed the country, becoming available in every town and city, other dramatic advances were also reshaping the production of homes. House-building itself was central to the American economy throughout most of the nineteenth century. In every city, private expenditures for construction, both residential and commercial, and developers' or communities' outlays for public services—including roads, sewer systems, water works and fire departments—constituted the single most important contribution to the nation's economy. Although the proportion of national and family income that went into housing began to decline by the end of the century (and dropped even more at the beginning of the next), production of housing units remained high, and was crucial to the growth of American industry.[1] There were jobs not only in construction but also in affiliated fields, from the production of building materials and furniture to plumbing equipment and kitchen utensils. Although the depression of 1873 slowed housing starts in most cities, these other industries continued to expand.

As the nation's population rose—increasing almost threefold between 1860 and 1900, with the urban population increasing fourfold—new housing stock was urgently required. Growth in the Midwest was especially rapid. Chicago's population rose from 300,000 in 1870 to 500,000 ten years later, and to twice that by 1890. In large part, this remarkable boom occurred because the city was emerging as a national center for almost every aspect of the flourishing housing industry. Chicago had become the third-largest producer of manufactured goods in the country by 1880. The number of factories there almost tripled over the next decade; the number of factory workers more than doubled. The value of the products from these factories rose more than 100 percent.[2] Chicago became the country's principal source for raw materials for housing—especially lumber, but also brick and stone; it produced great quantities of plumbing fixtures and window glass; it was the nation's largest manufacturer of furniture. Chicago was also the distribution center for all of these goods. The large department stores of Chicago, especially Marshall Field's, and the mail-order companies of Montgomery Ward and Richard Warren Sears, serviced every town and large city west of the Alleghenies. The major railroad lines converged there. The railroads also brought the latest pattern books and architectural magazines from the East Coast. But by the 1880s, when Chicago became one of the principal publishing centers in the United States, local companies began to add their own texts and journals on housing. In hundreds of ways, the city was central to a pattern of industrial expansion which affected the production of houses.

In Chicago, as elsewhere in the country, the number of people who could be considered middle-class was on the rise. Clerical workers, salespeople, government employees, technicians, and salaried professionals increased in the census figures more rapidly than the old middle class of business entrepreneurs and independent professionals; more rapidly, in fact, than the population of the nation as a whole.

National income was, consequently, increasing too, from $237 per capita in 1870 to $309 in 1880, to $492 by 1900. While families were insecure about their social status and financial future in many ways—since the major earners were generally in someone else's employ—they could rely on steady incomes at these salaried jobs. A clerk in an insurance firm in Chicago earned about $1,500 a year in 1880, and $1,800 by 1890. A lawyer in a small firm might be earning $4,000 by 1890. (In contrast, many skilled workers brought home only $500 to $800 in a year, and most working-class families lived on less than that.)[3] These income levels and occupational groups defined the middle classes.

But so did home ownership. By American standards, as expressed in the popular builders' texts, women's domestic guides, and other literature of the late nineteenth century, the "middle-class family" was recognized by home ownership, and by the quality of that home, as well as by the man's employment. Certainly the range of middle-class families I have just cited were able to buy their own homes, often in the outlying suburbs by the end of the century, and to furnish them fairly stylishly—although probably only the young lawyer could consider a professional architect's services in designing his home. Most of the families who, by their own definition, were middle-class would either work with a local carpenter (who asked only a flat fee to interpret a pattern-book design) or purchase a speculatively built house from a builder or from a previous owner who was moving.

However, home ownership was not as widespread as many Americans wanted to believe. A survey which was first made part of the census in 1890 showed that, nationwide, only 48 percent of American families owned their own homes; in cities of over 100,000, that figure dropped to 23 percent. Chicago's 29 percent was, consequently, slightly above the national average.[4] Renting was, after all, quite profitable to those who had the capital to invest; returns were commonly about 10 to 12 percent annually, and could be as high as 40 percent. (It was, in fact, the importance of these urban land rents that led Henry George to propose his famous Single Tax land-reform scheme which became so popular at the end of the century.)[5] Thus, when builders like S. E. Gross began to offer "easy payment" systems of financing for houses that cost between $1,000 and $5,000 (plus financing charges and land), they indeed seemed to offer an opportunity to expand the ranks of the American middle class by making inexpensive suburban homes more widely available. A family with a yearly income of only $1,000 could consider becoming suburban homeowners and taking on middle-class status. Consequently, when the Chicago journalist George Ade asked why the city's "fortunate" middle class had "a monopoly of the real enjoyment," he could duly note the advantages of home life, as well as employment status and economic stability, which pertained to "all those persons who are respectably in the background"—Ade's definition of the middle class.[6]

The availability and the very appearance of these homes were made possible by recent industrial advances. A new range of machinery allowed builders to apply the architectural complexities of the Eastlake or the Queen Anne or the Moorish styles to relatively inexpensive dwellings. It was not, however, industrial production itself that was new. Since the 1850s, American mills had produced machine-cut moldings and kept them in stock for builders, but the moldings had been fairly plain and coarse. The advent of steam power permitted the use of equipment that made such ornament faster and in greater variety. By 1870, 70 percent of the lumber-milling firms in this country that made stock blinds, window sash, doors, and ornament relied on fast, heavy steam-powered equipment rather than on foot-velocipedes for each machine. After 1871 there was a flood of inventions for even faster, cheaper machines. The 1876 Philadelphia Centennial featured a display of woodworking equipment, almost all of it American, which fascinated foreign visitors unfamiliar with such technology (fig. 15).[7]

By the late 1870s, much of the decoration for the stylish middle-class dwelling was already being produced in a factory, shipped across the country by railroad, and then simply tacked onto the dwelling. Strips of detailing were produced in an increasingly wide assortment of shapes, sizes, and grades. They were mostly in wood, although there was also factory-produced ornamental work in metal, plaster, and terra-cotta (fig. 16). A great variety of more delicate shapes replaced the old jig-sawn, straight-edged ornament of the pre–Civil War "gingerbread age," crafted by the carpenter on the site. Carpenters' pattern books continued to show how to carve imaginative ornament, but in the back of the same books were advertisements for the latest woodworking machinery.

Shingles, cut to resemble fish scales or snowflakes, or left rough-edged and "natural," could be produced cheaper and faster by a factory. Moldings were available in elegant beading or floral designs,

Figure 15. American woodworking equipment on display at the Philadelphia Centennial. (From *Scientific American,* 1876.)

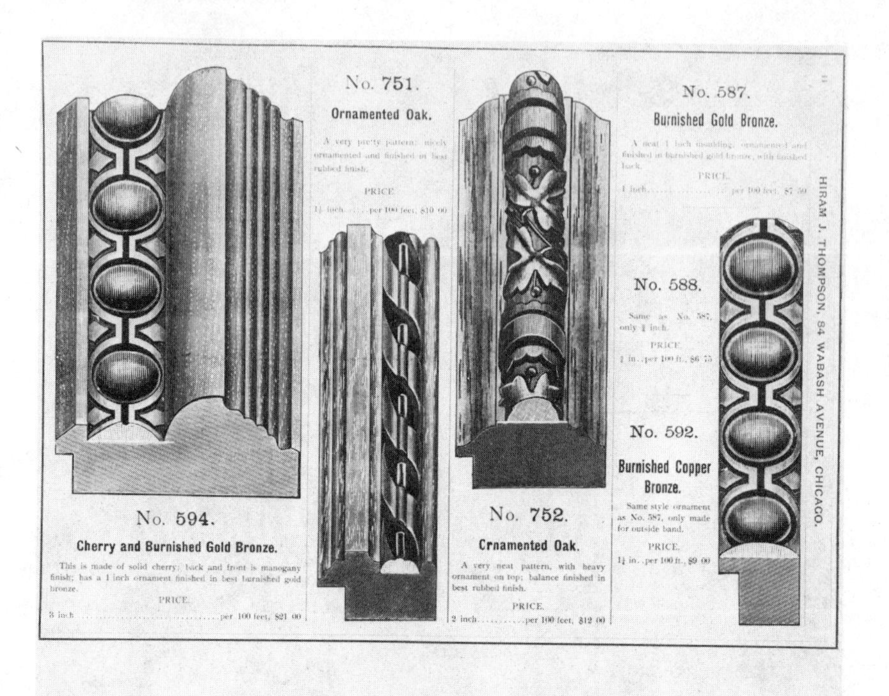

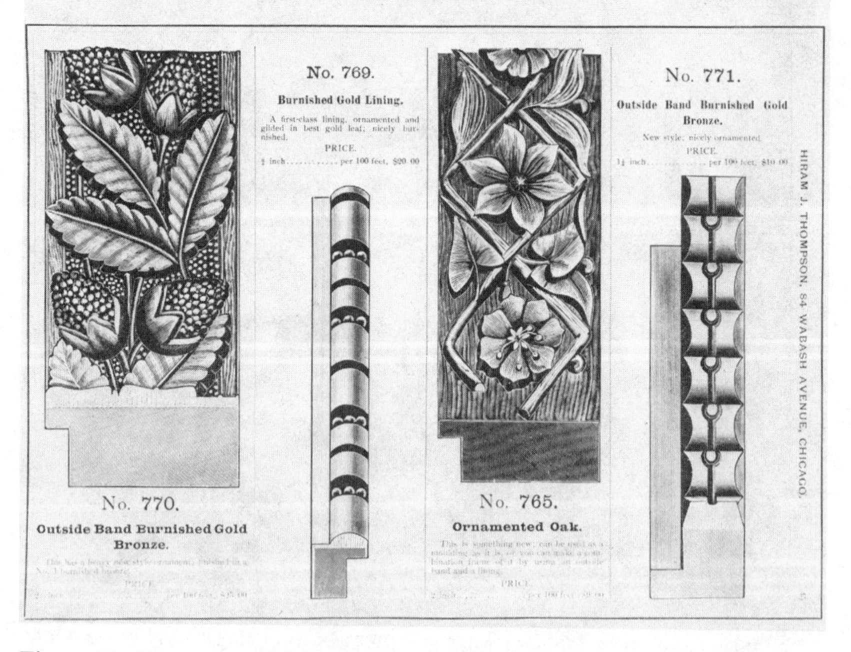

Figure 16. Factory-produced moldings. (From the catalogue of the Hiram J. Thompson Company of Chicago. Courtesy of the Chicago Historical Society.)

always regular and precise. Spindles in delicate cylindrical shapes, Venetian blinds with beveled slats, capitals in every order and disorder came from architectural supply companies. The pieces had only to be bradded and glued into place. Most doors, frames, window sash, and wainscotting panels were produced in the mill. Entire porches and stairs could be ordered from catalogues. Increasingly, the interior finish work was relegated to the planing mill as well, for there it could be kept perfectly dry to season, and free from dust for varnishing. By the end of the century, F. E. Kidder's standard textbooks on building construction reported that it was only in the rare case of a small quantity of work being done in a special pattern that lumber did not arrive dressed from the planing mill, moldings were not struck in the molding mill, and doors did not come from the stock pile. These economies, he noted, were essential in any house costing less than $4,000—that is, any moderately priced middle-class home.[8]

The major difference during the 1870s and 1880s was not mechanization per se, but the greatly increased output and variety. Mechnization of house-building and decorating did not arrive all of a sudden, spurred by a particular fashion or even an ingenious inventor. Devices like lathes and templates had been used in woodworking for generations. But now productivity improved dramatically with new precision equipment. Higher-grade steel blades allowed the steam-powered machines to be used at full speed, without cease, with no danger of metal fatigue. Interchangeable blades and tilting tables expanded the possibilities for speed and variety still further in the 1880s. By 1898, the commissioner of labor, Carroll D. Wright, reported that with mechanical saws it now required only four hours to produce irregular forms in wood that would have required 110 hours with hand processes.[9]

New machinery also speeded up and systematized the production of other building materials. A factory worker could cut recessed panels in stone, embellishing the blocks with flat arabesque ornament modeled from templates. Since brick had become more expensive (doubling in price just two weeks after Chicago's 1871 fire, then rising more gradually), brickworks soon shifted from handmade to machine-made products. By 1880, the number of Chicago brick manufacturers had tripled. They now produced a machine-made "Chicago common," much harder (since it contained less limestone) than earlier products. And there were new varieties: smooth dry-pressed bricks (three to five times as expensive as the common, but of better quality); molded bricks to create an arch or a beveled string course; thin Roman bricks; shiny glazed and enamel bricks. All of these were available in a wide spectrum of colors, in cream, buff, yellow, crimson, even metallic sheens and glosses which supposedly resembled the moist hues of lichen and moss. Fireproof terra-cotta blocks and ornament were also being manufactured in factories like the Chicago Terra-Cotta Works. After the fire, Peter B. Wight began turning out hollow tiles for fireproofing at another local factory. New processes for grinding tints and mixing mineral paints or oil stains expanded the range of colors that could be used to adorn any house. Paint and sand combinations were also used to simulate other materials, for instance, giving galvanized sheet metal the rough texture of sandstone.[10]

The new techniques encouraged extravagant display, while making ornament more accessible to American builders and homeowners. In fact, by the late 1880s, architects and builders were demanding some restraint. John Root protested the "disastrous effects" of the fast-expanding range of colors and textures available in manufactured bricks, terra-cotta, and paint, condemning the metallic sheens, the glaring clashes of colors, the artificiality of the products. The carpenter Fred Hodgson was encouraged by the spread of Richardsonian motifs, with their simple, unadorned lines.[11] Most people were still delighted with the spectacle of complex shapes and varied materials, however.

Industrial processes were transforming the inside of the house too. There were large assortments of wooden latticework screens, stairway balustrades, and plaster rosettes. During the 1880s, as the use of steam power and new machinery revolutionized the plaster industry, it was also easier to have a smooth, plain surface for a wall. Hand-applied plaster, like brick mortar, had required time and skill. After being mixed on the site, the combination of lime, sand, and animal hair had to wait "in stack" before it could be "wet up" and readied for use. With patented chemical plasters made in a factory, quality could be controlled and time saved on the site, since the materials could be transported wet and ready to apply. By 1896, when it was said that 99 percent of the homes in the United States had plastered walls, ceilings, and partitions, workers relied almost solely on factory-produced plaster, wire-lathe, and mortar.[12]

The production of plate glass also emerged over these decades. Before 1875, almost all American window glass had been imported from France or Germany, for American glassworks had consistently proven financial failures. But by the mid-1880s, high quality and inexpensive window glass—plain, stained, or ornamentally cut—was being profitably manufactured at home. Recent improvements in furnaces, fuels, and additives for molten glass, as well as more exacting rolling machines, would cause the volume of American-produced glass to increase more than tenfold between 1880 and 1919.[13] Lumber dealers, as well as specialty stores began to carry stock windows to fit their stock sash. Builders could now respond more easily to the vogue for walls of windows in a house.

Perhaps the most conspicuous and most discussed improvement in domestic building technology was in heating and plumbing fixtures. Basement hot-air or hot-water furnaces, connected to a maze of flues and registers, were still fairly expensive in 1880; but they were being introduced into some middle-class homes (although stoves were still the norm and fireplaces were a highly symbolic additional source of heat). Furnaces had to be frequently stoked with coal, and the register in each room adjusted by hand, until automatic controls became available in the early twentieth century. These systems were thus troublesome as well as expensive. Nonetheless, room stoves, registers, and even furnaces were displayed as proud possessions and works of art. Whether in the parlor, the kitchen, or the basement, heating appliances were encrusted with ornament to make them artistic. The popular "Crown Jewel" or "Art Garland" stoves were advertised as beautiful objects. Chicago's J. A. Colby and Sons and the Tobey Furniture Company designed and made furnaces on commission, while the less expensive John M. Smyth store on the West Side instituted installment buying to encourage customers to choose elaborate models of furnaces, room registers, and stoves.

Plumbing was an even more complicated matter. Although drainage systems were still primitive (pipes usually emptied into cesspools or pigpens rather than municipal sewage lines) and hot water was a luxury, more careful planning for sanitation was taking place. Manufacturers of plumbing equipment reported soaring sales in the 1880s. Changing public attitudes about home sanitation, directly related to fears about germs and "sewer gas," stimulated the technological advances. These manufacturers were able to utilize the fledgling health theories profitably. Although there had been only 44 plumbing firms in Chicago at the time of the 1871 fire, 187 existed by 1885. Richard T. Crane and Company, the largest firm, produced and distributed thousands of porcelain and painted cast-iron bathtubs, flush toilets, sinks, and lavatories, as well as valves and pipes in lead and iron, all during a single year. The year 1880 had been epochal, according to the *Architectural Record;* after this date, "true sanitary plumbing" began, with porcelain fixtures, exposed pipes in galvanized wrought iron, and careful specifications issued by architects and builders.[14] The outdoor privy and indoor earth-closet seemed primitive now; the modern flush toilet, developed about 1778, came into general use a hundred years later. The practice of installing washstands in every bedroom, with porcelain or tile "splashers" on the wall behind them, was often discarded in new homes. By the end of the century, the bathroom would no longer be looked upon as an effeminate luxury. Toilets would no longer be isolated outside the house's walls. Taking a bath would not be considered potentially dangerous. Of necessity, the new plumbing systems for fresh water and for waste were now connected to municipal sewage and water supplies in the major cities and well-to-do suburbs. The older systems periodically overflowed with the vast amounts of waste water emptied into them.

Both the municipal services and the more refined home-fixtures greatly increased the homeowner's average expenditures. The cost for plumbing an average (that is, $3,000) American house in 1860 had been estimated at about $250; by 1890 similar estimates ranged between $500 and $1,000, often reaching a fifth of the total cost of the house. Americans were willing to pay. They had come to trust the manufacturers of their plumbing equipment and the sanitary engineers with their health.

The impact of technology on the late-nineteenth-century dwelling also extended to public transportation and the construction process itself. The expansion of American cities in the 1870s, while remarkable, had been contained by the still primitive public transportation networks of slow horsecars and infrequent, expensive railroads. In Chicago, in the aftermath of the fire of 1871, which had destroyed three and a half square miles of the city center, residential settlement began to move outward. But the process was gradual and the new neighborhoods were often congested. Investment proved, however, quite profitable. In Hyde Park and Englewood, to the south of the city, but still fairly close to the downtown area, investors reaped benefits of 1,000 to 15,000 percent in five or six years. A belt of frame workingmen's cottages, erected by development companies or building and loan associations and owned by their inhabitants, formed a semicircle around the outskirts of Chicago to the south and west, although the ring was a narrow one.[15] Strict municipal legislation preventing the use of wood construction within designated fire limits prompted much of the new building. Since stone and brick were so expensive, many builders who specialized in moderate-cost dwellings concentrated on the nearby suburban towns or undeveloped areas rather than increase their construction costs.

But it was difficult, at the time, for many families to take on the expense of a suburban home. This usually entailed a large down payment with the remaining money (and 5 percent interest) due in five years. Banks foreclosed if payment was not on time. Furthermore, most working-class men, women, and children, whose employment was irregular and poorly paid, had to remain near the central city. So did many salaried workers. All the same, Chamberlin's guide to Chicago of 1874 could claim that "ninety-nine families in every hundred will go an hour's ride into the country, or toward the country, rather than live under or over another family, as the average New Yorker or Parisian does."[16] This estimate, far from accurate, even for the city's upper classes of the time, nonetheless reveals a widely shared sentiment. The middle class, in Chicago and other large American cities, wanted privacy, contact with nature, and self-sufficiency, all qualities they hoped to find in a suburban home.

The difficulties of existing transportation did contain Chicago's expansion of the 1870s to a mere half-mile beyond the existing limits. But there were experiments going on which would change this pattern, in hundreds of cities, within a decade. The introduction of the cable car in 1882 was followed by the electric trolley in 1888 and the first elevated railroad in 1892. Chicago quickly installed each of these services, but the major commitment was in electrifying the municipal streetcar lines in 1889. This made commuting on the streetcar from the suburbs easy and much faster. Speeds were twice those of the old horsecars, even if conditions were crowded. In 1890, at the insistence of commuters, the legal rate of speed for the suburban streetcars was increased from ten to twenty miles per hour in the city, and up to thirty miles per hour outside the city limits, cutting the time even more. Railroad service was soon extended to match the new competition. The Blue Island Land and Building Company, in operation since 1869, developed Morgan Park on the suburban branch of their Rock Island Railroad. By 1905, there were fourteen daily trains each way from Morgan Park to downtown Chicago, thirteen miles away; it was a daily round trip of from thirty-five to fifty minutes, with a monthly ticket costing only $2.25, about the price of a new pair of men's pants and within a middle-class family's budget.[17]

The proliferation of these services, together with the relatively inexpensive fares and faster speeds, allowed formerly urban middle-class families to commute to work or shopping from the suburbs. The streetcar lines brought thousands of Chicagoans to the small, ornamented, romantic houses going up outside the city. In making suburban life available to so many families, the streetcar service brought about an extraordinary increase in the size—both population and area—of many cities. The city limits of Chicago swelled outward after the improved transportation facilities were installed. To provide for necessary services, new territory was annexed, increasing the municipal tax base. In 1870, the outer limits of Chicago were five miles beyond the main downtown corner; by 1890, the combination of new transportation networks, record construction figures, a fourfold increase in the city's population, and a massive annexation of land to the west the year before, had pushed the limits to twelve miles.[18]

The expansion was controlled and manipulated by a few private investors. Yet because of the enthusiastic public support for the suburban services, city councils made great concessions to those businessmen who provided the services. Charles Yerkes centralized the transportation lines in Chicago, for instance, and thus became one of the most powerful of a new breed of American streetcar magnates. Together with a group of aldermen known as the "Gray Wolves," he made a fortune by investing in transportation companies and real estate. By 1893, after eight years of dealing, Yerkes owned not only most of the five hundred miles of streetcar tracks in and around Chicago, but he had been able to sell the land along the routes he had planned. The situation was similar in many other American cities—Omaha, Denver, Oakland, Minneapolis—where unprecedented population increases and the almost desperate demand for transportation services gave such entrepreneurs a free hand, at least for a time. The progressive reform campaign at the end of the century would later turn against the traction trusts, and in Chicago's case, force Yerkes to leave the city. During the 1880s and early 1890s, however, he seemed to promise much the same package as most popular builders: the rediscovery of nature, the escape from the city's problems, the preservation of the family. He assured Chicago of health, individuality, and freedom in the suburbs, made possible with streetcar commuting.

The reaction against the consolidation of trusts was, of course, connected to the rise of the progressives' criticism of inequalities in American society. They harshly condemned the loss of individual initiative and free enterprise for workers at every level. The traction trust was one glaring example of a profound reorganization taking place in the late nineteenth century. The nature of work was becoming more specialized, more centralized, more highly managed. Each level of the housing business underwent a transformation. Architects, as we have seen, organized into a professional body in an attempt to define their rights and responsibilities more exactingly. Real estate interests shifted toward larger consortiums, controlling banking and transportation as well as land, and these promoters also began to work with larger general contracting firms. Manufacturers looked for ways to gain a greater control over their markets in order to assure a larger turnover of their goods. They formed "combinations" or trusts in the supply and distribution of materials.

Chicago was the likely center for this kind of concentration in the building trades, for it had been the world's largest lumber market since 1856. Along the river, boards were piled up twenty and thirty feet high: pine from forests of Wisconsin, Michigan, and Minnesota, whitewood and black walnut from Tennessee, ash from the Deep South. By the mid-1880s, the nearby forests were fast becoming depleted, and taste had moved toward lighter woods; Chicago dealers expanded their reliance on the railroads over the canals, and began to move up cypress and white pine from the South to the Chicago mills. More than two thousand men worked in these local mills, turning out doors, sash, dressed lumber, and ornamental detailing for houses around the country. Several mill owners organized combinations of lumberyards, lumber mills, freight lines, and local contracting firms. A single man could import wood, have it finished, turn the ornament, and either use it for his own contracting firm or have it shipped at special rates. Campbell Brothers, a manufacturing and contracting firm with over two hundred employees in their main Chicago branch, had a sizable advantage in the local market since they could make and distribute products quickly and cheaply. D. Wade and Company, founded in 1883, produced entire ready-made houses, cut, fitted, marked, and shipped in large orders as far away as Buenos Aires. Small operators, both retail and wholesale, were forced out of a powerful, well-organized enterprise centering in Chicago: the lumber trust.[19]

Larger manufacturers in several other building-materials fields now found it advantageous to work together to promote their wares. In 1884, in downtown Chicago, a consortium of contractors and architects, under the leadership of Henry Lord Gay, opened the Permanent Exhibition and Exchange of Building Materials and Improvements. (A few years later, it would be officially renamed the Institute of Building Arts.) Here were elaborate displays, open to the public, showing the range of materials and ornamental work available, particularly the products of the larger firms that could afford to buy prominent space and pay attendants to hawk their wares. On the upper floors were a large architects' library (open to members of the profession and to builders who paid dues), together with assembly rooms for professional architects' and builders' organizations in the city.[20]

The National Association of Builders was established in 1884, largely under the impetus of the major Chicago builders. Their first meeting was held at the Permanent Exhibition building. Here Samuel E. Gross, B. F. Cronkite, and William F. Kerr, all of Chicago, spoke out about the need for industrialization and the problems of the building unions. They insisted, for example, that industrialized construction required uniform specifications in materials, designated by the architect or builder rather than by the workman on the site. Cautiously at first, they condemned the building unions as disruptive, socialistic forces dangerous to American industry and society.[21] Actual industrialization of the building industry proceeded slowly and was poorly managed, but it emerged early as an issue for builders. The concerted hostility toward the building trades workers, and their unions in particular, already cast them as the major impediment to progress.

This organization of builders was a new and significant event for the country. Although the basis of the American construction industry would remain local, small builders now declined as the urban building companies organized to protect their interests and to advance rationalized, large-scale developments. A large builder could complete a package deal of half a block of houses on a ninety-day loan from a bank. Especially during the building boom that was launched in Chicago in 1889, with the announcement that the city had been chosen as the site for the great 1893 World's Columbian Exposition, builders worked frantically to cut their expenses and time on residential construction. But the increased pace and greater reliance on industrialization had begun earlier in the decade. A rapildy increasing housing market made cost-efficient methods of building imperative. The apartment house was one result, and many were built in the larger cities during these years. But the production of small frame houses also became a more industrialized process.

The building-workers' organizations and their tactics were also undergoing major changes. Within the unions, there was a new drive for centralization and concerted political maneuvering. The aim of the workers, or certainly of their leaders, was to protect jobs and to secure decent wages, and also to protect high-quality construction. In 1887, the bricklayers' union began construction on an architectural manifestation of that determination: a labor temple in which all the building workers could find a symbol of their unified strength. The temple was a twelve-story "skyscraper," comparable in height to the other business structures rising in Chicago's downtown area. It was completed in 1889, at a cost of $50,000. Within the solid stone, brick, and terra-cotta building (it did not use the revolutionary steel-frame construction that was just being accepted in Chicago), were ground-floor stores, an auditorium, a larger hall to seat three thousand, small assembly rooms, a mechanics' library and reading room, and a hotel.

Here, in 1890, the Council of Building Trades was founded, a union of all building workers: first the stonecutters, carpenters, painters, plasterers, derrickmen, hod carriers, lathers, gas fitters, galvanized iron and cornice workers, slaters, steamfitters, stairbuilders, and bricklayers, and eventually the twenty separate groups which were required on a large construction site. They all agreed to support one another in securing what they considered to be adequate wages and reasonable working hours, to maintain the union representatives' control of work on a site, and to resist the rapid industrialization of their crafts—the specialization, the loss of autonomy, the speedups in production and cutbacks in the number of workers employed on a job. With equal fervor, they opposed the substitution of poor-quality, factory-produced ornament, structural materials, and technological equipment for homes as well as for larger buildings.[22]

For most of these many union workers, the production of houses was as important to their trade as the construction of office buildings or department stores. One indication of this importance can be found in the records of the plumbers' union. At first the introduction of new plumbing equipment into the home had stimulated a great respect for the skilled plumber. Pipes had to be installed carefully, for it was widely held that angles would allow poisonous gases to be trapped within the house.[23] For this reason, the pipes were left exposed in the kitchen, the basement, and the bathroom, so that the residents could be assured that no gases were escaping and accumulating in closed places. But the principal responsibility lay with the plumber who installed equipment. And, since the fixtures were visible, installation was a matter of aesthetics as well as sanitary precautions. In 1885 plumbers of Chicago formed an organization to encourage high-quality work. The officers of the Master Plumbers' Association prevailed upon members to experiment, to read, to improve installation techniques and promote public health. They saw themselves as skilled workers: both sanitary scientists and designers. The association even offered an annual prize for the best essays on ventilation and drainage. They welcomed the Western Association of Architects to the city, and expressed their respect for these other designers who hoped to establish higher ideals of residential architecture.[24] The building workers firmly believed that they were critical to the production of good housing.

Despite such efforts, the autonomy of building workers on the construction site was declining. The architect's or builder's specifications for materials became increasingly detailed; the manufacturer's stipulations for installation more precise. The emphasis in product design and even installation was shifting from the worker's skill to the manfacturer's precision. Safety and comfort now resided in the product itself, not with the person who chose and fitted it. Quality was a matter of industrial techniques in the factory, with fewer provisions for judgment and variation on the site. The carpenter and builder now faced each other across a formidable barrier, as the split between architect and builder, between architect and engineer also widened.

This loss of individual autonomy and general skills was not the only problem. In the end, the industrialization of housing production was not fully realized; with true industrial reorganization, there could at least have occurred a remarkable advance in the numbers of units produced and a significant decline in their cost. But the building industry, and especially its housing sector, were scarcely models of rational organization. For one, divergent local building codes, stringent union requirements, high transportation costs for shipped materials, and financing constraints kept construction much less efficient than in other major industries. Nonetheless, during the last quarter of the nineteenth century, residential building was being industrialized as never before, even if the process was piecemeal and unsystematized.

The Home as Retreat from Industry

This rapidly expanding world of industrial production supported a rich, complex imagery for American residential architecture. The popular styles of the 1870s and 1880s held the public's fancy in large part because the forms supposedly represented and reinforced an ideal of the home and family. The celebration of home, family, and womanhood—now known as the cult of domesticity—took shape in the early nineteenth century. And it flourished. Later, toward the end of the century, with the opening of the suburbs to many middle-class families and the dramatically increased production of ornament for facades and furnishings for interiors, it was easier to celebrate the individual distinctions between families and the more general distinction between homes and the tall buildings going up in downtown areas. What had been a rhetoric proclaiming "the home" and "the world" as separate realms now became much more of an actual physical reality.

At the same time, the presumably personal touch that women were to bring to their homes became far more tutored. Although many domestic guides continued to insist nobly that the American middle-class home was more comfortable than the expensive villa of a wealthy family—being more individualized, less ostentatious, and even healthier—it was undeniable that these same guides applied pressure on their readers to purchase "artistic" objects for their homes.[25] In order to have the home seem to be a haven from the world of business and industry, it was necessary to bring in industrially produced furniture, bric-a-brac, curtains, and wallpapers, and to learn from department-store displays, manufacturer's advertisements, and books of advice how to arrange these things. The crowded display rooms at every exposition, the drawings and photographs in pattern books, the model rooms that interior decorators set up in the large department stores, all of these prototypes stressed to the middle-class housewife that her own taste and her own handmade decorations were simply not sufficient for a good home. Moreover, this advice increasingly tended to look toward the wealthy and their architects for ideals. The elaborate shapes of rooms, the Queen Anne living hall, and the Eastlake mantelpiece of the fashionable, individualized, middle-class dwelling were miniaturized versions of architecture that had been originally conceived for sumptuous estates. By the late 1880s, most sources of decorous taste were explicitly instructing readers and clients about how to imitate the rich, explaining what to buy and how to arrange the purchases for the best effect of tasteful elegance on a limited budget.

The guides extolled the benefits of a clear distinction between the home and the rest of the society. This dichotomy was obviously an idealization. With the rise of suburban living after the 1880s, women as well as men were able to take streetcars into town, where they could take in department stores, club activities, and entertainment. Many families continued to live in the cities, of course, even if they could afford to move to the suburbs, and the end of the century saw a great increase in the construction of flats and apartment-buildings.

In fact, it was the industrial production of goods and the commercialism of their presentation to the public that allowed the very ideal of the home as a separate world to flower as it did. Yet, the two worlds of Victorian men and women did have their own distinct aesthetics now, representing symbolically their opposite, symbiotic systems: the skyscraper and the Queen Anne cottage; one soaring high, of stone, plain and functional; the other low to the ground, of wood, and ornately decorated.[26] Each kind of architecture relied upon advances in American industry, and each, in its turn, was a reaction to the pressures of the industrial, capitalist city.

The elaborate architectural iconography of the model middle-class home relied absolutely upon the industrial production and commercialism the home supposedly transcended. Yet the home was sentimentalized in popular novels and elegant critical essays as a refuge from that world. Home was to be the institution that would preserve the essential human qualities of love, spirituality, and respect for others, since these values could not easily be sustained in the demanding competition of business enterprise (fig. 17). The appeal was broad. To the atheist, home was the source of all altruistic values. To the religious, following the sermons of Chicago's David Swing or Dwight Moody, the family was the unchanging, God-given human institution. Even academics corroborated these ideals. Edvard Westermarck, for instance, published *The History of Human Marriage* in 1889. This popular anthropological treatise purported to prove that the monogamous patriarchical family was the natural and universal state for all humanity.[27]

Obviously, many people in Victorian society were concerned that this supposedly universal family order was in danger of being subverted by industrial values and products. This was particularly true in the United States, where the drive for success, according to many observers, was the most notable national characteristic. How could this ideal American family produce individuals who could compete successfully and still remain above commercialism? The only hope seemed higher ideals, embodied in houses and in the women who tended to those houses. A richly symbolic architecture and a pure, protected womanhood would keep domestic values intact. Such was the promise of countless ministers, art critics, educators, physicians, and other prominent figures. Architects, builders, and interior decorators echoed their sentiments. In this crusade, as each author took care to stress, women could count on the reinforcement of an elaborate, deeply symbolic residential architecture. The connection meant, first, the continued embellishment of the middle-class home. Second, it meant that women would inevitably experience that home in a different way than their husbands and children would. A writer in *Appleton's Journal* was explicit about this duality:

> It is not her retreat, but her battleground. . . . her arena, her boundary, her sphere. To a woman, the house is life militant; to a man, it is life in repose. . . . She has no other sphere for her activities. . . . [W]oman by the very necessities of her existence, must have a different idea of home than what man has.[28]

And so the argument went, in innumerable other books and magazines and sermons: Women were fundamentally different from men, more delicate and more altruistic. They should, therefore, be protected in their homes. From this "battleground," women would be able to uplift the characters of their families and improve "the welfare of society as a whole."

Thus, we are left with many weaknesses in this idealized portrait. Most conspicuously, the personal, individualized domestic setting was made possible by advances in industrial production and a loss of autonomy for the worker. Although the aim was houses and parlors that embodied the personal creativity of the housewife, the carpenter, and the skilled artisan, the fact was that the ornament within and without relied on fast-paced factory production and skillful advertising. The tensions of industrial expansion affected the construction business.

The social strains of industrialization also promoted the desire to

Figure 17. Domestic images of home and family. (From Pye Henry Chavasse's *Woman as Wife and Mother* [1878] (left) and Emma C. Hewitt's *Queen of the Home* [1892], both published in Chicago.)

HOME
TRAINING

make each home an escape from the driving commercial world, a task that was patently impossible. The idea that women, from their homes, should improve the state of the society came into direct conflict with this enforced segregation, just as the facts of industrial production belied the supposed individualism of each dwelling. For a time, though, middle-class men and women could revel in the pleasures of home as, indeed, private retreats for family togetherness—for this idea was not simply a commercial device but a deeply felt desire. Moreover, the elaborate architecture and fastidious furnishings took some of the pressure off of the inhabitants, especially the women, for whom these domestic issues occupied most of their time. At least temporarily, the image of the Victorian home stilled some of the doubts about the power of the home to make the family truly secure.

But while many families invested in symbols of status and stability—inglenooks and bay windows, bricks and wallpapers—others began to rebel. By the 1890s, protests against the cult of the home, with its privatism, its limitations on women, its expense, and its sham ornament, would become outspoken. The way in which houses were being produced, their use and appearance, came into question. Elaborate images of domestic stability and industrial progress were no longer sufficient.

PART TWO

REORIENTATION

1893–1903

4 THE HOMELIKE WORLD

Chicago has for the last fourteen years been the centre of the communistic and anarchistic agitation in the United States and . . . [of] social reformers, who imagine themselves in possession of an infallible receipt to perfect not only all human institutions but also human nature.

Richard Michaelis, *Looking Further Forward, an Answer to Looking Backward by Edward Bellamy* (1890)

Soon after Frances Willard, professor of aesthetics at Northwestern University in Evanston, just north of Chicago, assumed the presidency of the Woman's Christian Temperance Union in 1879, she set the organization on a new course. No longer would temperance be its sole cause, the single solution. One reform alone could not improve enough people to make a substantial difference in the quality of American life. By the 1890s, her "Do-Everything Policy" included support for labor unionization (especially for the tactics of her close friend Terrence Powderly, president of the moderate Knights of Labor), as well as agrarian Populism, Christian Socialism, suffrage reform, Bellamyite Nationalism and "home protection." This last cause was Willard's phrase for a revised ideal of domesticity. Women had to have the ballot and political power, she argued, if they were going to uphold the values that the culture associated with the home. Furthermore, they needed places in the commercial world from which to carry on their various municipal reform crusades, such as the Woman's Temple Willard commissioned for downtown Chicago from the firm of Burnham and Root in 1892. Home was still central to Willard's ideal of womanhood, but the Victorian image of the passive, delicate, reclusive female had become outdated. The mission of her new woman was "to make the whole world Homelike."[1]

Willard's policies illustrate a reorientation of American values about the home as a social setting and a physical environment. Many of the concepts had been expressed in the 1880s. But it was the decade of the

1890s that inaugurated a period of almost frenzied reform activities, programs for participation and efficiency in every area of American life. Both housing itself and the rhetoric of domestic values were central to many of these reform campaigns, including the movements for tenement laws, public health, women's rights, temperance, and countless other causes. There was, for instance, a sudden, uncomfortable awareness of the appalling condition of housing for the nation's poor. In addition, there were drives to improve the quality of middle-class homes, making them more healthful, easier to keep up, simpler and less pretentious. Willard and others backed women working outside the home and tied this to the need for more efficient dwellings; her praise for Bellamy extended to the "architecture of Nationalism": apartment buildings and standardized row houses.[2]

A vision of a community of simpler, similar homes replaced the earlier focus on privatized, perfect dwellings, each one the haven of a separate family, each one a world unto itself. Concurrently, the leaders of numerous reform organizations decided to connect their goals and tactics for better homes with those for better cities. They would bring the values of the home into the city, they claimed, in order to solve its problems; they would use a combination of popular participation and rational organization to accomplish the task, but the driving force would be the widespread desire for better homes and families. From these concerted efforts would come what was to be called the progressive movement.

Progressivism itself is an ambiguous term, used by countless individuals of the late nineteenth and early twentieth centuries to emphasize their forward-looking views. As a movement, it stood for an intellectual critique of the excesses of capitalism; a political drive for greater popular participation in government; an increased social awareness of poverty and privilege; a middle-class effort to reorganize and rationalize the institutions of American life, fitting them to modern conditions; and a professional effort to restore a healthy order to the cities.[3] Theodore Roosevelt's Progressive party of the 1910s was simply a later, more tightly structured and professionally dominated aspect of a broad reform effort which took shape in the 1890s, during a period when the country faced a major depression, intense and violent labor organizing, and the shocked recognition that neither the family, the government, nor industry were functioning as the previous generation had hoped.

The place to begin reform was the home; but now this meant ambitious programs to reorganize that setting, making more housing available, making all homes healthy, enabling women to have more time for reform campaigns—and thus bringing the values of the home to the world. It is not that the values of Victorian America were cast aside. Rather, they were brought out of the individual home into the community. Here groups of people, mostly middle-class suburbanites and urban reformers, took advantage of the sense of suspended time and confused values brought on by the depression. They asked how the home should change, what should be discarded, what collectivized, what preserved. It was clear to these progressive reformers that some change had to happen. Many of the tensions which had been kept suppressed by the Victorian ideals of woman, worker, home and nation, were now transformed into demands for reform.

Of course, there were many ways of responding to the disorientation of the 1890s. It was a time of great and lavish wealth, displayed in magnificent American castles and charity balls. Some of the most stupendous wealth came from the monopolies that were formed during the decade. As we shall see, the splendor that wealthy families demanded, combined with the hard facts of a depression economy, drew many professional architects toward a grandiose vision of Beaux-Arts chateaux and magnificent civic centers celebrating America's businessmen. But the 1890s was also a time of experimentation and innovative programs for reform in architecture, as in literature and politics. Demands for a simplified, standardized domestic architecture reached a crescendo as not only professional architects but various nonprofessional groups, too, took up the cause. From Oakland to Philadelphia, and especially in midwestern cities like Cleveland, Omaha, and Chicago, the early progressives sponsored projects for improving the environment. They upgraded streets and sidewalks, planned parks, statues, and municipal playgrounds. Above all, specific proposals for improvements in housing for every class of American now abounded.

This chapter will present the four major forums in which architectural change was demanded for the American home. In each case, professional architects were at least marginally involved, although the thrust of the movement came from nonprofessionals. Usually these groups were interconnected, and some especially active people—notably, Jane Addams, Henry Demarest Lloyd, and the Reverend

Graham Taylor in Chicago—participated at every level of housing reform. The most vocal category included the "housers" and philanthropists who advocated tenement reform and low-cost suburban housing for workers. Then there were those who emphasized specific public health improvements—considerations of water supply, sunlight, ventilation, and cleanliness. Such improvements were to be enforced in middle-class as well as working-class homes. The third category consisted of those reformers who wanted to concentrate on the middle-class home, modernizing and simplifying its form and decoration. Loosely identified as the arts and crafts movement, this campaign had far more ambitious goals than the preservation of handicrafts. Architects, journalists, and many others interested in issues of industrial production, public education, and aesthetic reform came together. One of their principal professed common goals was to promote better houses for every American.

While each of the other categories of reformer actually represents a formal organization, the fourth does not. Yet, in a sense, the nonprofessional critics of American home life who edited and wrote for popular magazines had the greatest impact on housing styles and decor, and on attitudes about the home and family. These widely read aesthetic crusaders advocated simpler, more efficient houses; they also demanded changes in the social structure. While not themselves designers, Edward Bok of the *Ladies' Home Journal* or Herbert S. Stone of *The House Beautiful* saw domestic architecture as a valuable symbol for the larger society. As influential journalists, they frequently used architectural descriptions to heighten their critiques and enliven their visions of the future.

Before presenting the architectural and social platforms of these progressive groups, let me stress how important the language and the concept of the home became in the 1890s. Willard's concept of the "Homelike world" was always central in the progressives' diverse apocalyptic visions for better American cities. The new rhetoric of "humanizing politics" and "domesticating the economy" appropriated the culture's hitherto exclusively domestic values, applying them to the political and economic world. Henry Demarest Lloyd, the Chicago journalist, insisted that political economy could never be considered a universal science until it acknowledged the political and economic significance of the family, the home, and the community. The "social housekeeping" argument adopted by many women reformers also followed from Willard's phrase. Louise de Koven Bowen, a prominent Chicago philanthropist, told one audience that women were clearly entitled to express their opinions publicly—at least on questions of garbage disposal, cleanliness of the streets, the care and education of children. "If a woman is a good housekeeper in her own home," she explained, "she will be able to do well that larger housekeeping."[4] Feminists in turn relied upon the larger definition of the domestic sphere in their attempts to enter professions, universities, unions, and political leadership. Suffrage activists used the same argument to support women's right to vote, claiming that they would bring morality to governmental office.

The spirit of "practical idealism," invoked by so many progressives, had certainly existed before the 1890s. But it was during this decade that a new consciousness of urban problems and a new approach to their solution clearly emerged. The decade saw the rise of the Populist party, an agrarian-based movement against political corruption, low farm prices, and the special privileges of big business and big finance. Populism centered in the Midwest. In 1896 William Jennings Bryan delivered his "Cross of Gold" speech at the Democratic party's Chicago convention and gave forceful expression to many of these formerly third-party issues. The Populist "mutterings of discontent"[5] were echoed in the cities by an urban progressive reform movement, essentially a separate affair, which shared, nonetheless, many of the ideals of the agrarian Populists. The urban progressives were, for the most part, middle-class professionals, together with the wives and daughters of such families, although the influence of the nonprofessionals (often the women in an organization) gradually declined. They were committed to city living, but were horrified by the injustice, the poverty, and the disorder they saw in cities. Attacking laissez-faire capitalism, they called for government to control the trusts, while extending necessary services to the needy poor. They wanted to patch up the system of American democracy. They would make it work by bringing down the top and raising up the bottom, chastizing the powerful and Americanizing the immigrant. The ideal was essentially one of a universal middle class, made up of small independent capitalists, bound together in a responsible community and overseen by judicious administrators.[6]

The middle-class insecurities were real enough. Issues of status had, by the end of the century, become more complicated, more diffuse. A man's employment, his bank, and his education; the kind of house his wife kept and whether they owned or rented; their neighborhood and family; and the woman's involvement outside the home in civic affairs all helped define a family's place in the social structure. Incomes too were becoming less equal. Between 1890 and the First World War, the wage differential between skilled and unskilled workers widened. The difference between the wage-earning middle-classes and the very wealthy, in terms of incomes and daily lives, was even greater. Most of the nation's nonfarm working population had become wage-earners by this time; no longer self-employed, they had little control over their earnings or even the tasks they did on the job, although there was obviously greater independence for white-collar employees. And, although real wages did not rise during these years, prices certainly did. In Chicago and across the country, the cost of living increased 35 percent over the two decades following the depression of 1893.[7] Stability was definitely hard to come by.

The progressives expressed concern about three sets of problems: the poor and their needs, the rich and their abuses, the middle class and their insecurities. Each problem they saw primarily as a social and political conflict. However, in the search for concrete solutions, they often cast these abstract issues in environmental terms. The principal environment, to which the progressives returned again and again in rhetoric and specific programs, was the home. All American homes needed improvements, to make them healthy, efficient, comfortable, and stable. Disparities had to be lessened so that equality between the classes would be achieved. Many reformers demanded that government improve domestic as well as political institutions, upgrading housing and stabilizing the nuclear family. Academics such as John Dewey and Charles Henderson began to investigate the problems of the home. Settlement workers like Jane Addams and Mary McDowell organized poor neighborhoods to insist upon specific improvements for their apartments and streets. Demands for public health, community life, women's rights, for modern efficiency and better consumer products, were translated, with varying amounts of detail, into proposals for reform in domestic architecture.

The very availability of housing was an issue. The depression of 1893, the worst the nation had ever known, had an especially harsh impact on residential building. Although other sectors of the construction industry declined from the high figures of 1890, housing was particularly affected. Residential construction, nationwide, reached a low of 189,000 units in 1900, down from 381,000 starts in 1892. Chicago, which had enjoyed a great boom in the years preceding the World's Columbian Exposition, was especially hard hit. Housing starts were down to 3,500 in 1900, from a high of 13,100 in 1892. Both nationwide and in Chicago, construction did not begin to flourish again until 1905, when housing starts rose to 507,000 for the nation as a whole and to 8,000 for Chicago.[8] The slowdown in housing starts, in Chicago as elsewhere across the country, posed a sizable impediment to general economic recovery, for many secondary industries, from brick production to porcelain manufacturing, were also set back. Furthermore, the lack of new housing stock pushed up rents and the cost of buying a home in cities and suburbs alike.

Whether they lived in the suburbs or in the city, middle-class persons were generally frightened by the changes they saw taking place in the cities of the 1890s. The recognized that the problems were directly connected to the economic situation. The depression brought unemployed men and professional "tramps" wandering from one area to another, sometimes organized, as in Coxey's thwarted march on Washington, but more often in small, desolate bands or on their own. Congregations of immigrants were, if anything, even more unsettling to most native-born middle-class Americans. By 1900, 60 percent of Chicago's population was made up of immigrants and the children of immigrants. Moreover, these immigrants were no longer mostly familiar German, Irish, and English stock; Eastern Europeans, once an obscure fraction of the immigrant population, now made up a quarter of Chicago's foreign-born. The labor movement, especially after the riots at Homestead and nearby Pullman, seemed frighteningly anarchistic, violent, and destructive to middle-class observers, and to a number of workers and their families, too. In 1894 alone, nearly 750,000 working men and women in the United States went out on strike. Two years later, the Boston settlement-worker Robert Woods first publicized the term "city wilderness."[9] It expressed a general impression. The reformers saw alarming disorder and confusion in the cities, and they wanted to rectify at least some of the problems.

Many intellectuals now experienced a new calling: they were to formulate the moral goals and social means for democratic progress. Henry Demarest Lloyd's famous exposé of the Standard Oil Company, published in 1894, called for a "new conscience" of scientific humanism to guide politics, academic research, social work, and aesthetics to a higher plane.[10] Enlightened experts in these fields would provide models for a well-run, egalitarian society. Documentation of the quality of streets and tenements, the course of diseases, the trends of population and family patterns emerged as the principal method of investigation. Most of the people who collected empirical information about environments analyzed the homes of the poor. A study carried out by the U.S. Bureau of Labor in 1892, the first of its kind in this country, described the habitations of working-class families in four American cities, including Chicago. Carroll D. Wright, director of the bureau, acknowledged that the study only considered subjects that were quantifiable, never inquiring about possible reasons for poverty. Still, in the hands of nonprofessional reformers like Jacob Riis, Lewis Hine, and Robert Hunter, flashlight photography, invented in 1887, often added a more emotional visual supplement to the statistics.

By the mid-1890s, novelists and academics, bureaucrats and physicians were expressing a heightened awareness of the influence of one's surroundings. Frederick Jackson Turner's famous address on "The Significance of the Frontier in American History," read before the American Historical Association in Chicago in 1893, forcefully expounded a theory of national institutions, from literature to government, arising in part from the availability of public lands and the range of sectional differences. Hamlin Garland's *Crumbling Idols,* published the following year by the young Chicago firm of Stone and Kimball, called for "local color" to enliven American literature. Lester Frank Ward's *Dynamic Sociology* (first published in 1883, but really popular only after 1890) was one of the many texts connecting environmental factors to income, intellectual stimulation, and social position, stressing their decisive role in individual achievement.[11] Soon Ellen Semple introduced the study of geography as a human science to the University of Chicago, a science suggesting how the environment might determine cultural behavior. These academic reformers, however, moved beyond the scientism of a strictly Darwinian awareness of environmental adaptation and stages of development. They agreed, for the most part, that social problems could be prevented if knowledgeable experts could understand and manipulate the basic institutions of work, politics, social life, and family. The reorganization of the physical environment, and especially the planning of homes, was the obvious way to begin.

Even those academics who looked askance at liberal programs for reform pointed to the environment as a powerful cultural symbol. Thorstein Veblen, the notorious, brilliant professor of economics at the University of Chicago, saw architecture as evidence of a nation's material conditions and cultural expectations. Such institutions, he wrote, acted on individuals to reinforce directly the cultural values the institutions represented symbolically. *The Theory of the Leisure Class*, published in 1899, documented the ways in which "conspicuous consumption" was replacing conspicuous leisure as the most visible means for demonstrating an individual's cultural reputation. And architecture constituted a definite part of this trend: styles were usually based, he charged, on pretense and display, as well as on shelter and personal expression. The values of waste, expense, and elevation from "familiarity with vulgar life" represented the principal determinants of form.

Domestic architecture was meant to look especially whimsical, lighthearted, unconcerned with practical, everyday matters of economy or convenience. Windows, plans, and facades were designed either for useless novelty or for pretentious imitation, but seldom for the comfort of the inhabitants. The blank walls on the backs and sides of buildings, Veblen contended, usually proved to be their best features. The efforts of his fellow Chicagoans in the Arts and Crafts Society seemed to him not reform but new versions of old symbols. The sham serviceability of unadorned fences and fireplaces, the stylized imperfections of imitation handmade furniture, the studied naturalness of rustic wood and stone were all artifice in the name of sincerity.[12] These "simpler" styles, as he recognized, were indeed replacing earlier, more ornate Victorian expressions of status, but the same economic forces of display—not inherent utility—made them fashionable.

Hostile toward Veblen's criticisms, most social and aesthetic reformers in Chicago were smugly convinced that he was wrong. They were on the right course toward a rejuvenated community and stable family life through environmental improvements. But environmentalism could, of course, place a limit on the reformer's understanding of other people's problems. As Veblen had in fact pointed out, this approach to reform relied on the image of improvement rather than on real substance. Similarily, the gathering of statistics on environmental problems was spurred by the hope that information could, by itself, raise awareness and generate solutions for every problem.

In a sense, the familiar nineteenth-century reformers' absolute trust in the ability of the American public to recognize the best model had reappeared. This generation also shunned governmental regulations and insisted that education could assure improvements. The intentions of activists in universities, settlement houses, and the thousands of organizations which sprang up during the 1890s were often commendable. However, they wanted to improve housing, family life, and government only on their own terms. The underlying premises for their sociological studies and educational campaigns came from their middle-class backgrounds. The newly popular fashion for architectural simplicity and rational organization of the household, together with the long-standing insistence on isolating each nuclear family from outsiders, quickly became absolute standards for housing. The reformers' belief that a normal home life could not develop in "abnormal" environments frequently led to a rigid definition of what was normal and even permissible, as much as it inspired sincere efforts to upgrade the dwellings of the poor.

Improving the Homes of the Poor

Once reform-minded men and women began to look around them, conditions in American cities of the 1890s left little doubt about the need for environmental improvements. The issue was how to go about it most quickly and efficiently. The fierce speculation in the new Chicago suburbs had produced acres of nearly identical, poorly planned and cheaply constructed cottages, set along unpaved streets. Only board sidewalks and occasional saplings relieved the monotony of the gridiron, and there were few controls over the quality of construction. But the problems in the slums of Chicago—Goose Island, the Near West Side, Packingtown near the stockyards—were far worse.

Settlement houses had recently appeared in such areas, supplementing churches and missions as connections between middle-class reformers and the poor families who lived in crowded tenements or tumbledown shacks in narrow back alleys. Hull House, the first settlement house in Chicago, was established by Jane Addams and Ellen Gates Starr in an old mansion on the Near West Side in 1889. Inspired by the example of Toynbee Hall in London, Addams and Starr wanted to provide services and political representation for their Chicago community. Doctors, educators, and social workers contributed to the classes and the campaigns launched by the Hull House residents. Allen and Irving Pond designed and supervised twelve buildings, extending Hull House to an entire block by 1907. Dwight Perkins and his wife, the artist Lucy Fitch Perkins, worked there as well, before going on to erect the University of Chicago Settlement in 1899. The university community saw the settlements as a way to promote and extend the educational goals they upheld. John Dewey and, later, Sophonisba Breckenridge—social welfare professor at the University of Chicago—as well as their colleagues Grace and Edith Abbott, were all active in Hull House. The Reverend Graham Taylor, director of the University Extension's Social Science Center for Practical Training in Philanthropic and Social Work, founded the Chicago Commons, and Charles Zueblin, a professor of sociology, founded the Northwestern University Settlement. Between 1895 and 1917, Chicago reformers established a total of sixty-eight settlements.

A common aim of the settlements was that of kindling the ideal of the middle-class home and community in the city's slum areas. As Taylor wrote: "The settlement house is really an addition to every little tenement home. Its books and pictures, the nursery and play spaces, the lobby and living room, the music and flowers, the cheery fireplaces and lamps, the auditorium for assemblies or social occasions and dancing, are an extension of all too scant home equipment of most of the neighbors." The settlement was to be an "idealized home,"[13] inspiring the new immigrant to reproduce an environment of cultured taste and healthful order. Connected to the settlements were organizations providing visiting nurses and volunteer "friendly visitors" to come into tenement apartments, where they would teach women how to care for their homes and families. It was hoped—indeed, firmly believed—that any family with access to the right models could reproduce a tiny but immaculate middle-class home.

The settlement workers and their supporters wanted to encourage middle-class life in more direct ways as well. In 1897 a group of settlement residents, charity leaders, and sociologists met at the Northwestern University Settlement to consider which steps were essential to relieve the city's tenement problem. Good models were simply not enough. Three years later, with the backing of wealthy businessmen and society ladies, they founded the City Homes Association. Their aim was to coordinate the separate reform activities in the city, especially those concerned with housing. Under Robert Hunter, the Investigating Committee produced a monumental compendium on *Tenement Conditions in Chicago* in 1901; the Small Parks and Playgrounds Committee lobbied for "breathing space" in the crowded slums (and, in several instances, persuaded the city to tear down much-needed but poor-quality housing); the Model Tenement Committee tried to interest private investors in building exemplary tenement housing; two other groups concentrated on the creation of a new housing code and a municipal lodging house.[14] If information were a first step, here it was in abundance.

Even though improved housing for the urban poor was a critical issue for these reformers, they all believed that the only good home was a single-family cottage in the suburbs. Addams made this point to the City Homes Association. However, she insisted that their job was to mitigate the evils of tenements rather than to dream of suburbs. Carroll D. Wright and the statistician Adna Weber were most responsive to reforms that would help working people acquire small homes of their own outside the city. They lauded building and loan associations, cheap rapid transit, and shorter working days (which would allow for commuting time). Most Chicagoans agreed with them. As one historian of the city wrote, "Every city, the majority of the citizens whereof are householders, is safe, not from riots, but from successful riots. . . . Building societies are the best form of special police and civic, unarmed militia. The dangerous classes are nomadic."[15]

All the same, most reformers were wary of too facile a solution to a major housing problem. They were all too aware of the fiascos which had resulted from the housing promotions of the early 1890s, when some developers had used brass bands, fireworks, and excursion trains to sell cheap houses on swampy land to syndicates of working people.

Despite such misgivings, an image of a good home for the worker had begun to crystallize: it was in the suburbs, with a tiny yard and fresh air for growing children. The small, simply built square cottage was standardized, both for economy and as a reaction to what Weber called the "exaggerated individualism" of the middle-class and their houses.[16] It seemed possible to point builders in the right direction, to prove to them that it was profitable to construct decent small houses if they accepted an austere aesthetic. This image was not only an expression of the reformers' hopes for the working classes. Rigorous simplicity was fast becoming the middle-class ideal.

"Germ Cultures"

While some reformers concentrated on the housing needs and social problems of the poor, others were concerned about the home life of the middle classes. One reform movement clearly bridged all classes, however. Public health advocates recognized that health had to be a citywide, indeed, a national concern. It was impossible to have the best health in only some of a city's homes.

The period between 1890 and 1910 has been called the "golden age of public health" in America.[17] During the preceding empirical stage, physicians and statisticians had concentrated on collecting information about sanitary conditions in the nation's cities. In the 1890s they began to work effectively with politicians, political reformers, home economists, and sanitary engineers toward the scientific control of communicable diseases. The acceptance of the germ theory of disease provided the ammunition of scientific proof, if not specific remedy. After 1883, Pasteur and Koch's experiments in bacteriology reached an American audience through the publications of the Chicago physician Dr. Henry Gradle.[18] After the isolation of various bacilli that caused specific diseases had made matters clear to the general public, the environmental conditions most conducive to the growth of germs suddenly became a focus of attention, even paranoia. Municipal and state boards of health, which had recently been advice-giving bodies at most, were granted great authority. Municipal control of services—sewage, garbage collection, water supplies—was brought into most parts of the larger cities. Legislation was introduced to upgrade housing conditions, especially in the tenements, insuring fresh air, sunlight, sanitary facilities, and adequate space, although provisions for enforcing the standards, particularly in existing housing, were usually minimal.

The principal focus, however, was on education. Public health officials inaugurated massive campaigns in an effort to teach individuals the practices of personal and domestic hygiene. Manufacturers of household goods immediately seized on the idea of the individual family's self-protection against germs; advertisements for soap products, plumbing equipment, casement windows, and furniture often featured the spectre of a dying child or a tubercular wife looming out of a dark background. Public health had indeed passed on to a new stage.

The germ theory displaced old myths of hereditary disease. Public health advocates looked for effective ways to control germs and prevent illness. Tuberculosis, now labeled a "house disease," was a principal target. During the 1890s municipal authorities instituted the first popular education programs, public exhibitions, and provision for home visits in infected areas. Cleanliness and order—in municipal services, but even more in individual dwellings—was the focus of educational and legislative campaigns. Keeping one's home clean and up to the highest standards of health imposed a mighty burden upon the housewife. So, while there were significant improvements in curbing certain sicknesses, new myths about the causes and prevention of disease replaced the older ones. Most women had learned one set of explanations in their youth. Now they read everywhere about the dangers of dirt, dust, darkness, and lurking germs. What should you do to keep your family's home from becoming a "germ culture"? advertisements asked.

There was even less possibility of control over public environments. Consequently, suggestions of contamination from public services abounded. Even the *Architects' and Builders' Magazine* intimated that books from public libraries could harbor disease germs; by the early 1900s, popular magazine articles carried such precautionary titles as "Infection and Postage Stamps" and "Disease from Public Laundries." Writers who described germs as "dangerous elements" and "foreign elements in the air" were clearly upset about certain populations they believed were contaminating other citizens.[19] Even domestic servants were suspect. Quarantine of the middle-class house became the favored precaution; the strongest criticism of removing services like cooking, washing, ironing, and sewing from the home was that any item could be infected from outside.

Fears about health were based upon real dangers, even if promoters of soap products and Spencerians who blamed diseases upon the immigrant poor did play upon the general public's anxieties. Epidemics and infant mortality threatened every home. In 1893, 45 percent of Chicago's deaths were infants under five (a decline of 14 percent since 1873, but five times the rate today). Typhoid, diphtheria, and tuberculosis were still menaces to anyone in the city.[20] Readers therefore carefully heeded the surprisingly consistent advice of scores of journals. The professional public health press concentrated on architectural suggestions for better ventilation and foundations. More fastidiously, writers for popular magazines condemned, on health as well as aesthetic grounds, the plush furnishings, intricate woodwork, and even the picturesque site-planning that had been fashionable in the 1870s and 1880s.[21] Any family could take certain steps to prevent illness.

An architecture of visible health emerged in many domestic guides and home magazines. Draperies, upholstered furniture, wall-to-wall carpets, and bric-a-brac—all "abiding-places for germs"—were evicted from the home. Since dust was thought to be a principal carrier, any place where it could collect was suspect. The purifiers urged that doorways and window casings become simpler; moldings and statuary niches disappear; cornices and irregular corners be eliminated. The "rambling structures" of the Queen Anne came under their attack. Not only did such houses depart from the rigid sanitary aesthetic, they were also expensive to heat properly and difficult to keep clean.

Other architectural improvements brought in light and air. However, there were a few comfortable dark corners to be found. Numerous writers on the home still praised the fireside inglenook as a cozy place for comfort and warmth, shielded from drafts.[22] Simultaneously, many more windows now became a goal in every kind of housing; even in the cellar, they were larger and more prominent. Often grouped together along an expanse of wall, wide casements or large doublehung windows let in the maximum of sunlight and fresh air. The sleeping porch, considered an excellent promotor of health, became quite popular in every climate. Wide, whitewashed verandas for dining and entertaining—often screened in summer and glazed in winter to become "sun-rooms"—opened every domestic activity to the out-of-doors (fig. 18).

The most important addition during the 1890s, the bathroom, now became a standard fixture in middle-class homes. Reformers publicized the issue of sanitation in the tenements, and this increased the middle-class awareness of plumbing facilities. Utility companies and large plumbing supply companies pressed builders to provide bathrooms in every home. The production of enameled sanitary fixtures doubled in the first few years of the twentieth century.[23] The compact arrangement of equipment in a five-feet-by-five-feet bathroom unit became more familiar, although many older homes still provided a fair amount of space for bathing and toilet activities, since the owners had converted bedrooms for the purpose.

The clearest symbol of cleanliness was the color white. By 1900 it

Figure 18. "Sun Parlour" porch. (Reprinted by permission from *House Beautiful* Magazine, ©copyright 1902 The Hearst Corporation. All rights reserved.)

became popular for numerous interior spaces. White was the sign of visible sanitary awareness. Concrete basements were whitewashed, and soon the living room and dining room walls were white as well. Descriptions of model kitchens began noting that the walls must be white. Wall coverings made available for kitchens and bathrooms in the 1890s—washable tiles, less expensive enameled sheet metal, lightweight oil cloth, enamel paint—were always specified as white. If possible, a light-colored linoleum covered the floor. Even the appliances had touches of shiny white porcelain enamel added to their sides and splashbacks. Things not only had to be clean, they had to look clean.

Municipal health campaigns for cleanliness were carried out, as were the advertisements, with great fanfare. When Chicago added 130 square miles of annexed land in 1889, the city passed a multimillion-dollar bond issue for a sanitary and ship canal to reverse the Chicago River and prevent it from further polluting Lake Michigan. Over the next several years, hundreds of miles of water mains and sewers were laid, thousands of miles of wooden sidewalks were built, and gas streetlights and fire-alarm systems were installed in the newly annexed territory. Taxpayers usually accepted these expenses willingly.

In many cities, a favorite indication of the new attitude toward cleanliness was the position of garbage men. In 1896, George E. Waring, Jr., who had recently been appointed head of New York City's Department of Street Cleaning, led his 2,700-man force, dressed in their new white uniforms and pushing their white garbage cans, down Broadway. Crowds cheered the parade of "Waring's White Wings" from the sidewalks. Chicago followed with several similar parades. In 1904, two major reform associations, the Commercial Club and the Merchants Club, hired a Boston sanitation expert, Richard T. Fox, to stage a sanitation extravaganza and win support for new municipal ordinances. He assembled a force of "White Wings" to clean the streets in the Loop area. Several of the city's major businessmen took up brooms for the occasion. But not every part of the city received the same attention, as Jane Addams made clear. She enlisted residents of the Near West Side to clean up their own streets—and she herself was photographed with them sweeping the sidewalk.[24] Cleanliness was becoming a media event, a public occasion, as well as a private responsibility.

Public health advocates were concerned with mental health as well as physical health. Earlier writers on environmental controls had been preoccupied with quantifiable measures—with temperatures, air circulation, and candlepower. In the next decade, domestic scientists would turn the desire for healthful environments into commodities. But for a time, during the decade of the 1890s, architectural answers to issues of good health were less important than the simple asking of questions. Most reformers did not really insist on any absolute, emphatic solutions to any of the problems they considered; the voice of the expert, defining once and for all the "one best way" still sounded tentative.

This same relatively open approach also characterized some academic social-science research of the time. Charles Henderson—minister, reformer, and professor of sociology at the University of Chicago—pioneered a "participant-observer" approach.[25] The passive situation of the public—as consumer, as citizen, as worker—emerged as a major issue for these reformers. A few of the home economists who held appointments as Henderson's colleagues at the university carried this idea still further, to the point of claiming that women were not in fact in charge of their households. Sophronia Maria Elliott, for one, insisted that women could never ensure healthy houses, no matter how thorough their training, since "most of us don't live in a house built for us."[26] Consequently, she proposed a massive reorganization of training and an exchange of ideas; architects and builders needed to work with ordinary families to find out about their needs; politicians should listen to consumers in order to pass more effective legislation covering all residential construction. Finally, her women students should not have to take the full brunt of creating healthy, happy homes; she warned them not to set unattainable goals for themselves but instead to work through collective action. Her approach is indicative of the widespread reexamination of the central issues of research, especially when it concerned the home and family. Many of these early progressive men and women understood that, even in public health. issues of comfort, privacy, social pressure, and political action were just as important as measures that could be quantified. In looking at the health problems affecting the home, it was worth considering elusive subjects like expectations and education.

Environments for Rational Beings

The early progressive reformers were aware of problems that extended beyond quantifiable matters of health, although their language often described such problems in disease terms which implied a cure for the problem. In particular, seemingly stable traditional expectations about the home and family became topics of widespread concern in the 1890s. Many Americans worried that their very homes had become infected with a "virus" of disillusionment. The family, and especially its women, seemed to be undergoing sudden, startling changes. Articles on "The Home in Peril"—always a mainstay in American periodical literature—multiplied in the popular and sociological journals of the decade.[27] Alongside them were testimonies about the dissatisfactions of middle-class women. Writers often cast their frustrations and demands in revolutionary terms. Margaret Deland, the Boston Unitarian reformer, described the *"prevailing discontent among women,"* their spirit of "Restlessness! Restlessness!" Ella Wheeler Wilcox, a popular author, wrote that "My mountain of mail is often a volcano of seething unrest."[28] In *Cosmopolitan,* novelist and radical feminist Olive Schreiner proclaimed that women's chief demand now was the right to work and to prepare for that work. In *Scribner's,* accompanied by Charles Dana Gibson's drawings of the fashionable modern woman, Judge Robert Grant echoed that demand for women's work, and suggested that the modern home, "intended for everyday use by rational beings," could help women live comfortably in two worlds.[29]

The increasing number of middle-class women working outside the home, participating in clubs and philanthropies, pursuing adult education courses, seems clear evidence of women's desire to leave behind the Victorian middle-class ideal of the female secluded in the home. In 1870, less than 15 percent of all American workers were women; by 1910 they would make up almost a quarter of the work force.[30] The figures for Chicago are even more striking, for the female population exceeded the male and the social strictures of the East had less influence. Five times as many women were in the labor force by 1890 as had been in 1870; by 1903, one person in ten (one woman in four) was a working woman. Many women also joined women's organizations. Chicago had the country's second largest women's club. The Illinois Federation of Women's Clubs, established in 1894 by delegates from fifty-four clubs, had two hundred fifty-one affiliates by 1903, and twenty-five thousand women attended their meetings.[31]

Some observers found benefits in these figures. Feminists were pleased with women's growing economic independence. They strongly endorsed simple, efficient houses and apartments to help the working woman with her domestic tasks. But the editor of the *Ladies' Home Journal,* Edward Bok, crusaded against women working outside their homes and even against their joining clubs, charging that they would tend to neglect their duties at home. Still, Bok was a sage enough journalist eventually to include articles on houses planned for working wives, "business-girls," and women who wished to add to the family income without leaving their homes.[32] Even those who railed against women working accepted the fact.

It was not only new employment patterns that affected the home, bringing about architectural as well as social accommodations. The work and even the social life that had once taken place within the family had been steadily moving outside, taken over by industry and by professionals. Fewer products were made at home by the turn of the century. Women in the cities bought their bread, vegetables, and canned goods from a grocery; their furniture, their husband's clothes (if not their own), medications, soap, and linens were other products women bought rather than made themselves. They often sent their laundry to commercial enterprises. The department store, an institution established after the Civil War, became more prominent in the 1890s. The great establishments of Chicago's Loop—Marshall Field and Company and Louis Sullivan's 1899 masterpiece of ornament, Schlesinger and Mayer (later Carson, Pirie and Scott)—featured magnificent display windows suggesting the tantalizing goods within. Enticements to buy came from many directions. When postal rates were again reduced, the number and circulation of magazines tripled in a decade. The practice of advertising on billboards, streetcar ceilings, in magazines, and on wall posters also increased remarkably. Images of new products spurred rapid changes in fashions, in home decor as in clothes. The modern housewife had less to do in her home, everyone agreed, and fewer things to make there, but had much more to buy and more difficult decisions to make about those purchases.

It was all too easy to connect the new conveniences to the divorce rate, which was rising, and the birthrate, which was falling off, at least among white middle-class women. Women, it was held, could take advantage of many new products and services which freed their time. Edward Bok and Chicago's Dr. Mary Melendy protested that women now shirked domestic responsibilities. One outcry entitled *The Domestic Blunders of Women,* by "A Mere Man," lamented the general lack of knowledge about economics, household management, and home design, brought on, the author claimed, by the mindless ease of modern conditions of homemaking.[33]

Many time-consuming tasks of home life were undergoing changes. Even the child's education was being subsumed, more and more, by outside institutions: day nurseries, kindergartens, compulsory high schools.[34] Critics and conservatives alike now asked rhetorically, What was left to be done in the home? Was there a new opportunity for individual fulfillment outside the home, and therefore greater family harmony within the home, as some claimed? Or was the family crumbling in the modern home, which had less work to draw its members close together? Few observers were certain of progress. Most of them saw the birthrate, the divorce rate, and other statistics as evidence of sudden, impending crisis in American family life. Few were able to see the pattern which had actually begun early in the nineteenth century. It was not that the family was less stable, as it seemed, but that there were more possibilities for change and variation. It was the mother cult of the late nineteenth century that was declining, not the family itself. But the quantity of recently collected data on family life made the contemporary situation seem apocalyptic.

Sociologists and social critics, radicals and conservatives, agreed that the family could not be left to its own devices. Regulation was necessary to curb its seemingly self-destructive tendencies. Even William Graham Sumner, a Social Darwinist who opposed reform efforts, believing they crippled the natural process of selection, maintained that "the part of our social code and social creed which wants re-examination and reconstruction is that which relates to the family."[35] Jane Addams discussed how industrial expansion could lead to the simplification of houses and thereby create a more "common lot" that would symbolize egalitarian democratic values.[36] Most observers accepted the need to regulate homes and make them more alike in order to reinforce certain values in all American families, although each person drew the line somewhere.

To the most conservative, apartments seemed "communistic." Even cooperative housekeeping services, then emerging as a widely discussed experiment, had dangerous associations. The New York clergyman James C. Fernald, together with the well-known dispenser of domestic advice, "Marion Harland" (Mary Virginia [Hawes] Terhune), attacked the political and moral failings of these experiments. In their "barracks vs. homes" argument, these two claimed that only "individualized homes" could simultaneously combat communism and stabilize the family. All the same, even Fernald and Terhune acknowledged that these private homes had to appropriate some of the rational, efficient planning of modern life in order to survive.[37]

Almost every major American social leader of the period took a stand on the need to standardize and thereby improve the nation's homes. Lyman Abbott, elder statesman of the Social Gospel movement, edited two books on the subject during the 1890s and a third in 1906. Abbott himself emphasized the need for pleasant surroundings which would reestablish the home as "the basis of civilization" (meaning Anglo-Saxon culture) and the "natural destiny" of every woman.[38] Yet even he insisted that kindergartens, building legislation, and women's philanthropies facilitated social stability.

Other contributors to his textbooks described specific architectural and social developments that related to a modernized domestic life. Helen Churchill Candee gave a thorough presentation of the business as well as the architectural side of housebuilding, although she dealt for the most part with more expensive, architect-designed houses.[39] Candee emphasized the good sense in cutting down on ornament. She recommended built-in furniture and an open plan, especially for the more mobile younger family just starting out. Mary Gay Humphries turned the familiar article on "House Decoration and Furnishing" into a call for the reorganization of the dwelling, making it much more efficient. "A busy woman," she wrote, "is accustomed to say that her idea of the house of the future is one that can be cleaned with a hose."[40] Humphries advocated substituting washable materials—tiles, mosaics, enamel brick, simple oil paint—for wood and wallpaper, and using only a painted stencil for ornament. The easy-to-clean house, she explained, would shelter the family, make home life more pleasurable, and still give each member time for activities outside the home.

These suggestions were not original. The criteria of comfort, convenience, simplicity, and good sense appeared as the familiar guideposts of the popular arts and crafts movement of the 1890s. The movement merits special attention here, for the generally acknowledged center of its activity in America was Chicago. The aesthetic and social roots of the movement lay in the ideals of "tasteful" art and individualized craftsmanship espoused by Ruskin and Eastlake a generation earlier. Later partisans in England, Scotland, and then the United States, went back to the original texts of these aesthetic renegades, turning away from the ornate architecture and furnishings that had been popularized under their names. Again, the goal was to reform society through art. And again the place to begin was in the home.

The term "arts and crafts" came into use after the establishment of the London Arts and Crafts Exhibition Society in 1888, but the principles had been the creed of a group of designers who had followed William Morris since the 1850s. Adherents of the movement never actually settled on a style, but they did share principles of use and design.[41] Because they were concerned with the production of objects for daily use, they advocated simplicity of forms, generated by the active participation of the worker/artisan in the design process. National or regional sentiments were important considerations. So too was an "honest expression" of the materials chosen. Whether in England or Scotland, California or the Midwest, there were particular forms and local materials favored by each group of designers. Equally important was the reaction of the user, who should find an object or a house convenient, pleasurable, and comfortable.

These guidelines, of course, were general enough to cover a wide range of artifacts. And, consequently, many styles could be graced with this label. Yet there were differences between the styles, and significant ones at that, both aesthetically and politically. The English movement was particularly interested in the condition of the working classes, those who suffered the most from the industrialism the movement so detested. William Morris, Charles Ashbee, Walter Crane, and their followers—all of whom were also involved in socialist politics—focused their work on the involvement of the craftsperson in design and the improvement of workers' housing.

In the United States, the tale was told quite differently. Industrialism had brought about problems, but many people believed that it was still possible to use industrial techniques in a positive way. Machine production, after all, was an inescapable part of life, as the Chicago Arts and Crafts Society, among others, contended. It was therefore imperative that designers take over this production, in order to turn out quality goods. Some of the Americans in the movement were interested in traditional handicrafts, the production of charming, individualized goods for the wealthy. Others wanted to teach the poor as well as the middle-class family to appreciate simple lines and fine quality in any product, whether it had been made by hand or by machine, so that they would not succumb to the shoddy goods on the market. Both groups believed that educated consumers could turn the course of production. And therefore, in most cases, their emphasis was on the final product rather than on the process of making it or the persons who did the work. It is not surprising, then, that the vast majority of American objects in the arts and crafts style, as well as the houses that bore this label, tended to be for the middle class rather than for workers.

Despite such differences, the ties between the midwestern movement and the one in England were numerous. Jane Addams and Ellen Starr had visited London and seen arts and crafts training in the workshops of the settlement houses there. Crane and Ashbee, who taught in the London settlements, visited Chicago in 1891–92 and 1900–1901 respectively. Morris fabrics, wallpapers, and furniture were available to well-to-do Chicagoans beginning in the 1880s at Marshall Field's department store, and after 1900 at the Tobey Furniture Company. By that time, however, the city had evolved a structure of commercial production and distribution for handicrafts and its own concept of what "arts and crafts" meant.

The Chicago Arts and Crafts Society, founded in 1897, was the third to be established in this country.[42] The people who assembled at Hull House for the society's meetings included architects and designers, of course. Frank Lloyd Wright, Marion Mahoney, the Pond brothers, Myron Hunt, and Dwight Perkins were all charter members. But many of the other members were not designers at all. They included society and business moguls, lawyers and educators. The journalist and professional reformer Henry Demarest Lloyd joined, seeing another opportunity to promote industrial reform. So too did sociologist Charles Zueblin, who was in the process of establishing the Northwestern University Settlement House and was active in numerous civic art societies. The *Chicago Herald*'s art critic, Lucy Monroe, attended, as did her sister Harriet, the poet and architectural critic, an outspoken opponent of Wright. Oscar Lovell Triggs, a Whitman scholar at the University of Chicago—together with Zueblin, Lloyd, Addams, and Starr—insisted eloquently that the society's purpose was to make the industrial worker a creative and satisfied artisan. As Triggs wrote, "Instead of mechanicalizing [sic] society by applying industrial principles, is it not possible to humanize society by socializing industry?"[43]

Despite such aims, the group's programs reveal the distance which separated these reformers from the actual situation in manufacturing, construction, and every other trade. There was never an attempt to affiliate with local building-trades unions or furniture makers, for instance (although Addams and Zueblin, as individuals, did try). These workers' groups were then battling to preserve in their jobs the same artisanal skills that the Arts and Crafts Society eulogized. As the actual tasks of the industrial worker became more specialized, the middle-class members of reform groups began to promote general education and integrated work. But they did not connect their goals to the demands of the building workers. Thus, such goals amounted largely to abstract ideals. In practice, the Chicago Arts and Crafts Society kept art and politics quite distinct.

Proponents of the arts and crafts were actually more concerned with the relationship between the machine and the woman—the woman as consumer. They hoped to improve the quality of goods on the market, working from two directions. According to Wright, for one, if the designer—whether the idealized artisan/worker or the trained design professional—could take control of industrial production, then goods would certainly improve. At the same time, it was necessary to educate the public to appreciate these better goods. Not only the privileged few deserved them—those who could afford handmade Tiffany glass, Grueby pottery, books from the Roycroft Press, "New Furniture" from the Tobey Company of Chicago. People who had to shop in department stores and from mail-order catalogues, where they would never find handmade articles, were a major focus of this campaign to upgrade public taste. The society displayed a model tenement room, fitted out with exemplary built-in cabinets and simple, sturdy furniture, at their joint exhibition with the Chicago Architectural Society in 1900.[44] They sponsored classes and exhibitions on bookmaking, cabinetmaking, weaving, and pottery in the public schools and settlement houses (fig. 19), in an effort to preserve the traditional crafts of the immigrants. Articles appeared in every kind of popular magazine—from *The House Beautiful* to *Cosmopolitan*, the *Architectural Record* to *Good Housekeeping*, extolling the virtues of plain furnishings and decor. This middle-class audience proved to be the main sponsors and benefactors of the American arts and crafts movement.

The style espoused by the movement did, in fact, reach a remarkably large and diverse group of Americans. The Chicago-based mail-order companies were responsible, in large part, for this phenomenon. By the early 1900s, Sears and Ward began producing "New Art," "Craftsman," or "Modern Mission" goods of all sorts. Rather than disguising the almost spartan construction of tables, chairs, and cabinets in their catalogues, the mail-order companies now played up the fashionably severe lines and minimal ornament. Of course, there was a world of difference between a table that was simple and plain because it had been painstakingly handmade at a Hull House workshop and a similar piece that had been mass-produced to imitate this simplicity. The mail-order companies in fact betrayed the aesthetic philosophy of the arts and crafts movement in numerous ways. A Montgomery Ward's catalogue of 1905 could proudly advertise "Mission furniture," but it was stained brown to resemble oak and fitted

Figure 19. Exhibit of work by members of the Chicago Arts and Crafts Society, on display at the Women's Temple, Christmas 1901. (Reprinted by permission from *House Beautiful* Magazine, ©copyright 1901 The Hearst Corporation. All rights reserved.)

with imitation leather to keep it inexpensive. At every step along the way, the original principles of the arts and crafts movement were chiseled away as the style gained acceptance.

Yet the forms did take hold, especially in the Midwest. By the turn of the century, it was fashionable for a young couple to have a relatively unadorned parlor, at least in comparison with that of their parents. It would be fitted with squared-off, built-in cabinets, furnished with a minimum of rigidly rectilinear tables and chairs, perhaps with a hand-knotted rug on the floor and a Navaho basket on the wall to show their appreciation for other simple cultures. The aesthetic of "New Art" sparseness had replaced Eastlake elegance as the latest moral domestic architecture.

In addition, the major mail-order companies soon advertised a larger version of the arts and crafts aesthetic. By 1900 the houses available from Ward or Sears, shipped precut from their warehouses in Chicago to any part of the country, reflected one further interpretation of the principles espoused by the Chicago society. These factory-produced, unadorned wooden boxes were certainly spartan and strictly utilitarian. They offered owners the possibility of installing their own heating and plumbing fixtures, and of embellishing the shell and the interior with a variety of decorative fittings (fig. 20). Such efforts had to be considered handiwork. The catalogues' suggestions to "do-it-yourselfers" and the illustrations of owner-built kitchen nooks and living room fireplaces, all assembled from factory-produced parts, clearly relied on arts and crafts stylizing. "Substantial, lasting, comfortable" had become widely used labels for the newly acceptable minimal decor and facade. The up-to-date, economical package had a great appeal. By 1905, Sears could advertise that "enough houses have been built according to our plans and with our materials to shelter a city of 25,000 people."[45]

The arts and crafts movement was not simply a matter of educated middle-class aesthetes spreading an established gospel of good taste to working-class consumers. It had, undoubtedly, its strongest impact within the middle class itself. In meetings and publications, architects, reformers, and housewives had to listen to one another. Many of them recognized shared concerns that were, in part, aesthetic; but there was more. The widespread interest in simple, functional environments could be interpreted as a social statement as well. Women had their say about matters of upkeep and health. Social reformers developed an argument for greater standardization and economy in house-building. Architects learned from these people outside their profession who spoke with such vehemence on matters of residential design.

The changes in Frank Lloyd Wright's own home reveal that influence. Still attached to a late-Victorian ideal of interesting clutter in 1897, he moved toward an emphasis on uncluttered open space after several years of exposure to the Chicago Arts and Crafts Society.[46] His famous lecture on "The Art and Craft of the Machine," delivered at a Hull House meeting in 1901, was in many ways a restatement of Triggs's vision of greater democracy through artistic machine-made products. In Wright's case, however, and with most of his colleagues, the end product was far more important than the process that went into making it. The problems of industrial production—specialization, repetition, drudgery, loss of initiative and control over one's work—would, he claimed, be overcome by an ideal: the artist's conception of beauty.[47] Change required the architect's leadership.

The interaction between various groups, all interested in domestic

Figure 20. Living-dining room and (opposite) precut model house. (From *Modern Homes,* a catalogue of furniture and prefabricated houses available from Chicago's Sears, Roebuck and Company. Courtesy of the Chicago Historical Society.)

architecture and decor, left perhaps the most significant legacy of the American arts and crafts movement. For many architects, these societies provided their major exposure to progressive thought and to other professionals involved in social reform. They garnered new ideas from the societies. At the same time, the reformers outside the field sharpened their aesthetic images of an improved American home. Even more than the architects, these nonprofessional men and women placed their confidence in the power of modern domestic settings to transform American society.

Crusaders for Democratic Homes

Several American publications tried to overcome the separation between aesthetics and politics established by the Arts and Crafts Soci-

MODERN HOME No. 264P229

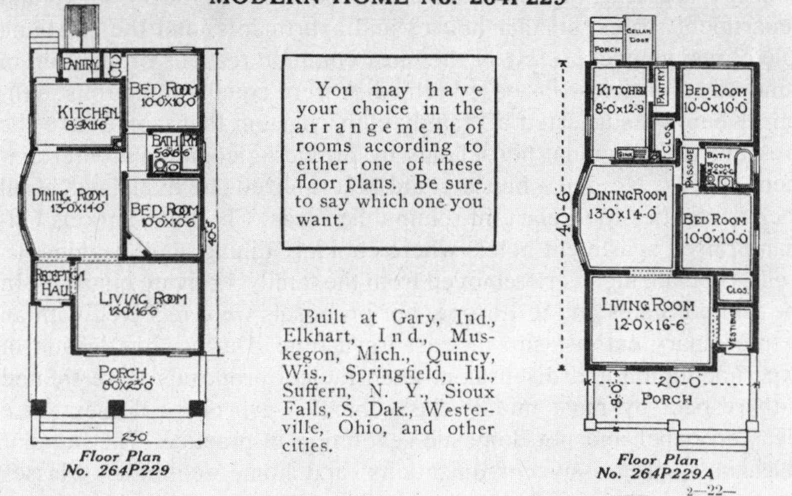

Floor Plan No. 264P229

Floor Plan No. 264P229A

ety. The rhetoric of their proposals often explicitly proposed architecture as a social and political tool, even if the constructions the editors fabricated to demonstrate their analysis were frequently naive and flimsy. Popular monthly magazines, enjoying lower prices, sizable circulations, and the heyday of interest in muckraking journalism during the 1890s, seized on housing as a favored topic. Even more adamant were women's homemaking journals. Publications which might today seem to us complacent, homebound, demure, restricted to the most ordinary tales of family life, became engaged in social and even political issues.

The House Beautiful, the *Ladies' Home Journal*, *Cosmopolitan*, and *The Craftsman* led a crusade for women's rights, city planning, and public participation in every aspect of government. Most of all, they championed better housing for all Americans. Underlying the discussions of architectural styles, with the repeated emphasis on simplicity, was a bold declaration of social and political values. Or, to qualify the statement, the declaration was bold for publications that addressed a conspicuously middle-class suburban audience.

Almost everyone agreed on the need to rethink the home. Urbanization, the streetcar, the telephone and electric light, grocery stores and department stores, smaller houses and apartments, and the changing role of women were a few of the most common reasons brought up in hundreds of articles. Proposed remedies were equally numerous. William Kempton suggested a "family club" system that would take the pressure off individual households by providing communal entertainment spaces. No one's house could be criticized, he explained, if all social activities took place in semipublic areas. Charlotte Perkins Gilman praised apartment hotels where cooking, dining, and cleaning, as well as socializing, were removed from the family's private quarters. In the United States and in Europe, her proposals were received with an extraordinary enthusiasm, at least for a time. During this decade of experimentation and discussion, even radical proposals were treated with respect by most middle-class liberals—especially if they were ideas on paper and not domestic revolution in practice. The popular magazines, progressive organizations, and home economics classes covered a wide range of radical critiques of American domesticity and a surprising range of counterproposals. As Jane Addams later said, "The decade between 1890–1900 was, in Chicago, a period of propaganda as over and against constructive social effort; the moment for marching and carrying banners, for stating general principles and making a demonstration, rather than the time for uncovering the situation."[48] But at least the propaganda was heard.

In the 1890s, it was as if every opinion on the subject of housing really counted for something. *Cosmopolitan,* for instance, sponsored a contest for the best essay on "The Organization of a Home" in 1899, soliciting ideas from its women readers. Edith Elmer Wood, who would later become a prominent housing reformer, won the prize for the category that considered the homes of those on low incomes (incomes of between $1,500 and $2,500 a year and, therefore, above those of unskilled workers). She dealt with the subject directly and outlined how economies preceded ideals in such households. The second prize went to a committee of fifty young women who worked for the National Cash Register Company in Dayton, Ohio. In flowery language that expressed their conviction of a rosy future for modern homemakers, they likened the home to a business where a hierarchy was necessary, meetings were a spur to good rapport, and the "purchasing agent" was a specially trained worker.[49] Such enthusiasm for management techniques in the home would soon become the principal approach to domestic reform. But now it was only one voice among many.

Domestic architecture, like housekeeping standards, was a major issue during this decade. Critiques of opulent, expensive houses were vehement, even if proposals for alternatives lacked the same intensity. The fiery Populist Ignatius Donnelly equated the trappings of such houses with concubinage in his melodramatic *Caesar's Column* (1891). The midwestern minister Charles Sheldon condemned the rich man's house as "a palace of luxury" in the best-selling novel *In His Steps* (1896). John Burroughs wrote on "The Vanity of Big Houses" for *Cosmopolitan,* and warned the prospective homeowner, as well as the architect and the builder:

> But the moment he goes beyond the simplest structure—plain, undisguised wood or stone—and begins to build for looks, for position, or from the pride of a full purse, that moment there is danger that the gentler divinities will foresake him, that the quiet, nonassertive, open-air standards will be outraged, and the discordant, the meretricious, will take the place of the humble, the harmonious, and the assimilative.[50]

Writers still evoked elusive domestic values and the delicate guardians of such values, but they now called upon the muses of simplicity, restraint, and community to watch over all good homes. Clearly, the arts and crafts aesthetic of natural materials, simple lines, and forthright economy had gained a foothold. Many people firmly believed this to be democratic, egalitarian art.

To see the emergence of an aesthetic and ideological shift in attitudes toward the American middle-class home, one can also look to the *Ladies' Home Journal*. Edward Bok, who became editor of the magazine in 1889, saw the reorganization of the American home and the preservation of the traditional family as his crusades. He asked professional architects to design "model *Journal* houses" for the magazine, much as Sarah Josepha Hale had requested "model *Godey's* houses" fifty years earlier. Fiercely nationalistic (to the point of condemning Parisian clothes for American women), Bok looked to these architects for housing models that would embody both the recent middle-class demands for efficiency and the long-standing American reverence for self-sufficiency. Together, Bok hoped, he and the designers could refine the new needs and the old traditions into a truly American domestic architecture. His own stipulations were few: every servant's room (if there were one) was to have a least two windows for cross-ventilation; a living room or library was to replace the unnecessary parlor; "the morals of the bathroom" dictated one for every house; and no "senseless ornament" was allowed.[51] For some years, however, no architect would take Bok up on his offer; this was a builder's job, designing prototypes to be duplicated, and a violation of the architect's professional integrity. But the depression of 1893 altered the standards of professionalism, making any job opportunity seem attractive.

For the first model *Journal* house, published in the winter of 1895, the Philadelphia architect William L. Price showed a $3,500 Elizabethan cottage. In the following issues appeared a Colonial Revival house by Ralph Adams Cram, an inexpensive shingled cottage by Edward Hapgood, a neo-Palladian edifice for $7,000 by Bruce Price, "Some Artistic Little Houses" of Colonial sentiment by Joy Wheeler Dow, and several Shingle Style residences by Arthur Little.[52] All in all, these architect-designed model houses were quite traditional. They followed established historical styles. Moreover, the costs tended to be fairly high for a middle-class budget.

Bok also recognized artistic innovation that went beyond his prerequisites for good American residential design. In 1901 he published two of Frank Lloyd Wright's model houses, designed for his magazine the year before. The first, "A Home in a Prairie Town" (fig. 21), was, in fact, a more mature expression of Wright's just-emerging Prairie house idea than the actual commissions he had recently undertaken for clients. The floor plan and the interior sketch showed the rooms flowing around a large central hearth; in one variation, the space extended up to a second-floor gallery overlooking the living room. Likewise, the facade was strikingly modern, with a low forceful roofline, leaded casement windows, and continuous planes of low walls.

There is no reason to think that the editor or his readers protested against these innovative forms, for Bok continued to feature Wright's work, as well as the houses of his colleagues in Chicago—George Maher, Richard Schmidt, Robert Spencer, Charles White, and Myron Hunt, in particular—even before the professional architectural press was willing to give them such attention.[53] Yet the model house Wright published in the July *Journal* backed away from the earlier architectural experimentation.[54] In the text, Wright blamed the "average homeowner"—partial, he claimed, to a traditional gable roof and willing to let economies rule out the handsome two-story living space—for the self-imposed conservatism. The title of this model, "A Small House with 'Lots of Room in It,'" suggests his disdain for popular sentiments about home design. Wright refused to admit that respect for his daring new aesthetic could come from the general public. Although he took the opportunity to publicize his practice and spread his ideas, he seemed to resent what he saw as the inevitable aesthetic backwardness, even cowardliness, of the *Journal*'s readers.

Yet Wright had drawn many of his ideas from the surge of general interest in housing during the 1890s, from the suggestions of the domestic scientists, public health workers, arts and crafts enthusiasts, and progressive reformers he encountered. He incorporated their desire for economical and efficient space-planning, open areas, space-saving built-in furniture, large expanses of windows, natural "organic" materials, and modern technology. He also responded to the more abstract desires for family stability, community life, and the preservation of individuality, all symbolized in residential design. Wright raised the architectural expression of these concerns to a remarkable, unquestionably innovative aesthetic level. But his houses were not as bizarre or disliked or out of place as he sometimes implied. Well before

Figure 21. "A Home in a Prairie Town" and plan (opposite), Frank Lloyd Wright's first model house for the *Ladies' Home Journal,* 1901.

the third of Wright's model *Journal* houses appeared in 1907, the builders' press had recognized his work and the effect he had had on suburban housing design. The *National Builder* published a photograph of his Fricke house in Oak Park in 1905, and of the Heath house in Buffalo the following year.[55] Commenting on the second, Hodgson remarked that such composition and practical interior space-planning were, happily, becoming "typical." One of the principal reasons for the acceptance of the Prairie house by such a wide-reaching audience was the exposure given the *Ladies' Home Journal* model-house designs, for that magazine had almost reached the hitherto unheard-of circulation of one million readers when the designs appeared.

As a professional architect, Wright's response to the fact of a prototype design was deeply ambivalent. The texts which accompanied his *Journal* houses referred to the need for conceptual clarity in the model-house design, so that the future adaptations of the model would faithfully represent the original ideas. He also expressed a strong desire for actual control over any houses that would be built from the designs. If there were going to be duplication, he wanted it either to be an absolutely perfect copy of the original or else a project whose execution he would be called upon to supervise.

Wright also recognized that the issue of the individual model house implicitly raised the larger problem of planning. He therefore carried his particular concept beyond the single dwelling. Above the first

model *Journal* house, he showed a site plan for four identical houses on a single suburban block (fig. 22). The "Quadruple Block Plan" stipulated that each floor plan would be exactly alike, for the sake of economy and also for artistic control. The facades would be almost identical, although each dwelling could incorporate some distinctive features in its ornament. Like the estimated cost of the model ($7,000, exclusive of land and architect's fee), the site planning also suggested a strong desire to single out a democratic aristocracy as the clients for his model houses. The four almost identical houses were spread over a generous two-acre site. In one arrangement, they were grouped close together at the center of the site, while another offered spacious yards on all sides of maximum privacy. Over the next forty years, Wright kept coming back to this kind of arrangement, insisting on the need for land and privacy for the model American home.[56] This combination, offering neither independence nor community, was to become characteristic of middle-class suburbia.

Another popular journal of the period, Gustav Stickley's *The Craftsman,* made the associations between architecture and social reform more explicit. Early issues in 1901 consisted largely of a paraphrasing of Wiliam Morris's ideals and articles on handicrafts. The editorial statements vowed to uphold the interests of applied and fine arts, worker and designer, family and society. These lofty ambitions, in Stickley's eyes, directly related to one another. He would lead his readers on a campaign for total reform, ranging from the individual home to the city plan, with beauty—and especially beautiful

Figure 22. Quadruple block plan by Frank Lloyd Wright, from the *Ladies' Home Journal,* 1901, showing ideal site planning for his model house design.

houses—as their weapon. Accordingly, coverage became more diverse. *The Craftsman* carried articles on slum conditions in New York City, Kropotkin's utopian anarchism, factory working conditions, village improvement societies, and Chicago's Municipal Art Society, which sponsored civic sculpture. The expectations of immediate, lasting social harmony through good design were obviously unrealistic, but a sizable audience wanted these assertions. Moreover, Stickley was particularly interested in and fairly well-informed about residential architecture, the preferred reform approach of many Americans of the time. This increased his credibility. Professional architects even wrote on style for his journal: Frederick S. Lamb on the Gothic, A. D. F. Hamlin extolling the Beaux-Arts or attacking Art Nouveau, and Louis Sullivan (rehabilitated, if briefly, by Stickley's support) on his own vision of a modern democratic architecture.[57] However, the magazine usually presented less professional approaches.

In 1903 Stickley began to publish "Craftsman Houses" in his journal. These cottages he described as "well-built, democratic, well-planned houses belonging to their owners, suitable for resolving the problem of the lack of servants thanks to their simple, pleasant internal layout, and able to satisfy the needs of all the members of the family."[58] The description thereby promised that ths modern approach to residential design could indeed remedy almost every problem facing the American family. Here again, Stickley tied architecture to political values, social goals, and psychological needs.

The rhetoric, in general, proved loftier than the designs (fig. 23). The principal elements of houses in Stickley's journal were low rooflines, overhanging eaves, simple built-in furniture, a strong emphasis on the surfaces of native stone and wood, and a central fireplace, often with a surrounding inglenook. Many of these model dwellings Stickley designed himself, while others were done by enthusiastic supporters of his campaign (including Claude Bragdon, E. G. W. Dietrich, and Harvey Ellis) and by amateur architects across the country. Clearly, there is a continuation of the Victorian builder's approach to residential architecture in these designs; the image of the harmonious family, close to nature, in its protective, naturalistic, "democratic" home had been reduced to the simplest essences. However, unlike the earlier American builders, Stickley did not insist that every dwelling have a highly personalized design. Domestic architecture, to him, meant greater availability of homes, and therefore economy as well as standardization. He was enthusiastic about the benefits of industrialization.

All the same, at an average estimated cost of $5,000, these prototypes were scarcely available to everyone. In 1905, Stickley therefore began to publish "Craftsman Cottages" (at an estimated cost of $1,000, and with 1,800 square feet, as compared to the 2,500 square feet of a typical house). These, he explained, would solve the housing needs of the working class. The elimination of extras and the simplification of detail were carried to their full measure in these plain little dwellings, which were, in effect, drastic reductions of his idealized middle-class home.

Stickley's promotion of social and architectural reform had great weaknesses. The programs were simplistic, and so was the aesthetic. Occasionally, his drawings have a real charm but more frequently they are awkward and rather rigid. The reliance on "natural materials," whether in the sturdy Craftsman furniture Stickley himself popularized, or in the rugged brick, stone, and board-and-batten construction he favored, was a formula open to misuse. These materials in themselves could never assure either a comfortable setting or a harmonious architecture.

A more stable publication, with similar intentions, was Chicago's *The House Beautiful*. Founded by the engineer and part-time architect Eugene Klapp in 1896, the magazine represented an ideal of simplicity even in its name. The title was taken from a Robert Louis Stevenson poem which described "A naked house, a naked moor, / . . . Such is the house I live in, / Bleak without and bare within,"[59] The following year, Herbert S. Stone, editor of *The Chap-Book*, bought *The House Beautiful* and set it off on a campaign for architectural restraint and

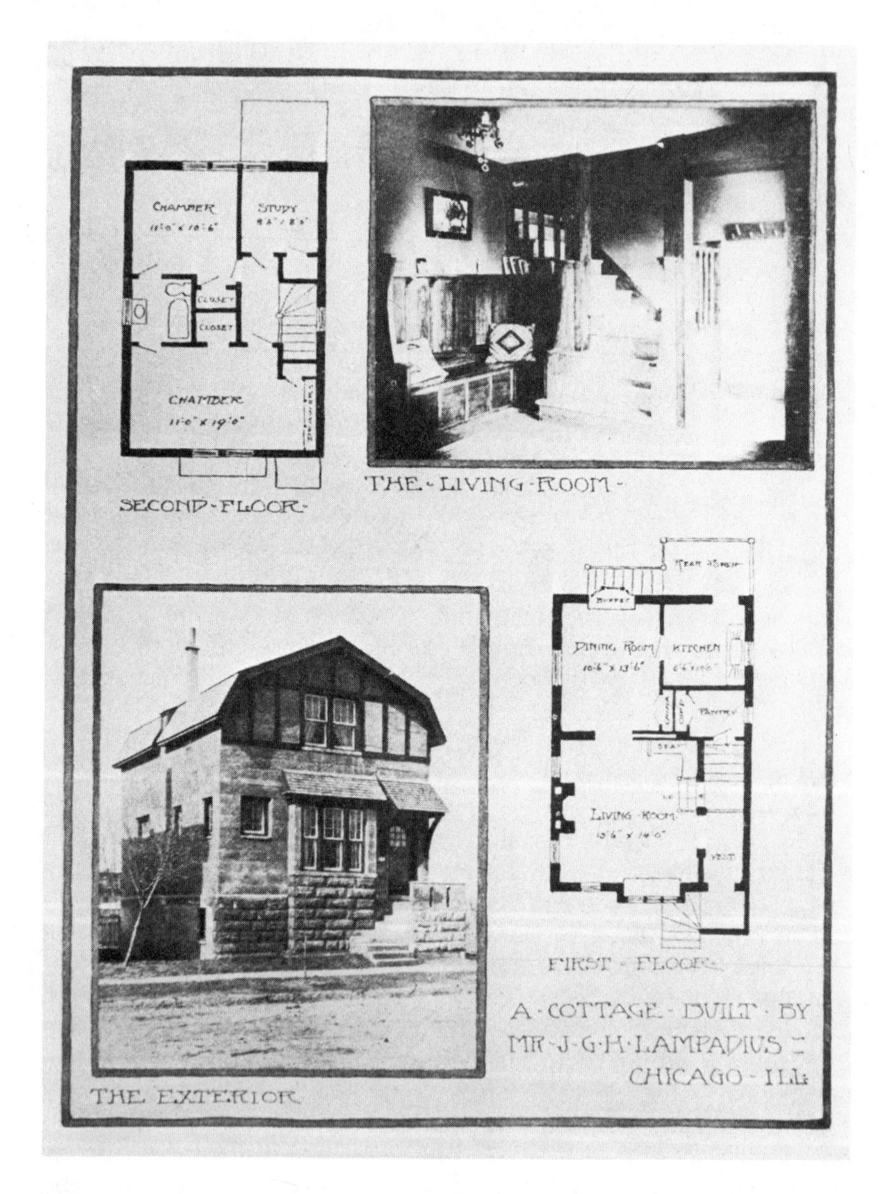

Figure 23. A cottage designed and built by J. G. H. Lampadius of Chicago (featured in *The Craftsman,* 1903), and (opposite) another typical stairway and hall interior (from *The Craftsman,* 1905).

popular participation in design, a campaign that included a cautious endorsement of progressive politics.[60]

The cover announced a crusade of "Republic Building." That goal was linked to a plain, economical architecture for homes. Moreover, such an aesthetic was best defined by the users themselves. *The House Beautiful* featured articles on public health and tenement reform, although, like the magazine's designs, these articles were more restrained than Stickley's examples. Nonetheless, the magazine covered a range of domestic issues which embraced, in passing at least, all classes of homes. Other articles backed the women's suffrage movement and women's active involvement in every aspect of work and civic life. Ellen Henrotin, president of the Chicago Woman's Club and then national president of the federation of woman's clubs, wrote a regular column entitled "The Woman's Forum."[61] She described connections between home and community, giving accounts of women working in factories, the Consumers' League, and city-planning associations. However, considering the causes for contemporary industrial problems, Henrotin railed against the labor unions, claiming that they sought to improve workers' lives according to their own principles of self-interest, rather than recognizing the universal benefits of middle-class liberal reform politics. This position is scarcely surprising, for Henrotin was the wife of a leading Chicago stockbroker.

Her limits were, in many ways, those of Stone himself. His project for political and social reform through widespread participation in housing issues was actually limited to the middle-class families who had the time—and the moral fervor—to join the crusade. Yet he was devoted to the magazine and its potential, even selling out his share in *The Chap-Book* in order to give himself more time for *The House Beautiful.* (He maintained his position as head of a small publishing house which specialized in midwestern authors, including Hamlin Garland, George Ade, Laurence Gronlund, and Eugene Klapp, the last of whom wrote *Successful Houses,* a book based on articles, written under the pseudonym of Oliver Colemen, from his early years as editor of *The House Beautiful.*)

Stone derived many of his ideas from William Morris, as did Stickley and many activists in the arts and crafts societies. Since his student days at Harvard, Stone had been a follower of Morris's aesthetic philosophy, and even his brand of democratic socialism. The political stance of antiprofessionalism and belief in broad-based participation in design—a stance Stone applied directly to residential architecture in his journal—followed closely from Morris's credo. *The House Beautiful* took a fervent antiarchitect position for some years, in fact. One article on sanitary reform complained that architects were "very much better fitted at the end of their course to design palaces for kings than dwellings for common folk." A review praising the English architect M. H. Baillie Scott and his elegant designs from *The Studio* was careful to add the disclaimer that most people could not afford to have an architect design all the right built-in furniture; standardization and mass-production would have to supplant individualized designs, if meaningful artistic reform were to become far-reaching.[62]

Many articles showed the work of men and women readers. Nina C. Kinney began a series on "Housekeeper's House Plans" in 1898. She featured drawings—mostly very simple rectangular floor plans—of inexpensive, convenient houses either designed from scratch or adapted over time by housewives. In the same vein, the assistant editor, Virginia Robie, published an enthusiastic article about the Chicago house designed by a Mrs. Knowlton Mixer: it was an austere box of rough-cast, gray stucco with an open floor plan.[63] A few years later, another nonprofessional, Robert G. Work of Chicago,won a competition for the best $3,000 cottage (fig. 24). His design was, in many ways, a refinement of Stickley's "Craftsman" aesthetic at a more reasonable price. The living room and dining room were open, and he gave special attention to convenient storage, a well-equipped bathroom, and a good-sized kitchen. The facade of this cozy box presented a pleasant mixture of Tudor half-timbering and tiny squares of stained glass, creating a mosaic pattern. Yet the most important factor in these house designs was not aesthetics per se, but economical construction, efficient planning, and the assumptions that people knew what they wanted and needed in their homes.

Most of the work published in *The House Beautiful* had an acknowledged debt to other architectural and social reform movements whose leaders were also fond of the Tudor style. The English arts and crafts tradition and the emerging garden city movement in England provided respected models for this American journalistic crusade. Raymond Unwin and Charles Ashbee were frequent contributors to the Chicago journal. American writers praised Garden City Exhibition cottages and the model workers' towns of Bourneville and Port Sunlight for their sensible, inspiring architecture.[64] A distinct visual ideal was emerging here: simple, easy to maintain, healthy cottages of low cost, with a feeling for traditional home comforts as well as modern interior planning. The majority of the American homes favored by Stone strongly resembled the quaint Tudor cottages built for workers in English garden cities, although they were of course considerably larger, better-equipped technologically, and almost always owned by the occupants, rather than rented.

When the Chicago journal began to print the work of local "progressive" architects—including Frank Lloyd Wright, Myron Hunt, Robert Spencer, Charles White, and Lawrence Buck of the emerging Prairie school group—the accompanying texts stressed their adherence to garden city principles of simple residential design and their radical break from the Beaux-Arts tradition then dominating the profession.[65] In fact, the majority of local architect-designed houses featured in *The House Beautiful,* like the owner-designed residences, were variations of the fanciful Tudor cottage mode. The more radical houses of the Prairie school architects, with their stark, geometric composition, seemed less appealing, for they lacked sentimental associations. As with the Arts and Crafts Society, the Chicago housing crusaders in journalism were quick to seize an acceptable architectural style and claim that it represented their social goals. And, despite all the discussion of community and class equality through a modern, standardized architecture, the houses these journals presented were almost uniformly detached, middle-class dwellings, except for those in the illustrations for propagandistic articles on housing exhibitions and social reform. There was really very little concern with the condition or the participation of people outside this class. In sum, *The House Beautiful* and its sister journals in other cities backed efficiency, economy, a minimalist aesthetic—and the full participation of a suburban middle class.

Figure 24. Model house design and plan (opposite) by Robert G. Work of Chicago, winner of a competition for the best $3,000 cottage, sponsored by *The House Beautiful,* 1902. (Reprinted by permission from *House Beautiful* Magazine, ©copyright 1902 The Hearst Corporation. All rights reserved.)

All the same, Stone's interest in architecture as a social and political phenomenon became fairly explicit at times. In a series which began in 1904, he enlarged his attack on corrupt builders and sycophantic architects, whom he had previously held responsible for poor-quality housing. Even more than these groups, he now contended, the wealthy

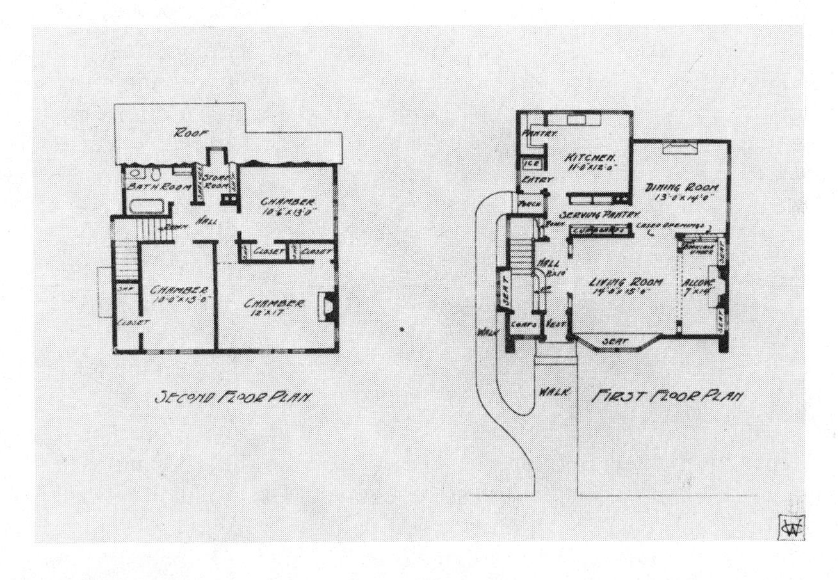

bore the blame for bad housing, since their taste was generally based on ostentatious display rather than on more rational criteria, and others followed their taste.

"The Poor Taste of the Rich" railed against excesses and opulence. The rich, Stone declared, fostered the high cost of middle-class housing, the poor health and cluttered disorder of most urban and suburban homes, as well as the more serious problems of the poor and their inferior housing (although this last point seems to have been of less concern to him). Stone did not criticize the fashion-hungry people who imitated the rich. The blame rested with those who set the fashions, for he could lead out of the wilderness those who had aped them. The first three installments of the series singled out houses in New York and Boston, giving the names of the owners, and photos of particularly extravagant rooms. The fourth presented typical rooms in the excesses of Turkish and Renaissance splendor. "Costly ugliness is a crime," wrote the disdainful editor. American millionaires had not lived up to their civic responsibilities; they did not provide high standards of taste for others to follow. The aesthetic indictment only thinly veiled a political statement: these families deserved the fate of Louis XVI. When the series continued with an exposé of "Poor Taste on Moderate Incomes," the text had become restrained, only gently chastizing, less implicitly a political metaphor.[66] Readers were advised to throw away their bric-a-brac, draperies, and all unnecessary paraphernalia. They should not emulate the undeserving rich. Instead, it was imperative to launch a progressive aesthetic of simplicity and comfort. Stone clearly agreed with the statement Henry Demarest Lloyd had recently made in *Wealth against Commonwealth:* "If our civilization is destroyed, as Macaulay predicted, it will not be by his barbarians from below. Our barbarians come from above. . . . [w]ithout restraints of culture, experience, the pride, or even the inherited caution of class or rank."[67] Attacking the taste of the wealthy was a variation on the progressives' resounding condemnations of the political excesses of the rich.

The editors of popular magazines for women and their families used housing descriptions to reinforce political statements about class inequalities, the need for community, and citizen particpation. The same themes of housing and home values colored the rhetoric and the programs of innumerable progressive causes. The popular journalsim shows all too well the often strained political arguments being made about a universal domestic architecture. Although it is indeed true that these journals endorsed and, to a large extent, encouraged a dramatic change in middle-class housing and in attitudes about housing problems, the editors—like their readers—did not really question whether this new model was available to and desirable for every class in American society. Eventually the imagery of the modern, simplified model overshadowed the original social aims of the crusaders. When architecture and furnishings changed, the change was only a matter of styles, for the principles of community action, popular participation, and women's rights had been obscured.

In the narrowness of their understanding of class and in the breadth of their claims, these popular progressive journalists resembled adherents of the arts and crafts movement, the public health movement, and the settlement house campaigns to upgrade all American homes. Their aspirations, their methods and their limits were also similar to those of another housing reform movement that rose to prominence during the decade of the 1890s. As Henrietta Goodrich of the Department of Household Administration at the University of Chicago insisted, no real benefits for the home, the family, or society were possible "till the home in popular conception shall embody something more than the idea of personal relationships to individual homes."[68] The home economists of the time also saw their great task as the reform of the American home.

5 MODEL HOUSEWIVES AND MODEL HOUSES

The seclusion of home is bought at a dear price.

Caroline L. Hunt, "Homes for the Greatest Number," *The Chautauquan* (1902)

In the 1890s, home economics made a decisive break with its rural roots in homey advice-giving. A new generation of women and men decided to make the home—its architecture, its upkeep, its production, its social life—the center of the modern industrialized world. The movement attracted the chemist Ellen Richards, the educator Marion Talbot, the economist Helen Campbell, and social reformers, including the University of Chicago professors Charles Henderson and Sophonisba Breckinridge. Even a few architects, notably Frank Chouteau Brown of Boston and Nathan Ricker of the University of Illinois, joined in. The home economists' cause was monumental. So was their determination. They recognized that social and economic conditions of their time demanded different conceptions of housing and home life: more women wished to work outside the home; the household was changing in size; more goods for the home were produced by industry; the costs of construction and furniture manufacture were spiralling upward. Marion Talbot's lectures at the University of Chicago, beginning in 1893, would document the effects of such changes. "The result," she declared, "is that the activities of the home are no longer controlled within its walls."[1] The question then was, who controlled the home and family? Although they did not answer the question directly, home economists now acknowledged that the control was not exercised by individual housewives.

The earliest stage of an organized educational campaign in household affairs came about during the 1870s. Publicly financed training in domestic arts and sciences was one aspect of the post–Civil War advances in women's education. Addressing the special needs of war widows, courses tended to emphasize housekeeping economies. Women learned to improve the quality of goods they made in their own homes. Associated with the midwestern land-grant colleges (coeducational by charter) and the cooking schools of the large Eastern cities, this stage of home economics focused on the individual home as a center of production. By the 1880s, with heightened middle-class consumerism, supported by a romantic, passive ideal of domesticity, this campaign for specialized domestic education fell back to a predominantly rural base. Even many agricultural colleges dropped their departments of household arts.[2] Women in the cities and suburbs now relied on the increasing number of books and magazines for advice on keeping house and making household purchases.

In Boston, however, several women were initiating a campaign for a more scientific, professional approach to the house and its functions. Ellen Swallow Richards received her degree in chemistry from MIT in 1880; four years later she was (somewhat begrudgingly) given the title of instructor in sanitary chemistry and a small basement laboratory for her research on microbes in common foods. Under her instigation, the Boston Sanitary Science Club, the Boston School of Housekeeping, and the Women's Educational and Industrial Union were soon founded.[3] In such groups educated middle-class women began to discuss how they might use modern science to improve their homes, how they might control commercialism and involve other women like themselves in useful work outside their homes.

At the 1893 Chicago World's Columbian Exposition, under the auspices of the Board of Lady Managers, representatives of various women's groups from across the country, each concerned about conditions in the home, came together for the first time. This Women's Congress resolved that "matters pertaining to the household had not kept up with the procession of progress," implying that the home, unlike modern industry, had not been reorganized along rational lines. The participants founded the National Household Economics Association to remedy that lag. They declared their aims to be the promotion of: "(1) sanitary houses; (2) skilled labor in every department of the home; (3) and schools of household science and service."[4] These goals reflected fundamental differences between the assembled groups. The NHEA was dominated by the women's clubs, notably that of Chicago, the sponsoring city. These clubwomen were, on the whole, more interested in training capable servants than in themselves becoming involved with problems of housing construction and public health. But other events at the exposition were soon to steer the movement away from such class self-interest toward the scientific approach favored by Richards and her cohorts.

The handicrafts and art objects of the Inter-State Exposition and the 1876 Woman's Building at Philadelphia were still present in 1893, but were less prominent than they had been. In the new Woman's Building there were sentimentalized murals of *Modern Woman* by Mary Cassatt and *Primitive Woman* by Mary Fairchild MacMonnies, concoctions as varied as the queen of Italy's handmade lace and cigarettes rolled by Spanish women laborers, mementoes by famous American women nurses, authors, explorers, and inventors. Sophia Hayden's building was itself a study in decorous taste, the icing of its facade that of a pure, white Italian Renaissance palace. Within, however, many of the exhibits, mounted on simple, unadorned iron frames in the open central rotunda, told of other aspects of women's talents. The displays showed a mounting interest among America's middle-class women in technological invention and the new "scientific" approach to philanthropic work. Visitors found portable sinks and dish-heaters, portable bathtubs and mechanical dusters, all invented by women. Women exhibited their patented transportation systems, typewriters, and citywide waterworks projects. Participants built a model hospital ward and model kindergarten. Next door was the Children's Building, a child-care facility filled with the latest equipment for gymnastics and progressive education.[5]

If the emphasis of women's attention was still largely on the home, it was a different kind of home. Mrs. Coleman Stuckert showed the plans and model for her cooperative housekeeping project for Denver, which included cooperative kindergartens and trade schools, as well as a common kitchen and dining room for forty-four middle-class families.[6] Appliances in the model electric kitchen in the Chicago Woman's Building used Tesla's portable electric motor, invented only four years before. Nearby was the Rumford Kitchen, organized by Ellen Richards for the state of Massachusetts. It consisted of a tiny, wood-frame "model workingman's house" containing a prototype of an inexpensive collective kitchen from which nutritionists could feed the poor.[7] Several women, then, were already using the latest domestic technology to suggest major transformations in the kitchen as a setting and a workplace.

During the years following the fair, a massive educational campaign was the principal focus of the home economics movement. Homemaking departments under a variety of titles appeared in major colleges and universities, including Northwestern, Cornell, Vassar, Stanford, and the University of Illinois. Other schools added to their curricula fashionable courses in house planning, construction, and sanitation, in the economics of housing, the chemistry of foods, and the sociology of family relations. As early as 1897, the U.S. secretary of agriculture stated in his annual report that "among the educational movements which in recent years have engaged the attention of the public, none has been received with greater favor than the attempt to introduce into the schools for girls and women some systematic teaching of the arts which are practiced in the home." In 1890, only four colleges had domestic science departments, but by 1899 there were twenty-one that had them; and by 1916, 195 institutions would have 17,778 students studying the household.[8]

For some time, the emphasis continued to be that of teaching young working-class girls to become good household servants (and to keep up their own homes as well). A ladies' magazine of 1897 declared:

> Schools for domestic service are what we want in this country more than anything else. The solution of the servant-girl problem unquestionably lies in the application of education to it. . . . Intelligence opens the door to every known profession in the world today. And that is what we want and sorely need in our kitchens.[9]

Courses in household science, consisting of housekeeping and cooking techniques, were part of the industrial-training program instituted by the progressives in many urban public schools. Urban settlement houses and even factory managers sponsored similar courses for immigrant girls and their mothers.[10]

But this situation was under siege from several directions. Proportionally fewer women were willing to be servants in other persons' homes, for one, finding that even factory work gave them greater independence for about the same wages. Classes demonstrating a "professionalized" approach to housework and cooking were not going to change their minds. Those who did work as servants were more adamant about their rights. A union of domestics, organized in Chicago in

1901, demanded better hours so that the maid would have time to shop like the mistress. And not all home economists agreed that the lack of a servant class was a problem. Margaret Sangster, among others, was hopeful that housewives would be persuaded to take control of their own homes and the health of their families, an argument Catharine Beecher had made thirty years earlier. Lucy Maynard Salmon believed that the "servant-girl problem" was a good reason for rejecting large houses and cumbersome furnishings. "Girl-bachelor" apartments and cooperatives as well as professional services for cleaning, laundering, and cooking should not be considered aberrations, these women wrote. Such modern approaches toward homemaking were useful to women who did not work, as well as for those who did.[11] Perhaps, such articles now suggested, it was the middle-class woman, as well as her maid, who needed special education to recognize such modern opportunities.

In 1899, eleven women and men came together for the first Lake Placid Conference on Home Economics. Their aim was "to improve the conditions of living in the home, the institutional household and community."[12] Their methods were to be scientific research, professional training, and extensive public education in modern methods of homemaking. By 1908, when the group reconvened as the American Home Economics Association, with Ellen Richards as their president, this model of expertise dominated the national movement. Across the country, high schools and elementary schools had incorporated training in home economics, cooking, furnishing, and domestic architecture. The courses consistently emphasized rigid "scientific" standards, even though research procedures were by no means clear.

There was a frenzy of activity. Grade schools and organized playground associations followed syllabi for instruction in the history and variations of housing, and the students built tiny model houses (fig. 25). In college courses, the home economics teachers were sometimes assisted by architects, interior decorators, and other specialists who built their practice houses, their classroom buildings, and special laboratories, and joined them in the teaching. Contributions from firms as prestigious as McKim, Mead and White—which built the University of Illinois Women's Building (1903–5)—made the courses attractive to middle-class college students of both sexes. U.S. Government Bulletins and the Cornell Farmers' Wives Bulletins brought information to farm wives. One-week extension courses, notably at Columbia Teachers College, the Drexel Institute of Philadelphia, and the Uni-

Figure 25. Miniature suburb constructed by children at a Chicago playground. (From *The Play Movement in the United States,* 1922.)

versity of Wisconsin, brought in women with little time for regular coursework. So, too, did the correspondence courses, in particular those of the Chicago-based American School of Home Economics and the American School of Correspondence, both affiliated with the Armour Institute after 1904. By 1911, over ten thousand persons had enrolled in ASHE courses.[13] The middle classes were now learning to reappraise their own houses, their housework and purchases, and their cities too.

The Lake Placid group had grand ambitions. Its members wanted to modernize all American homes, to improve the work that women did in these homes, and to initiate a vaguely defined civic-improvement drive with these women as its base. As Richards phrased the aims of this group, home economics stood for:

> The ideal home life for today unhampered by the traditions of the past;
>
> The utilization of all the resources of modern science to improve the home life;
>
> The freedom of the home from the dominance of things and their due subordination to ideals;
>
> The simplicity in material surroundings which will most free the spirit for the more important and permanent interests of the home and of society.[14]

Thus the home economists were attempting to modernize the Victorian ideal of women uplifting society by giving women a new weapon: science. They were aware of the dangers of commercialism; they realized that relying on material solutions alone to solve domestic problems was simply fetishism. But the values and interest, the "ideals" to which they constantly referred were never made specific in their writings or their actions. Not unlike the domestic sentimentalists of the Victorian period, whom the modern domestic scientists criticized so harshly, these women also tended to fall back on a rhetoric of absolute, but vague, ideals. They assumed that everyone in their society agreed upon the same values for the home. Despite these presuppositions, the domestic scientists did bring a fresh spirit of inquiry to the study of the house and family. Given their commitment to the benefits of private family life, they were still eager to explore unconventional ways of housing the family and to subject the family to rigorous examination.

Radical Alternatives and Liberal Approval

The prominence of radical feminists in the 1890s—women demanding equal rights, the vote, and, in some cases, fundamental changes in the family and the class structure—was by no means perceived as a threat by these more moderate reformers. Popular home economics texts and moderate teachers were, on the whole, quite tolerant of alternative proposals that were designed to bring about major architectural and social change in the home. A wide range of alternatives were considered acceptable in this remarkable decade of questioning and experimentation. Even relatively conservative journals were at least prepared to discuss openly the merits and disadvantages of cooperative housekeeping, publicly funded child-care, standardized dwellings and apartments—and women working outside their homes. These same issues would not be so easily accepted a decade later. In the 1910s, attention would turn specifically toward suffrage, with less of a broadly defined interest in the home, women's work, and the problems of daily life. Moreover, by then, the group of domestic scientists now entrenched in the universities had made "science" into an absolute standard. They sought to control the disarray of conflicting ideas and proposals for domestic reform. By the 1920s, the feminist movement itself, like the alternative styles of home and family acceptable during the 1890s—at least in theory—would be almost forgotten. Americans seized upon the fancifully traditional (but technologically modern) dwelling and the lighthearted, youthful woman as symbols of their contentment. Few people would want to discuss alternatives.

The radical feminists of the 1890s seemed ready to spurn existing domestic arrangements. But they too tended to identify their goals with rigid endorsements of particular environments and social relations, which they assumed should become universal. Charlotte Perkins Gilman, in *The Home: Its Sphere and Influence* (1903), condemned the home, as it then existed, as an archaic holdover from preindustrial times and demanded that all its functions be either mechanized and collectivized, or discarded. In her many magazine articles and lectures, she called for apartment living, collective kitchens and dining rooms, and cooperative childcare facilities. Somewhat romantic about the benefits of extended family living among immigrants, farm and urban working-class groups, Gilman wanted to do away with the middle class's prized "false privacy" in nuclear units and to replace individual houses with hotels.[15] Others echoed her demands. The Englishman W. L. George attacked conventional American domestic architecture in *Woman and To-Morrow:*

> The home is the enemy of woman. Purporting to be her protector it is her oppressor. . . . I speak, of course, of the home as it is to-day; and I waste no thunder on bricks and mortar, dogs and drawing-room fenders; those things, which we need or choose to have, are the representatives of a system which must be attacked through them, and with it they must probably go, to reappear in civilized forms.[16]

On the one hand, the accoutrements of home life are insignificant baubles; but on the other, they are the symbols of a decadent culture. The radicals, like the moderate home economists, seized upon the actual physical environment as the expression of old ways of living and repressive institutions. However, both groups recognized that this environment could be appropriated to their own ends. Their proposals for social change could be made tangible with specific architectural suggestions. George, for instance, called for doing away with "unnecessary rooms" such as dressing rooms, dining rooms, kitchens, and basements. He advocated cutting back the size of the average house by 33 percent. Like Gilman, he proposed large blocks of forty to fifty flats set in a garden, over a common restaurant. He wanted to substitute these collectivized living arrangements for the acres of wasteful single-family houses in middle-class suburbs.[17]

But what was an "average house" with so much space, or an "average family" with three extra servants? Most of the well-known radical feminists of the time were discussing social change and architectural means which applied only to well-established upper-middle-class families. Yet they usually insisted that their alternative settings and their collective living arrangements should become standard for everyone. Not only did this attitude deny that many families might want to keep some of their cooking, entertaining, and child-care within their homes. It also concentrated on particular issues of excessive privacy, space, and ornament—clearly, problems that were relevant only to those who had too many of such luxuries. Certainly most working-class and poor families were not burdened with uselessly large and overdecorated dwellings. In fact, most female Marxists of the time emphatically stated that they wanted the benefits of family privacy and pleasant home life which a working-class family found hard to secure. Kate Richards O'Hare of New York, or Margaret Dreier Robbins of the Chicago Women's Trade Union League, by no means saw spartan, collectivized homes as a solution to the needs of working women. The concept of an escape from material objects, overabundant space, and wasted time at home was not everywhere an issue. The subject only became problematic as the middle-class women in American cities and suburbs decided that it was time to renegotiate the artistic trappings of class.

The home economists did have a somewhat clearer awareness of class issues, even with their middle-class biases and even though they concentrated their reform efforts on the institution of the middle-class home. They did not claim to be an avant-garde, describing a utopian future, a vision disconnected from the present and its dominant values. Wanting specific, immediate improvements, rather than radical change, these reformers began with what existed and quietly suggested ways in which homes might be modified. Caution encouraged them, for a time at least, to favor small variations within an established image of the home, rather than absolutist, pseudo-scientific models for housing or family life. This reserve made many of them more aware of existing social problems, if less visionary about possible alternatives. They could consider the common and the different needs of families that had no dressing rooms or servants to worry about, families that wanted their homes to be more than cells for sleeping. Ellen Richards stressed the need for privacy, quiet, and personal space in one's home. Helen Campbell, a feminist journalist and economist in New York City, was adamant about the need to plan for children's needs in the home, to provide sturdy furniture, open spaces, and easily cleaned materials. If Marion Talbot admitted that the home was no longer the center of the child's education, she still believed that certain valuable lessons would always be learned there. Talbot also emphasized flexibility, with every space adaptable to many different purposes. Calculations for the optimum size of a kitchen included allowances for visiting friends and children playing, as well as for efficient work.[18] Throughout the 1890s, this generation of home economists showed its appreciation for comfort and traditional activities associated with the home, even as it planned for modernizing that environment. In all likelihood, such attitudes expanded their sympathetic audience.

Yet home economists were more than apologists for the established order. Richards demanded a "*complete readjustment in accordance with modern conditions.*" She called for architectural change, for she wanted "the *ideal*...to be preserved, not the mere shell" of the home.[19] Like Talbot, she was enthusiastic about the possibilities of communal housing projects with shared gardens (tended by a trained landscape gardener, not by the individual families), shared kitchens, dining rooms, laundry facilities, and child-care. There was even room for utopian schemes in their courses and texts. Both women quoted the housing descriptions in H. G. Wells's *A Modern Utopia:* all home services are collectivized; all corners curved so as not to attract dust; all door and window frames of rounded metal impervious to drafts; and the only decoration of the smooth white walls is one faintly tinted line, "as finely placed as the member of a Greek capital." They praised Charlotte Perkins Gilman's books and Veblen's critiques, recommending them in their own textbooks. And they did not shy away from economics either. Readers learned about theories of rent and real estate as investments controlled by big finance, theories derived mostly from the liberal German political economist and statistician Ernst Engel.[20]

After Richards, the acknowledged leader of the home economics movement during these years was Marion Talbot (1858–1949) of the University of Chicago.[21] Talbot exemplifies the spirit of the movement at the turn of the century: the desire for fundamental restructuring of the home and its upkeep, the refusal to impose a single standard by which all families should live—in a word, liberal pluralism. Her ties with other reformers in the Chicago area and her efforts to spread her teaching outside the university demonstrate how closely home economics followed progressivism. Her architectural proposals show how resolutely the home economists endorsed the emerging modernist idiom of clean, unadorned lines and functional spaces.

Talbot was named to the first faculty at the University of Chicago in 1892, as assistant professor of sanitary science in the Department of Social Sciences and Anthropology, a department with only four members, headed by Albion Small. This group, the first university department of sociology in the country, soon became a major center of social-science research, especially in the study of cities.[22] Talbot's goal was to have the curriculum integrate research and policy on the home and family into the broader outlines of urban and political sociology. Her affiliation with these eminent colleagues was a significant one to her. "It implies," she wrote, "recognition that a very close relationship exists between sanitary conditions and social progress. Sanitation and sociology must go hand in hand in their efforts to improve the race."[23] Probably her colleagues would not have put it that way. But they did come to recognize the family and urban housing as crucial issues in their society.

Small made Talbot one of the editors of the *Journal of Sociology,* and she occasionally wrote articles for publication. But she herself acknowledged that hers was not a purely academic subject. This made it all the more her duty, she believed, to champion the university's stated policy of integrating practice with theory. She had the Rumford Kitchen from the Columbian Exposition set up in a dormitory so that students could continue to experiment with nutrition. She sent graduate students to live at Hull House and other settlements. One student, Caroline Hunt, worked with the Bureau of Labor Statistics to document the housing conditions of Chicago's Italian families and wrote a popular series of articles explaining why the middle classes should understand the facts about industrial production.[24] Within the university, where Talbot acted as dean of women until her retirement in 1925, she encouraged President Harper to add a department of public health and a department of social work. And she herself taught in almost every session of the university's correspondence program as well as the extension program in the suburbs.

Friends and colleagues outside her own field gave Talbot useful advice and theoretical direction. She invited Jane Addams to lecture in her courses and to contribute to her books. Sophonisba P. Breckenridge, a former student, joined her faculty in 1905 to specialize in housing for the poor and consumers' rights.[25] Talbot assigned the books of E. A. Ross, Charles Cooley, Edward T. Devine, and other liberal social scientists who called for a "practical sociology" in which research led directly to action. She also kept up close contacts with Chicago professionals, especially physicians, who worked on housing-related problems. She sought to use the progressive educational techniques of John Dewey. Two of her faculty, Ella Flagg Young and Julia E. Bulkley, held joint appointments in Dewey's Department of Pedagogy. Dewey, in turn, emphasized that the school (fig. 26) should be "a model home" that extended the practical training and moral environment of the family into the public sphere.[26] In 1904, Talbot's newly separate Department of Household Administration became part of Dewey's School of Education. Unfortunately, he left the university over a hiring dispute that same year, and the connection remained embryonic.

The home economists at the University of Chicago sought to apply the sociological and anthropological studies of their colleagues, notably those of Frederick Starr, W. I. Thomas, and Charles Henderson, all of whom stressed cultural differences between family groups. In turn, other members of the sociology department took an interest in the study of the home and family, recognizing that this sphere was central to their larger analysis of changes in social life and work relations. Charles Zueblin lectured on Chicago's housing problems and the range of the city's domestic architecture, from suburban cottages to urban tenements. He also appraised current environmentally based reform schemes in his lectures. These ranged from the proposals of the arts and crafts movement to the City Beautiful campaign. The Chicago minister, social reformer, and sociologist Charles Henderson even attended the Lake Placid conferences, where he stressed the role of home economics as a tool for urban reform.[27]

In Talbot's own work, she preached the need for improved housing, more effective housekeeping, and a new understanding of the many influences affecting home life. "The Citizen as Householder," a course she first offered in 1899 in both the college and the extension division, analyzed the public agencies, the commercial organization, the eco-

Figure 26. A class at the University of Chicago's Lab School making and furnishing play houses, ca. 1902. (Courtesy of the Regenstein Library of the University of Chicago.)

nomic and health factors, and other urban conditions which affected all of the city's homes. "A man's castle is not now a defense against his neighbors," Talbot declared, "but a possession which involves obligations to them."[28] She spelled out these obligations in a series of articles she coordinated for *The House Beautiful* between 1903 and 1905. Here were accounts of low-cost housing reform and public health legislation, working-class housing in Europe and the need for community planning in the United States. Her former student Mary Hinman Abel wrote a three-part account of cooperative housekeeping.[29] Other colleagues described the benefits of apartment life. One ridiculed an unnamed society of architects for their fears that apartments would destroy the family and lead women into frivolous idleness.[30] While Talbot did concentrate on reforms in middle-class, single-family houses, she never limited her focus to them.

The key to civic progress, Talbot believed, was the collective action of an informed public. Women could not depend on experts or professionals to make all their decisions for them. Except in the case of women's suffrage, she herself never believed wholeheartedly in progressive legislation. As she pointed out in lectures, legislation was too often written to benefit commercial rather than public interests. She did endorse municipal sanitation laws and tenement-reform measures.[31] But laws alone, she claimed, could never assure healthy houses, reasonable financing policies, efficient and responsible municipal government. Only educated, civic-minded men and women acting in concert could bring about lasting change.

The debate about participation divided home economists as it divided other progressive reformers. One of the points that distinguished Talbot was the implication that neither science nor law was value-free. Talbot certainly believed in scientific research and legal action, but she did not advocate absolute standards being imposed on all households for their own good.

Retraining the Housewife

Most home economists believed that one way to effect real improvements in domestic architecture was by training consumers to recognize good housing. The first step was to educate as many women as possible in house construction and planning. The campaign for housing education was not limited to the university. At the School of Domestic Arts and Sciences of the Armour Institute, organized in 1903, women could train for professional jobs based upon traditionally domestic duties such as nutrition, nursing, social work—and domestic architecture.[32] The low tuition and the scholarships, as well as correspondence course options, opened the studies to working women as well as middle-class housewives. The ties with Armour's Chicago School of Architecture assured qualified instructors and advisers in domestic architecture, including Hermann von Holst and Thomas Tallmadge.

Nonetheless, universities remained the prestigious locus for home economics as a serious profession. But there, too, during the 1890s, the leaders stressed popular education in all matters relating to the household. In a series of lectures organized in 1895 by Richard Ely in the Economics Department at the University of Wisconsin, Helen Campbell insisted that everyone should learn to draw floor plans. She cited Jefferson's designs as proof of the ingenious solutions which could come from amateur architects.[33] Isabel Bevier, head of the new Department of Household Science at the University of Illinois, took over courses on the history of architecture and the history of plumbing and heating from the College of Engineering. She then asked several of the architects on that faculty, among them Nathan Ricker, James M. White, and Seth J. Temple, to assist in her lectures and her studios. Bevier taught all of her students to draw plans and to use graph paper so that their drawings would be to scale. She illustrated her textbook, *The House,* with student work, including proposals for $2,000 houses, and with practical cottages designed by their owners[34] (fig. 27). These were uniformly small, efficient, economical model homes. Other courses emphasized construction. Students learned to judge good plumbing plans and joints and sound building techniques. They tested the quality of mortar and appraised grades of lumber. They learned about ventilation and lighting. Following one syllabus on "Shelter" put out by the American Home Economics Association, students would acquire, through a combination of site visits, laboratories, and theoretical study, the equivalent of elementary training as a contractor.[35]

Most home economists wanted to educate a great many consumers rather than a few good women designers. Their more specialized students could, it was hoped, advise architects, developers, and building commissions.[36] The students' combination of technical knowledge and sensitivity to human needs would make them useful members of a team. But none of these housing reformers openly encouraged students or readers to become professional builders, contractors, or architects themselves. Perhaps they simply recognized the barriers to women in these vocations, and placed their hopes in more indirect approaches.

Unfortunately, this tactic kept home economists fairly distant from developments in the building trades. None of their textbooks or articles refer to the efforts of those carpenters or plumbers who also wanted to upgrade housing. Like the Arts and Crafts Society, home economists studied the production of domestic settings in a curious vacuum: they ignored the workers who built the dwellings. This deficiency was related to the home economists' tendency to generalize about universal values, both political and aesthetic. However, working-class women did not readily accept the ascetic, simplified model home or the industrialized image of the modern housewife. Similarly, building-trades workers resisted the "modernization" of construction. Both groups therefore appeared backward to the dedicated middle-class reformer.

There were certain principles of design that the home economists did hold in common with forward-looking architects. First, they endorsed a radical simplification of the dwelling. The leaders of the movement emphatically refused to accept styles of decoration and architecture that might be fashionable but that were neither practical nor comfortable. They insisted that simplicity had to be the basis of all domestic design. Richards acknowledged the need for beauty, and even for luxury, but complained that many so-called advances in technology and decoration did not bring personal satisfaction or social welfare. As early as 1883, the Sanitary Science Club of Boston was citing William Morris on the benefits of simplicity and adaptability as primary aesthetic criteria. Helen Campbell also referred to Morris in her lectures, as did Talbot and Bevier, who quoted his dictum: "Have nothing in your homes that you do not know to be useful, or believe to be beautiful."[37] If they did mention Eastlake, it was by way of reference to his original text with its vehement attacks on artificial, unnecessary decoration; all of these women roundly criticized the pseudo-Eastlake ornament still so popular in the 1890s, charging that it was unhealthy, hard to keep clean, easily chipped, and generally ugly.

Instead of such pretense and extravagance, they wanted functionality to become the basis for all aesthetic decisions in the home. As Richards wrote, a main consideration in domestic design should simply be attention to the work that had to be done there. "Economy of labor has not been thought of in the construction of houses. In what other business would the coal supply be dumped on the sidewalk to be shovelled and wheeled into the cellar, only to be brought up again; the ashes carried down, only to be brought up and carried away."[38] Home economists wanted architects and builders, when they planned houses, to listen to the housewives' needs. There should be no crevices or cornices where dust could collect, they agreed. The materials should be smooth and easily washable. The windows had to be large and placed to maximize sunlight and fresh air. Women had to do their part, relegating unnecessary furniture, most bric-a-bac, displays of gifts and souvenirs to the attic—if there was to be an attic, which did not really seem necessary any more. But the principal responsibility was on those who had a hand in actual design.

All home economists wanted smooth surfaces and simple lines.

Figure 27. Owner-built bungalow and plan (opposite) in a Chicago suburb. (From Isabel Bevier's home economics textbook, *The House*, 1906.)

These same design elements would, in the early twentieth century, herald a radical modernist style among the architectural avant-garde in Europe and the United States. The home economists, too, were interested in new building materials such as reinforced concrete and porcelain enamel, and they speculated about as yet undiscovered substances. Even their rhetoric foreshadowed that of the architectural modernists of the 1920s. The home economists invoked an industrial aesthetic, the order embodied in "an office . . . the kitchen of a buffet car or a steamship, the arrangement of a laboratory [or] a store," wrote Campbell as early as 1895."[39] They liked to refer to model kitchens, dwellings, and apartments as "laboratories" or "experiment stations."

To many home economists of the 1890s, as to the architects of the European modernist movement in the 1920s, standardization seemed a necessary advance. Greater similarity between individual dwellings would create a more harmonious community plan. Most American cities, Campbell declared in frustration, were "frowsy checker-boards, stubble-fields of chimneys, wastes of monotony that is not regular and of eccentricity without distinction."[40] Greater standardization in American houses seemed a sign of democratic equality. That connection was made visible and emphatic with illustrations such as a row of identical Chicago bungalows, each proudly displaying its American flag, which appeared in *The Woman Citizen's Library* (fig. 28).

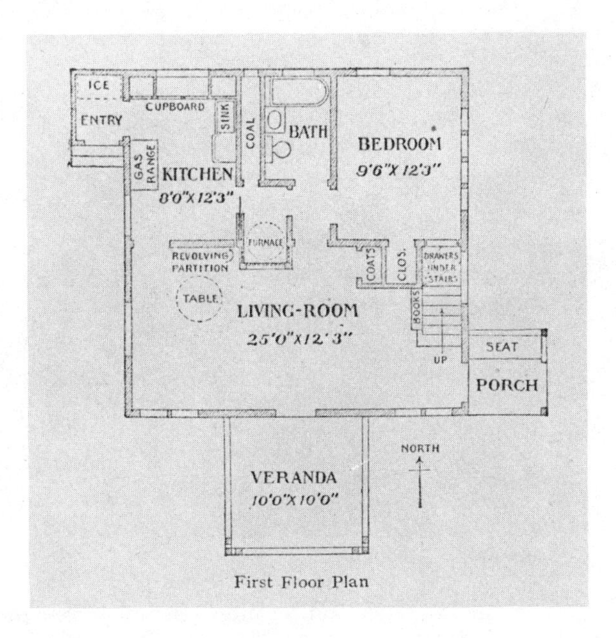

First Floor Plan

The home economists' bias toward the appearance of equality and self-restraint in domestic architecture derived, in large part, from the premise that such an image would help sustain an egalitarian society. This was clearly a naive assumption about the power of an environment. It was also based on a middle-class proclivity toward an almost ascetic moderation in all things. Wealthy families tended to spend their money on sumptuous houses and costly, beautiful objects; this seemed extravagant to the middle class. Working-class families proudly displayed cheaply manufactured decorative items and sentimental mementoes from their pasts in their homes; this seemed both unsanitary and tasteless. Liberal, middle-class home economists, like other housing reformers, were self-righteously committed to standardized simplicity in every home.

The home economists at the turn of the century did, however, want innovative simple forms. They looked to architects, particularly those of the midwestern Prairie school, for their models of modern homes. In the eyes of most home economists, it was the professional architect's duty—not the housewife's—to provide the ideal dwelling for modern family life. The home economists saw it as their job to popularize that

Figure 28. "An Inviting Outlook" on a Chicago street. (From *The Woman Citizen's Library,* vol. 12 [1914].)

model. Accordingly, Campbell had praised Frank Lloyd Wright's Winslow house in her *Household Economics.* She also cited Montgomery Schuyler's architectural criticism, which echoed her own call for aesthetic restraint and technological inventiveness. Bevier published houses by the Chicago architects Thomas Tallmadge, Robert Spencer (fig. 29), Walter Burley Griffin, and Lawrence Buck in the later editions of her textbook. She admired the clean lines of their chaste wood or stucco cottages. Other home economists drew from the more expensive and elaborate—but still resolutely classical—examples in Herbert Croly's *Stately Homes in America* and the calls for austerity in *Homes for City and Country,* a collection of illustrated essays edited by Russell Sturgis. They also looked to Joy Wheeler Dow's romantic tribute to the Colonial Revival, *American Renaissance,* and to the novelist Edith Wharton's *The Decoration of Houses.*[41] These texts could educate every reader in the principles of architectural design, just as they hoped their own home economics texts would instruct architects in more practical or everyday considerations.

In 1896 Helen Campbell wrote an article for the *Architectural Record* in which she asked both architects and housewives to put their dwellings to the same crucial test. Were they "in the lines of progress or against it?"[42] A progressive aesthetic, she implied, was almost identical for the two groups. Advanced thinkers among architects and home economists advocated similar principles of design: clean, unadorned lines; open spaces; functional considerations over mere fashion; greater standardization and community planning; a break with the stuffiness and the ornate styles of the past. In both cases, however, the moral and aesthetic arguments had their limits. The new progressive aesthetic was the aim of a middle class or, more precisely, an upper middle class. It addressed the practical needs and also the deeper emotional concerns of this class. Eclectic styles and effusive display were disconcerting, seen either as individualistic and reactionary or as dangerously anarchistic. Both groups were afraid that their culture might retreat into an unscientific and dangerously populist way of life. They wanted a distinct purge of historical fashions and excessive individualism. The professional home economist and the architect both saw it as their duty to define modern models for homes in order to usher in a new stage in American life. There had to be experts, with training and advanced views, who would guide the nation toward its future.

In the early period of the home economics drive, especially in the 1890s, there had been exceptions to this professional approach. Marion Talbot in particular had tried to combine scientific standards for the home—determined in the university laboratory—with encouragement for the active participation of women in community life and municipal government. She was opposed to any absolute, supposedly "scientific" approach to housing or home life because it would stifle the kind of involvement and exchange she wanted. For her, science produced information, and people then had to decide themselves how to use it. But most home economists, and most other reformers, had become more adamant about the need for scientific control of housing and family life by the early 1900s. They looked to experts—including themselves—and not public participation, to provide solutions that were to become standards in every situation. The recurring American effort to determine human behavior by environmental reform was updated with a modern scientific approach, absolute and authoritative, above the vicissitudes of culture and class. Scientific experts were supposedly above transitory fads and social biases. Some home eco-

Figure 29. Edward S. Bristol House and plan (opposite), River Forest, by Spencer and Powers, 1908. (From Isabel Bevier's *The House,* 1913).

nomics reformers now touted eugenics, or population control, as the most scientific means for creating a model society. But most of them still believed in the power of the environment to influence behavior. What was needed, however, were clear standards to modernize the home and thereby influence its inhabitants. Ellen Richards now coined a special term for such guidelines. For her "Euthenics," or "the science of the controllable environment," held the key to all other modern advances.[43]

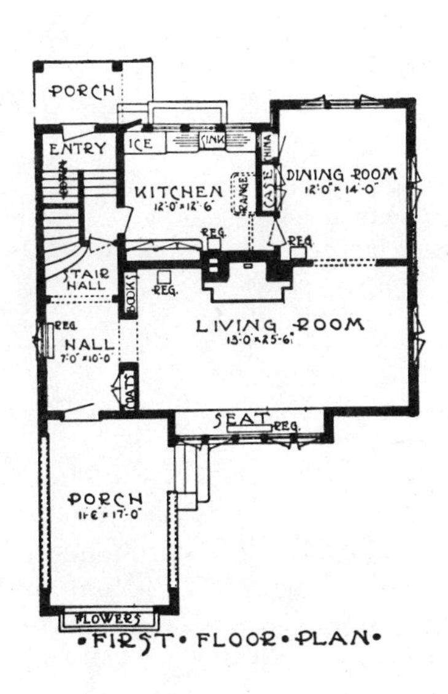

•FIRST• FLOOR• PLAN•

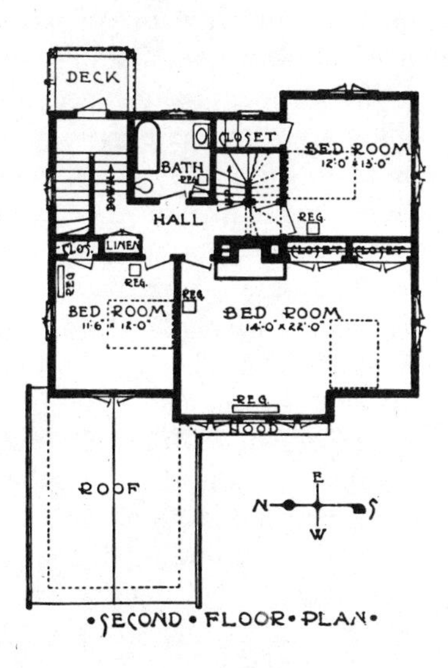

•SECOND• FLOOR• PLAN•

6 THE POLITICAL SETTING

There must be laborers and drones in every community. The laws of nature sanction this. The drone exists on the same principles as the rat, and the incautious laborer sinks in time to the level of the drone.
Industrial Chicago (1891)

The dominant American attitude toward the building worker changed profoundly during the last decade of the nineteenth century. Once romanticized, even in the professional architectural press, as a traditional craftsman preserving noble skills, the building laborer came to be seen as a petty tyrant holding up progress; a slipshod worker, little concerned with high quality or innovative technology; a pawn of corrupt unions, ready to cut off a city's supply of housing for ever-higher wages. Animosity against unionization in general was strong during these years. The violence at Pullman and Homestead frightened many people, and the Chicago daily papers were especially ready to whip up prejudices by linking unionists with anarchists. In 1901 the assassination of President McKinley in Buffalo by an anarchist intensified antilabor sentiment throughout the country, as the Chicago journalist Fred Hodgson noted with regret. Soon afterward, the president of the National Association of Manufacturers took to the Chautauqua trail to denounce "The Mob Spirit in Organized Labor."[1] Building workers took the brunt of this hostility.

The change in attitude, like the changes in architectural form of the 1890s, had been evolving for some time. Throughout most of the nineteenth century, the construction trades had been respected though, except in times of middle-class anxiety and hostility when strikes or street violence occurred. From the middle of that century, American egalitarianism and Ruskin's mantle of dignity and medieval associations had protected the building worker from the harshest criticism.

Sentimental descriptions presented the carpenter and the mason as venerable craftsmen, preserving traditional building skills. One reason for the popularity of this medieval allegory was that it portrayed "the worker" as someone content with his place in the social hierarchy. The true craftsman would not demand any sort of radical restructuring of society. This illusion was hard to sustain during strikes.

The very celebration of supposedly handcrafted detailing on buildings was, of course, also an artificial contrivance. Architectural evidence of the noble worker's skill was increasingly likely to consist of ornament and entire sections of buildings that had been produced in a factory. However, most architects insisted that craftsmen execute the fine ornament. The fact that the nation's wealthier families did have handworked ornament for their homes kept the illusion alive for some people.[2] Early issues of the *American Architect* had emphasized the importance of craft skills for the elaborate eclectic styles of Queen Anne and Ruskinian Gothic which were then popular.

Those who wrote on labor issues also praised the traditional crafts and rejoiced in the many opportunities for restrained self-expression available to the skilled carpenter. Architects who reviewed pattern books clearly favored the idealized craftsman over the upstart builder who professed to design entire houses in his own imaginative way, with no knowledge of refined techniques, no appreciation for tradition. Frequently, architects likened the relationship that existed between the contemporary professional designer and the building worker to that of their medieval counterparts constructing a cathedral. In both instances, one article glowingly stated, a mutual esteem, derived from a shared respect for traditional styles and orderly work processes, united these good men. Such mutual regard, this writer went on, had become more necessary in his own day. The "bond of sympathy" would make workers less likely to be drawn into political activity and unions. They should see that there was no real separation of interests between the worker and the architect.[3]

During the 1890s, the social and political tensions which had built up in the later Victorian decades often flared out of control. The resulting shift in attitude toward building workers also related indirectly to contemporary fashions in architectural styles. Popular Victorian-era builders' pattern books, women's magazines, and other kinds of literature too had presented domestic architecture as a celebration of the individual carpenter and mason, as well as of the individual housewife. From the mid-1890s, it was no longer considered so fashionable to regard a house as such a personalized creation. At the same time, houses had in fact become noticeably less flamboyant and more visibly similar.

As ideas of how the family functioned, of how the home should be constructed and what it should represent, were being reformulated, so too did architectural metaphors change. Like the Victorian home, the minimalist modern home of the turn of the century represented one expression of the dominant culture's ideas about the family and about the workers who constructed houses. Of course, it could be argued that the transformation of styles of domestic architecture was a purely economic issue. However, it was not necessarily more expensive to have ornamented dwellings. The late-nineteenth-century stage of modern industrialized building had generated a theretofore undreamed of variety of shapes and motifs, rather than the simple forms supposedly intrinsic to industrialization. In fact, the radically simplified houses of the early twentieth century were actually more expensive than the late Victorian houses, in large part because of the new technology and also because the cost of materials and construction had risen so rapidly. (Similarly, it might be mentioned, the "New Brutalism" of the 1960s and 1970s—raw concrete, exposed pipes and ducts—is generally more expensive than conventional construction, even though the buildings give the appearance of rock-bottom budgets.)

Houses of the 1890s and early 1900s were reactions to the *idea* of individualized dwellings and expensive, handcrafted detailing. Instead, the modern dwellings would embody the ideas of minimalism, efficiency, and economy. Yet a sheer minimalist aesthetic—the least expensive product possible—was never the fashion for moderate-cost houses on the private market (and not even for company-owned housing in industrial towns).

The Battle over the Building Craftsman

The building workers' antagonism toward the industrialization of their trades mounted to a new ferocity in the 1890s. A dedicated social reformist strain also continued to hold its own. The leaders of the trades, notably the carpenters Hodgson and McGuire, sought to establish an organized program for housing reform that would keep housing costs low, availability high, and still allow the workers to retain control over their jobs. But the rank-and-file of the building unions were often impatient with such broad-based reform measures. Carpenters, sheet-metal workers and woodworkers complained bitterly that "greenhorns"—women, children, or immigrants, trained to do only one specialized task and forced to work for very low wages—were taking their jobs and bringing down the quality of construction. Unskilled workers could make many products in a factory and even affix them to a building for wages half those of more diversified craftsmen.[4] Jobs in the factory and on the site became increasingly specialized by the 1890s, for contractors preferred to pay a worker who did only a few specific tasks and therefore commanded a lower wage. The building unions in Chicago, as in other large cities, tried to resist industrialization in an effort to assure jobs for their members.

From the late 1880s, resolutions had been passed restricting the use of machinery in construction. Sympathy strikes were started over pipe cut in the shop rather than on the site; over nonunion materials; over cutbacks and speedups determined by specialized workers' rates. The stone-cutters' union even refused to have its members work for any contractor who used certain machinery in his yard, and other building unions backed their demands. The unions designated "business agents" or "walking delegates" to oversee treatment of workers on construction sites. These representatives would prevent contractors from hiring nonunion labor for specialized tasks. By 1890, over a hundred cities had such building-union agents patrolling construction sites.[5] The delegates bolstered the workers' own self-esteem, for, like old-time carpenters, they wore the same clothes as the employers, priding themselves on high collars and silk hats.

In general though, the building workers fought with one another as well as against their employers. The delegates often prevented the use of "unfair" materials produced in out-of-town factories. But there was local friction, too. The allegiance between skilled workers and factory machinists in the same area was tenuous, at best. The changing production system was especially likely to lead to conflicts between skilled craft workers and machinists, who had generally been taught only a few unrelated techniques. Throughout the 1880s and 1890s, in fact well into the twentieth century, most unions would only admit skilled workers who had served a long and all-around apprenticeship. They refused to recognize the semiskilled worker or the machinist who had been trained in only a few aspects of production. This tactic, in direct opposition to the increased specialization in industry, kept their numbers down in many instances, and their wages as well, for contractors could use workers who were refused admittance by the established unions.[6] As the machinists organized into their own unions in the late 1880s—sheet-metal workers, woodworkers, pipe fitters, for instance—jurisdictional disputes arose. The use of new materials where wood had once been employed happened so quickly that no one could be sure which union the workers in question should be under. Quandaries arose over iron and steel framing, metal staircases, metal and tile wainscotting, even plumbing pipe and toilets, all of which had once been executed in wood.

These battles took place in an urbanizing nation still, by and large, optimistic about the benefits of industrialization. In every major American city, prominent local capitalists came together to sponsor trade schools which would train future workers for just a few specialized jobs rather than for a complex trade. On-site apprenticeship, according to their arguments, instilled old-fashioned skills; it also perpetuated an ambiguously defined but overly smug and dangerous class identity. Between 1883 and 1893, fifty public school systems introduced manual training, although it was generally of a rather formal, abstract nature, intended to train memory and dexterity through repeated exercises.[7] Chicago's Manual Training High School, designed by Solon S. Beman in a Ruskinian Gothic style, was established in 1884. Well-known local businessmen, including Phillip Armour, Potter Palmer, Richard T. Crane, and George Pullman, served on the board of trustees. There boys learned to operate machines and do some kinds of more rewarding handwork. There was little emphasis on decision-making or experimentation, and a great deal on discipline. In 1890, under the state chapter of the AIA, a builders' school was founded. Classes in manual skills, drafting, and typing were taught at the contractor-dominated Institute of Building Arts. The emphasis here was on officework and a businesslike regulation of construction. In 1893, just before the depression, Phillip Armour presented the five-story Armour Trade Institute to the city of Chicago.

As the massive history of *Industrial Chicago* (1891) pointed out, all of this organization for training construction and machine workers was done without any direct participation from the building trades themelves.[8] Most trade journal editors were, in fact, quite opposed to official trade school education. *Carpentry and Building* expressed the prevailing sentiment well, citing a Massachusetts Federation of Labor resolution:

> We are opposed to trade schools . . . as objectionable, because they never learn [teach?] the practical parts of a business, only giving a smattering of theoretical knowledge that makes its victim a poor workman, incapable of getting a good job, and yet a menace to every other man in the craft.[9]

The unions represented the trade schools as places for training specialized rather than general craft workers, teaching skills for mindless industrial production. The schools, they charged, did not give an overall concept of the process, whether it was furniture-making, house-building, or any other established trade. There was a great deal of truth in their criticism. The mechanization of plaster-making, the factory production of woodwork, standard grading of lumber, mass production of porcelain sinks, tubs, and toilets as well as pipe fittings—these processes had taken away opportunities for the worker to make choices about materials, or to exercise a range of skills on the job.

The opposition was proud. Fred Hodgson wrote editorials insisting that the plumber or carpenter was just as good a person as the doctor or lawyer, and just as good a professional if he had been apprentice-trained.[10] But such attitudes now seemd anachronistic to most middle-class Americans. The unions themselves were an example of the benefits of organization, many progressives pointed out.

As the editors of *Industrial Chicago* explained, it was industrial technology that would make possible the worker's vision of owning a home for his family. Transportation systems opened up the suburbs to everyone, just as cheaper bricks and plaster cut the cost of construction.[11] Why try vainly to oppose modern organization and specialization? *Industrial Chicago,* whose editors were successful businessmen, went on to consider why workers might not understand that whatever served American industry would also be in their best interests. Since laborers did not have time to study economic laws and theories, it was held, their approaches to economic problems were bound to be misguided. The fact that workers' household purchases were too small, the argument continued, demonstrated that they did not understand good business practices.[12] This is but one example of the kinds of antilabor sentiments fermenting in the 1890s.

In order to understand the hostility against building workers that became so strong during the 1890s, it is important to compare this decade with earlier periods of union organizing and public reaction. Union activity among American building trades workers, always fiery, had begun early. Contractor disputes had arisen in Philadelphia in the

1790s, and the first journeymen's trade union was organized there. By 1800 carpenters' unions had been formed in most cities along the Atlantic seaboard. Conflict was frequent in Chicago from the 1830s; the intense demands for new building often set laborers and contractors against each other, and placed the skilled laborers in a strategic position. Since the building trades were, and continue to be, almost entirely based on local rather than itinerant labor and, in many instances, on locally produced materials, the union locals quickly became powerful bargaining agents.

From their early years, the building trades unions had been in the forefront of the labor movement. In the year of the Centennial, Chicago carpenters and lumber workers joined with railroad workers, tailors, and McCormick plant laborers in the strike by the Workingman's party for the eight-hour day and wage increases; the army was called in to break the strike. The following year, Chicago laborers took part in the nationwide Great Strike, in which a hundred thousand people left their jobs across the country in support of railroad workers' grievances; again national troops were called in. Reactions among the working class and the middle class were tense and angry. The Citizens' Law and Order League was founded in Chicago, with Washington Gladden and Lyman Abbott, two prominent Social Gospel ministers, among the national vice-presidents. In 1884, the Central Labor Committee of Chicago was formed, dominated by the carpenters, to prepare for local participation in the nationwide general strike of May Day 1886, which was being planned as part of the movement for an eight-hour day. The Chicago Haymarket Riot, which took place just a few days after the peaceful May Day demonstration in 1886, inflamed both the labor movement and the antilabor sentiments of the city's establishment press. Suspicions against the building trades unions were especially keen, for Louis Luigg, one of the organizers of the carpenters' union, had been arrested as a prominent anarchist and charged with the fatal bombing. (One of the eight convicted, he killed himself with an explosive in his cell.)

By the middle of the 1880s, Chicago had become the center for labor activism in America. The city provided the greatest concentration of membership in the Knights of Labor and was also the base for socialist Eugene Debs and the railroad brotherhoods. Radicals debated the "Chicago Idea," a blend of Marxism and syndicalism, inclined toward revolutionary violence. Armed workers' militias trained in the streets, until they were outlawed and forced underground. The German worker-intellectuals who controlled the Central Labor Union and wrote for *The Alarm* or the German-language *Arbeiter Zeitung* demanded with great force that workers' grievances be met and the "ruling class" be overthrown. (Louis Luigg wrote frequently for the *Arbeiter Zeitung*.)

Many middle-class people feared that organized labor would precipitate more strikes and class violence. The Chicago National Guard Armory, built with a public subscription that was quickly raised after the Haymarket Riot, and completed in 1890, was a visible sign of a fearful mood. A rough gray stone fortress by Burnham and Root, it was architectural evidence of mounting tensions. Over the next decade, the armory was filled with stocks of firearms in anticipation of coming class warfare.

Hostility against the building trades had other sources too. The demands of the building unions seemed economically, as well as politically, precarious. For instance, in 1877, the year of the Great Strike, some twenty thousand loans for rebuilding after the 1871 fire came due, the city's largest savings bank failed, and many depositors lost their property. Local papers blamed the strikers for the depression economy and held the building workers directly responsible for the city's inadequate supply of housing.[13] The building trades in particular took the brunt of anger and fear about many of the city's problems. The men who were supposed to be building up Chicago and its wealth were in fact jeopardizing progress for their own interests. The power of the city's building unions would continue to incur the wrath of Chicago journalists, architects, builders, real estate interests, and bankers, while the general public wavered, according to the political situation, in its affections.

During the 1890s, the local building trades organizations became even more powerful. They affiliated with national unions—and with one another—seeking to maximize their strength. The unified Building Trades Council, formed in 1890, saw to it that 80 percent of the city's building workers belonged to unions.[14] The council, which was invested with great power by the approaching construction deadline for the Columbian Exposition, also saw that the unions won their demands. The threat of sympathy strikes on an issue affecting one group usually forced the contractor or builder to settle with that union in order to keep construction going apace.

In turn, each of the groups that had dealings with the building trades workers turned unequivocally against them in the early 1890s. The architectural press, for instance, now contended that workers were primarily responsible for the declining quality of all construction work, houses and public monuments alike. The assumption that the building workers had lost the competence and sense of responsibility they had once possessed became standard fare in the *American Architect*. Writers there insisted that quality was now only possible with factory-produced materials which had been made under exacting conditions:

> In certain points, carpenter's work, for example, was generally more skillful a hundred years ago than it is now. In those days there was little wood-working machinery, and carpenters had to work mouldings, plane large surfaces, and do many things that are now done "at the mill"; and, as good hand-work is smoother and more delicate than machine-work, the old hand-wrought panellings and cornices excite the expert's admiration. . . . It is not controverted that our cements are infinitely superior to anything that our forefathers knew; but some think that the masons of a hundred years ago could mix lime, and wield the trowel, more skillfully than those of the present day, and the hardness of the old interior plastering gives some color to this notion. They also used bricks more liberally than we do, but their bricks were very inferior to ours, and certainly no better laid. The *Tribune* appears to think that our ancestors did not build any "defective flues," and that the destruction of houses by sparks or heat straying from a fireplace into regions unsuited to such visits was a rare occurrence.[15]

While the author did, at least, dismiss the idea that there had been few fire hazards in old houses, he wrote as if the building workers had chosen to use millwork, and the plasterers to mix inferior grades, because they had lost the old skills. The truth, of course, was that they were fulfilling the contractor's specifications. And they were performing the kinds of jobs they might have learned in a trade school.

The depression of 1893 further aggravated this situation. In October, with the exposition over, thousands of transient laborers as well as many of Chicago's own population were left unemployed. (One estimate, by Major Harrison, put the number of unemployed in Chicago that winter at two hundred thousand.)[16] The mood was despondent. The impact of the depression was hard felt in the construction industry. Nonetheless, the unions remained strong. By 1900, thirty-two unions participated in the Chicago Building Trades Council, with a total membership of more than thirty thousand.[17] However, they now faced a more organized opposition. Earlier speeches presented at the annual meetings of the National Association of Builders had professed a common interest between builder and worker, but this stance had been abandoned by the mid-1890s. Now the builders adamantly backed industrially produced materials over on-site work wherever possible, and vowed to resist the demands of skilled construction workers who wanted to keep their jobs as they had been.[18] At the same time, producers sought to increase their output and keep in business, despite the reduction in sales with the depression, by using speedups and by marketing over greater distances. For six years, beginning with the onset of the depression, a dangerous overproduction of building materials flooded a market in which there was very little construction activity.

Then, in 1899, the contractors who mediated between the producers, the builders, and the workers on a construction site decided that they had to take greater control of the situation. Chicago's Building Contractors' Council (originally the Building Employers' Conference Committee) emerged as the first organization in the country made up exclusively of contractors. Many of them were facing bankruptcy. Although the declaration of war against Spain had signalled a rise in profits in other sectors of the national economy the year before, conditions did not improve so quickly in construction, where there was little to export. That winter, Chicago faced another building strike over the workers' right to oversee apprentice training and materials selection on the site. The Building Contractors' Council decided to call for a citywide lockout. Union obstinacy, the contractors protested, meant that they were "not able to call their souls their own."[19] They would withhold all materials until they regained what they saw as their right—control of all construction sites in Chicago. This act was the beginning of what became the greatest building hiatus in the experience of Chicago, and of the country, up to that time. The next year, 1900, saw the lowest number of dwelling units under construction in either Chicago's or the nation's recent history.[20] Several hundred local manufacturers had to close down their factories, since there was so little demand for their products—and since the unionized mill woodworkers had voted to join the building trades workers in their resistance.

Negotiations between contractors and labor remained at a standstill from late 1899 for more than a year. There were fifty to sixty thousand workers out, and two thousand contractors, as well as thousands more in related industries. Independent contractors were intimidated by the Contractors' Council, and strikebreakers were handled even more harshly by the unionists. Attempts to mediate the conflict came from several sources: the architects Henry Ives Cobb and Irving Pond, the settlement worker Graham Taylor, the moderate Samuel Gompers of the American Federation of Labor. Finally, in April 1901, after a year and a half of only sporadic building in Chicago, the matter was settled. Under Gompers's influence, union resistance had been reduced to limited demands for wages and hours, nothing more. The contractors clearly had the upper hand. Union working rules were under their absolute jurisdiction; there could be no sympathy strikes or restrictions on materials, machinery, hours, apprentice training, or the jobs a worker was told to do.

The group of building workers who had voted to disband the Council and accept the employers' terms in the lockout was blatantly corrupt. Martin B. "Skinny" Madden of the Steam Fitters Helpers had taken over the Council just before 1900. The graft that contractors had once given Madden as "strike insurance" now became regular payment. Gompers's power to negotiate unilaterally for all the union membership also marked the rise of a professional leadership in the unions and defeat for the socialists among the rank-and-file who had called for direct public intervention and broad political reforms. The public's image of the building worker had undergone another definitive change. He was no longer so much the fiery radical but rather the backward, stubborn, and corrupt laborer, interested only in his own monetary reward and an undemanding job.[21]

The Building Worker's Defense

At this point, construction in Chicago had been at best negligible for seven years, held back first by the depression, then by the demands of the building trades unions, and finally by the retaliatory action of the contractors (and, to most observers in the middle class, the obstinance of the unions). The issues involved had not been simply economic or political in a narrow sense. Throughout the 1890s, the unions had upheld their commitment to a social program which included protection of the crafts, public education, tax reform, land reform, tenement and factory inspection, and municipal ownership of public utilities.[22]

The declining quality of construction and the high cost of housing had been implicit issues in the conflict, too. The building workers had tried to hold back the shift toward industrialized specialization, in part as an effort to uphold sound construction techniques, and in part to protect their jobs. They accepted some industrialization as inevitable, or course, but they also accepted it because they realized that it could help keep the cost of the average house at a reasonable level. The issue of more housing was by no means an abstract point. Between 1890 and 1900, there was an actual increase of only 66,000 dwelling units in metropolitan Chicago, and the city needed housing for 139,000 additional households (over and above those who were already poorly housed in crowded, unsanitary conditions).[23]

One attempt to solve this problem had come from the building trades unions themselves, who held regular assemblies and sponsored collective union action during the depression years. Late in 1893, at the Bricklayers' Hall, the executive board of the State Federation of Labor adopted a resolution condemning the lack of homes and jobs in Chicago. Their remedy included a plan to set up rural colonies for unemployed workers and their families. The first was to be in the San Joaquin Valley of California: a four-square-mile tract divided into small fruit farms (each with a maximum of ten acres), to be known as Cosmopoles. The architectural features of the colony, drawn up by members of the building unions, represented an effort to "retain the social features of urban homes, coupled with the charms of country life. The dwellings, 224 in number, will form a double row of cottages. Within the circle of dwellings will be the storehouses, school, shops and other necessary buildings of the community." All tools and equipment would be owned collectively, and a communal tract of three hundred acres would provide food and operating revenue for the entire community. The sketches of the proposed community of Cosmopoles and its buildings have been lost, and the project never materialized, yet there was abundant enthusiasm for the scheme in all the daily papers.[24] While the decade of the 1890s was a time of crisis, it was also a time of daring, innovative plans.

The plan for Cosmopoles was a serious attempt to solve several problems of the 1890s. Another way one can read the debates over building standards and workers' responsibilities is to survey the trade press at the turn of the century. These journals had quite a wide circulation for their strongly stated views on the future of American construction policies. The *National Builder,* for instance, could boast 9,000 subscribers by 1900, and 29,000 by 1910; *The Carpenter* had 15,000; the *Building Monthly* 16,000; and *Shoppell's Modern Houses* 18,000 by that date. By comparison, the *Inland Architect* had only 4,000 and the *American Architect* 7,500.[25] (The figures for the builders' journals are probably conservative ones, for the building workers were more likely to have shared a journal among a group of friends than were the architects.)

The journalists for the building magazines were, first of all, not Luddites, unthinkingly opposed to rationalization and machines. Of course, they wanted to protect skilled jobs. But the editors, like their readers, would not simply accept "expert" advice from industrial management specialists as unquestionably definitive statements about techniques and materials. However, one does often find a somewhat obstinate, traditionalist stance against new approaches in these journals. An editorial in *The Carpenter* could state: "Workmen have no use for complicated machinery with intricate cogs and wheels in labor organizations. The simpler it is the better understood."[26] Even in this case, though, to read the criticism of "complicated machinery" merely as stubborn resistance to modernization is to miss the principal point of the piece. Here simplification meant continuing the guild basis of the unions, promoting respect among all the members, ensuring a democratic base. It was not an unequivocal statement that building workers should ignore or oppose all industrialization. Even if such statements were also self-serving, they were nonetheless efforts to keep alive the idealistic vision of the nineteenth-century carpenter-builders, a vision of hopes and promises for democratic equality.

Frederick Thomas Hodgson (1836–1919), a self-trained Canadian carpenter-builder who had come to New York in 1880 to edit the *American Builder,* was especially adamant about that vision by the time he moved to Chicago in 1893 to take over as editor of the *National Builder.* Workers, he insisted, had to accept new kinds of work organization and new skills in order to preserve their independence. Unless they could master modern practices, the contractors and large builders would have total control of the building site. He pleaded his case in many places. In 1899, Hodgson wrote an article for the *Architects' and*

Builders' Magazine in which he claimed that upward mobility for building workers was only possible if they would accept the new methods and machines designed to economize labor and materials.[27] This did not imply, by any means, that workers should foresake traditional building skills. Hodgson's series on "The Superiority of American Machinery" in the *National Builder* posed an ideal of skilled crafts traditions combined with the latest equipment. Accepting new technology, he insisted, did not mean abandoning skills but adding new ones. In 1900, he began a series called "The Apprentice's School Room," with articles on drawing, tools, traditional and modern construction methods; he followed this with "The Steel Square," a series which explained new building and measuring devices to readers.

A prolific writer, Hodgson produced more than fifty books on construction techniques and architectural styles in his campaign to preserve and modernize the various building trades. He described a range of fields, from carpentry to finish work, plastering to upholstery, writing for lay audiences of do-it-yourselfers as well as practitioners of the trades. *The Builder's Guide and Estimator's Price Book,* a compilation of prices for lumber, hardware, and labor written in 1882, was an early effort to prove the benefits of standardization in building. But Hodgson certainly believed in the integrity of building trades. *Modern Carpentry,* first published in 1902, eventually went into seventeen editions and expanded to include a second volume on joinery and a supplement on house plans. The text was marked by a reverence for the skilled carpenter. Hodgson also prepared similar home-study textbooks on plastering, stone-cutting, and woodworking. Chicago's Sears, Roebuck and Company distributed special editions of many of his books as part of their efforts to reach a middle-class home-builder and improver's market.[28] And the American Building Trade School of Chicago put out an *Encyclopedia of the Building Trades* in six volumes, edited by Hodgson, in 1907.

On several occasions, Hodgson went beyond practical education to write on architectural history and style. He believed the well-educated building worker should know about the artistic side of his trade. An appreciation of ornamental and architectural styles was one of his justifications for the worker's right to make decisions about a building. *Easy Steps to Architecture and Architecture of Antiquity, for Home Study* first appeared in 1907. Next was *A Treatise on the Five Orders of Architecture,* Hodgson's tribute to the great interpreters of classicism, from Palladio and William Chambers to McKim, Mead, and White.[29] For years, the *National Builder* carried "Pages from the Editor's Sketchbook," "Easy Lessons in Architecture," and "Our Grammar of Style." These departments featured Hodgson's own drawings of typical decorative motifs, furnishings, and architectural details from other countries he had visited or read about (fig. 30). At least he considered them to be typical. The representation was sometimes naive and even inaccurate. Hodgson did not always grasp the difference between Japanese details and Chinese, Elizabethan and Jacobean. His efforts to teach his readers to be cultivated could occasionally seem somewhat desperate. But he tried to fill the void of general artistic education for building workers as best he could.

There were examples of contemporary avant-garde architecture in Hodgson's journal as well as lessons from older architecture. He printed illustrations of residential work by Chicago's Thomas Tallmadge, Richard Schmidt, George Maher, and Frank Lloyd Wright, with perceptive comments on their innovative style and their commitment to good modern houses. Later, California bungalows by Arthur Heineman, Hunt and Eager, and Helen Lukens Gaut caught his fancy with their simple lines, sensible open plans, and low costs.[30] Several interiors by M. H. Baillie Scott were features of the early 1900s; Hodgson was perhaps most enthusiastic about the aesthetic and practical potential of these "New Art" interiors (fig. 31). Here was a simple, elegant aesthetic, he explained, based on natural materials and handsome detailing that went beyond the limits of the American arts and crafts fad. The English arts and crafts designers and those of the Austrian *Sezessionstil* understood the principles of combining art with industry. In these projects, there was a respect for the worker, whether in the factory or on the site, and sometimes a complete unity between designer, machinist, and craftsman.[31] These "New Art" interiors were the embodiment of Hodgson's goals for American building design: the craftsman could use both new technology and traditional skills to create beautiful, useful objects of quality.

Not all of the men in the building trades endorsed Hodgson's ideal of a housing standard determined and upheld by those who built homes.[32] Not even all of the unions backed this reform policy. Yet, in his own way and to a wide audience, Hodgson articulated the desire which existed among many building workers who wanted to improve the housing they were charged with building. For over thirty years, with

Figure 30. Fred T. Hodgson's interpretation of "Our Grammar of Ornament—Japanese." (From the *National Builder*, 1905.)

Figure 31. "New Art" interior by M. H. Baillie Scott. (From the *National Builder,* 1903.)

real determination, he insisted that it was his readers' duty to uphold the quality of American homes by the standards they enforced.

In the *Builder and Woodworker,* he had stressed that American architecture must "aim at the benefit of the million," not at the elite. Residential architecture, he told his readers, could become America's "first general artistic success," while providing the foundation for a stable and egalitarian society, if the men who built houses took up the challenge.[33] This residential aesthetic should not be ostentatious or expensive, he had pointed out in the 1880s. It had to be straightforward and plain, but well-crafted and dignified. The best way to achieve far-reaching success was to encourage the participation of all Americans in the design of homes. Public education should include instruction in the principles and practice of architecture and construction. Women in particular should take on careers in these fields in order to share their skills.[34] Together, the public and those who constructed houses could create a new kind of model home, a "republican" dwelling.

With the 1893 depression, Hodgson became even more dedicated to his cause. He tried to keep up the building worker's morale, despite the hard times. His editorials assured readers that economic constraints would lead to better-quality houses, since home-builders knew that contractors had to compete for work. He was aware of and hopeful about the complementary campaign for general education being undertaken by the progressives, the domestic scientists, and the Arts and Crafts Society. Hodgson tried to emphasize the common purpose of reformers and workers. He specifically connected the workers' political demands for better jobs and the demands for better homes. The principles, he insisted, were the same. Workers should take the time to educate themselves, he pleaded. They should hold firm to their responsibility to build housing they knew would provide the best possible homes for themselves and for other Americans. The desire for higher wages should never force the building worker to compromise the quality of the homes he produced. The "thousands who want to earn a living and a home" had two complementary duties, and two related goals.[35]

Hodgson recognized that one major impediment to his ideal was the growth of trusts in building materials. Small, local machine shops, sawmills, brick- and tile-producing establishments, and furniture workshops were disappearing under the competition of larger industries.[36] Paint, plaster, plumbing fittings, furnaces, stone panels, terra-cotta ornament, and wood finish-work of every sort arrived from the factory ready-made. In 1890, for the first time, the value of American manufactured goods had surpassed that of agricultural commodities (although farm products were then at an all-time high). Hodgson and others recognized that the problem was not so much the workers in these factories, but the profits of those who monopolized these industries and drove up prices. This situation forced the contractor to try and cut down the amount of on-site work, and it pushed up the cost of housing for every class.

A few companies now dominated the manufacture of most essential building products. A lumber trust, controlled by the Weyerhaeuser Timber Company, had been powerful since the mid-nineteenth century. By the 1890s, there was more effective control and planned production of every building material, as of other durable goods. The Sherman Antitrust Act of 1890, declaring that joint action in restraint of trade was illegal, outlawed "injurious combinations"; but the definitions were so vague that monopolies of important industries continued to expand. By 1900, there were 180 major American trusts, and in 1905, there were 305; by then almost 70 percent of all manufacturing employees worked in corporation-owned establishments. Henry Demarest Lloyd, Ida Tarbell, and other "muckrakers" focused the nation's attention on the excesses of the trusts run by the most wealthy and politically powerful American capitalists—the Rockefellers' Standard Oil Company or Carnegie and Morgan's U.S. Steel Corporation, a merger of 138 former companies which controlled 70 percent of the national output of iron and steel.[37]

Many economists admired the great trusts, of course, seeing them as symbols of strength and organization for modern American industry. In its turn, the *American Architect* nodded appreciatively at the "benefits arising from association" for manufacturers and distributors of building supplies.[38] Occasionally someone expressed fear that the trusts would deplete existing natural resources and force construction prices unbearably high. The timber trust came under the *Chicago Tribune*'s attack as early as 1880.[39] But only the editors of building trades journals systematically set out to prove that the great increases in the cost of construction at the turn of the century were the result of increases in the cost of materials, provoked by excess profits, and not of arbitrary increases in workers' wages. *The Carpenter* in Philadelphia railed against the trusts. Hodgson, in the *National Builder,* investigated the formation of building-materials trusts and computed their profits. Major electric, plumbing, and glass manufacturers reaped profits of 100 to 160 percent a year, and this during a severe depression. The lumber trust (Weyerhaeuser owned a quarter of the lumber then standing in the North and Midwest) had become the fourth largest of the country's great manufacturing interests. Domination by a few companies had forced up the price of lumber until the cost of a frame house was almost that of a masonry house.[40]

The goal of such exposés, as with most muckraking articles of the time, was to rid the American cities of profiteers, wrongdoers, the few who seemed to be standing in the way of a smooth-running system for the many. Hodgson did not look back to a romantic, preindustrial past; but he did believe that conditions had been more democratic when he had begun his career. The organization of construction work had once benefited building workers and the public more than producers. To men like Hodgson, the materials trusts had turned modern techniques against the workers by blaming the latter for higher costs. Equally damning was the fact that the monopolies were raising the cost of a house beyond the reach of more and more American families.

Hodgson was more verbal than visual in the kind of housing he actually endorsed. But he did try to present an ideal aesthetic for domestic architecture. It should, he wrote, derive from "'fitness of things'" rather than "miscalled 'original'... fads." Architects were unlikely to provide the needed models because of their ethics, which, he claimed, made it impermissible to alter another architect's designs, limited professional competitions to expensive monuments, and set minimum fees.[41] It was up to the builders to provide models, and he tried to give them guidelines. The "Economical Use of Space" was based on good materials, quality construction techniques, and practical arrangements of plans and built-in extras. "Simple Elegance," rather than ornament, should be taken as the evidence of skill. Considerations of sanitation and convenience were as important as beauty itself. Square plans were best, he went on; they allowed the freest circulation of air; they were the most economical to build and the easiest to keep up; and they had a stately grace.[42]

By 1897, many of the dwellings shown in Hodgson's journal—whether small cottages, large suburban houses, two-family dwellings, or small brick apartment buildings—had simple, rectilinear outlines. They used only one or two materials for their facades. The interior decoration had been cut back to paint and wallpaper, rather than layers of elaborate molding. George Garnsey's "Crescent Cottage" (fig. 32), a model of the plain aesthetic, was estimated to cost only $1,060 without a bathroom (or $50 to $75 more with one of the bedrooms converted into a simple bathroom). Robert Rae's Colonial Revival cottages of this decade (averaging $1,000 to build) were another popular interpretation of the drive for simplicity, regularity, and economy. (See fig. 45.) So were his rows of Romanesque city houses (fig. 33). These popularizations of Richardson's larger urban mansions were able to preserve the dignity and grace of the original at a much smaller scale and affordable price. Foursquare plans and minimal ornamentation kept costs down to about $1,500 or $2,000 for most small houses of 1,700 square feet; Rae in particular also provided the *National Builder* with several cottages estimated to cost only about $700.[43] Nonetheless, picturesque Queen Anne suburban designs—most of them by Chicago's George Garnsey, New York's E. G. W. Dietrich and the Grand Rapids carpenter

Figure 32. "Crescent Cottage" and plan (opposite) by George O. Garnsey. (From the *National Builder,* 1897.)

D. S. Hopkins—continued to appear well into the early 1900s, although they did become noticeably simpler in outline and decoration from about 1898. And, whether large or small, even the most undistinguished houses were never completely anonymous. There was always some distinguishing craftsmanship. This was, after all, a journal for building craftsmen.

Not all of the houses Hodgson published were successful designs. Many were awkward and austere, like Robert Seyfarth's little cubicle, which appeared in 1905 (fig. 34). Leaded glass windows and foliage could not relieve this stark plainness. The designs published in Hodgson's own pattern books—*Practical Bungalows* and *Hodgson's Low-Cost American Homes*—seemed uncomfortably balanced between modern minimalism and the kind of handcrafted, rustic ornament that had become popular at the end of the nineteenth century[44] (fig. 35). In many ways, Hodgson's favorite houses were variations of Stickley's crude Craftsman cottages, although they tended to be more spindly and less sturdy in their construction details, and somewhat more puritanical in their feeling for materials. Even if his editorial statements were

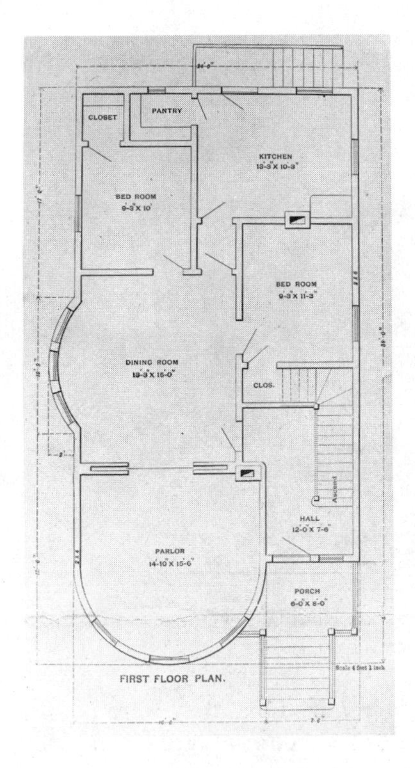

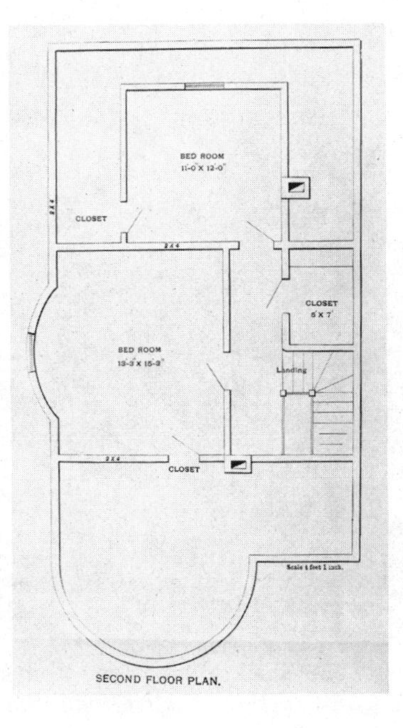

sharp and clear, Hodgson never evolved an aesthetic to embody his ideals of ornament or of the dwelling itself.

The most important aim in Hodgson's diverse campaign for architectural reform was not housing reform, in a purely aesthetic or even a political sense, but the general education of building workers. He wanted to encourage them to preserve their traditional crafts, to improve those crafts with new knowledge, to master recent technological advances rather than to fear them. The possibility of government-sponsored workshops combining art and industry for the public good (such as the German examples that he described) seemed an improbable solution in this country.[45] Hodgson recognized that the building workers would have to take the initiative themselves. By the early

Figure 33. Block of limestone Romanesque Revival rowhouses in Chicago by Robert Rae. (From the *National Builder,* 1897.)

years of the twentieth century, as he realized that they were not doing so, the tone of his educational articles and editorials grew more melancholy. He continued, all the same, to instruct readers in new techniques and in the uses of the latest equipment, as well as in traditional skills, tools, and attitudes. But it was clear that he suspected that the crafts were neglected. A series on "The Lost Art of Framing" attempted to avert such a decline; it was also an admission that the trades workers themselves were indeed losing their command of their calling.[46] They were unable to teach the younger carpenters a full range of skills. Information on factory-produced building products now began to appear with greater frequency in Hodgson's journal. Discussions of building as a major political and social issue for Americans, a crusade for the construction workers, became rare. Hodgson did what he could to spread knowledge about recent techniques and the history of the old. But he spoke against the times. And he knew it.

A worker with a general education in the arts and sciences, with autonomy at the work place and a respected place in the political arena seemed an impossibly romantic notion by 1900, even to the building

Figure 34. "A Neat Little Dwelling House" by Robert Seyfarth of Chicago. (From the *National Builder*, 1905.)

unions. The fact that a style of handcrafted (or seemingly so) decoration continued to be acceptable—indeed, to be a minor fad in certain parts of the country—did not, by any means, indicate that Americans still believed that building workers deserved their respect. Not even

Figure 35. "The American," a model cottage design and plan (opposite). (From *Hodgson's Low-Cost American Homes,* 1905.)

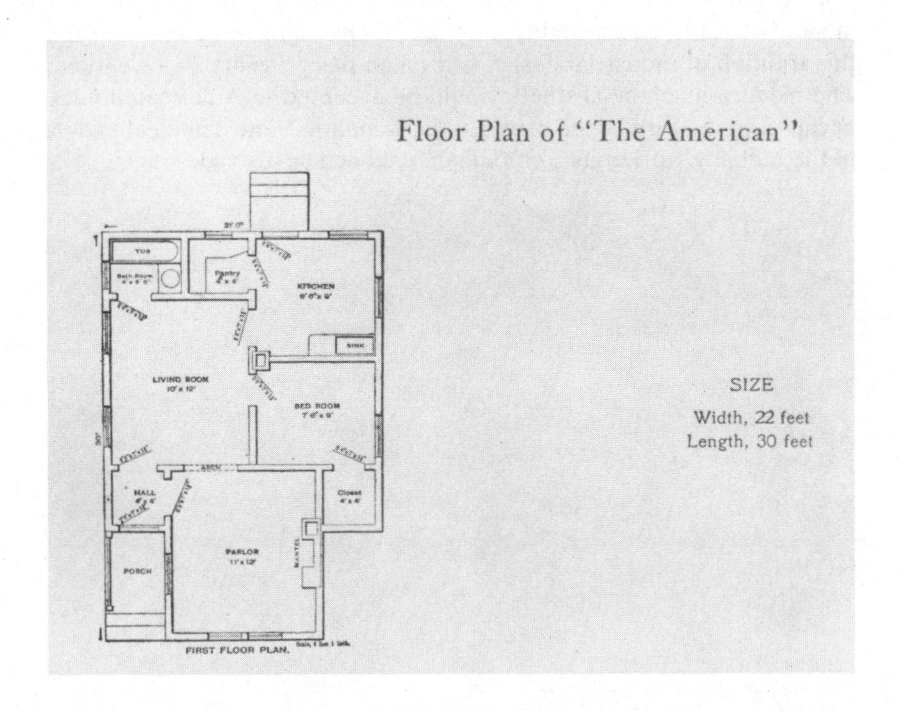

the workers themselves advanced such a position. House-building, even if it had a romantic look to it, was industrial production.

By the 1920s, the fascination with the machine rather than with the hand would produce a new romance. The expert with scientific knowledge and the modern technology at his command would rule. The anonymous industrial-design look eliminated all evidence of individual effort or skill by the workers who turned out houses or radios or any other industrial products. Modernists glorified a clean and conspicuously machine-made aesthetic. To be sure, the 1920s were also the heyday of the miniaturized romantic cottage in the suburbs—in Elizabethan Tudor, French Chateau, Italian Mediterranean, or Spanish Colonial Revival style. These provided an alternative of sorts. But everyone knew that factories produced the imitation thatch and false half-timbering which gave the cottages their charm. Within these houses, the reliance on modern materials and appliances (and on interior decorators to arrange them) provided indisputable evidence of a modernist aesthetic sensibility once again. One of the preconditions for this triumph of industrial design had taken place twenty years earlier. The modern machine aesthetic could be accepted in American homes because, at the turn of the century, the romantic Victorian idealization of the building worker as a craftsman had been destroyed.

7 THE PROFESSIONAL MOOD

The result is that these lower-cost houses are largely beyond the influence of improvement.

"The Architecture of the People," *Architecture and Building* (1899)

In 1889, two young New England architects, John Calvin Stevens and Albert Winslow Cobb, published a pattern book of their house designs. Entitled *Examples of American Domestic Architecture,* it contained, despite the national reference, mostly sketches of shingle-covered resort homes built along the Eastern seaboard. In the text, Stevens (the writer for the two, as well as the better designer) discussed what was, in fact, a national phenomenon: the call for reform in American domestic architecture. Transformations in housing, he wrote, should not simply be stylistic (although he did endorse a modified Colonial Revival), but explicitly social as well. With fierce, indeed Calvinist, language, he protested against the extravagance of the 1880s: the "degrading luxury" of mansions, "unwholesome hiving" in apartments, and the "painful contrasts" of class. A fondness for ornament and display, he charged, had led to a sinful "Magnificence in American Architecture." The profession, concerned only with splendid buildings commissioned by wealthy clients, was "flourishing like some rank, luxurious weed."[1] But Stevens did see an alternative to this decadence. There was a mission for the socially conscious architect. Homes of simple, unpretentious form, therefore available to the entire population, could become "a powerful helping agent in the process of sharing the fruits of labor equitably among all, and so promoting public health and happiness."[2] Better housing could, in effect, bring about necessary social reform.

Stevens and Cobb shared with many of their less outspoken colleagues an assumption that the environment could determine social life. But the tone of their book, with its harsh criticism of the architectural profession, was nonetheless too severe for most of their readers at the time it appeared. In a review published in the *Inland Architect,* Robert McLean faulted the "indiscreet haste" of this mission. He dismissed the references to inequalities of class, to luxuries indulged in by the wealthy and their architects, as "unscientific generalities."[3] The architectural profession, he acknowledged, needed to reexamine its values and responsibilities. But McLean could not accept beginning from so negative and, to him, alarmingly populist a position.

In the following decade, most American architects found that they could no longer avoid such troublesome issues. The men, and the few women, too, with professional training had to ask themselves, as Stevens had done, what they should do to help create the kind of society they wanted. American architects decided that it was necessary to define their profession more explicitly—in both the abstract sense of an identity and a clear set of responsibilities, and a more precise sense of educational priorities and legal boundaries.

How did Chicago architects and, by comparison, their colleagues in other regions deal with the question of professional identity during the tempestuous decade of the 1890s? Some retreated to visions of order and stately grandeur, a world of chateaux and monuments, of universal laws of beauty and powerful clients who could support their magnificent visions. It was, undeniably, a defensive conservatism, for these same architects still claimed that their designs would somehow address the nation's urgent social problems. Others looked forward, often focusing on housing issues, sometimes working with the many other groups that were also interested in rethinking the home. Architects were never as involved in the progressive movement as other professionals—doctors, lawyers, teachers, ministers, and social workers—tended to be. Yet the fact that so many people were advocating environmental reforms required that architects take some account of these popular campaigns. Moreover, like other Americans, architects cared deeply about the very real problems they saw in the cities, in the government, and in the family. They were certainly aware of the confrontations between contractors and building-trades workers which often held up construction on their own projects. And many of them, because of the depression, faced drastic reductions in the commissions they received. In these circumstances, some architects began to experiment, spatially and socially. Often their experiments followed directions similar to those being taken by the nonprofessionals who were demanding environmental reforms. The result was an infusion of new ideas for the architects but also an even stronger need, as they perceived it, to define, publicly and firmly, their professionalism.

Underlying the forms these architects explored and the proposals for professional goals they championed was a deep ambivalence. At the very time when there was an unusual amount of exchange with people outside the profession, architects in Illinois renewed their efforts to pass the country's first law restricting entry to their profession. During a period when new approaches were possible and new professional paths wide open, many architects cautiously stayed committed to safe, familiar, nonjarring forms. Overwhelmingly, they shied away from too partisan a stance in their writings and speeches, continuing to claim that their designs were universal and their clients "typical."[4] At times their statements even seem to echo the populist builders' ideal of designing for all Americans. Yet the architectural profession could not hide the fact that their principal clients were, in fact, an elite, a very small group of wealthy patrons. Nor could the democratic rhetoric disguise the architect's desire for total control over these grand projects which, he promised, would benefit all Americans. Whether it was Daniel Burnham with an academic ideal of universal beauty that infused his plan for Chicago, or Louis Sullivan with his "democratic" office towers, or Frank Lloyd Wright with his daring model houses for the modern family, the architect declared that his beneficent intentions required complete autonomy if he were to fulfill them. This assertion that architects could design to meet all needs—if they had sufficient control over building—was the profession's rallying cry during a turbulent decade.

A Program of Grandeur

Even though the architectural press never directly addressed the nation's dire economic state during the 1890s, the depression had a resounding effect on this profession. The building industry in Chicago, as in every part of the country, was severely shaken in 1893 and did not, as we have seen, begin to recover until 1901. Residential construction, especially for low- and moderate-income housing, felt the hardest blow. Many architects found that they had to concentrate on larger commissions, such as public buildings, stores, offices, and houses for the wealthy, if they wanted work. The ties between the profession and the wealthy families of America strengthened, for the architect was now even more ideologically bound to those who had the money to build, those who wanted to buy the assurance of beauty.[5] At the same time, many architects, especially younger ones just starting out, suddenly found themselves out of work—or, more politely, "self-employed."[6] Even the *Architectural Record* admitted that the architect of 1897 had to "hustle for a living."[7]

It was evident to most people that the national economy and the society were in crisis, and that architectural styles, as most aspects of American life, would have to be altered to respond to these larger forces. More and more journalists described the cities in a language that gave architecture a political meaning. Walter B. Harte, for instance, writing in the *Arena*, the professional social-work journal, contrasted residential areas of Boston to show the "lessons in political economy in bricks and stones."[8] Even the architectural press now discussed style in vaguely economic terms. The *Record* allowed that the popularity of simpler styles was, in part, an accommodation to economic conditions: "Architects know, what the public does not seem to have found out, that the recent classic revival has not been a matter of choice, but of necessity. . . . The classic formulas are . . . the greatest labor-saving devices of which the history of architecture gives any account."[9] The article, like many others, praised the recent aesthetic trends toward simplification. Yet, by this account, only professional architects understood the simpler classical styles or the real reasons for having them. Unappreciative, "ignorant laymen" only clamored for " 'an original style of architecture.' "[10] The professional press, and many of its readers, were anxious to preserve the distinctions of rank. They faced a depression, a drastic cutback in construction, vehement criticism of the profession; moreover, a sizable and outspoken array of people had asserted the right to speak out about environmental issues. Architects had to make their professional identity more assured and respected.

Most American architects continued to assert that firm standards of beauty and competence were the best ways to protect their profession. Yet few of them were prepared to define those standards precisely. Their stance presupposed an elite, trained in the esoteric rules of universal beauty. They would experiment within carefully delineated formal limits. In a few daring cases, someone would even carry the laws to a new level of expression, although most of the confederation's members were committed to upholding the existing interpretations of those laws. The best of what the architects did, the argument continued, would quietly filter down to the population below them. An appropriately lofty position, however, was necessary in order to preserve the respect due art and the artist. If the nation and its builders sincerely revered these superior artists, and followed their example, then their shared built environment would become beautiful and stately.

A major question for architects, given their professional priorities, was, What were they to do at a time when new construction starts had been sharply cut back? There were large mansions and apartment houses, office buildings and public institutions going up, and this scale of work was popular. If possible, an aspiring architect affiliated himself with the increasingly larger firms that specialized in such projects. Daniel Burnham's Chicago office had a hundred draftsmen by 1900, for instance. Burnham's firm, unusual in its scale, was an indication of the "plan factory" or "combine" approach toward which the profession was moving.[11] Architects in such firms would be assigned to one aspect of a particular kind of building, whether site planning for civic centers or foundations for steel-frame office buildings. And there was little residential design in these larger firms. Early in his career, Burnham, for one, had confided to Sullivan that he was "not going to stay satisfied with houses; my idea is to work up to a big business, to handle big things, deal with big business men, and to build up a big organization, for you can't handle big things unless you have an organization."[12] In this scheme, the design of houses (except for the mansions of a few important clients) would be left to the builders.

Bravado and businesslike organization offered one approach to hard times. Still, no one characterization can accurately describe the professional architect's viewpoint during this or any decade. The disposition which unified them was a critical attitude toward outsiders. The reformer interested in environmental issues and the builder who claimed too large a part of the diminished construction market were both the targets of the profession's ire.

Builders and real estate speculators took the harshest verbal abuse. Architects criticized them for the "barbarism" of America's urban and suburban environment. John Wellborn Root had recently attacked indulgences like " 'rooflets' " and " 'fixings' " in galvanized iron favored by midwestern builders. The only hope for a "wholesome reaction," he wrote in *Scribner's,* would come from the increasing number of architects trained in the East Coast or European schools. He gave no credit to the changing taste of clients. Nothing could still Root's scorn for builders and their products. Crying "'all which flams is flamboyant,'"[13] he indicted even those who tried to imitate the restrained compositions of trained architects. Builders who copied serious architectural compositions, Root contended disparagingly, were no better than those who created thier own mad inventions; neither group could fully understand the meaning of the forms.

In another article, also published in *Scribner's,* William P. P. Longfellow regretted the pitifully low standards of taste in his country. "The things which attract our people to art are the ornamental and the realistic," he wrote; each of these concerns was equally crude. By such accounts, there had to be a sharp distinction between "architectural" work, concerned with ideal beauty and its laws, and mere "building." Building was the work of nimble but uneducated designers. To some architects, such designers played upon the desire for symbols of status and stability, while to others they never rose above mundane considerations of utility and economy. As Longfellow put it, "Interest in architecture there is among architects; in building among the public. . . . [A] real architectural interest is almost as esoteric and professional as an interest in abstract law or medicine."[14]

Reliance on concepts of universal laws to mark a distinction between architect and outsider became more pronounced during the depression decade. C. E. Jenkins of Chicago was among those who insisted there were such laws: "That there are recognized styles in architecture which should be considered, recognized conditions which have come to us from generations back, which exist as emphatically as the laws which govern science, no reasonable person questions for a moment."[15] Respect for the academic traditions of architecture was evident in every aspiring professional's work, including that of Frank Lloyd Wright. His Blossom house and his Winslow house show this classical discipline of forms he was assimilating before veering off in a new direction with his "Prairie House" of the early 1900s.[16] Even the architects who called for stylistic revolution believed strongly in absolute laws of form which they had comprehended, after arduous study, and would now reinterpret in their own way.

Occasional calls for what seemed social and aesthetic revolution were, in a similar way, statements about formal principles. Louis Sullivan's appeal for an "architecture of democracy" was, in fact, quite abstract as a program. He castigated the classical tradition as inherently aristocratic and claimed that the American architect who followed this tradition was not a truly "democratic citizen."[17] But when Sullivan demanded an architecture that would accurately represent a society which had progressed to a new level of equality, he was actually referring to ideal forms that would *symbolize,* in his eyes at least, such a society. He did not speak of specific architectural or political means to extend actual benefits of health or comfort more equitably, or with greater particpation in the process of decision-making. For him, democratic architecture would, instead, bring uplifting ideals of beauty and manly strength to great monuments, and all the populace together could gaze proudly upon these monuments.

Furthermore, in Sullivan's eyes, it was only the architect, the man of genius and determination, who could decide which forms were democratic. To him, only the true architect was privy to the universal laws of nature and beauty, laws which the Beaux-Arts had emasculated. "The people" would intuitively recognize this universal beauty—but it did not come from ordinary builders. The chosen few who could interpret their culture and comprehend the laws of nature should dare to search for higher forms. But they had to select their work carefully, so that their buildings would clearly reveal these laws. For aesthetic rebels like Sullivan (even though he had to take on smaller commissions as his career declined later in life), and certainly for conservatives like Burnham, highly visible, majestic public buildings were deemed especially suitable subjects for the superior form-givers, the true architects of a society.

From one end of the professional spectrum to the other, architects of the 1890s moved ever farther away from a concern with the small house as an architectural problem or a social need, even though many of them, of course, continued to design and build such houses. But the profession's interest, as expressed in official publications, organizations, and school curricula, turned now toward larger monuments and grand city plans. In 1894, Robert McLean, editor of Chicago's *Inland Architect,* announced that "Building News," a report of current construction in the Midwest, would no longer carry notices of buildings costing less than $5,000. This policy, in effect, cut off reporting on most of the housing being built in Chicago and other cities. The need for small houses was reduced to "the cottage question," a debate about architectural styles for resort towns and well-to-do suburbs. At the onset of the depression, McLean asserted that the cottage style was "now gradually going out of vogue," except in the suburbs and for the seaside, and was being replaced by more formal academic structures in Classical or Renaissance Revival styles. *Architecture and Building* magazine, once considered a proponent of utilitarian values, echoed this position in an article of 1899. The editors declared that there existed a line of cost below which an architect could not go. They did not stipulate the amount. However, they seemed to eliminate all moderate-cost houses, since the authors suggested that, in these cases, carpenters should follow the designs architects had conceived for more costly projects, reducing the scale and simplifying the decoration as the budget required. Formal solutions had to come from above; but it was not the responsibility of those at the top to provide for "The Architecture of the People."[18]

Such statements about cottage architecture clearly implied assumptions about the profession. Anyone could design a small house, these critics intimated; if only they restrained from showiness and followed established guidelines, the results would be acceptable, if necessarily unoriginal and uninspiring. It was, however, just these qualities which marred the work of the builder. Such unoriginal enterprises were not architecture and not the architect's responsibility. Only trained designers could masterfully carry off more complicated buildings such as large public monuments, office towers, or splendid villas, the kinds of structures upon which the professional journals were now focusing most of their attention. Such commissions were the architect's special province, for they required originality and experimentation, tempered with skill and training. This professional stance dismissed the issue of small houses, their construction and design, as well as their availability. It also sidestepped a critical architectural problem implicit in this larger scale—that of standardization—by simply disregarding the need for quality mass-production of moderate- and low-cost housing.

Originality and standardization were troublesome issues for architects, points of contention and ambivalence throughout the decade. Professional critics characterized both builders and the public as licentious in their stylistic taste, and then turned to find fault with the monotonous sameness of the American city. Not even within their own ranks were architects of one opinion about the limits on originality. They all agreed that the architect should have the right to artistic invention. The Beaux-Arts principles which most professionals esteemed so highly supposedly embodied a respect for order and propriety; the architect was trained to draw from established canons of academically approved styles. The desire for decorum was so strong in the 1890s that even younger members of the profession who experimented too liberally drew sharp censure. As C. E. Jenkins wrote in the *Inland Architect* of 1896:

> That *style* is the outcome of the genius and study of great minds, the result of the best thought and intellect of periods when certain standards were lived up to and made lasting by a purity born of concentrated effort in one direction, should be a sufficient reason certainly for young architects to lay aside that "most sure-to-be-a-failure" condition of striving for "absolute originality."[19]

During this decade, in America at least, the academic tradition emerged as a bulwark against formal change and implicitly against social change as well.

Four themes, then, were especially potent for the architectural profession as the country faced the decade of the 1890s: suspicion of sudden change, either formal or social; the desire for authoritative control; fascination with order; and respect for the larger, monumental scale. The impetus for the formal grandeur which characterized the decade for architects, and which embodied all of these themes beautifully, was the example of the French Ecole des Beaux-Arts, or, more precisely, the American profession's esteem for the Ecole and the desire of American architects to imitate its practices. Their emulation resulted in a formalism far more dry, rigid, and grandiose than that of the original. Yet the products most representative of that academic grandeur, especially the great World's Columbian Exposition of 1893, brought architects throughout the country, and especially in Chicago, a prestige and respect they had not previously enjoyed.

It was in Chicago that America delivered its highest homage to the Ecole's tenets of style and design. Few people expected such magnificence from this brash midwestern city in 1889, when Congress announced that Chicago would be the site for the World's Columbian Exposition of 1893. The outcome was a magnificent, if less than perfect, tribute to Beaux-Arts principles of design and planning, and to the Ecole's portrait of the architect as *chef d'affaires.* The imperial majesty of the exposition obviously had little bearing on the moderate-cost dwelling, the middle-class suburb, or the tenements of the poor. But, that was just the point.

The spectacle not only represented a compelling grandeur for the profession, it also captured the country's fancy. Even many reformers keenly interested in housing issues were swept away in their enthrallment with this orderly beauty. They then explained, writing for every popular magazine read by an American audience, how the lessons from the "White City" could bring about the reforms they wanted to see in American society. The University of Chicago sociologist Charles Zueblin, a specialist in city planning, praised this alternative to civic "anarchy" and eclectic individualism. The Chicago exposition, "a miniature of the ideal city," was to him the beginning of American civic improvement. "For the first time in American history, a complete city, equipped with all the public utilities caring for a temporary population of thousands . . . was built as a unit on a single architectural scale . . . the most socialistic achievement of history." The poet Richard Watson Gilder eulogized Burnham's vision as well: "Ah, silent multitudes, ye are a part, / Of the wise architect's supreme and glorious art." Other writers carried the White City into the future. In William T. Stead's utopia Chicago in the twentieth century was a remarkably efficient, beautiful metropolis where "perfect control" reigned. William Dean Howells, whose "Traveller from Altruria" had marvelled at the exposition, saw in its efficient planning the model for a coming socialistic society, a planned state dedicated to the common good rather than individual gain. Henry Demarest Lloyd agreed. In his short story "No Mean City," Lloyd described the exposition as the genesis of an experiment in enlightened social planning, a movement which, in the story, grew until the old city of Chicago was finally destroyed, for it had become impossibly backward.[20] Lloyd wrote Burnham of his appreciation for a spectacle which "revealed to the people, possibilities of social beauty, utility, and harmony of which they had not been able even to dream. No such vision could otherwise have entered into the prosaic drudgery of their lives, and it will be felt in their development into the third and fourth generation."[21]

Accounts like these attributed the unity of the vision to a collective approach in planning. It seemed that the individual genius of each architect and designer had been merged with the group in the interest of the greater good. With battalions of experts to guide city planning, it then followed, the same results would be assured. In fact, however, this supreme prototype for the future city had not been a city at all, but a world's fair—rapidly constructed in plaster staff on an empty field with massive sums of money, an imaginary world of progress and pleasure where everyone could share the benefits equally, but only for a moment. In the delight with what appeared to be a solution to urban problems, almost every observer overlooked this disparity.

The rapturous musings on the final product also ignored, by and large, the reality of Burnham's tight control, the rigid academic standards he imposed, his absolute authority. Occasionally a critic of art, or of the Beaux-Arts, spoke out against that authoritarianism. Louis Sullivan decried the exposition as the worst possible event for the development of an indigenous American architecture. The cynical Henry Adams mocked the rhetoric of uplifting beauty:

> The artists and architects who had done the work offered little enough encouragement to hope for an improved public taste; they talked freely enough, but not in terms that one cared to quote; and to them the Northwest refused to look artistic. They talked as though they worked only for themselves; as though art, to the Western people, was a stage decoration; a diamond shirt-stud; a paper collar.[22]

Even the architectural critic Montgomery Schuyler, while enthusiastic about the display, cautioned readers of the *Record* not to see the exposition as real architecture pertinent to the needs of modern America.[23] Henry Van Brunt, a participant in the massive design production, also warned that this single stylistic formula should not be taken as an absolute—at least by trained architects. However, there were those who needed its restrictions:

> many uneducated and untrained men practicing as architects, and still maintaining, especially in the remote regions of the country, an impure and unhealthy vernacular, incapable of progress; men who have never seen a classic monument executed on a great scale, and who are ignorant of the emotions which it must excite in any breast accessible to the influences of art. To such, it is hoped that these great models, inspired as they have been by a profound respect for

> the masters of classic art, will prove such a revelation that they will learn at last that true architecture cannot be based on undisciplined invention, illiterate originality, or indeed, upon any audacity of ignorance.[24]

The example of the White City would, it was hoped, impose some restraint and respect for authority on this group of "illiterate" builders.

From these varied accounts of the exposition, it seems clear that there were felt to be, at the time, two separate, parallel aesthetic imperatives for America. Educated architects should continue their search for progress, their efforts to create a modern set of design principles. For them, the example of the exposition, with its uniform stylistic requirements, should be an inspiration but never a limit; armed with an understanding of the past, they could plan for the future. But builders were another case. They should restrict their experimental efforts and abide by clear-cut rules, such as those which governed the exposition. Architects and reformers alike, for the most part, praised the orderly image they discerned in the White City, bound by specific design criteria, cast in a defined set of styles, symbolizing an ideal planned community. The architectural critics then went on to call for a suspension of that carefully regulated conformity—but only for a few architects and their clients.

By the late 1890s, all over the country—in Kansas City, Cleveland, San Francisco, in small towns and suburbs with active local improvement societies—there was evidence of the exposition's impact. Architects wore the laurels of the public artist, and enjoyed the respect which they had so coveted. Enthusiasm soared for majestic planned settings on a grand scale. Businessmen sponsored stupendous civic construction projects. No longer isolated buildings or sculptures, the monuments were organized into Haussmanesque plans which altered large sections of a city or its surrounding landscape. The image of architects, artists and business leaders working together for the greater public good was based directly on the success of the exposition. It had been the prototype; now the City Beautiful movement would provide the infrastructure for a perfect, planned society all over America.

The best-known and the grandest of these endeavors again came about in Chicago. The plan for the city, like the exposition itself, was overseen by Daniel Burnham. In 1896, he had begun campaigning for a

South Park system to preserve the exposition grounds and develop the lakeshore. With the backing of several local businessmen's clubs, progressive organizations, and political leaders, this system quickly grew into a scheme for reorganizing the principal institutional buildings of the city into a grand civic center, rationalizing the entire traffic system, and beautifying the lakefront. Addressing the Chicago Merchants' Club that year, Burnham promised the businessmen that they could rely on economic returns from this systematic aesthetic program, for "Beauty had always paid better than any other commodity."[25] The ideal and the practical would be unified—or at least the architect's and the businessman's concepts of what was best and what was necessary would be united.

The conspicuous missing element in Burnham's scheme was housing, particularly improved housing for the city's poor. Some Chicagoans were dubious about the merit of a plan that ignored this problem. The nineteenth-century ideal of pure beauty, inspiring and uplifting individuals, raising the spirits of the poor out of their material circumstances, elevating those of the bourgeoisie above their materialistic concerns, seemed shallow and callous, especially during a depression. Mary McDowell of the University of Chicago Settlement House criticized Burnham's lack of planning for the housing and recreational needs of the families that lived in the stockyards district near her. Even Richard T. Crane, the local plumbing baron and a member of the Merchants' Club, doubted if this was the best way to improve the city. "I have no quarrel with those who would make the city more beautiful than it is," he wrote the *Chicago Tribune,* "but I would have all such schemes begin at the bottom. I would not put money into boulevards and statues and fine bridges and elaborate public buildings until the immediate surroundings of the poor are made better and decenter."[26]

Burnham tried, rather awkwardly, to rebut these criticisms. He briefly explained that the best way to prevent slums was by cutting through wide streets, letting in disinfecting sunlight. His plan, he contended, offered all the city's residents a vision of uplifting beauty which they could share equally as Chicago citizens.[27] Although his defense was weak, the appeal of a grand visionary city center carried more prestige and brought in more money than cautious programs for municipal housing reform. Civic grandeur was the architectural course toward progress in which most city officials chose to invest.

Defining Professional Standards

What were other Chicago architects doing in the 1890s, those who could not aspire to Burnham's scale of operations? While there was no absolute in style or identity that was accepted uniformly by all professional architects—indeed, most of them varied both style and statements about their work according to the client at hand—the period was nonetheless characterized by prevailing themes and aesthetic preferences.

All professional architects hoped to share some of the recent pomp and glory, capitalizing on the heightened respect for their profession which was the great legacy of the exposition. This meant intensifying the fight against the builders, who could still call themselves architects and dissipate this professional prestige. Now it was time to use legal sanctions as well as angry words.

Actually, the movement to create legal restrictions on who could practice architecture had begun during the 1880s. A state licensing and registration bill had been introduced in 1884 at the first meeting of the Western Association of Architects, and Dankmar Adler presented the bill in the Illinois state legislature the following year. It was tabled, but finally, in 1897, after thirteen years of lobbying (mostly by Adler, Nathan Ricker, and C. W. Nothnagel, a Chicago architect elected to the state legislature the year before), Illinois became the first state to require a license for the practice of architecture.[28]

The registration bill had to address a knotty question—What was architecture?—and provide some reasonably specific answers. Even then, however, the legal definition, drawn from the WAA lobbying committee, was surprisingly technical, administrative—and vague.[29] The licensing board created by the bill (composed of architects chosen by the AIA and state officials appointed by the governor) granted permission to practice to any graduate of an accredited university architectural school and to those who passed an examination showing their competence in the subjects taught in most such programs. The process was obviously subject to changing interpretations as the board took on new members. The one thing made clear was the scale of building that required an architect's expertise and control. Special provisions allowed anyone to design his or her own dwelling, or to build a single house for another person's habitation (but only if that person were presented with a certificate warning that the designer was not registered). There was no such freedom of choice in larger commissions: churches, monuments, public buildings, apartment buildings, office buildings, or factories, for instance. Only the licensed architect had the right to these jobs, because only he could properly supervise other workers and direct a major project. In essence, then, architecture was . . . what architects did.

Advocates of the bill argued that some form of regulation was absolutely necessary for the public safety in a time when buildings were ever larger and more complicated. Still, even most architects openly acknowledged that the economic pressures of the depression and the pride of their profession were also motivations. As the *American Architect* admitted, "Among architects, however, it [the registration bill] was almost entirely urged as a measure for raising the general standard of the profession and particularly of eliminating that large element of contractors, real-estate agents and young draughtsmen, who without any particular professional education or experience," declared themselves to be architects.[30] There was opposition to the bill, in Illinois and other states, from architects, builders, and other individuals who saw it as unnecessarily exclusive and restricting. Fred Hodgson wrote in the *National Builder* that the licensing law was in fact designed to control prices and restrict competition from those who had not been trained in professional schools. Builders and carpenters, if they wanted to construct more than one house at a time, were forced to accept the architect's control over their legitimate right to design and erect homes.[31] (As a conciliatory gesture, the bill contained a grandfather clause, granting licenses to builders who had already established steady practices, upon payment of a $25 fee; but, henceforth, all builders would have to apprentice for a much longer time than architectural students, in order to be qualified to take the examination.) However, the stipulation on construction projects requiring a licensed architect cut two ways. This legal definition further distanced the profession as a whole from moderate-cost residential design, which had been relegated to the category of mere "building."

The Illinois registration bill was the culmination of decades of bitter fighting between architects and builders. As the lobbying intensified during the 1890s, individual architects everywhere were facing the questions raised by the bill: What scale, subject, and style comprised the best and most professional architectural work? Surveying the issues of the *Inland Architect* for this decade, one finds numerous letters, editorials, and accounts of official meetings which confront these issues. The plates and the articles give a good indication of professional opinions and activities in Chicago—or at least an indication of the kinds of opinions and the types of designs that were considered exemplary.

The focus of the journal was on buildings that the editors conceived to be technically and aesthetically more demanding than the small house. Of course, architects continued to design and build small or at least moderate-sized houses. And a few of these continued to be published, especially early in the decade. There were notes of simplification in many of them: George Maher's Cochran house, Georgian-inspired and academically correct; his Wheeler house (fig. 36), which

Figure 36. Mrs. A. D. Wheeler House, Edgewater, by George W. Maher, 1894. (From *Inland Architect,* 1894.)

combined classical features, a medley of building materials, and a Dutch Colonial gambrel roof; or the hewn logs and rugged stone of

W. W. Boyington's "Ravine Lodge" or Maher's MacMeans house, both glorified rustic cottages.[32] The editors juxtaposed picturesque country cottages, more regularized Queen Anne dwellings, stately Classical Revival homes, elegant Romanesque Revival and French Renaissance mansions. At no point did a single stylistic idiom dominate absolutely. The houses W. L. B. Jenney built at Buena Park, Illinois, also published as a set in the journal, show the range of styles and inventive handling of them which was still considered acceptable in 1890.[33]

Over the decade, one can watch the styles and the architect's freedom of interpretation change dramatically. After 1892, majestic commissions and more academic Beaux-Arts projects eclipsed simple forms and the smaller house. George Maher bridged the transition with his formal houses; during the 1890s, the *Inland Architect* featured more illustrations of his work than that of any other architect. With the onset of the depression, there was less small residential building under construction. There was even less discussion of it in the schools and the journals. While the *Inland Architect* never embraced European monuments with the fervor of the *American Architect,* there were travel notes from abroad and occasional illustrations of celebrated American and European historical buildings for the edification of readers. In both publications, the monument became the principal focus. Illustrations of current American work turned more and more toward large commercial, ecclesiastical, or public structures or prestigious estates. Van Brunt and Howe's Renaissance Revival clubs and office buildings often appeared. American fantasies of French chateaux in François I splendor (or, more accurately, in imitation of Richard Morris Hunt) became the favored models for houses.

The architectural schools followed the lead, and the *Inland Architect* soon noted with pride the great proficiency shown by students at the Chicago School of Architecture in their sketches of country clubs and chateaux (fig. 37).[34] The exhibitions of the Chicago Architectural Sketch Club also showed the same sudden domination of the Beaux-Arts academic ideal, although the club's leaders never ousted all other kinds of work. The American interpretation of the Beaux-Arts clearly reigned as the favored approach, offering both a role for the architect and a satisfactory definition of the architectural problem he faced. In 1894 there was still a mixture of styles and philosophies in the drawings exhibited at the club's annual show: monumental Beaux-Arts-inspired

Figure 37. Chateau design by F. G. Mueller of the Chicago School of Architecture. (From *Inland Architect,* 1896.)

railroad stations and library buildings, quaint colonial furniture and Queen Anne residences (including several watercolor renderings of Frank Lloyd Wright houses). By the next year's show, the balance had shifted undeniably toward the imposing monument, including several *projets* sent over by Chicago students at the Paris Ecole. A drawing the following year showed a chateau design by Lawrence Buck, who would later make his name as a Prairie school architect specializing in simple, small houses.[35] As the depression wore on, subjects became more elaborate and fanciful: "A Villa in Tennessee" (fig. 38) and "A Casino on a Private Estate" appeared in 1897. Not surprisingly, since there was so little real work to be done, many of the entries, and especially the more grandiose fantasies, were not actual commissions. They were dreams to sustain architects through a time of all too ordinary doubts and banal work. Published commissions like the Tennessee villa promised magnanimous clients who appreciated those lofty ideals.

By 1900, the architectural climate warmed toward simpler, smaller, and more realistic projects. In journals, exhibitions, and classroom studios, a new set of methods and concerns came to the fore. A one-day sketch problem for a gate lodge from the Chicago School of Architecture (fig. 39) reveals an alternative to the preoccupation with grand country villas and casino staircases which had marked most of the decade before. That year, the exhibition of the Chicago Architectural Club featured six Frank Lloyd Wright residences, settlement houses by Pond and Pond and by Dwight Perkins, and an exhibit on improved working-class housing.[36] Here indeed was evidence of a less grandiose vision of the architect and his or her product. Once again, the small house was considered a valid architectural problem.

It is evident that the Beaux-Arts approach, or an American version of it, dominated the architectural schools and journals and the official professional organizations of the 1890s. All the same, in considering the overall change of mood after the exposition and the depression of 1893, one should not overestimate the impact of the Beaux-Arts. Even though professional architectural schools, journals, and societies posed the academic ideal as "True Architecture," these bodies represented only a small number of people. Although they were extremely influential in the profession, the academicians did not by any means dominate all building in America. In spite of the prestige of the Beaux-Arts Society (founded just after the exposition to promote training at the Ecole and to combat the "vagaries and abuses" of current architecture), Burnham and his Chicago colleagues in the society found it difficult to raise funds to send students to the American Academy in Rome.[37]

Moreover, students in American architectural schools could make only a minimal impact on the country's actual environment. True, institutions like the Chicago School of Architecture (a joint program offered by the Armour Institute of Technology and the Chicago Art Institute that was established in 1889 by Louis Millet, a former Ecole student) were strongly oriented toward the Beaux-Arts. That school's catalogue made its priorities clear, claiming that "the genius of the American people is so mechanized that the danger in this country lies in placing too much emphasis in architectural education upon mathematics and construction, and too little upon artistic elements."[38] But, as late as 1896, there were only thirty-nine students in the Chicago School of Architecture. Two years later, with nine schools of architecture in the entire country, there was a total of 384 students enrolled in degree programs of those schools. And several departments, notably at Illinois and Cornell, maintained a strongly "practical" bent, although they did integrate a Beaux-Arts orientation into their history and ornamental design courses.[39]

Architectural journals could claim only half the circulation of the builders' journals, and a fraction of what the popular monthlies claimed. Even in the professional architectural press, especially the more iconoclastic *Inland Architect,* there were disputes about the absolute authority of the Beaux-Arts approach. In 1894 that journal reprinted a debate (it appeared originally in *Engineering* magazine), between an advocate of "Beaux-Arts Principles" and an opponent who

Figure 38. "A Villa in Tennessee" and plan (opposite) for Mrs. Eugene Davis, by Howard and Cauldwell. (From the *Catalogue of the Tenth Annual Exhibition of the Chicago Architectural Club at the Art Institute,* 1897. Courtesy of the Chicago Historical Society.)

favored "Practical Training." The first, Arthur Rotch (a graduate of the Ecole), insisted on the need for a "mental attitude" which would provide immutable principles in the face of ambiguous, often conflicting, design criteria. "The young architect requires a pure aesthetic code to guide him," Rotch maintained, "when bewildered by specious influences." The rebuttal by Robert D. Andrews (who had apprenticed with Henry Hobson Richardson) discussed some of these specious influences. He allowed that increased contact with Europe, made possible through new systems of transportation and photography, was indeed beneficial for architects. But, he asked, did Americans want to repeat the experience of ancient Rome by imitating her architecture (itself an imitation of the architecture of a more advanced culture),

·HAWTHORNE·RIDGE·
·VILLA·FOR·MRS·EUGENE·DAVIS·
LA·FOLLETTE·TENNESSEE

using this imported beauty "as a cloak for luxury and mental idleness"?[40]

Andrews proposed that schools emphasize structure over history, and craft over art, in order to break the hold of European aestheticism. He went so far as to suggest joining a building-trades school to every architectural department so that design would be, of necessity, more

Figure 39. Gate-house study by Arthur Mackie of the Chicago School of Architecture. (From *The Chicago Architectural Club, Book of the Exhibition of 1900.* Courtesy of the Chicago Historical Society.)

practical and economical. No one implemented such utilitarian programs for any longer than a short trial period,[41] yet they were current topics of debate. The Beaux-Arts model might have been the authoritative reference for the scholars of the American profession throughout the 1890s, but it did not determine all that was being built or all that was being said about architecture.

Conduct and Conscience

American architects everywhere were in a strangely ambiguous, ill-defined situation in the 1890s. They were, as a group and individually, cautious about responding too directly to the public's interest in architectural issues; they also avoided the polemics of European designers who evoked moral rationales (criticizing the degeneracy of ostentation) or political purposes (demanding more government-funded low-cost housing) to justify their designs. In general, American architects tended to be reserved about the avant-garde European movements of the turn of the century. Even the English arts and crafts movement, with its strong political overtones and emphasis on working-class housing, was suspect.[42] The undulations of the Art Nouveau never caught on with the enthusiasm the style generated in France or Belgium. Herbert Croly, editor of the *Architectural Record,* described Art Nouveau as an expression of "'fin-de-siècle' sensationalism, which tries to whip jaded sensibility into new life by violent stimulation."[43] The Austrian *Sezessionstil,* crusading for a radical purge of architectural ornament, was here reduced to a few conspicuous geometric motifs.[44] By and large, few American architects expressed much of an interest in theory. Xenophobia was extreme. American architects and architectural writers criticized European professionals who seemed to have become too decadent and sensual, just as they found fault with those who were too politically engaged. They stayed on the middle ground, not leaning too precariously to one side or the other.[45]

Those who admired the absolute authority of the Beaux-Arts found there a firm professional identity. But others, suspicious of such absolutism, especially if it derived from European sources, found themselves still searching for a role and a system of design that could take fuller account of what was going on around them, of the technological advances and social reforms of their time. Sometimes with misgivings, these architects turned to the progressive groups in their cities, the reformers who were campaigning for an architecture that was relevant to social and political concerns. A shared interest in modernizing the American home provided architect and nonarchitect with a common language, even if their purposes were quite different. The architects did not usually donate their services as designers or even, with a few exceptions, as teachers. In fact, one motivation architects had for joining these organizations was an expanded search for private commissions. Yet they were exploring architectural ideas then current *outside* their profession, discussing something very different from universal principles of beauty.

Chicago architects interacted with one another and with many nonarchitects in a variety of forums during the 1890s. The range of their exchanges with nonprofessionals is remarkable, for it represents a significant departure from the aloofness of earlier years. While some architects simply handed down expert opinion on artistic matters, others began to share their ideas with and listen to the city's artists, reformers, political leaders, domestic scientists, housewives, and even with one another, as they had not done before.

Architects spread their specialized knowledge in many ways. Nathan Ricker's program at the University of Illinois at Champaign-Urbana included special courses for builders and carpenters as well as those exclusively for architectural students. With two other members of his faculty, Ricker taught in Isabel Bevier's household science department and gave advice for the architectural and historical sections of her textbooks. Chicago architects, on the whole, steered clear of the domestic science field and the building trades. Unlike Ricker and his associates in Champaign, most of them did not become involved in courses that reached these groups, nor did they take part in the home-study programs offered by the Chicago-based American School of Home Economics. (It was a young Boston architect, Frank Chouteau Brown, who became a contributing editor to this organization.) However, two local architects, Hermann von Holst and Hugh Garden, did teach in the newly integrated architecture and engineering program at the Armour Institute branch of the Chicago School of Architecture. And these two also joined with building specialists, including Fred Hodgson, to produce the massive *Encyclopedia of Architecture, Carpentry and Building,* a twelve-volume treatise which the American School of Correspondence (an affiliate of the institute) finally published in 1907. While von Holst and Garden emphasized architecture as a fine art, explaining the classical orders and defining historical styles, they extended this specialized information outside the confines of professional academies. Preparing the *Encyclopedia,* they discussed the relationship between aesthetic issues and the economic constraints and technical issues which interested the other editors.

It was in keeping with the prevailing professional identity to give advice about the city's civic architecture, and to do so from positions of prestige. W. L. B. Jenney therefore became a member of the Chicago Art Commission in 1894. This body recommended or vetoed art works and other improvements for public places. Louis Sullivan, Peter B. Wight, and James Gamble Rogers joined the board of directors of the Municipal Art League when it was founded in 1899. This group unified the city's sixty local art clubs and suggested civic sculpture, parks, and school programs on art. Dwight Perkins, a conservationist as well as an architect, also joined the league board as the newly appointed head of the city's Special Park Commission, which was delegated to create an overall plan for Chicago's recreational needs. By these gestures, the artist served the public, if only by the example of a learned opinion or the gift of a beautiful monument.

Chicago architects also offered consultation to the public on a more practical level. They campaigned for and often drafted laws and insurance regulations that determined municipal building practices for theaters and office buildings, tenements and houses. In the early 1890s, Dankmar Adler and Henry Goetz began working with the Chicago Underwriters Association to establish a policy on standards for slow-burning construction. Insurance agents then agreed to grant lower rates to local builders and architects who met the standards.[46] In 1893, the National Board of Fire Underwriters' Laboratory was established at the Armour Institute. Architectural students as well as those in engineering observed materials tests.

The Illinois State Association of Architects began to work with the Chicago Citizens' Association for improvements in municipal building laws.[47] Charging that existing building regulations were in effect useless, since appointments to the board of examiners were based on political favors, the association acted predominantly as a political organization. However, the architects in the association did offer advice. This led to a new code, approved by the Chicago City Council in 1898, which extended requirements for tenements and apartments (as well as theaters and offices) and called for examiners to be appointed on the basis of experience. (The code was less stringent than New York's primitive law of 1879, and inspection was at best minimal.[48] Nonetheless, architects did recognize and discuss the need for legal measures that would improve building.) The debate over regulations occasionally found its way into the pages of the architectural magazines and the meetings of their organizations, but it was more effective to deal with the issue directly, talking with outsiders.

Other ways to spread professional expertise to a sizable audience emerged during the 1890s. For instance, one of Chicago's popular educational programs was the Central Art Association, founded in 1894 by the philanthropist Mrs. T. Vernette Morse, the sculptor Larado Taft, and the novelist Hamlin Garland. This organization was dedicated to general education and sought to spread art throughout the Midwest, beginning with Chicago. Within a period of four years, some three thousand paying members were attending Chautauqua-like lectures and traveling exhibits on architecture, industrial art, house decoration, and municipal improvement, as well as more traditional courses in painting, ceramics, and history. Among the lecturers were Ellen Gates Starr, who described the arts and crafts programs at Hull House, and the interior decorator Candace Wheeler, who addressed a Chicago audience on "Art and Its Relation to Commerce and Manufacture."

Louis Gibson and his wife Emily Gilbert Gibson gave a study course in architectural theories at the CAA. George R. Dean offered a correspondence course on English domestic architecture adapted to American conditions.[49] Frank Lloyd Wright (elected a member of the Board of Directors of the CAA) read a paper entitled "Art in the Home" to a session in 1898. He pleaded that "A process of elimination is the necessity now; to get rid of the load of Meaningless things that choke the modern house; to get rid of them by teaching the teachable that many things considered necessities now are really not so." Consumers could affect the market, he claimed, if they learned to demand the correct kind of housing. But it was necessary to trust all to the architect, rather than to suggest the style or decor.[50] Other local architects made similar qualifications. Dwight Perkins presented his opinions on "Criticism of Architecture by the Public." He praised the growing popular interest in his field, but cautioned that the architect's freedom was too delicate and precious to be abused.[51] Robert Spencer, speaking on the issue of a national style, nodded approvingly at popular demands for fresh air and simple forms, if they were "within reasonable bounds."[52] When architects took to the public speaker's platform, they made the same points about exclusive authority and esoteric laws of beauty that they expressed in professional conclaves. Their exchanges with the public never extended an unambiguous invitation for greater participation from clients.

Another effective medium for teaching the public the principles of residential design was through the already well-established women's magazines. These also provided a source of income for the educators. Perkins, Spencer, and Alfred Granger wrote for *The House Beautiful*. Sullivan wrote numerous articles for *The Craftsman*. Most of all, as we have seen, the *Ladies' Home Journal* could provide a major forum for the progressive midwestern architects, once they realized that teaching the public to respond to innovative architecture could indeed help their business and their cause.

Almost every prominent Chicago architect joined a club and met, generally weekly, with local artists, journalists, writers, with businessmen and political leaders. Here the exchange of ideas was, in theory, among equals. Here again there were new ideas for the architects to consider.[53] The "Little Room," Chicago's most accomplished club of the time, brought the Pond brothers, Howard Shaw, and Hugh Garden together with Hamlin Garland, Henry Blake Fuller, Lucy and Harriet Monroe, Robert Herrick, Jane Addams, and Herbert S. Stone. Among this congregation, the subject was art, not practical pointers on domestic economy. But it was a modern definition of art: realism in the novel, the poem, the building, and the city plan. Architects and writers discussed the need for a new set of aesthetic values, criteria for art drawn from real life rather than abstract laws, although the various perceptions of "real life" tended to fit into exceedingly orderly categories which strongly resembled laws. When there were ensuing commissions from the friendships made in these groups, such as the austere brick house Hugh Garden built for Robert Herrick in 1900, the influence of these new values was perceptible.[54] Garden's architectural style was here as unsparingly precise and unrelenting as Herrick's prose.

In other organizations that architects joined during these years, art played less of a role, although architecture and planning appeared again and again as topics of discussion. Allen and Irving Pond were consultants to the City Homes Association and were deeply involved with the settlement house movement (so appealing to liberal professionals that it too might be considered a club). The two architects also became members of the Municipal Voters League—an organization founded to challenge the neighborhood bosses' political control—as well as of the City Club, the Commercial Club, and the Merchants Club (that is, after these societies voted to accept professional men as members). In these political reform organizations, the architects promoted parks and playgrounds, public health regulations, smoke abatement, municipal reform, and the Burnham plan for the city. They talked with academic reformers like Charles Zueblin, George Vincent, and Albion Small, all three from the University of Chicago's sociology department, with the builder Henry Ericsson and the businessman-philanthropist Charles Henderson. In all of these progressive business clubs, the principal topic was the reorganization of the entire city along modern, rational lines; the shared assumption was that this approach would benefit industrial progress and eradicate social problems.[55] Participating in the discussion, these progressive architects enlarged their vision of how best to use their skills for the public good.

A quickening of thought and greater exchange of ideas also took place among the architects themselves. With residential building greatly reduced and many architects out of work, there were more opportunities for discussion, writing, and even formal organizations, opportunities that had not existed in the previous, busier decade. With small groups of like-minded colleagues, architects began to explore what path their profession might take. Sometimes it was simply a case of sharing space and talking informally at the office. In 1896, one group, composed of Wright, Perkins, Spencer and Myron Hunt, later joined by Walter Burley Griffin, the Pond brothers, and several other younger architects, took a common space as "associates" in a downtown Chicago building called Steinway Hall. In 1897 Wright added a studio onto his Oak Park home, which quickly became a second communal drafting room and debating forum. This group of architects, one member later recalled, deliberated over Henry George's Single Tax program, the goals of the Progressive party, the future of Robert La Follette, and Herbert Spencer's theories of Social Darwinism.[56] They also began to evolve together what would come to be called Prairie school design.

Lectures and organized debates often provoked heated discussions during these years. Sullivan spoke to the Chicago Architectural Club on "The Principles of Architectural Design" and Wright described "The Practical Nature of the Artistic." There were also talks by outsiders interested in social reform through architecture, notably Jane Addams's 1900 presentation of the "scientific planning" research undertaken by Patrick Geddes in Edinburgh.[57]

Another organization even challenged the established profession, although its policies were equally vague. Largely through the initiative of the younger members of the Chicago Architectural Club, the Architectural League of America was founded in 1899. This league represented an effort to bring about more cooperation between the professional clubs in various American cities. Sullivan was the idol of the group and a paper he had written, "The Modern Phase of Architecture," which called upon the younger architects to regenerate the art with new ideals and values (based on the universal laws of nature and not human luxury), brought down the house at the first meeting, held in Cleveland.[58]

Following that lead, over the next two years, the Chicago delegation to the Architectural League staged a series of protests against what they saw as the conservative orientation of their profession. "Pure design," or studies of abstract geometric forms, should replace academic reconstructions of classical monuments in architectural education, they insisted. "Progress before Precedent" should, they urged, be adopted as the league motto.[59] This stance was scarcely a call for actual social reform or a politically progressive role for the architect. Rather, it was one more attempt to define a modern professional aesthetic and identity within the carefully restricted bounds of formal preferences. But, as in so many architectural debates, there was an implication of social "progress" associated with the aesthetic crusade. All the same, the resolutions were defeated. It was now the end of the depression decade. With economic recovery more certain, and the enthusiastic public response to the City Beautiful movement seeming to promise many grand commissions for architects, protest against the established profession had less appeal.

The 1890s had been an epoch of soul-searching, for architects as for other Americans. Although the profession was by no means unified, there had emerged powerful symbols of order, authority, and grand scale, interpreted in various ways by different individuals and groups. These symbols, and the determination to incorporate them in their architectural practice, united those who envisioned Beaux-Arts monuments and those who pursued the idea of a modern American home and city. As professional architects, the members of both groups wanted to be charged with overseeing the American environment, changing it to fit their aesthetic and social vision. At a sufficiently large scale of operations, their architecture could seem to be unifying opposing factions, responding to different groups in the society, and giving the architect his due position of respect.

PART THREE

A NEW ORDER

1903–1913

8 THE MINIMAL HOUSE

The home is the acme of simplicity, and yet it is beautiful in its appointments, for it contains nothing that does not tend towards the pleasures and comforts of its inmates.

Mabel Tuke Priestman, *Artistic Houses* (1910)

At the turn of the twentieth century, almost every kind of literature concerned with the home—including professional architectural and engineering journals, builders' pattern books, promotional brochures for real estate companies, women's journals, domestic science textbooks, and popular monthly magazines—reconsidered the familiar topic of domestic architecture. Their common aesthetic position was one that called for a radical simplification of the dwelling, although there were very different interpretations of how far to carry this process and why to promote it. These conflicts became even more apparent as houses did, indeed, take on a different appearance than that of Victorian dwellings. With a barrage of similar images and related ideas from all directions, there occurred a sudden and dramatic change in the outward appearance of the average American dwelling, in the technology that equipped it, and its formal relations to its neighbors. The varied expectations for social change and professional prestige associated with the architectural forms were seldom realized. The organization of household work and family life certainly remained essentially the same. But the trappings of the suburban dwelling had undeniably been altered.

Beginning in the 1890s, contemporary with the increasingly sumptuous estates and chateaux fabricated by some architects and architectural students, there had been evidence of a shift toward smaller, much simpler houses. By 1900, the reorientation was perceptible at every level of residential design. It is not that a minimalist aesthetic was something drastic, revolutionary, unthought of before this time. Of course, the homes of families with little time or money for elaboration had always been simple. But the sudden, widespread acceptance, even fashionability, of that aesthetic was startling. Middle-class families had as much of an effect on the change as architects and builders did. Since their sensitivity to design issues had been heightened by innumerable magazine articles, classes, and discussions during the 1890s, these families had a distinct idea of the kind of houses they wanted. The people who designed houses, whether for clients or a speculative market, knew this.

The aim of designers and clients was that of a balance between luxury and austerity, between individualized private dwellings and communal arrangements. As one commentator expressed the idea of moderation:

> There have been two extremes in later American home architecture—overornamentation and absolute disregard for appearance. The first arose from a feeling that every dollar spent in the interest of art (!) should be so geegawed to the outer world that all who passed might note the costliness and wonder. The second extreme had its birth in an elementary practicality that believes anything artistic must be both extravagant and useless.[1]

Others discussed balance in terms of planning, and called for an equilibrium between necessary rationalization and treasured privatism. Katherine Busbey spoke for those who condemned apartment living as the "most dangerous enemy of American domesticity,"[2] but who recognized that private homes had to adopt some of the principles of apartment design and maintenance. In sum, then, most Americans seemed to want private houses in planned groups, houses that offered health, efficiency, and security, with some artistic grace; houses that gave them a sense of being modern, up-to-day, social, and "progressive." All of these words could now be applied to a certain kind of architecture.

Many observers saw the popular demand for modified simplicity and standardization as the wind of progress, soon to reach designers and clients at every level of society. A few younger architects even acknowledged a common bond between themselves and the builders who advocated a modern minimalist design. In 1903, writing for *The Brickbuilder,* Robert Spencer gave an account of recent residential work by Chicago architects. It was all, he explained proudly, "distinguished by its simplicity and severity. This severity, however, lies particularly in an absence of ornament and the use of simple, almost cheap materials."[3] Even the city's wealthiest families, he claimed, were turning against the palatial magnificence which still characterized New York and Paris. This shift in taste was especially important, according to Spencer, because the wealthy set the fashions for other families, as their architects set the example for builders. But more of that simplified example was still needed. Architects had to take on the challenge of creating an economical, elegant aesthetic for less expensive houses. It should be based, Spencer later wrote in *The House Beautiful,* upon skillful massing of the parts of a house, judicious arrangement of openings, and the use of texture rather than applied ornament. Yet "even composition of masses must be subordinated to the economy which has demonstrated that a plain square or oblong box is the cheapest form," he asserted. It should be possible for the builder or the architect who explored ordinary building to achieve "economy . . . dignity and simplicity" for everyone.[4]

Almost every architect, builder, and social reformer of the period recognized that a change was taking place in American ideas about the home. They united in condemning the ornately decorated, individualized Victorian dwelling, indicting the era of Eastlake and Queen Anne as the "American Decadence" and the "Reign of Terror."[5] But not everyone sensed the fresh breezes of modernity coming from the same direction. Herbert Croly, editor of the *Architectural Record,* contended that the decade of the 1890s had been the turning point for American suburban architecture; designers and clients had rejected "freakish," "out of place," and "*meaningless* eccentricities" for more stately and subdued dwellings. However, he was primarily impressed with the reforms in the "better class" of homes, those costing over $8,000. Less expensive houses were shaped by the necessities of economics, not aesthetic choice.[6] Frank Lloyd Wright later looked back to "the new dwellings that appeared upon the prairies from 1893 to 1910," but he was seeing only the houses that he and his colleagues of the midwestern Prairie school designed during these years.[7] Both men recognized an important shift in residential design and dated it correctly, yet they limited the revolution to a restricted group of architects and their forward-looking clients. In fact, similar formal changes were evident in the houses of builders and architects alike, in the model homes of domestic scientists, of women's magazine editors, and of carpenters.

Popular writers of the early twentieth century agreed, for the most part, with the architectural profession's scathing indictment of the Victorian era in housing. They were even more explicit in tying what now seemed visual disorder to social problems, blaming excessive architectural diversity for family tensions and even for political conflict. Katherine Busbey railed against the suburbs and their "labyrinth of unreason with grotesque details supposed to represent the 'latest styles.'"[8] Other critics charged that houses conceived as display encouraged class differences and individualistic competition between neighbors. To us, it may seem simplistic to reduce the problems of ethnic immigrants, the appeal of socialism, the goals of feminists, or the limitations of early monopoly capitalism to the lack of a proper model for suburban housing. But that was, in effect, the claim of many reformers. The metaphors linking architecture to social and political ends were taken very seriously.

In part, then, the motivation for formal changes in American domestic architecture came from social reformers. The progressives of the 1890s and early twentieth century insisted that there was a strong correlation between certain architectural forms and the social changes they sought to bring about. In part, too, the changes derived from designers; however, this group included builders and amateurs as well as professional architects. The architectural details and cultural issues which dominated model-house designs in *The House Beautiful*, the *National Builder*, or *Domestic Engineering* were remarkably similar in concept and appearance. If the editors of these journals often recognized the quality of domestic design among the progressive midwestern architects of the Prairie school, they also realized that a new aesthetic was emerging on several fronts at the same time.

In essence, the shared aesthetic of the early-twentieth-century minimalist model house relied on five principles. Each of these ideas had been explored in the 1890s by many groups, and then became the basis for new construction in the 1900s. The technological system became more complex, more costly, and more important as a criterion in house design. The kitchen became a central focus for the designer, and a different kind of room. Houses became simpler in outline and ornament, inside and out. Square-footage was dramatically reduced and, as the number of rooms and partitions declined, the floor plan opened up. Finally, houses became more alike in their plans and their general appearance, as the individuality of each dwelling (and, supposedly, that of the occupant) became less frantically emphasized. These same points are evident in the work of almost every class of designer, especially in their projects for middle-class houses.[9]

Investing in Domestic Technology

New domestic technology was central to the aesthetic and the cultural redefinition of the modern home. The systems brought into the home regulated its temperature, air, and light and supplied it with power and services. By 1901, Henry Demarest Lloyd, writing in the *Congregationalist,* could extol the benefits advanced technology would bring to every American household:

> Equal industrial power will be as invariable a function of citizenship as the equal franchise. Power will flow in every house and shop as freely as water. All men will become capitalists and all capitalists co-operators. . . . Women, released from the economic pressure which has forced them to deny their best nature and compete in unnatural industry with men, will be re-sexed. . . . The new rapid transit, making it possible for cities to be four or five hundred miles in diameter and yet keep the farthest point within an hour of the center, will complete the suburbanization of every metropolis. Every house will be a center of sunshine and scenery.[10]

Everyone, it seemed to these enthusiasts, could share the infinite power of electricity equally. According to the observer, women would be able to work because they were free from household drudgery, or able to return home from outside work with increased economic abundance. Bringing greater ease of home life, technology seemed to promise a return to "life as it should be," the progressives' cherished but vague ideal of universal middle-class existence. As one writer in *The House Beautiful* expressed the sentiment:

> The suburban house expresses freedom from restraint; it is the home of children; it means purer air; it means more room to move around in; it means gardens; and it implies a social life which years of city living may never engender. . . . The suburban house is a type of progress.[11]

With such hopes, many middle-class American families were ready to change their houses to incorporate technological improvements for their better health, efficiency, and comfort.

Production of sanitary fixtures increased markedly after 1900. Porcelain toilets, bathtubs, and sinks began to be mass-produced in sufficient numbers and at a low enough price to reach most of the American middle-class market.[12] The bathroom usually included each of these items, and perhaps a sanitary toothbrushing basin for the household that was especially conscious of hygienic fashion. The convenient bedroom washstand passed out of production altogether. By 1904, Fred Hodgson could write that no house should be without a bathroom or at least a tub in a separate room, if there was no running water for the other fixtures. (All the same, his pattern books still included less expensive plans for bathroom-less houses. But such houses implied subsistence living.) Soon Sears advertised plumbing systems which the "American Husband Who Wants His Wife to Have the Best There Is" could install on his own.[13] While privies and cesspools were still common in many small towns and in the poorer areas of large cities, unincorporated suburbs often passed ordinances forbidding them, and cities like Chicago tightened their inspection policies for new developments. Household sanitation had reached a higher level of perfection, and that level quickly became the standard.

At the same time, improvements were occurring in every phase of home technology.[14] Many middle-class homes were equipped with portable hot-air furnaces; if water under pressure was available, a hot-water system (or perhaps a steam system, although this was far more expensive and troublesome) could be installed. Around 1900, there were experiments using cork, sawdust, or quilts of seaweed for insulation. Architects' experiments in fire retardation, carried out during the slow years of the 1890s, quickly became standard construction techniques after the turn of the century. The use in houses of fire stops between wood studs and metallic lath for ceilings, of asbestos or mineral wool between floors, were among the suggestions Chicago's Peter Wight made in the *Fireproofing Magazine*, which he edited between 1901 and 1907. (These techniques had first been used for apartments and commercial structures.) And there were advances in the technology of concrete, which Frank Lloyd Wright, Bernard Maybeck, and Thomas Alva Edison, among others, used as a fire-preventive building system for homes.

Cement stucco became the favored surface for house facades, available in a multitude of textures and tints. It cost less, in most cases, than other surfacing techniques, while giving fashionable uncluttered lines.[15] Chicago's Radford Architectural Company insisted on stucco's advantages in their pattern books, which featured titles like *Radford American Homes* (1903) and *Radford Ideal Homes* (1905). Several companies, including Radford, also began to produce sheets of gypsum wallboard to replace interior lath and plaster.

Finally, the advances in small appliances were plentiful. Ammonia-cooled iceboxes were on the back porch, a gas cooking-range stood in the kitchen (or perhaps a combination gas-and-wood stove, just in case the gas failed), maybe a telephone in the hall, and a hand-cranked washing machine to replace the washboard down in the basement.

In each case, there was initial resistance to the new technology, and then rapid general acceptance of the latest standards for the efficient modern home. However, these improvements consumed space—space for the equipment itself and space taken out of the total square-footage of the dwelling in order to reduce construction costs. There had to be room now (usually on the second floor) for at least one 8′ by 10′ bathroom—soon reduced to a spartan 5′ by 5′. The basement, the storage niches on the first floor and under the stairs, the ample room in some houses once given over to the bathroom, all these were usually absorbed into or reduced in size by the larger amount of area given over to furnaces, pipes, and equipment of all sorts. A large portion of the basement, plus room registers and then radiators for the areas not immediately above the furnace, had to be planned around the heating equipment. Furthermore, since hot-water heating required 25 percent more radiating surface than steam, a house with low ceilings and fewer rooms or alcoves outside the basic compact plan would help economize on both installation and fuel costs. What would later be called the "servant spaces" of a building now became more important for the average American house.

The new technology required a substantial investment on the part of the speculative builder and the homeowner. One writer estimated in 1905 that increased sanitary requirements for housing had doubled the cost of a given enclosed space over the past fifteen years.[16] Housing economists have estimated that construction features and equipment present in the bulk of American houses of the early twentieth century, but absent in most of those built before 1890, amounted to between 25 percent and 40 percent of construction costs.[17] The fact that the average cost per unit did not rise too sharply during this stage (national averages were $2,400 in 1890; $2,275 in 1905; $2,650 in 1910; while averages for Chicago were slightly higher)[18] indicate that cuts were certainly being made elsewhere. Conventional wood-frame construction became lighter, often to the point of being flimsy, less soundproof, less well-insulated. The trends toward smaller, less ornamented, more standardized houses also helped balance the mounting expenditures for domestic technology.

Despite the expenses and the changes required in their homes, most Americans considered the technological advances to be necessary improvements. As the Chicago sanitary engineer and associate editor of the *Sanitary News*, Jonathan Allen, wrote:

> The American people are accumulating material wealth so rapidly that they now demand many conveniences which a generation ago would have been considered unnecessary, and others which even ten years ago would have been considered luxuries which only the very rich could afford. The modern American home must have a perfect system of hot and cold water supply; an inoffensive and sanitary system of disposing of household wastes; an adequate system of automatically controlled heating combined with ventilating; and a convenient and complete scheme of artificial lighting.[19]

Allen was among the domestic reformers who believed that technical improvements would protect every family's health, preserve their privacy, and stimulate the economy. The possibility of "a perfect system" for plumbing or for family life seemed beyond doubt or question.

Robert Thompson, a Philadelphia educator and political economist, was one of the more radical reformers who hoped that industrial technology and scientific planning would not, in fact, preserve existing culture but rather bring about dramatic changes in the structure of the American home and family. He wanted to see standardization of architecture, believing that it would cut construction expenses and promote a sense of community likeness rather than individual differences. In his writings on the future of the household, he called for centralized services, with cooking, cleaning, and child-care moved outside the home, so that individual dwellings would harbor only the emotional and social aspects of domestic life.[20] A few voices were more cautious about the dangers of investing in technological solutions to all problems. George Harvey, writing in *Harper's Weekly,* called for "elimination of household possessions, and not . . . increase of household machinery."[21] But even the wary critics of American materialism, and certainly most progressive liberals among the housing reformers, felt that the unprecedented reliance on domestic technology was here to stay. It was not a fad.

The sudden prominence of the kitchen itself points up the fact that the cult of technology and simplification was, in part, an expression of a growing interest in scientific values and rational planning for every sphere of life. The kitchen became the center of the modern house (fig. 40), the focus of attention in most pattern books, and certainly in domestic science textbooks and women's magazines. It replaced the parlor as the favorite subject of housing guides and books of decorating advice. For instance, *Carpentry and Building* reprinted a series on planning the model kitchen by the Chicago domestic scientist Nina C. Kinney, a series originally published in *The American Kitchen. Indoors and Out,* a fashionable journal of upper-class country life, described the "office" of the country estate where the housewife carried on her communications with the world outside, complete with a telephone, mailbox, filing cabinet for bills, and a telescope for watching approaching visitors. Isabel McDougall, describing "An Ideal Kitchen" in *The House Beautiful,* used all of the latest metaphors: "something on the lines of a Pullman-car kitchen, or a yacht's galley, or a laboratory . . . [or] the scientific cleanliness of a surgery."[22] If in 1898 Eugene Klapp could publish a book on *Successful Houses* with chapters on halls, drawing rooms, smoking rooms, and bedrooms but scarcely a mention of the kitchen, this had become impossible a decade later.[23] Every article or book on the home reiterated the point that the kitchen was the most important room in the modern house.

The main reason for this prominence was that the kitchen, more than any other space, was supposed to be scientifically planned and run. The model kitchen was now compact and square, approximately 11′ by 11′ (much smaller than it had been during the nineteenth century).[24] A commodious kitchen dresser (or "Hoosier Cabinet," the most famous brand name) stood in one corner, with rows of open shelves alongside; a central work table faced the sink, which was to have windows above it. By 1910, even the pantry seemed an unnecessary waste of precious space, and more kitchens had efficient built-in cabinets. The "kitchenette," "dinette," and even the "pantryette" caught the public's

Figure 40. Kitchen (From Sears, Roebuck and Company's *Modern Homes*. Courtesy of the Chicago Historical Society.)

fancy as feminine diminutives of scientifically scaled-down and well-organized work places.[25] Surely here was evidence of a rational household, a modern planned home.

The Elegance of Restraint

Most American architects, builders, and popular writers on housing favored the elimination of anything that seemed superfluous ornament. For them, simplified living was not so much a return to basics, however, as a dramatic movement forward, a system of producing dwelling units and their equipment directly and efficiently. To some observers, modern habitations seemed, in turn, a means for producing rational men and women, well adapted to an advanced industrial society.

The increase in apartment living in the larger cities, quite noticeable since the decade of the 1890s, offered food for thought to advocates and opponents of the apartment. According to Robert Thompson, for instance, apartments were a clear sign that people accepted a new kind of dwelling if it simplified the tasks of daily life.[26] Consequently, as he told the many social reformers who preferred single-family houses, the only way for them to proceed was by applying to new homes the advantages of efficient planning, centralized services, improved technology, and the reduced space and ornamentation he so admired in apartments. That reaction to apartment life, whether the approval was enthusiastic or grudging, was one of the many issues that made simplification of all homes the most widely accepted trend of turn-of-the-century residential design.

In interior design, the new aesthetic of simplification was especially noticeable. American builders, the editors of popular magazines, and their respective clients and readers kept apace of the architects, for they were more certain of the effect they wanted inside the house. Everyone agreed: the "black walnut and haircloth period" of heavy furnishings was emphatically over.[27] Plain, unadorned walls of light color became popular. Painted stencils formed a border (fig. 41). Paneling, if used at all, was of the utmost simplicity; the grain of the wood (either left natural or with a slight stain) was considered sufficient display. If columns emphasized an entrance or an interior doorway, they were either Doric or Tuscan. Not only were these capitals plainer, but they could be easily turned in wood; the ornate Ionic or Corinthian capital was more expensive, since it had to be modeled in papier-mâché or composition. Stairway balustrades became almost severe, like rectilinear screens or even fences, replacing the elegant curves and carving of the earlier living hall.[28] Journals for every audience and houses in every suburb showed the signs of restraint—or at least the fashionability of restraint.

In magazine models and in actual builders' drawings, modern, built-in conveniences were specified for every room: bookshelves and cabinets, window seats and cupboards, fold-down tables, benches, and ironing boards. By 1900, these adaptations were no longer taken as the signs of economizing on space and investment. The *National Builder*, the *Ladies' Home Journal*, and *The House Beautiful* featured interiors with handsome built-in wooden furniture. They praised the efficient, economical use of space for inexpensive cottages and for elegantly modern, architect-designed estates. Beauty was now in the object of

Figure 41. "A Room in Blue Wood" by Arthur Heun. (Reprinted by permission from *House Beautiful* Magazine, ©copyright 1902 The Hearst Corporation. All rights reserved.)

daily use—the built-in medicine cabinet, the clever fold-out bench, even the plumbing fixtures[29]—rather than in the merely ornamental detail. Not all of these items remained regular features, however. By the later 1910s, as the cost of on-site construction continued to rise and the cost of manufactured furniture dropped, the only built-in fads to remain basics were closets and cupboards.

I do not, all the same, want to imply that a minimalist aesthetic became absolute for all the suburban houses built or published. The lure of the opulent and exotic became, if anything, more intense with the increasing number of household goods being brought in from the Far East, the Philippines, and Europe. The lively interest in folk art, especially textiles, also brightened up American interiors. The "Turkish corner" or "oriental box," a fad of the late 1890s, featured a canopy over a pile of pillows and fabrics, often with an intricately carved wooden screen to one side.[30] But, even in a sumptuous house, this was only one corner of an environment that had, by and large, become almost spartan in comparison to the abundant display of furnishings, art objects, and architectural ornament of the 1880s. And the oriental fad was to lose some of its opulent, slightly decadent allure by the early 1900s, when it too became plain and restrained.

A more sedate orientalism had actually intrigued Americans for some time. Japanese styles in particular fascinated artists, architects, and many consumers. The traditional Japanese house, or "Ho-o-den," that was constructed for the 1893 Chicago exposition charmed thousands of visitors. By 1903, Annie Howes Barus, a member of the University of Chicago Department of Household Administration, praised the pervasive Japanese influence in American housing. "Probably one of the greatest boons we shall get from an increasing familiarity with the habits of Asiatic life," she wrote, "will be the orientalizing of our tastes toward the standards of extreme simplicity which give the charm and aesthetic quality to Japanese home life."[31]

In another way, the romantic interest in rustic living, rugged materials, sleeping porches, and camplike architecture accentuated this appreciation of the simple life. The mood spread to furniture fashions, as well as architectural styles. The Chicago exposition had introduced new kinds of furniture into the middle-class home, redefining the appropriate kinds of objects for home, work, and recreation. Equipment for the office, especially multipurpose chairs and tables, came into the kitchen, the man's "den," and the family room. Throughout the house, furniture was lighter, more like outdoor summer equipment in wicker, rattan, or bamboo. The sturdy Mission and Craftsman furniture of oak (or stained pine), so popular in the early 1900s, was plain to the point of austerity. Collapsible camping equipment—hammocks and canvas chairs and folding tables—became fashionable even for the living room. As porches came to be a more integral part of the house, their comfortable, informal styles of decorating entered the rest of the dwelling. The parlor furniture of a decade before was criticized everywhere as being uncomfortable, ungainly, difficult to move, and unsanitary.

The same process of restraint and elimination altered the facade, although here the process was less assured. Even the colors of builders' houses became more subdued by the late 1890s. Since the time of the Chicago exposition of 1893, Beaux-Arts monuments and mansions most often had facades of white marble or limestone. Smaller buildings soon followed suit, if not in white, then in softer and subtler tints.

Builders as well as architects put aside the deep browns and variegated red bricks of the 1880s for soft ivories and buffs, pale yellows or grays, set off by some darker woodwork or golden Roman bricks, by a door painted red or shutters a vivid green. Natural brick with raked horizontal joints, thick clapboards, rough stone, stucco roughened with sand, gave the only texture.

In the houses of the 1900s, the number of projecting wings, dormers, and porches declined drastically, leaving a simple rectangular box shape, often close to a perfect cube. Rambling plans and ornament were no longer considered necessary signs of natural home life. Every part of the dwelling became quieter. A simple hip or gable, perhaps crossed once at the center, replaced the complicated roofline of the 1880s. Careful fenestration and interesting placement of a porch could provide sufficient interest to the passerby, for a demonstrative individuality no longer seemed acceptable. Windows could also be grouped at the corner of a room, giving the appearance of a bay, without the expense of having the carpenters turn several extra corners. Or they could be grouped together along a wall so that the metal edges or lead decoration in the casements created a pattern against the plain surface. All of this was simple, quiet, and unpretentious.

Making the Most of Less Space

Square-footage was cut back dramatically in these modern, simpler houses.[32] The number and size of rooms declined. Extra or single-purpose rooms such as libraries, pantries, sewing rooms, and spare bedrooms had expressed the Victorian family's sense of uniqueness and its daily pastimes. By the late 1890s, these rooms had been discarded in most new middle-class homes. By 1900 popular housing magazines usually showed only three downstairs rooms in a moderately priced house: the living room, dining room, and kitchen. Often the front hall, once a formal presentation area and a living space as well, was omitted. The stairs, in that case, would go up directly from the living room. The dining room diminished in size, a reality of economics explained as "scientific planning" based on the average size of a dining-room table. That scientific justification, in fact, was used to put forth explicit standards of size, shape, and finish, as well as use, for every room.

The second floor and above conformed to the contractions below.

Bedrooms became small alcoves, essentially for sleep and privacy, no longer receiving rooms for one's guests and children, as they had been for nineteenth-century women. The attic disappeared as the roof became flatter. Water was usually piped throughout the house from a central system of city-supplied services, rather than stored above in a cistern so that gravity could send it through the pipes. Even if there were more built-in closets, for clothes and linens upstairs as for foodstuffs and utensils below, total storage space was, in fact, dramatically reduced. In pantries and halls, spare rooms and attics, space was cut back and, at times, reduced to nothing at all.

As these rooms became smaller, their functions changed, and so too their use. Housing studies attempted to relate the reduced square-footage not only to rising construction costs but to the decline in domestic production of goods as well.[33] There were no longer places for storing away quilts and home-canned products for future use. Consumers still needed space for the goods they bought. But since the fashions were changing quickly, and faster distribution of food meant that the kitchen did not need to be stocked for long periods of use, these spaces were relatively small.

This commercial promise of freedom was true in the parlor as well. Buying goods for the home was no longer a matter of filling the front presentation rooms with artistic objects. The modern products were useful, comfortable, and replaceable. In fact, a campaign against the parlor as a useless and old-fashioned space was mounted from all sides around 1900. *Carpentry and Building* declared "The Parlor Doomed."[34] Bok launched a drive to promote the family living room over such specialized social rooms. The *Ladies' Home Journal* offered quality reproductions for the walls, furniture approved by the editor, and advice on "Good Taste vs. Bad Taste" for every purchase.[35] Stiff formality was no longer fashionable, in rooms or clothes. A dark, overstuffed, poorly ventilated room could no longer be considered healthy. A room that was seldom used meant a waste of precious household space. The multiple-purpose living room absorbed the variety of settings for entertaining of the Victorian dwelling—the parlor, living hall, sitting room, family room—into a single space.

If that single living space was smaller than the former combination of rooms, it was often as large as any single room in the presentation area of a comparably priced Victorian house. One of the principal ways in which builders, as well as architects, accommodated the reduction in square-footage for a house, and especially for its living area, was to open up the floor plan. If speculative builders were more cautious than some architects, anxious about a market that might not want too much openness between rooms, they nonetheless cut back on the number of partitions as they cut down on the number of rooms. Hodgson, in his 1905 pattern book, featured an inexpensive cottage in which all of the living space flowed around a central double-sided fireplace and staircase.[36] There were no partitions at all in the living and dining area. In other examples, only an arch or a screen separated the downstairs rooms, except for a solid wall and door to close off the kitchen. With fewer walls, houses could still seem spacious, even if they were, in fact, growing smaller.

Enforcing Aesthetic and Social Standards

Given the similarity in the demands for reform in American housing styles and in the vehement criticism of the individualized Victorian dwelling, a greater uniformity in houses of the early twentieth century was perhaps inevitable. If the plainer, smaller, more anonymous houses indeed represented an advance, then the new aesthetic should become a standard throughout the country. Since part of the appeal of the new fashion was the appearance of commonality among dwellings, then standardization should become a requirement.

More practical considerations also encouraged uniformity, of course. Standardized plans, similar handling of detailing inside and out, could, to some extent, keep down costs. A builder who erected ten or twenty houses in one development, working at the fastest pace he could organize, found scheduling easier if the individual units were fairly much alike. A large part of the appeal of standardization was that it seemed to assure more economical houses, for builders and the public. Standardization implied a modern, industrial approach to housebuilding.

Most architects, builders, and housing reformers accepted the fact of standardization. The Chicago architect Hermann Valentin von Holst strongly endorsed the trend toward "The Uniformity of Modern Floor Plans" in his 1912 pattern book of Prairie school designs, for instance. Throughout the book, floor plans were rectangular and regular, no longer featuring idiosyncratic bays, alcoves, nooks, and corners. The facades, for the most part, offered slight variations of the stucco-covered box, with a small porch here or a band of windows there to give a quiet distinctiveness. (There were a few Tudor and Colonial cottages with more fanciful ornament.) The texts accompanying the numerous $1,000–$6,000 cottages—most of them by Frank Lloyd Wright, Lawrence Buck, Robert Spencer, Joy Wheeler Dow, and Bruce Price—repeatedly stressed the need for greater standardization of facade and floor plan in the smaller house, in part for the sake of economy and, even more, for aesthetic control. One plate, to which von Holst called special attention in the preface, showed how several different facades could be erected from a single plan; another presented five "basic" three-room house plans for the modern builder.[37] In fact, many builders were already using these tactics suggested by the architects: reversing a plan or adding a porch here and there, or using several different styles of facade for identical plans. The goal, in practice as in theory, was the appearance of controlled individuality for an entire block or neighborhood.

As standardized housing became more accepted, the social implications of this architectural uniformity were often discussed. Reformers who were not designers—Jane Addams, Graham Taylor, Marion Talbot, Robert Thompson, or Charlotte Perkins Gilman, for instance—were especially eager to champion the need for common architectural standards. Such a vision of similarity would, they believed, reinforce a balanced, egalitarian social life for a community. Advice in most home magazines and pattern books reiterated the theme and added an aesthetic note: "If the unusual is emphasized in a design," warned an article in *American Homes and Gardens,* "there must be a lessening of the artistic qualities." Chicago's Radford Architectural Company estimated in one 1905 pattern book that "75–90% of the people to-day wish to build . . . economical, standardized, simplified homes."[38]

Nonetheless, there was a certain resistance to uniformity. Most architects still believed unquestioningly in the unique, custom-designed dwelling for those clients who could afford the expensive experiment. Frank Wallis praised the "leaven of sound and needed scholasticism" which now "dominated the faddish individualization of the past generation." But he had even loftier encomiums for the "brilliant group doing excellent individual work," for these architects were breaking new stylistic ground.[39] Most builders, too, still emphasized some variation in each dwelling in order to present the product to the potential buyer as a "home," and not merely a house. Even more hostile toward uniformity was the well-known city-planning authority, Charles Mulford Robinson, who spoke out strongly against the "Social Deficiencies of Standardization" in his popular guide to planning.[40] Because all people in a community are never alike, he argued, standardization of settings and of social expectations would lead to misfits and widespread maladjustment.

As with those who welcomed increased architectural uniformity, these critics assumed an inevitable relationship between the amount of variety in the environment and the possibility for differences among the residents. Thus, the debate about standardized housing centered on the need for planning in the residential suburbs, the need for more houses and people there, and the degree of social conformity that was desirable. Discussions of standardization were confrontations between those who wanted greater control of American society, represented in strict housing standards, and those who sought to guard individual freedoms and privileges, again through housing design. But that conflict had, in fact, been implcit in debates about American domestic architecture for quite some time.

The tendency toward greater similarity in house plans and facades was a visible trend in American housing design, but it was not at all an absolute fact. In and of themselves, minimalism and technological advances did not even constitute a style, much less a set of rigid guidelines. The differences between professional architects and speculative builders present one set of distinctions. In and around Chicago, the architects associated with Frank Lloyd Wright—including Robert Spencer, Charles White, Myron Hunt, Arthur Heun, Richard Schmidt, Thomas Tallmadge, William Drummond, Marion Mahoney, and Walter Burley Griffin—developed individual variations of a very particular style.[41] Their shared aesthetic was based on abstract geometric forms and "organic" decorative motifs that were sparingly placed to accentuate the volumes of the architecture. Although these concerns fit into the larger trend of simplification, their self-assured aestheticism was not the norm. Robert Spencer's 1903 house for Mary Wiekeuson of Hyde Park (fig. 42), published and praised in several architectural guides and magazines, was almost resolutely free of ornament.[42] But it projected an austerely self-conscious restraint, and not merely attention to fashionable plainness or necessary economies. The small suburban houses that Spencer, White, Tallmadge, and others in the group

Figure 42. Mary Wiekeuson House, Chicago, by Robert Spencer, 1903. (From Herbert Croly and Harry W. Desmond's *Stately Homes in America,* 1903.)

designed for clients in Oak Park or River Forest to the west of Chicago (fig. 43) were usually variations of the standard stucco box, but these

Figure 43. Mrs. Charles E. Simmons House, Oak Park, by Charles E. White, 1905. (From *Ladies' Home Journal,* 1910.)

too were always distinctive.[43] Each one gave the impression of a decidedly stylized austerity.

Builders did not, except in rare cases, organize these familiar modifications of simplicity and standardization into something approaching a clearly defined style of their own. Their boxlike versions of the Classical Revival, the arts and crafts, or even the new style of the midwestern Prairie school—which they began to imitate immediately (fig. 44)—usually proved to be more tentative as well as less refined than contemporary architects' work. While cutting back dramatically on the ornament they used, and on the unusual shape of a house, builders still tried to emphasize whatever decoration or eye-catching detail that they retained, rather than to recognize the inherent decorative possibilities of the geometric planes themselves. Their primary aim was not to create a new style; it was to cut expenses while pleasing a public that seemed to want a careful balance between uniformity and individuality.

So, while the demure, standardized dwelling of the modern minimalists dominated the housing market at every level, confusion and caution about styles remained. In fact, there were several versions of this new minimalism, and some of the styles harked back to earlier

Figure 44. House at Morgan Park. (From the *1911 Chicago Real Estate Show* catalogue. Courtesy of the Regenstein Library of the University of Chicago.)

housing history. The bungalow (see fig. 27), derived from the late-nineteenth-century American vacation home, was one popular variation on the plain, more anonymous box.[44] Its large front porch (usually running the width of the building), open living area (with tightly fitted bedrooms and a kitchen squeezed to the sides), and romantic exposed wood and brick or stone surfaces inside the house also expressed an interest in simplicity. However, this was simplicity of a poetic, romantically rusticated sort.

For many Americans, the architecture that epitomized both the new simplicity and the established traditions they hoped to preserve was the "Colonial" (fig. 45). Historical legacy, predominantly of the New England colonies, but with regional variations of Dutch Colonial, Spanish Colonial, and Mission Revival as well, lent dignity to the modern small house. Of course, the style had been a popular one since the time of the

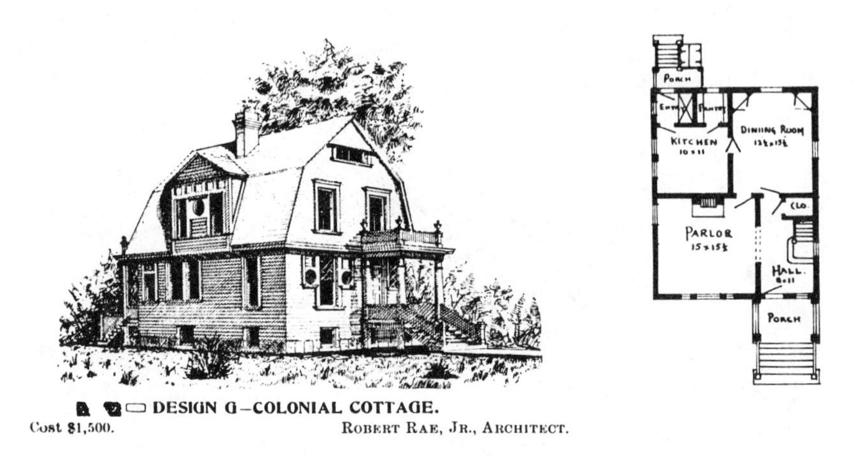

Figure 45. Colonial Revival model house by Robert Rae. (From the *National Builder,* 1897.)

Philadelphia Centennial, when the simple foursquare lines of the Georgian house became a visual inspiration to architects and to builders alike. During the depression years of the 1890s, that style gained even more popularity, for it seemed economical as well as sensible. When the hard years came to an end, the reign of the New England Colonial did not cease. Joy Wheeler Dow's articles on American architecture, collected as *American Renaissance* in 1904, documented the resurgence of neo-Georgian classicism all over the country. He stated emphatically that this kind of architecture was more conducive to a stable social order than any other style. It restrained the vulgarity of popular display which had characterized the "rabid democracy" of Andrew Jackson's presidency and the nineteenth-century builders' houses.[45] (Dow linked Jackson and the builders as political and architectural representatives of ill-bred populism.)

But when *Carpentry and Building* magazine proclaimed the "radical reversal toward old colonial principles" in 1900, the editors presented the New England houses as part of the entire country's common heritage of democratic good sense and egalitarianism.

> The people really want better art than they can get, or could get heretofore; for it is the fault of the architects themselves that we have a gingerbread architecture. The people really want a combina-

> tion of wholesome, strong, simple effects, and especially good, liveable things, with fair and moderate cost. And that is what the present generation is getting at last.[46]

By this account, the recent enthusiasm for the Colonial was a sign of the American public's stronger insistence on houses that were economical, efficient, simple, and dignified. Practicality and common sense—and not the architect's prestigious example—made the style popular. Smaller and simpler modern houses could boast a respectable democratic heritage. Consequently, they could remind Americans of traditional political and social values, as well as modern possibilities for progress.

Despite such statements of bold purpose, the loss of the nineteenth-century builder's sense of a mission, and of the building worker's pride and independence on the construction site, were all too evident in the cautious hesitancy of most of the plain styles of early twentieth-century domestic architecture. Builders neither fully abondoned old forms and arrangements nor fully accepted the innovative styles then available to them. The houses in the new suburbs and the growing cities were indeed simpler and much more similar than Victorian houses were. Yet there was still very little effort on the part of most builders to plan at a sufficiently large scale to assure either significant economy for buyers or real improvements in domestic work for the women who kept these modern houses. The styles had changed. That much was undeniable, even if it was not absolute. But the hoped-for social reforms had not arrived. As this became clear, the progressive enthusiasm for popular participation in housing design and civic reform declined.

9 EXPERT ADVICE

The average citizen will have but narrow means, and the beauty of his dwelling will be in its modest forms, its studied simplicity, its well-bred restraint; but every citizen is a shareholder in the commonwealth and by his citizenship becomes part of all that the city is, of all that the city does.

Allen B. Pond, "A Gospel of Beauty" (Lecture delivered before the Chicago Literary Club, 1909)

Many reformers of the late nineteenth century—including architects, building-trade unionists, feminists, settlement workers, and journalists—had hoped to find a new prototype for the American home, a model that would, in turn, support their larger social and political goals. Certain formal themes had been common to their visions. Throughout most of the century, individuality, self-expression, practical planning, and closeness to nature had been emphasized; then, during the 1890s, an interest in uniformity, restraint, and economy modified this exuberance. By the early twentieth century, a shared aesthetic of "studied simplicity" had made its mark. At almost every level of American society, houses were noticeably different from the late Victorian dwellings, inside and out. But what happened to the conflicting social goals that these diverse groups had attached to their architectural proposals? And how did each group respond to the widespread acceptance of the minimal house?

The metamorphosis which occurred at the turn of the century involved more than just a reformulation of the dwelling as an isolated object. There was a shift in conception, in every reform group's proposals, from the single model house to the entire model suburb. The larger scale of planning, each group claimed, necessitated a shift in policy from participation and diversity toward greater reliance on expertise and uniform "scientific standards."

The larger setting for homes entailed a new architectural perspective, and different social tactics and goals as well. It was no longer sufficient to invoke a vague image of natural diversity embracing and harmonizing all the individual homes; a well-defined plan for each dwelling, a visible order imposed over the entire neighborhood and the city itself now seemed imperative. Control of nature through social and physical sciences replaced the earlier image of harmonious natural processes. Thus, considerations of cleanliness and professional organization, together with a notion of the family as a "social product," as one author put it,[1] displaced Victorian sentiments about the isolated private family and the ethereal woman's "influence." In reality, however, the scientific imagery did not disrupt either the nuclear family or the housewife's role; it only made them seem more modern.

Since so many Americans still assumed a powerful connection between architectural setting and social life, the focus on uniformity raised larger issues, too. Those who promoted greater reliance on planning and controls insisted that architectural uniformity would reinforce social equality and shared community life. But other Americans feared that rigid architectural standards for houses would lead to social conformity and a loss of individualism.

The conflicts, it seemed, could be allayed in the suburbs, where private property would strengthen individual independence. Within an exclusively residential community of similar families, minor differences in dwelling style would not seem unplanned or disorderly. The planning provisions incorporated into the new suburbs were more specific and legalistic than the loose nineteenth-century controls of fire and health laws, vernacular traditions, and architectural fashions had been. Socially, legally, and aesthetically, the suburban community now received more attention from American architects, developers, reformers, and academics than ever before. It was the middle ground, the compromise between the crowded city and the individual homestead, between the socialistic society and the private retreat.

But agreeing upon the need for planning standards was not enough. Were the modern standards to be the popular concerns for efficiency, economy, health, and community that the progressive reformers had espoused? Or were they to be, simply, the definitions of good design put forth by the architectural profession, now spread throughout the middle-class suburbs? Or the tactics for political and social control which made the suburbs—once considered the hope of the cities—in fact only sheltered preserves for middle-class families?

Underlying these questions were issues of political power as well as aesthetic philosophies. By 1910, the progressives' argument for participatory government and design had become a part of the suburbanites' demand for autonomy from the cities. Real estate interests and middle-class residents wanted to decide themselves how their suburbs should look, how they should be run, and certainly what and who to exclude. They did not necessarily want a residential environment open to all citizens alike, a suburban solution to the nation's urban problems. As architects, builders, domestic scientists, and social scientists debated about standards for the model suburb, they sought an alliance with these suburban groups.

In any case, most reformers had shifted away from the earlier rhetoric of participation. Each group advocated objective, scientific analysis to determine the authoritative standards for community planning. And each claimed to have the needed experts in housing and family life who could manage the participation of ordinary citizens and present the best guidelines for them to follow. In the process of defining planning procedures, the various organizations of housing designers and reformers each became more professionalized. Two groups led the field. Architects found what seemed a fitting role as comprehensive planners for large metropolitan and suburban areas. And social scientists, rather than lay reformers without credentials, issued definitive statements about family patterns and community organization, and related these to design criteria. The proposals of these social and design experts seemed, certainly to the popular and the professional press, to offer the best way of organizing the cities and the suburbs for the maximum benefit of the country as a whole.

Scientific Management of the Suburbs

By 1910, dissatisfaction with the fragmented planning and diverse architecture of the nation's existing suburbs and with the competitive individualism of most suburbanites had become a familiar topic. The *Nation* railed against the tendency to extend what were, it agreed, good qualities in business—namely, experimentation and independence—into suburban domestic architecture.

> The results of this attitude toward the business of house-building everywhere confront us. Our cities and country districts are crowded with houses and villas that reflect, in endless and bizarre

> confusion, the capricious ignorance and fantastic bad taste of their owners. . . . But if the individual is not to be reached, public opinion has not yet arrived at a point where it can impose restrictions and assume authority to pass upon all plans before the builders are permitted to proceed.[2]

The need to impose some standards on the suburbs, even in democratic America, seemed overwhelmingly clear.

Many of the midwestern progressives readily accepted the premise. Frederic C. Howe, the liberal Ohio senator and an advocate of urban welfare programs, called for scientific planning to decide what should be "The American City of To-Morrow." Trained experts, he declared, could realize the earlier progressives' dream of making the "city like a home."[3] Emil Siedel, the Socialist mayor of Milwaukee, regretted that home planning was so often left to the inexperienced. City planning and home-building, he wrote in *Case and Comment,* are specialized skills which must come under collective agencies rather than disparate individual controls.[4] Over and over again, the critics evoked scientific planning, objective standards, and unbiased experts as the only recourse in solving America's urban and suburban dilemmas.

What went almost unnoticed in the so-called "City Scientific" movement, with its emphasis on municipal services and strict legislative controls, was the reorientation of reform efforts from the cities themselves to the suburbs. The problems confronting the cities, from epidemics to traction trusts, were not as severe in these outlying areas. But since so many reformers still saw the solution to urban dilemmas as an expansion of the suburbs to house more people, they extended their scientific approach to them too. Benjamin Marsh, who had organized a New York City committee to study urban congestion, became the secretary of the suburban-oriented Society to Lower Rents and Reduce Taxes on Homes in New York. Frederic Howe expanded that vision to a national goal in *The City: The Hope of Democracy:*

> Moreover, the housing problem, the greatest problem of city life, is largely dependent upon transportation. The price we are paying for bad housing, with its vice, misery, and sickness, is awful to contemplate. Unless relieved, this condition will constantly grow worse. It cannot grow better. And one of the means of relief for our huddled, herded masses is through cheap, easy transit to the open fields of the suburbs. . . . For the open fields about the city are in-

> viting occupancy, and there the homes of the future will surely be. The city proper will not remain the permanent home of the people. Population must be dispersed.[5]

Howe had gone beyond wistfully hoping that building and loan associations, together with inexpensive public transportation, would solve the urban housing problem. He wanted scientific controls to disperse the population in an efficient and orderly manner. He even imagined particular architectural criteria for these residential utopias. A "higher order of organization" for "this brick and mortar life" would come from "a unified treatment of architecture." Standardized design and minimal ornament reduced the cost of houses and thereby increased the supply of suburban homes.[6] Such ambitions could no longer be left to chance and individual taste.

Chicago reformers agreed, for the most part, with Howe's analysis. Concerned with the problems of "vast, undisciplined Chicago," as H. G. Wells characterized the city in 1906,[7] most of them now demanded systematic planning. A city planning commission, the third in the country, was established by ordinance in 1909. But even before this official act, there had been concerted efforts for greater control over building and land use. Debate centered on which standards to enforce and how extensive an area to bring under regulation. The question of the city government's authority in the suburbs, and of the urban reformer's respect there, generated special controversy.

The municipal government eagerly extended its control over all kinds of construction. In 1903 and again in 1910, the city council revised Chicago's building ordinances, setting up a department of building, headed by a mayor-appointed commissioner. (He had to be an architect, a civil engineer, or a building contractor. Efforts to avoid graft by closely regulating officials was one aspect of civil-service reform.) The new code requirements for class III, or residential buildings, reinforced the minimalist, uniform tendency in architectural styles. Fireproofing standards, stipulations on the quality of materials, special regulations governing the size and fireproofing of appendages like bay windows, porches, and skylights,[8] all these controls made construction more expensive and promoted simpler, more uniform shapes.

Under the leadership of Albert Beilfuss, the city council sought to protect "home streets" from business and industry. It authorized a special Committee on Residential Districts and passed an ordinance in 1911 limiting the right to build or convert for nonresidential purposes in a "neighborhood."[9] Thus, legislative efforts to rationalize construction techniques went hand in hand with a progressive campaign for direct democracy and local control.

Despite the shared awareness of the need for land-use regulations, the suburbs were generally reluctant to accept the municipal government's standards. This refusal was disconcerting to the reformers who wanted to improve the entire region systematically. The newly annexed territories received services to bring them up to code. City coffers opened to build sidewalks and sewer lines, to pave streets, to install gas street-lamps, and to provide fire and police protection in exchange for tax revenues and votes. But suburban communities outside the city limits resisted annexation. Their policies seemed obstinate and self-serving, for the city still provided many services for these outlying areas. The public transportation lines which crisscrossed the city aided the suburbanite who wanted to come into the downtown area to work or shop. Yet the suburbs did not provide transportation or housing at a sufficiently low cost to meet the needs of any but the middle and upper-middle classes from the cities. Suburban governments refused to sanction the city's efforts to plan at a regional level. Equally aggravating to the urban reformers, who considered their codes and regulations to be the indisputable results of unbiased research, the outlying areas did not accept that lead gladly. Instead the suburbs flouted municipal regulations governing construction. They saw control in different terms.

Attracted by lower insurance rates, more tolerant building codes, and cheap, undeveloped land, real estate development had focused on the outlying areas, rather than on the central city, for some thirty years now. Even if the suburban governments did not heed the strict municipal building ordinances, they employed definite control mechanisms. However, here the intent was primarily to decree *who* would be allowed in, rather than *how well* a building had to be constructed. Common law offered three ways to control land use: covenants; easements and profits; and "natural rights" to light, air, and access. The restrictive covenant now came into widespread use as real estate developers attempted to designate certain classes of suburbs and to emphasize the residential nature of their subdivisions. With this tool, the developer could guarantee a homeowner that other houses would be of approximately the same size, and other neighbors of the same economic and social class. As the suburbs expanded, such controls became more frequent and far-reaching. In 1913, the legislatures of Illinois, Wisconsin, and Minnesota passed laws enabling certain cities to establish strictly residential districts, at the will of the district, where manufacturing and commercial establishments would be banned. Governor Dunne of Illinois vetoed the act as unconstitutional. Yet major real estate interests and suburban lobbies in Illinois, New York, California, Massachusetts, and other larger, heavily populated states were still able to cut off any efforts to promote regional planning, diversified land use, or economic mixes of population.[10] The suburbs implied exclusion of the city's problems, both legal and social.

In the cities, the rallying cry of all reformers became that of efficiency. The way to achieve it was through rational organization and scientific standards. Municipal reform campaigns centered around hiring qualified civil servants and appointing commissions of specialists to give expert advice on government decisions at the municipal, the regional, and the national levels. (The suburbs, the progressives reasoned, would eventually recognize the superiority of this guidance.) The various clubs and organizations of the early progressive movement restructured themselves according to rational principles, often consolidating for efficiency and increased political leverage. In 1904, one such national consortium, the American League for Civic Improvement, with Charles Zueblin as its president, encouraged Chicago's varied reform organizations to follow its lead. The league took a census of Chicago organizations involved in city improvement, and found there were 342 such societies within the county limits. A civic council was immediately organized to classify the groups, promoting cooperation and, wherever possible, consolidation between them.[11]

Among the most active reform organizations and the most committed to a modern "scientific charity" approach were the Chicago City Club and the more recently founded Chicago School of Civics and Philanthropy. Julia Lathrop, Edith Abbott, and Sophonisba Breckinridge, all Hull House residents, directed this later institution, a social-work school that stressed how social science could rationalize progressive reform. The Chicago City Club was an organization of business, professional, and academic leaders who sought to reorganize municipal government. Charles Merriam, a professor of political science at the University of Chicago, ran as a reform candidate for mayor in 1911 with the club's backing.[12] Merriam ran as a Progressive, for there was now a formal political party, with specific social and political goals, which had emerged from the diverse progressive efforts of the 1890s. When the national Progressive party convention nominated Theodore Roosevelt for president in 1912, the platform would include provisions for improvements in housing, especially tenement controls and planning commissions. In each of these instances, the proposed solutions came from specialists in a particular problem who based their programs or models on highly acclaimed objective research.

By 1912, anyone eager to be systematic referred reverently to an engineer by the name of Frederick Winslow Taylor. Taylor's *Principles of Scientific Management*, a compilation of his twelve years of experiments in the steel industry, had appeared the year before. It brought about a nationwide efficiency craze. Scientific experts analyzed wasteful procedures in education, business, house-building, or homemaking, and prescribed alterations. Twentieth-century urban planners and reformers wanted to appeal to the business and middle-class suburban constituencies who were so enthusiastic about Taylor's methods. By citing scientific management procedures, they could insist that their proposals were based on objective research, not subjective opinions. One article published in *The American City* openly explained why planners should rely on statistical research. "This method of work," explained the anonymous author, "systematized, standardized, 'Taylorized,' as it is, has most decidedly proved its worth. It appeals strongly to the businessman . . . and convinced everyone that the experts have real knowledge on which to base their recommendations, and are not presenting mere dreams, pretty but impracticable."[13]

The Chicago reform clubs brought in outside experts to counsel them about their planning proposals for the modern city and its outlying suburbs. In general, the advice was to hire and appoint more experts. George B. Ford, the New York architect and housing specialist, spoke to the National Conference on City Planning when it met in Chicago in 1913. He called for statistical surveys and standardized aesthetic controls. Competitions limited to a few of the best designers, he told his audience, would assure a high quality of residential architecture and provide just the needed amount of individuality.[14] In 1909, Benjamin Marsh spoke to the Chicago City Club on "City Planning in Justice to the Working Population." He called for the city to follow the German approach to planning, exemplified by Frankfort on the Main, by standardized living conditions at the highest level of social and aesthetic amenity. Current American practices, Marsh claimed, took the lowest acceptable conditions and made them uniform for an entire city.[15]

The advice was abstract, but George E. Hooker, secretary of the club, decided to investigate Marsh's model. In 1910, he went to the Berlin City Planning Exhibit and toured the German cities. He returned determined to organize an American exhibit on housing for the city and the suburb. Hooker wanted that conference to be in the West, even though he considered his own part of the country to be even farther behind European city-planning trends than New York (where Marsh had organized exhibits in 1909 and 1910). Yet Chicago and the surrounding cities of the Midwest had, Hooker believed, particular problems and innovative planners to solve them.[16]

It would take several years for the City Club housing exhibit to materialize, but during that time Chicago's architects and reformers learned more about what a scientific approach to planning might entail. In fact, demands for scientific expertise in city planning were one aspect of a transformation taking place in the progressive movement as a whole. By 1910, talk of community centered around the efficient, well-organized plan, rather than around grass-roots participation in civic life. The emphasis was still on improvements, and particularly on housing, but now the guidelines would come from objective experts.

Most progressives did modify their attraction to scientific techniques by continuing to pay homage to universal principles of art and social organization. These laws, too, were laid down by experts, notably architects and academic social scientists. The goal was a synthesis of art and science, using statistics and abstract principles of beauty or social order to plan homes and government, streetcar routes and budget allocations. Even if Burnham's master plan for Chicago gave far more weight to the aesthetic factor, ignoring funding for social surveys carried out by planners (such as those of George Ford or Frederick L. Olmsted, Jr., for Newark, New Haven, Pittsburgh, New York, and other cities), there were minor proposals for analyzing Chicago's environment and the city's needs.

A few Chicagoans, although endorsing the common vision of an orderly plan for urban and suburban development, expressed strong opposition to the standardized, centralized planning schemes that were now emerging. The landscape architect Jens Jensen was one of these. As chairman of the City Planning Committee of the Chicago City Club,

Jensen wanted to encourage some degree of centralized urban planning. But he also wanted clear limits on that control. He was critical of grandiose "City Beautiful" plans wherever they might be applied, but especially in the suburbs. An associate of Frank Lloyd Wright and the Prairie school architects, Jensen envisioned a suburban city that preserved some sense of individual detail and diversity within the larger whole. In 1911, writing for *The Survey* (a professional social-work journal which had developed from Graham Taylor's *Charities and the Commons*), Jensen criticized the "show city" of Burnham and the City Beautiful planners as inhuman, imperialistic, and undemocratic. His contention was: "The more formality in design, the less democracy in its feeling and tendency." A city should be based, he continued, not on commercial benefits but on ideal homes. "The American home is the foundation upon which the world's greatest democracy rests. . . . A city should first of all, then, be homelike."[17]

Yet even Jensen believed that the best way to achieve "ideal homes" was through a system of legal regulations and the advice of unbiased experts. He called for a municipal department of civics, "consisting of the best talent in art and science."[18] That department would see to utilitarian planning matters, such as the width and layout of streets. It would also organize neighborhoods, first by its power to approve new subdivisions, and even more tellingly by its commitment to create neighborhood centers based around schools, churches, settlement houses, clubs, and—an usual proposal for the time—workplaces. Not only offices but factories, too, would be integrated into Jensen's model neighborhoods in order to make work life more pleasant and home life more wholesome for all classes in the ideal society. Not even the suburbs could be exclusively residential, he reasoned, if real community were to evolve there.

The concept of the neighborhood, the ideal community of homes, was the basis for most progressive planning visions of the early twentieth century. Social reformers extolled neighborhood organizations and improvement societies as the link to past small-town community and as the forum for modern urban politics. Jane Addams, Mary McDowell, and Graham Taylor saw their settlement houses as institutions designed to restructure local groups, respecting the diverse ethnic traditions in the immigrant communities while they remolded those populations—Americanizing, socializing, and Christianizing the most promising individuals.[19] The university-based reformers had similar sentiments. At the University of Chicago, John Dewey, George Vincent, W. I. Thomas, Charles Merriam, Marion Talbot, Sophonisba Breckinridge, Grace Abbott, and perhaps most of all the new group of urban sociologists beginning with Robert Park, all endorsed a "new parochialism," based on the "immediate community."[20] They took their theories from the work of the German sociologist Ferdinand Tönnies and the Americans Edward A. Ross, Charles Cooley, and Simon N. Patten. As Ross had explained the emerging understanding of community functions, only art in the service of "the social garden" could remedy the erosion of *Gemeinschaft*.[21] And only "centralized administration by experts," specifically sociologists, could successfully direct this social experiment in community-making.[22]

Academics and nonacademics alike shared similar principles of modern neighborhood planning. To Jane Addams, George Hooker, or Frank Lloyd Wright, as to Charles Cooley or Charles Merriam, the complexities of the modern city required that academics and architects, politicians and planners, observe how people really lived in groups; then they would redirect these basic patterns to achieve a more balanced, moral society. For both these groups, research about social community now focused as often on middle-class suburbanites as on working-class people in the city. Studies of ethnic communities in the inner cities continued to appear, of course, notably the *Hull-House Maps and Papers* and Thomas and Znaniecki's classic analysis of the Polish peasant.[23] But more and more academic and social reformers now concentrated on the organization of community in the suburbs, rather than on applied social science in the city. Suburban life was considered the norm for human behavior. Hooker, for instance, was adamant about the need to document the movement of industries to areas outside the crowded urban center. He believed such a study would promote the trend by demonstrating the economic advantages to industry. This, in turn, he felt sure, would multiply the working-class housing available in the suburbs, by increasing the demand. Graham R. Taylor, a second-generation Chicago reformer, concurred, and in his *Satellite Cities* trumpeted the advantages of suburban industry.[24]

The Woman's City Club of Chicago also concentrated on well-planned suburban solutions to urban problems. As one member wrote, "'Womanly Activities'" were their principal concern: "The keeping clean of the city, the consideration of public health, the welfare of children and the inspection of schools and playgrounds."[25] Although most members of the club lived within the city limits, they looked outside its boundaries for models of good community planning. Favorite comparisons in their educational campaigns were contrasts between American cities and the planned cities of England and Germany, and between Chicago and its suburbs.

Harriet Park Thomas, wife of the sociologist, and Anna E.Nicholes, the club's civic director, planned a City Welfare Exhibit in 1913 to encourage better planning in and around Chicago. They designed posters which encouraged greater participation in government, especially for women, and also stressed the need for stronger controls over every public service, from garbage collection to school curricula (fig. 46). Several of the displays explained the benefits of centralized community-planning experiments in Germany. This show of city planning progress reached ninety thousand people in Chicago, and then traveled to Portland and Pittsburgh.[26] The message in the displays was clearly stated. Improvements in housing—and therefore, the posters pointed out, in sound family life as well—had to come from cooperation between citizens' groups and planning experts, a unity of art and science, and integration of city and suburb.

One of the most important Chicago institutions to take up the crusade of modern planning was the Municipal Museum, founded in 1904 by the Commercial Club and the City Homes Association. Today the concept of a municipal or social museum may sound strange, but such organizations appeared alongside the great art and science museums of the City Beautiful movement. During the first two decades of the twentieth century, reformers and philanthropic industrialists in Berlin and Paris, at Harvard and Chicago, saw these museums as a way to spread the latest ideas on city planning, health, housing, labor relations, and community life. Charles Zueblin, as president of the American League for Civic Improvement, had first suggested the Chicago organization in 1901. In a speech that year, he insisted that "we can not live happily in an environment of smoke, hideousness of home architecture and decoration, and dearth of nature, recreation and elevating occupation, the products of unrelieved commercialism."[27]

An inspiration for remedying those problems, in his opinion, would be a huge public display of city planning progress. The first installment was the "Model Street" which Zueblin proposed for the upcoming Louisiana Purchase Exposition at St. Louis. The Philadelphia architect Albert Kelsey, who had recently completed a major renovation of the

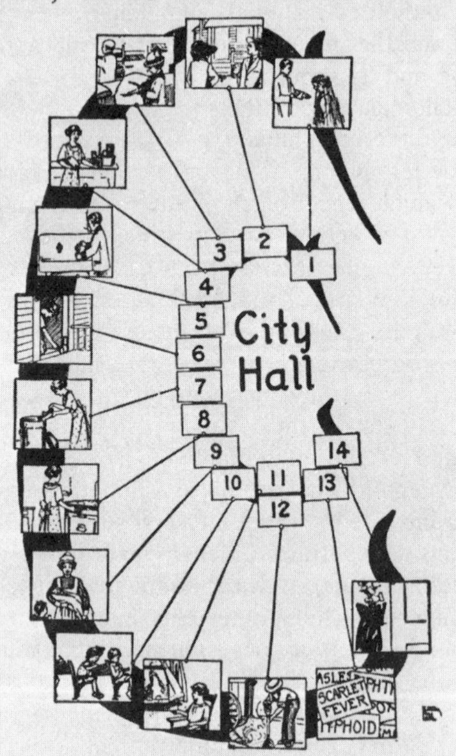

Figure 46. Poster from the Woman's City Club Housing Exhibition of 1913. (From *The Woman Citizen's Library,* vol. 19.)

Chautauqua, New York, summer settlement, carried out the project with the backing of organizations like the Chicago Commercial Club. When the fair closed, Zueblin had already drawn up plans for this "object lesson" in city planning, together with all the exhibits and brochures on urban issues from the fair, to be brought together in a permanent display of city life and progress. This was Chicago's Municipal Museum.

Howard Van Doren Shaw, a traditional stylist, found the calm, reassuringly familiar Colonial Revival lines of Kelsey's buildings from the St. Louis fair to be his idea of a suburban model. He became a member of the board of the Municipal Museum, specializing in housing exhibits, serving along with Zueblin, Jane Addams, George Vincent, George Hooker, and Mayor Edward Dunne. Over the next ten years, the group sponsored eleven exhibits, most of them at the city's public library. There were eighty-four conferences and five hundred free lectures in conjunction with the exhibits, carrying information to the suburban neighborhoods. The subjects ranged from park and city planning principles to lively debates about the effect of housing on tuberculosis rates and the role of domestic science in housing reform. The topics included almost every major reform cause of the period, from orderly municipal government to public health, tidy kitchens to majestic civic centers.[28]

As much as any other local organization of the time, the Municipal Museum bridged professional and political barriers, bringing together conservative architects with innovators, academic radicals with businessmen. More than any other consortium of reform interests, it was dedicated to environmental change as the way to effect lasting social and political progress. Housing received as much attention as other more public, collective aspects of urban life. The home and the city were viewed as microcosm and macrocosm, sharing the same aesthetic principles and facing the same problems at different scales.

A Modern Basis for Reform

Many reformers tried to uphold the earlier progressives' ideal of a city plan based on domestic virtues. They also incorporated a more rationalized approach to their jobs that was drawn from scientific management. Walter D. Moody, a propagandist for the Burnham plan, wrote in his manual for the city's schoolchildren (and their parents):

> As our city is only our larger home, to decide what is the great thing we are to do for Chicago we can take a lesson from facts familiar to us in our homes. Each of us knows that at home the first step to economy is good order. We know, from observation, that the wasteful household is the one in which the furniture is always disarranged and in which the rooms are untidy. We know that waste and extravagance in the home goes hand in hand with disorder. Imagine how time and effort would be wasted in our homes if things constantly used about the stove in the kitchen should be stored in the front hall, if pianos should be permitted to obstruct narrow hallways, if our iceboxes should be kept in attics and our dining tables in the sleeping apartments.[29]

In the city plan, the factory plan, or the house plan, the principles for order and improvement were supposedly identical. City planners used homey references to compartmentalization in order to make their larger zoning proposals seem more acceptable and familiar; home economists spoke of the need for scientific housework procedures and architectural standards, determined by unbiased research, to justify their own authority. The leaders of many different groups now relied on a shared language of efficiency and expert guidance. These principles supposedly determined the form of the model city and suburb.

Even the arts and crafts enthusiasts took up the banner. Oscar Lovell Triggs, for instance, had praised a Morgan Park improvement association as a model social institution as early as 1903. The town, he explained to readers of *The Chautauquan,* "is perhaps the most democratic of American political institutions."[30] The individual improvement society combined aesthetic education with suburban home rule. Local professional people—who understood the principles of modern management—oversaw everything here. The perfect place to realize the arts and crafts ideals was, not surprisingly, the suburbs rather than the workplace. Triggs and other local leaders of the movement now openly condemned the building unions, despite the fact that the two groups supposedly stood for similar principles—general education, preservation of handicraft skills, beneficent industrialization with respect for the artisan. As Triggs wrote, somewhat opaquely, "The union which has been effected in the labor world is in like manner [comparing it to the business corporation or trust] superficial and partial. . . . Combination is the order of the day; but the union of the conflicting elements with the public has yet to take place."[31] The major obstacle to such unity, according to the suburban reformers, was class. By this, they meant that workers had not yet learned to appreciate middle-class values. The building tradesmen should be the willing recipients of their benefactors' good taste, Triggs insisted, not the instigators of political change. The arts and crafts movement belonged in the suburban classroom and the community center, not on the urban construction site.

By 1910, the American arts and crafts movement's refusal to take the role of a political force even vaguely reminiscent of its English antecedents had become obvious. Furthermore, the leaders could no longer sustain their earlier promise that a minimalist aesthetic could make good houses available to every family. Stickley had been forced to admit that he had never built any of the houses which appeared in his magazine. More important, they would probably cost about twice as much as he had claimed.[32] The major repercussion of this admission (other than the eventual failure of *The Craftsman* and Stickley's empire) was a further loss of faith in a populist solution to something as complex as housing. The arts and crafts remained a decorative fashion, a way of personalizing simplified, minimal dwellings with folk art. But it was merely a suburban fad now. It was obvious now that the Craftsman style of rough-hewn natural materials for homes offered simply an illusion of simplicity and economy.

The building trades, after the debilitating strike and lockout of 1900, faced head-on the demise of their crafts and of their autonomy. The builders were now considered the experts at suburban development, and the workers as troublesome drones. By 1910, not only the contractors but many of the union leaders as well had been won over the the builders' side. Union management, now openly affiliated with the political bosses and major developers, accepted specialization and standardization—as well as large sums of money—in exchange for the prevention of sympathy strikes. Even journals like Hodgson's *National Builder* dropped their educational campaigns. The advertisements for correspondence courses no longer promoted general knowledge; the new promise was instant expertise in a specialized field for those with little schooling. Articles and editorials in formerly progressive magazines were perfunctory accounts of the latest materials and unimaginative presentations of basic techniques, rather than the social tracts they once had been. The reform impetus, the pride in craftsmanship, the call for those who produced houses to make sure they were of good quality and still inexpensive, all these higher goals had disappeared.

The most telling evidence of this change in attitude is the way the construction unions and building press accepted the scientific management routines first laid out by the New York contractor Frank Gilbreth. Taylor himself praised Gilbreth's *Bricklaying System* (1907) as an excellent example of the first principle of scientific management: decision-making should be separated from manual work. One of the favored slogans of Taylorism was "the substitution of science for rule of thumb," which obviously meant, in this case, that the contractor or builder should make the decisions a skilled carpenter, mason, or plumber had once assumed were his. The building-trades press did not, as it once had done, try to analyze and combat such efforts to define and demean construction work. Hodgson recommended Gilbreth's books to his readers so that they might become more efficient workers.[33]

Other journals on the home and family were changing their image and their content too. No longer did *The House Beautiful* or *The Craftsman* present simplified, economical houses, designed or at least modified by their owners, as the soundest basis for American domestic architecture. In fact, Stone moved his journal to New York City in 1911, and then resigned two years later, leaving Virginia Robie as editor. Robie, who had studied art and decoration, had long been the magazine's associate editor. But she did not have the political goals or even the literary appreciation of her predecessor. Under her, *The House Beautiful* published a chatty series of articles on small-house planning by the Chicago architect Charles E. White, Jr., illustrations of work by Prairie school architects, and extensive coverage of the English garden city movement. But it no longer published examples of houses or community buildings designed by those who used them. Instead there was expert advice on home decoration and gardening, garages, and the latest domestic appliances. Here again was the formula for the modern home: "science with art builds therein temples to the Ideal."[34]

These women's magazines had become conservative and proper, usually abandoning their earlier campaigns for community development and jobs for women. The positions had been reversed; now it was architects and professional reformers who spoke of community planning. The abrupt change in the message of these journals signaled a reorientation in the women's movement itself. Although the liberal home-economics teachers and women's magazine writers had tried to address the housing and the family life of a diverse range of groups, their assumption that improving the home environment would bring about major social change had proven unfounded.

Now the leaders of the various women's reform organizations advocated "managed participation" rather than direct popular participation in home and family-related issues. Enthusiasm about participating in housing reform campaigns declined sharply. Feminists turned toward the suffrage movement as their greatest hope, and in 1913 Illinois women won the limited right to vote. The Woman's City Club turned its attention from city planning and housing to women's education in government procedure. A campaign overseen by Jane Addams prepared women for their new role as citizens with ballots. But the role of the intelligent voter did not prove to be sustaining. Within a few years, as the club's biographer pointed out, a passive and disillusioned spirit replaced the earlier vigor.[35] And in other organizations, too, women reformers also turned toward legislation and more "scientific" or professional systems to solve the social problems which concerned them. However, those women who were volunteers in agencies often found their positions usurped by trained professionals as the drive for rational organization and expert management ousted the earlier participatory tactics of one movement after another.

In every field, from nursing to kindergarten teaching and social work, the process was the same. Training and a professional approach were considered the prerequisites for competent work. Even in the interior decoration of the average home there was a greater reliance on the new spirit of expertise. In Chicago, Alice E. Neale, Edith W. Sheridan, and Ida J. Burgess carried on the campaign Candace Wheeler and Elsie de Wolfe had launched in New York. Theirs was a profession, they claimed, not a mere talent. As Wheeler wrote, insisting on the need for trained interior design experts, "What will save woman from the 1001 mistakes of inexperience . . . the results of laws she has never studied?"[36]

Trends in home economics after 1910 presented another indication of the declining interest in popular participation and the rise of expertise in every aspect of home planning. The Chicago leaders of the home economics movement never endorsed outright the national trend toward scientific management and absolute standards for every home. Yet this had become the prevailing model in every women's magazine and in countless books on the home by the end of the first decade of the new century. New leaders had come into the movement now. The most prominent were Christine Frederick of Greenlawn, Long Island, and Mary Pattison of Colonia, New Jersey. Both of these housewives had recently declared themselves domestic scientists. As "Household Efficiency Experts," they appraised domestic architecture and furnishings, housework and family life by rigid and simplistic standards of efficiency drawn directly from experiments in industrial production. They developed their guidelines in their own suburban kitchens, which had been transformed into scientific laboratories or "household efficiency stations." Frederick in particular portrayed the housewife as a well-trained, conscientious worker who studied the management techniques of home organization in her tiny kitchen "office" corner.

Neither Frederick nor Pattison discussed the home as a social setting for the family or as a social cause for the reformer. According to these domestic scientists, the individual house was an isolated workplace. Here the housewife could exercise absolute control over her "professional" duties as "home administrator." Guidance for housewives came from books with businesslike titles: Frederick's *The New Housekeeping: Efficiency Studies in Home Management* (1912) and *Household Engineering: Scientific Management in the Home* (1915), Pattison's *The Principles of Domestic Engineering* (1915) and *The Business of Home Management* (1918).[37] References to Frederick Winslow Taylor were conspicious. In fact, the prophet himself even wrote the foreword to Pattison's first book. He compared her work on the home to Newton's *Principia* and Darwin's *The Origin of Species,* promising that "this new branch of engineering will do almost as much for mankind."[38]

The home economics movement as a whole had accepted scientific management by this time even though the acceptance was a reluctant one for some. Women's clubs had taken up the crusade for exacting standards of housekeeping. Most home economics departments had moved in that direction. At times, the new domestic scientists explicitly endorsed standardization, as when Frederick explained how uniform floor-plans would help the expert determine the "one best way" to proceed with dusting any house.[39] In general, metaphors of functionalism became ever more popular, rather than actual attempts to influence housing design. The dwelling, and especially its shiny white kitchen, was likened to the "domestic factory," the "laboratory," the "surgery."

The functionalist aesthetic was not derived from a consideration of the housewife's needs and experiences, but from the study of abstract models of efficiency and quite inappropriate conceptions of a productive factory setting. The domestic scientists wanted to produce trained workers who would operate smooth-running machines according to the precise instructions of the managers. Their expectations necessarily meant that housework would consume more of the woman's time and effort, as she struggled to keep up to the ever rising standards.[40] The semblance of modern functional planning became an end in itself. Few people stopped to inquire whose needs were actually being met in this arrangement.

Business Methods and Professional Propriety

How did American architects respond to the standardization proposed by reformers and domestic scientists? Most of them continued to criticize the variety of styles in the preceding decades as bastardized architecture, a pastiche of senseless ornament totally lacking in the fundamentals of good design, and ignored the popular campaigns for simplification and standardization on every side. Some architects wanted styles of impeccable historical accuracy; others, a new set of forms based on modern concepts of functionalism and abstract beauty. In Europe, Hermann Muthesius staunchly defended standardization as the direction for the profession to pursue in the twentieth century, but most American architects still balked at the idea that their designs should be mass-produced. Burnham, Maher, Sullivan, the Ponds, and numerous others worried about a loss of originality and therefore, they feared, of professional integrity. To be sure, Frank Lloyd Wright's 1901 speech on "The Art and Craft of the Machine" had endorsed the architect's tackling mass production, and he, along with Irving Gill and Frederick Ackerman, had carried this belief into practice.[41] But the architectural press and the schools remained suspicious and distant.

A few architects were aware that their profession viewed building production from a favored vantage. As Robert Spencer wrote in 1905, "But the schools [of architecture] do not teach economy of planning in the sense of cheap building. Their students are not hampered by limitations of cost, and their architectural flights are not hampered by considerations of mere dollars and cents."[42] Later, he expressed regret that so many architects considered themselves above mere house-building, and urged others to follow the lead of "the younger fellows in the big cities . . . looking for new suggestions, both practical and aesthetic, for new ideas, or for old ideas embodied in new and improved forms."[43]

But Spencer was something of an anomaly, ill at ease in a more specialized profession that was now optimistic with more prosperous times and bountiful clients. Office staffs grew ever larger, and business methods became the accepted way to organize the stages of production. As Herbert Croly, the editor of the *Architectural Record,* lamented, "The office of a prosperous architect is organized like any other business concern, particularly for the purpose of turning out in a manner satisfactory to their clients the designs of very many, too many buildings."[44] The Prairie school architect Charles White confided to Walter Willcox, a Seattle colleague, that he welcomed the business approach as the best and most interesting way to preserve the profession. He connected his attraction to the larger, more specialized firm with a desire to "broaden out, and get something besides dwellings." Residential and nonresidential design remained the strongest differentiation in the profession, at every scale of office. Furthermore, viewing themselves as businessmen with corporate clients, few architects were enthusiastic about exchanging ideas with the general public. White would continue to write popular magazine articles, but this was only, he confided to his friend, in order to supplement his income. His articles often eulogized the intelligent contractor, architect, or client who recognized the value of a rationalized, large-scale organization of production.[45]

Many architects quickly passed over the daring styles which had become available in the first decade of the twentieth century. Even some of the former innovators among the midwestern advocates of modernism now charted different courses. White and other colleagues turned toward simple, proper Colonial Revival houses around 1910, not only for clients but for their own families too. Spencer took up the Tudor Revival with enormous enthusiasm. Other Prairie school architects—Tallmadge and Watson, Eben E. Roberts, Richard Schmidt, and Hugh Garden—became more restrained in their designs and turned more often to nonresidential projects. The avant-garde itself eventually declined in influence. Wright left for Europe in 1909, placing the far more conservative designer Hermann von Holst in charge of his office. Similarly, in California, the Greene brothers and then Irving Gill eventually lost their upper-middle-class clients and the backing of the professional journals.

This turning away from radical forms was quite visible. H. Allen Brooks blamed it on the rising influence of middle-class women as they won greater access to jobs and suffrage rights; he claimed that these women, innately drawn toward more conservative historical architectural styles, were then able to have a stronger say in the choice of an architect for their family's house.[46] As we have seen, it was just these women, during the previous two decades, who had sponsored the modern simplified aesthetic for houses. They had connected the social reforms they sought to a more efficient and standardized model dwelling. The fact was not so much that clients were changing as that a shift was occurring in professional roles.

One of the clearest statements of the twentieth-century role for the architect, and for other American professionals as well, came from Herbert Croly. Between 1900 and 1909, he edited the *Architectural Record* and wrote several books on domestic architecture. Like so many others, when Croly examined the American built environment, relating what he saw to social conditions, he was dismayed with the evidence of chaos and disorder. He acknowledged the general concern with environmental issues that had motivated popular reform efforts, and recognized that the 1890s had been a pivotal decade. During this decade, he wrote, "Americans began to realize that their stock of buildings of all kinds was inadequate, or superannuated. Increased volume of business, improved standards of living, higher aesthetic ideals all demanded more buildings, in some cases larger buildings, and buildings of a different type."[47] However, the situation, in his eyes, had generated a hodgepodge of unrelated organizations and unseemly architecture.

To Croly, as to many others, the house remained the principal architectural means for social and aesthetic reform. In 1902, he wrote, "The suburban dwelling really interests more Americans than any other architectural product."[48] That generalized interest—evident in amateur dabblings in design, political reform campaigns, civic organizations, and occasional professional attention to models for moderate-cost houses—was certainly commendable. But the diversity of efforts also explained, in part, why national environmental reform, including better housing prototypes, had been so slow in coming.

Although Croly praised reform as a truly American tradition, he faulted the current means for trying to effect improvements. Too many diverse groups that lacked proper training were attempting to bring about social reform through environmental tactics. Moreover, the professional architects who did have the training to carry out experimental reform were dissipating their talents in too many small and scattered projects. Architects, he wrote again and again, should not limit themselves to minor and insignificant efforts to improve the environment. These could only produce buildings constrained by low budgets and uneducated, unaesthetic clients. Instead, professional architects should recognize the opportunities available to them by working for wealthy clients. Here they could experiment freely and discover modern forms, unrestrained by lack of funds or cautious taste. They could develop the principles for an architectural reform of the highest, universal order. Then, as the profession evolved a set of styles appropriate to the modern age and society, that architecture could be handed down to ordinary builders and middle-class clients. Then, and only then, a standardization of good design, a "nationalization of taste," could emerge.[49]

Croly's position on standardization was obviously an ambivalent one. He insisted on the need for experimentation, but only among the educated few, the experts. He wanted to see their ideas become a "nationalized" norm shared by everyone in the country. But in minor projects, a good architect's work was compromised and a bad designer's worst tastes were given free rein. Croly remained adamant about the need for professionally educated architects to remove themselves from the fray in order to work for the eventual improvement of the larger public environment and the national good.

Croly's model for the architect was intended to be used for other professions, too. In *The Promise of American Life*, published in 1909, while Croly was still editor of the *Record*, he extended the principles originally evolved for architects to defend a general philosophy of reform.[50] Centralization and strong governmental guidance from able leaders were critical to future progress. As he had done in architecture, Croly criticized piecemeal reform and unruly participation by the general public in social reform and politics. He claimed that government, like architecture, was the responsibility of those who had been designated true leaders. And it was the duty of these leaders, believing in a better society for all, to accept positions of authority. Croly's political philosophy, based on centralized organization, professional expertise, and scientific planning, stirred the country's major political leaders of the pre–World War I years. It offered a basis for Theodore Roosevelt's "New Nationalism" and later for some of Woodrow Wilson's wartime programs. The influence of his work on these political figures is a sign of the sudden turning toward expertise, rather than direct participation, in the progressive movement after 1910. Croly achieved this philosophy by considering the problems of professional identity and social responsibility affecting the twentieth-century American architect.

Croly's approach was an appealing one for the socially conscious architect. Specialization and large-scale projects did become far more common than they had been in the late nineteenth century, although architects, especially if they were working for any of the numerous small firms still in existence, continued to take on a variety of small projects. A reorientation of professional attitudes about housing and planning was quite evident. Croly's description of aesthetic reform filtering down from the top assuaged some consciences. His espousal of large-scale projects, in which the architect received his due respect as an expert, made these undertakings the preferred way to plan for the greater social good.

The architect was now more likely to design model communities of housing units as well as individual houses. The dwellings in these community plans were, as Croly had recommended, usually quite similar, and almost certainly of a uniform style. Attempts to improve society by environmental change still focused on housing, but the attention of the designer had shifted to the arrangement of units in a group: model apartments and tenements, bungalow courts, row houses, entire suburban developments, or at least large sections of such large projects. The Pond brothers in Chicago, Ernest Flagg in New York, A. Page Brown in San Francisco, and others designed apartment houses for moderate-income families, or occasionally working-class projects. In Los Angeles and nearby Pasadena, Arthur S. Heineman led the way in arranging bungalows in courts where community buildings would often be shared among the residents. The *National Builder*'s Fred Hodgson, fascinated with this California aesthetic, reproduced several of these courts, and the model spread through the Midwest, too.[51] Even in well-to-do suburbs, planning was more evident. Howard Van Doren Shaw's many houses in Lake Forest, north of Chicago, were sedate and decorous dwellings in English revival styles that fit gracefully with the earlier, mid-nineteenth-century dwellings. Croly, in fact, found Shaw's work exemplary for the reform-minded architect: his designs epitomized professional restraint and insight, the mark of "a national tradition, which is profoundly influenced by local conditions, while by no means divorced from a necessary and fruitful debt to the better domestic architecture of the past."[52]

Architects continued to debate issues of style and form, but most of them saw the dwelling, especially the moderate-cost dwelling, as something given, both in its social and technological aspects and, for many, in its formal aspects too. Now the challenge was in the arrangement of these units. Trained architects possessed the design expertise that was needed in planning residential communities.

Architects, and builders too, planned entire suburban developments according to precise aesthetic standards, aiming to control what Croly often disparaged as the evidence of an eclectic or disorderly amateurism. The more traditional stylists imposed a clear aesthetic formula. Even the architectural innovators like Wright, who had returned to Chicago, or William Gray Purcell and George Grant Elmslie in the Midwest, Henry Wright in St. Louis, or Irving Gill in California, worked within a definite stylistic range, often planning groups of dwellings as a unit. Walter Burley Griffin's subdivisions of the 1910s drew from the superblock planning of the English garden cities and from Beaux-Arts principles. The Wilder subdivision in Elmhurst and the Harvey subdivision in West Chicago had communal land set aside, to be shared by all the families in the groups of row houses and single-family dwellings. The designs followed firm guidelines to give a strong sense of architectural and social harmony. In Griffin's other community design projects of this period—notably the Trier Center Neighborhood in Winnetka (fig. 47), Clark's resubdivision in Grinnell, Iowa and Beverly Hills near Chicago—the common space was only implied, but the architectural style was nonetheless strongly controlled.[53]

Interest in planning became so widespread that some architects could claim that it was a priority for their profession. As Robert Spencer told the Chicago City Club in 1913, commenting upon the recent National Conference on Housing, the architects who had attended the conference had been disappointed at the lack of attention to

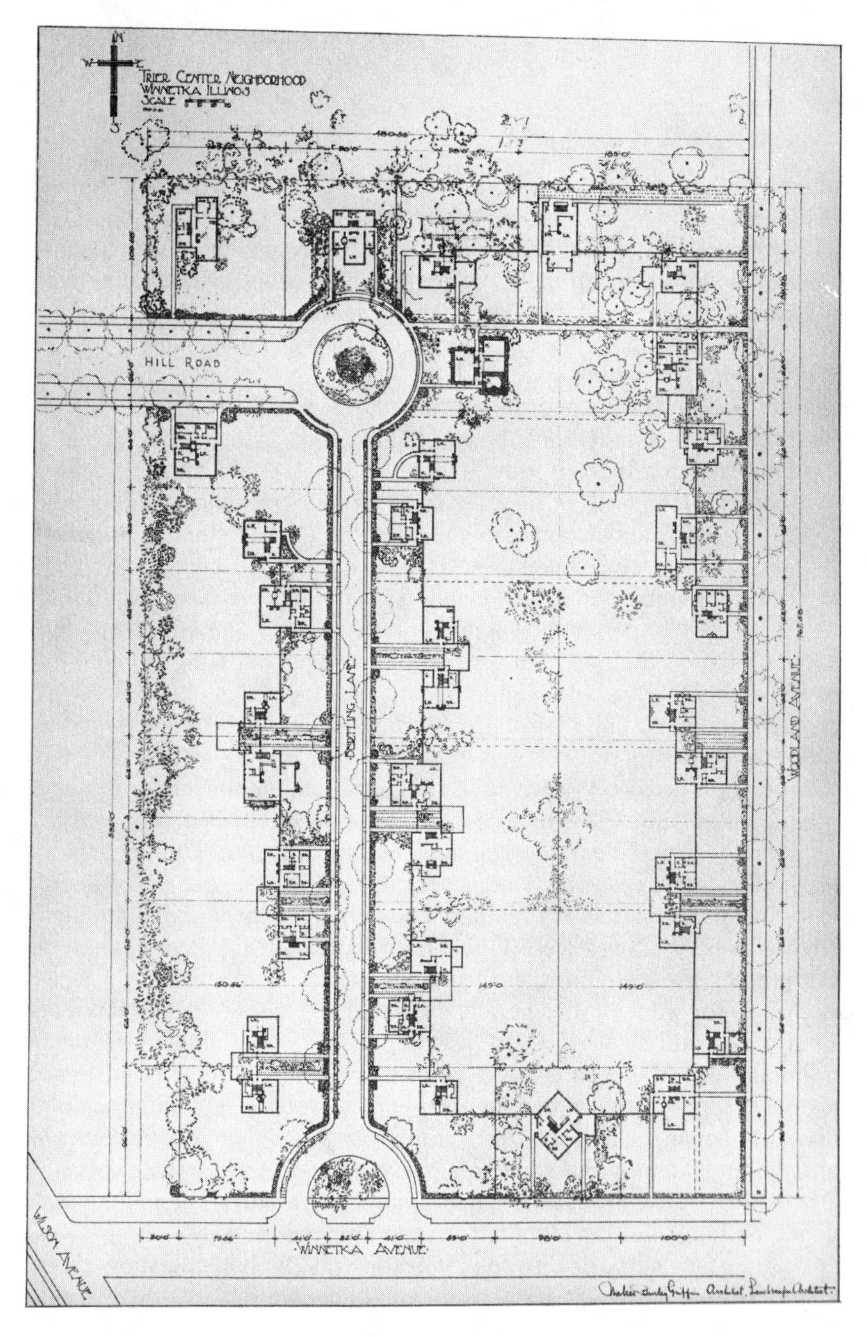

Figure 47. Site plan for the Trier Center Neighborhood, a planned development of thirty-five fireproof cottages at Winnetka, by Walter Burley Griffin, 1913. (From *Western Architect*, 1913.)

"the subjects of subdivision and neighborhood planning," which had become the profession's primary concerns.[54]

The best of the builders had already begun to plan at a large neighborhood scale, although many smaller builders continued to practice on a piecemeal basis. A few large developers now hired architects to design their basic model houses and help with the site planning, hoping to attract more customers with quality design. As with the architect's move into popular domestic literature in 1895, this marked another threshold. Here, too, it would be essential that the architectural profession clearly demarcate its own degree of involvement in large-scale developments, as well as its special areas of expertise outside such projects. Griffin, for instance, worked for the Chicago builder Russell L. Blount on several speculatively built houses in Beverly. At the same time, he perfected his Beaux-Arts planning skills and eventually left the country to oversee his winning entry in the competition for the design of Canberra, Australia, in 1912. By the early 1920s, the collaboration of developers with well-known architects in the totally planned upper-middle-class suburbs of Houston, Cleveland, Kansas City, and other large cities would become quite common.

To be sure, architects continued to design unique houses for upper-middle-class clients. This remained the basis of their residential work. They also designed custom dwellings for less well-to-do families when they had an interesting client, or simply needed another project to keep the office going. However, it had become quite acceptable for architects to take on community plans, either for actual developers or, with greater prestige, for reform organizations' competitions. These were plans for what were generally conceived as middle-class, or occasionally as a mix of middle- and working-class communities. The professional reformers emphasized that trained architects, rather than amateurs, should take on the planning of model suburbs. Similarly, the architects began to look to other professionals for "scientific" standards of site planning and social organization. Together, these experts, with their models for modern suburban communities, hoped to influence builders and developers.

An important mark of this collaboration was the housing show that George Hooker organized after his trip to Berlin in 1910. The City Club, aided by the Woman's Club, the Woman's City Club, the Chicago School of Civics and Philanthropy, and other local organizations, opened its exhibition in March of 1913. Posters and displays documented existing housing conditions in Chicago and innovative approaches to city planning in Europe. The favored examples were the English garden city of Letchworth, the planned corporate towns of Bourneville and Port Sunlight, and the German cities of Frankfort on the Main and Ulm, where the municipal government controlled land speculation and enforced high standards of housing construction. The Woman's City Club section emphasized the value of community participation in municipal health, garbage collection, child welfare, and the control of advertising. The City Club, on the other hand, stressed the need for expert guidance in these complicated matters. Irving Pond, George Hooker, and the businessmen on the Housing Exhibit Committee encouraged architects, sanitarians, engineers, and social scientists to suggest improvements for inner city and suburban housing. Housing had become an abstract problem to be solved with scientific research and centralized governmental control to enforce the results.

One part of the City Club housing exhibit was devoted to a competition for a model suburb in a quarter section on the outskirts of Chicago. The entries showed the range of acceptable architectural images for suburban housing. Or, more accurately, they showed the model community images, since details of actual architectural development were only a second, and unrequired, stage of the competition process, after an initial site plan and bird's-eye view of the whole. Most contestants focused their attention on site plans.

The program called for a mix of income levels, with the majority of units going to working-class families earning around $1,000 a year. Although the suburb was supposed to be distinctly residential in character, there was to be mixed land-use, with business and commercial buildings and a social center, as well as schools and churches. The program drew from the best of the English garden city concepts of community, using centralized social institutions to make up for the loss of space in smaller dwellings and to bring the residents together for a unified, well-organized social life. The City Club housing committee and the jury chosen for the competition were specific about their purpose. Entries were to provide good models for developers, the program stated, in addition to general information for the public. The object of the competition was to balance the plan Burnham had composed for the city with proposals for suburban development which gave "intelligent direction ... [based on] essentials for good housing and for neighborhood institutions."[55]

Participants were almost all design experts—architects, engineers, landscape architects—although a high school teacher and a doctor also submitted entries. They lived not only in the Chicago area but also in San Francisco, Boston, New York, Minneapolis, and Gothenburg, Sweden. Despite the diverse locations and backgrounds, there were four basic approaches among the forty-four finalists whose work was published: local Prairie school design with a strongly expressed theme of architectural and social community; more traditional revival styles set in ways to encourage exchanges between families, or a village approach; monumental, axially planned Beaux-Arts schemes, turning the neighborhood into a residential civic center; and rigid grid plans which advertised superior scientific and sanitary advantages, as well as the reassurance of familiar street patterns.

If the styles and philosophies were certainly distinct, every scheme did emphasize neighborhood planning, even if only a few designers discussed their theories at length. Still, the prominence given community over individual expression varied considerably. Frank Lloyd Wright submitted a noncompetitive design. He clearly stated that the business and social buildings provided a "background" to the housing, where life would be "quiet and clean."[56] Wright stressed the separation of houses from one another as much as the uniformity of their design. One theme represented privacy, and the other community. Workers' apartments and semidetached houses were on the periphery, facing the outside streets, almost exiled from the middle-class community which formed the core. The largest area went to a "residence park" based on the quadruple block plan. Here each family would be "protected" from neighbors, as Wright put it, for there was only one dwelling on each side of a block. While he acknowledged the mix of incomes in the program, Wright's scheme favored dwellings for the upper crust.

William F. Drummond's entry emphasized the collective aspects of his "neighborhood unit plan" (fig. 48), even though his structures showed the formal influence of several years in Wright's office. Everyone shared something here: "the Institute," or social center; common gardens in the back of houses and apartment blocks (fig. 49); party walls; sweeping vistas that called one's attention to the unity of the

Figure 48. Neighborhood plan by William Drummond for the Chicago City Club's model suburb competition, 1913. (From *City Residential Land Development,* 1916.)

whole rather than to any particular building. The "nucleus" of his cruciform site plan, Drummond explained, would be a public structure, either the Institute or, along one of the minor axes, a business or commercial block.[57]

The plan of Robert A. Pope, a New York City landscape architect, took a more conservative approach, at least toward design, with small Colonial cottages (fig. 50). But he also demonstrated a progressive attitude toward neighborhood planning. Using his recent working-class suburb of Forest Hills, outside Boston, as a model, Pope described how he had laid out almost identical houses around small interior courts.[58] The standardization would cut costs and also reduce competitiveness among the occupants, he declared. Moreover, the traditional forms (in fact, almost a builder's vernacular) would, he asserted, make the more radical communal ownership of the courts and parks seem familiar and less threatening. It was another case of an architect claiming that design could establish certain values.

Of course, the Beaux-Arts plans—notably those of Walter Burley Griffin, Marcia Mead, and the Chicago firm of Herbert and Lewis

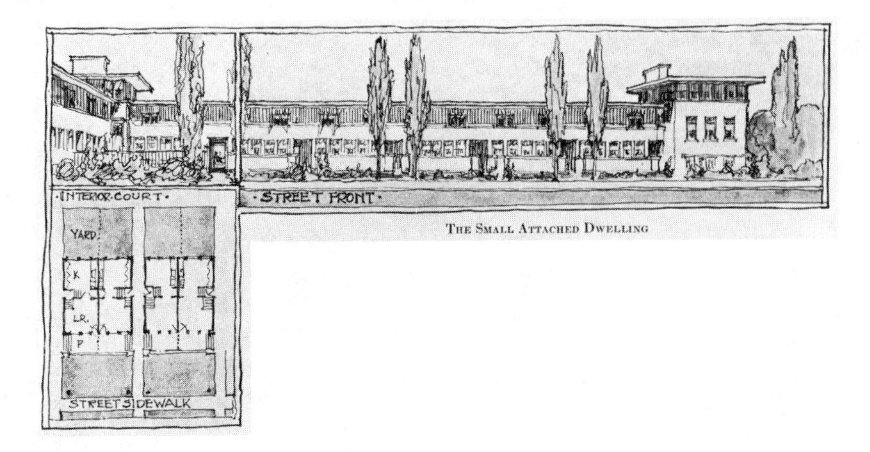

Figure 49. Apartment house prototype by William Drummond for the Chicago City Club competition.

Riddle (fig. 51)—relied on public monuments for their neighborhood focus. None of these designers provided detailed drawings of dwellings. The plan of the project as a whole was their concern. Civic feelings would consist primarily in the residents' pride in the splendor of the civic center, their texts asserted. Mead emphasized the elaborate pavilions at the entrance to the subdivision and a formal central plaza. Griffin designed a miniature city, with formal gardens and public plazas regularly placed at the intersections of major avenues. He eased the overall sense of a large capital city by providing narrow curved streets between the avenues and the largest amount of open space—parks and playgrounds and rows of tree-lined streets with wide sidewalks—of any of the competitors. Riddle and Riddle acknowledged that their aim was to recall Burnham's great municipal center for Chicago with the monumental columns and fountain of their scheme. Like him, they did not discuss housing needs in their model suburb proposal, but instead emphasized the grand gestures of Beaux-Arts-inspired urban planning.[59]

Even the two gridiron plans, one by a Chicago physician and the other by a local engineer (fig. 52), were presented as carefully thought-out neighborhood schemes. Dr. Tenney explained that his concerns for sunshine, ventilation, and stable construction would

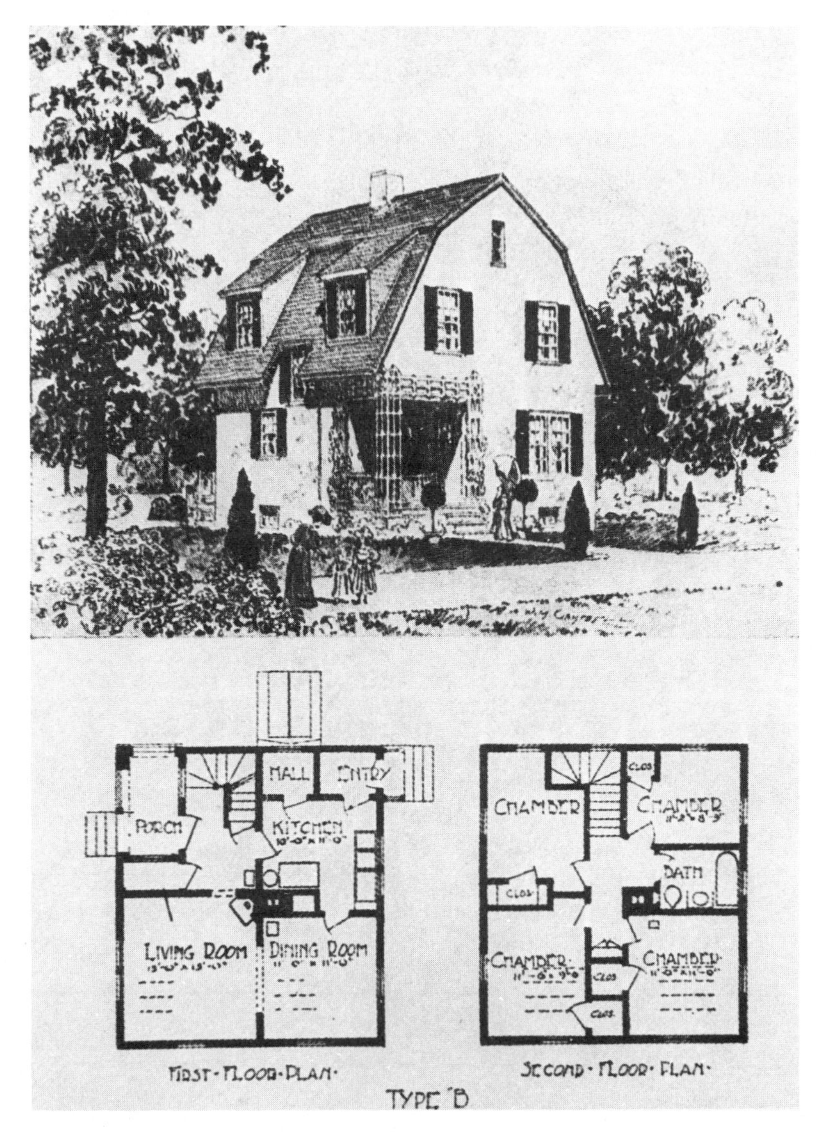

Figure 50. Colonial cottage prototype by Robert A. Pope for the Chicago City Club competition.

Figure 51. Perspective drawing and site plan (opposite) of model suburb by Riddle and Riddle for the Chicago City Club competition.

facilitate cooperative endeavors and pure thoughts among the healthy residents. H. J. Fixmer declared that the practicalities and efficiency of his self-sufficient suburb would instill "community" among people of small means and simple tastes.[60] The means might have varied considerably, but the goal and the language of each entry proclaimed the merits of a totally planned community.

Often the architect-planners, especially the Prairie school group, used innovative ways to achieve their community feeling. Every entry

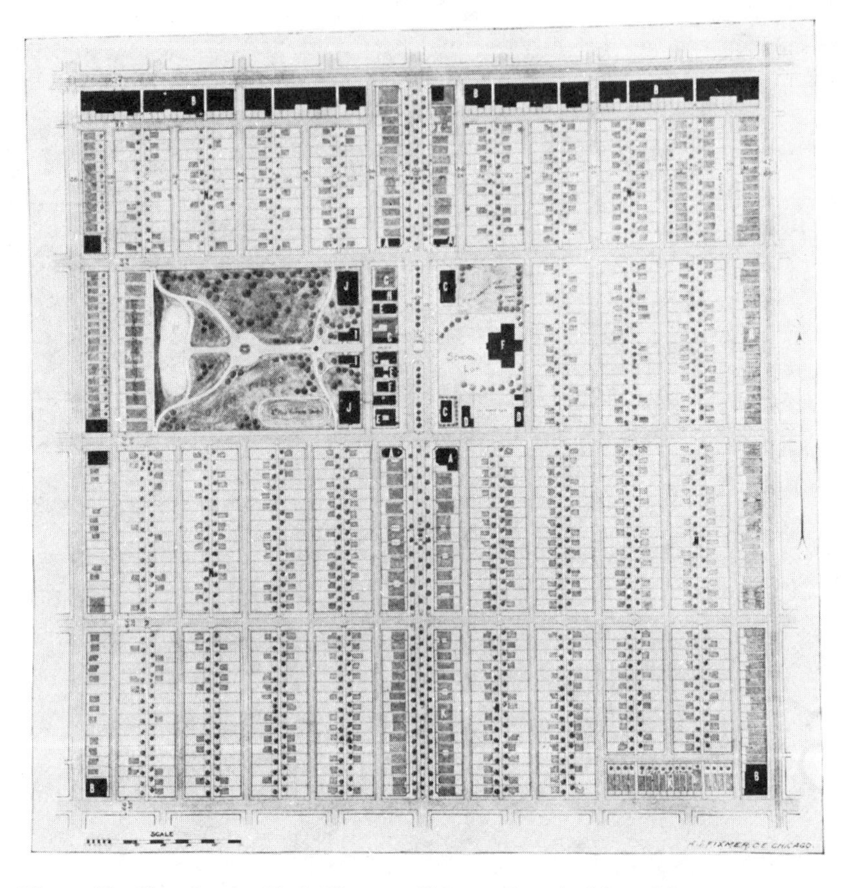

Figure 52. Site plan by H. J. Fixmer, Chicago Board of Local Improvements, for the Chicago City Club competition.

carefully zoned residential, commercial, and communal social areas. The Prairie school and Beaux-Arts schemes created large residential areas where there was no internal traffic, in effect, superblocks. There was some awareness of the fact that American reverence for private property stood in the way of community. Drummond addressed the property issue directly, praising the cooperative English and German garden cities over the American landholding system. Pope endorsed Kropotkin's system of collectively owned and maintained parks and playgrounds to reinforce the bonds of community.

But community centers were easier to plan than new property laws. In each entry, the planner centralized many of the social functions once carried on in individual homes. There was shared space for social gatherings, kindergartens, classes, clubs and adult societies, gymnasia and athletic fields, rooms for reading, workshops for music and crafts. Wright even included a domestic science center with the YWCA and kindergarten. Each of the designers shared the optimistic expectation that trained experts would supervise the social and educational life, even the political life, of the community. As Drummond expressed it, "The object of the Institute is to bring about healthful and vigorous participation in all those activities which could be systematically pursued through the employment of expert instructors, as well as to encourage voluntary religious, educational, recreational, and political activities."[61] These experts would choose the best kind of pedagogy and health, social life and political stance, or a limited variety of each philosophy, and then make these options available to the group as a whole.

All of the plans, to some extent, extolled the values of business and science. Wilhelm Bernhard's first-prize design had a community center which also included business and commercial allotments. Here, he pointed out, people would be sure to congregate.[62] Scientific studies to back the designs were considered a sign of professional objectivity. One plan was based, the designer claimed, on a sociological study of the habits of the Chicago population as a whole, so that it would reflect common traits. The gridiron designers were especially adamant about their scientific bases. One plan was derived from studies of sanitation; the other from consideration of ecological conditions.[63] Robert Pope wrote that "it is quite . . . feasible to determine the direction which pedestrian and vehicular traffic will take when streets and walks are laid down in given places."[64] Even the jury's comments stressed that they appreciated how the plans responded to the dominant values of the day. The designs, they wrote, were based on "ideals which make for efficiency . . . of the 'Young American.'" The planners, the report went on, had given their expert guidance to correct the excesses of individualistic initiative which had hitherto been allowed to rule in the suburbs. Although they agreed that most of the schemes did lack a certain "emotional expression" and variety, the overall planning provided a necessary order.[65]

All the same, in the end, the jury and special advisers could not decide which plan, or even which type of plan, they preferred. Albert

Kelsey admired the noncompetitive entry by Wright and deplored the grids. Irving Pond decried the "self-styled American school" of Wright, Drummond, and Bernhard. (Griffin, like many other competitors, had been content with only a site plan.) He indicted their designs as heavy, monumental, and unresponsive to existing popular tastes. It was "ungracious, even were it moral," Pond declared, "to force the free American spirit to dwell in a depressed and depressing cubiform environment."[66] He saw in these radical, abstract forms a denial of tradition and diversity, as well as a lack of sympathy or respect for average American aesthetic preferences.

In a perceptive sociological analysis, Carol Aronovici, an advocate of low-cost housing reform and secretary of the Suburban Planning Association of Philadelphia, lamented the lack of any real street life in the schemes. They were all too monumental, in his opinion, all too planned and perfect. The focus on the private home and its guarded yard prevented the development of community bonds. The plans that tried to differentiate public spaces failed, for mere labels defining a given area as communal land to be shared by surrounding residents were overly simplistic.[67] (It went without saying that the grid plans, which made no provisions at all for shared space or public use, offered even less of a solution.) Aronovici commended the attention many of the entries had shown to social issues; yet he recognized the insufficiency of an architect's simply designating a given area for particular social functions and then assuming that complicated sociological and political problems had been solved.

The jurors were in general accord about the basic problems facing the planner of a modern suburb, although their language did tend to be quite abstract and hesitant. They were in resounding agreement when they discussed the principles that planners should apply in addressing social problems: centralized organization of government and social services, community facilities, a mixture of private and public spaces, separation of land-use functions; in sum, rational social-science models and a unifying aesthetic order. While they debated fiercely about the best modern architectural styles, they accepted these principles without question. Moreover, the responsibility of the architect and the social scientist to work together to solve social problems had also become a commonly held assumption. These two had emerged as the experts for the joint venture of modern community planning. The conflicts that still remained centered around the specificity of the architect's sociological vision and the style that best exemplified modern community life. Aronovici alone doubted whether the designer had the ability to solve social problems.

Metaphors of Suburban Stability

By the time of the City Club competition, it had become quite apparent that a larger scale of architectural planning and a new concept of stylistic form had taken hold in Chicago, as elsewhere in the country. Architects, reformers, builders, and clients now tended to conceive of residential design in what they consistently described as a modern and more rationalized manner, even when there was also a sentimental attachment to more established styles. Yet the break with the past was not as radical as it may have appeared at the time. In fact, what seems to have happened is that many architects transferred the rhetoric and even some of the design principles once used to characterize the individual Victorian dwelling onto their modern suburban plans. The site planning of the subdivision itself was now picturesque and rambling, even in corners of Beaux-Arts schemes, while the dwellings had become "units," almost as if they were the mechanical conveniences to be plugged into the more artistic whole. The suburb was supposedly an organic entity, as the house had been in the 1880s. Bernhard expressed the general mood: "The organically developed suburb, strongly marked by an architecture of its own, able to impress its individuality on the district, will awaken in its citizens the love for beautiful surroundings, and will express definitely through its individuality the individual life of the citizens."[68] The inspiring influence of the community plan—simultaneously individualistic and democratic—closely resembled the aura the house itself once supposedly cast over its inhabitants.

The larger scale of organic metaphor did signal changes in environmental planning, however. For people like Frederic Howe—who compared the well-run city with the human body, also regulated and guided by the head—metabolic imagery provided a further justification for expert control and rational organization.[69] Nature had become a disciplined system in these metaphors. Divided into distinct, separate functions, and closely regulated, its tendency toward disorder and randomness could be held in check.

Despite differences, modern and traditional designers, radical and conservative social critics shared one conspicuous policy with each other and with their predecessors. Even in the highly organized and functional modern community, the home remained a primary basis for planning the larger social world. Homes might be much more alike now, but the belief in their power to influence behavior and values remained as strong as it had been in earlier eras. Although architects and social scientists now concentrated on the suburban community of similar homes and like-minded citizens, they had incorporated, almost directly in many cases, the nineteenth-century precepts of "home influence" and organic house design.

The deep belief in the home as the locus of moral reform remained unshaken. Now expertly trained architects, planners, and sociologists connected that original premise to an emphatic demand for planned communities of housing units. This modern ideology of residential design assumed the necessity of both the orderly neighborhood and the private house. As they integrated the earlier ideals of individualized prototypes into their larger schemes, twentieth-century design professionals, their advisers, and their collaborators all recognized that the symbol of the home remained potent for many Americans. They continued to use domestic images and rhetoric, therefore, but to serve different ends and at a much larger scale. Daniel Burnham, Charles Wacker, and Walter Moody, staunch believers in high art and grandiose projects, employed the homey imagery of house-planning to demonstrate certain virtues of the grand city plan and to justify the new zoning proposals. Frank Lloyd Wright, Robert Spencer, Walter Burley Griffin, and other architects who specialized in residential design could now tolerate the idea of a prototypical dwelling—provided that they had a strong hand in the design of the larger city or suburb where the model would be utilized. These architects and many others like them invoked both the traditional idealization of the model private home and the modern concept of the planned community, claiming that they would oversee both ends of the design problem.

The continuity of belief in the moral influence of the home reveals the power of that image for the American imagination. Even when the actual environmental changes have failed to achieve the reformers' stated aims, and even though the images representing the model home might be altered, the belief has endured. Consequently, few reformers have been willing to attack directly the causes for the problems they saw around them, whether the issue was social inequality, class antagonism, family instability, women's rights, or working conditions. Instead, they have tended to propose ideal social and architectural models that would, in their theories, bring about a situation where the problems would no longer exist. After an initial stage of public exposure, the model would duplicate itself automatically, because it was so obviously, visibly superior to existing standards. Whenever a given set of problems grew too unwieldy, someone would propose a better model home to alleviate the difficulties.

This approach to reform has been remarkably similar in architecture and in politics. In both cases, the American home and the idea of the model have been consistently important themes. Reformers have promised, again and again, that with these tools, they could solve conflicts in the society. Under the impetus of the progressives, for instance, the appearance of houses underwent a major transformation, as did many aspects of political organization. Liberal reformers, home economists, architects, and builders loudly proclaimed that modern residential planning could generate community action and protect individual freedoms—simultaneously and without conflict. In a similar spirit, other progressive reformers instituted mechanisms for participatory democracy on the one hand, and for a more rationalized or "scientific" approach to government and civil service on the other. Despite obvious failures, the simplistic, often self-serving claim that they could manage these architectural symbols or social institutions also gave these reformers much of their appeal.

Such an understanding of environmental influence and social reform is not particular to the period I have described here—a turn of a century and of a way of life. There is something peculiarly American about the campaign to define and publicize models for the home and to connect those models to other, larger social goals. It is too easy to smile at the extraordinary rhetoric of these earlier housing reformers, or at the rhetoric of the builders or architects for that matter, and thereby deny how central a value the model home has been and still is within our culture. Belief in the ability of the market to accept and disseminate the best available model—and, therefore, a corollary belief that government intervention would obstruct the process—has stymied governmental housing policy in America. Demands for individuality and self-expression in private homes have continually overpowered the widely professed complementary desire to equality. Collective efforts to retreat into rigidly controlled suburban settings, "protected" from the muddying influences of other groups and from nonresidential activities, have too easily fostered a deadening social uniformity and great difficulties for those who veered from the norm.

Campaigns for the model home have been typically American in what they have been and what they have not been. One chief characteristic is the basic denial of politics, power, and the diversity of the public domain. The image of the standardized model home has, nonetheless, been a rallying symbol for numerous social causes. It has stimulated various forms of political action, enlisting certain people to work together for such goals as better social services, economic equality, consumerism, public health, and democratic participation in government. To be a householder is to be a citizen. Yet, there has seldom been an acknowledgment of the complexity of the issues underlying these goals, or even of the issues which relate to housing quality and availability.

In the enthusiasm for symbols of domestic and social benefits, problems of cultural difference, political conflict, and economic control have consistently been swept away. Moralistic superiority is more easily tolerated when leaders or reformers have promised better homes. Most often, the emphasis has been on the technologically modern private home for a single family. It has long been considered the primary symbol of American cultural values and a direct way to stabilize the society. For many people, that image itself came to be seen as the fundamental personal or cultural value it represents.

NOTES

Introduction

1. Calvert Vaux, *Villas and Cottages* (New York: Harper and Bros., 1864), p. 128.

2. For analyses of these journals and their impact, see Frank Luther Mott, *A History of American Magazines,* vols. 4, 5 (Cambridge: Harvard University Press, 1957); *Victorian America,* Daniel Walker Howe, ed. (Philadelphia: University of Pennsylvania Press, 1976), especially Howe's "Victorian Culture in America," pp. 3–28; Henry F. May, *The End of American Innocence: A Study of the First Years of Our Own Time, 1912–1917* (New York: Alfred A. Knopf, 1959), chaps. 4–6; Ann Douglas, *The Feminization of American Culture* (New York: Alfred A. Knopf, 1977); Edward A. Bok, *The Americanization of Edward Bok* (New York: Charles Scribner's Sons, 1924); Stuart Ewen, *Captains of Consciousness: Advertising and the Social Roots of the Consumer Culture* (New York: McGraw-Hill, 1976); Larzer Ziff, *The American 1890s* (New York: Viking Press, 1966), especially pp. 120–45.

3. The *Oxford English Dictionary* gives 1812 as the year in which the term "middle class" first appeared, and the citation sounds familiar: "Such of the Middle Class of Society who have fallen upon evil days." In 1832 *Webster's Dictionary* gave a typically American reading: "Thus we speak of people of the middling class or sort, neither high nor low." The use of the word was a self-conscious yet general statement about moderation. In the 1860s, the middle class began to be divided into lower and upper ranks, yet the definition remained one of social position and relative security as well as of economic strata. See Burton J. Bledstein, *The Culture of Professionalism: The Middle Class and the Development of Higher Education in America* (New York: W.W. Norton, 1976), pp. 1–79; and Raymond Williams, *Keywords: A Vocabulary of Culture and Society* (New York: Oxford University Press, 1976), pp. 51–59.

Chapter 1

1. Henry Nash Smith, "The Scribbling Women and the Cosmic Success Story," *Critical Inquiry* 1 (September 1974): 47–70; Ann Douglas, *The Feminization of American Culture* (New York: Alfred A. Knopf, 1977).

2. For sources on nineteenth-century books, see Henry-Russell Hitchcock, Jr., *American Architectural Books: A list of books, portfolios, and pamphlets on architecture and related subjects published in America before 1895* (Minneapolis: University of Minnesota Press, 1962). On Downing, see Vincent J. Scully, Jr., *The Shingle Style and the Stick Style: Architectural Theory and Design from Downing to the Origins of Wright*, rev. ed. (New Haven, Conn.: Yale University Press, 1971), pp. xxviii–xlvii; and "Romantic Rationalism and the Expression of Structure in Wood: Downing, Wheeler, Gardner, and the 'Stick Style,'" *Art Bulletin* 35 (1953): 121–42. Another interesting attempt to interpret this architecture is Clifford E. Clark, Jr., "Domestic Architecture as an Index to Social History: The Romantic Revival and the Cult of Domesticity in America, 1840–1890," *Journal of Interdisciplinary History* 7 (Summer 1976): 33–56.

3. *The Architecture of Country Houses* (New York: D. Appleton & Co., 1850; reprint ed., New York: Dover, 1969). In 1841 Downing published *A Treatise on the Theory and Practice of Gardening Adapted to North America . . . With remarks on rural architecture* (New York: G. P. Putnam, 1841). The next year Putnam's published his *Cottage Residences;* between 1846 and 1852, Downing edited the *Horticulturist*, from which a group of his editorials was posthumously published, with an introduction by George William Curtis, as *Rural Essays* (New York: G. P. Putnam, 1853). See also George Wightwick, *Hints to Young Architects*, which contained a piece by Downing (New York: G. P. Putnam, 1847).

4. *The Architecture of Country Houses*, pp. 2, 31–35, 269–70.

5. ". . . Mr. Downing sounded his trumpet call, and henceforth repose was impossible and discipline distasteful," was the appraisal of "American Architecture—With Precedent and Without," *American Architect and Building News* (hereafter cited as *American Architect*) 4 (October 26, 1878): 139.

6. *Godey's* was published between 1830 and 1898, when it was merged into *The Puritan*. See George L. Hersey, "Godey's Choice," *Journal of the Society of Architectural Historians* 18 (October 1959): 104–11; Ruth E. Finley, *The Lady of Godey's: Sarah Josepha Hale* (Philadelphia: J. B. Lippincott, 1931); and Isabelle Webb Entrikin, *Sarah Josepha Hale and Godey's Lady's Book* (Philadelphia: Lancaster, 1946). For a complementary study of the Englishman Loudon, see George L. Hersey, "J. C. Loudon and Architectural Associationism," *Architectural Review* 144 (August 1968): 89–92. (In America, "Associationism" also referred to the followers of Charles Fourier; see Dolores Hayden, *Seven American Utopias: The Architecture of Communitarian Socialism, 1790–1975* (Cambridge: MIT Press, 1976).

7. John Bullock, *The American Cottage Builder* (New York: Stringer & Townsend, 1854); Gervase Wheeler, *Homes for the People in Suburb and Country: The Villa, the Mansion and the Cottage* (New York: Charles Scrib-

ner, 1855); Charles P. Dwyer, *The Economic Cottage Builder* (Buffalo, N.Y.: Wanzer, McKim & Co., 1856); Catharine E. Beecher and Harriet Beecher Stowe, *The American Woman's Home* (New York: J. B. Ford & Co., 1869; reprint ed., New York: Arno Press and the New York Times, 1971). Also see Scully, *Shingle Style,* pp. xlvii–lix; Clay Lancaster, "Builders Guides and Plan Books and American Architecture, from the Revolution to the Civil War," *The Magazine of Art* 41 (January 1948): 16–22. A complete listing of pattern books can be found in Hitchcock, *American Architectural Books.* For overviews of the period and its architectural expression, see John Brinckerhoff Jackson, *American Space: The Centennial Years, 1865–1876* (New York: W. W. Norton, 1972); James Early, *Romanticism and American Architecture* (New York: A. S. Barnes, 1965); and Donald Drew Egbert, "The Idea of Organic Expression and American Architecture," *Evolutionary Thought in America,* ed. Stow Persons (New York: George Braziller, 1956), pp. 336–408. See Chapter 2, above, for a comparison of these pattern-book writers with the professional architects of the late nineteenth century.

8. *The Architecture of Country Houses,* pp. 35, 257.

9. The quotations are from *The Seven Lamps of Architecture* (New York: John Wiley, 1849), pp. 165, 172–73, 188. On Ruskin, see Roger B. Stein, *John Ruskin and Aesthetic Thought in America, 1840–1900* (Cambridge: Harvard University Press, 1967); Henry-Russell Hitchcock, "Ruskin and American Architecture; or, Regeneration Long Delayed," in *Concerning Architecture: Essays on Architectural Writers and Writing Presented to Nikolaus Pevsner,* ed. John Summerson (Baltimore: Penguin Press, 1968), pp. 166–208; Kristine Ottesen Garrigan, *Ruskin on Architecture: His Thought and Influence* (Madison: University of Wisconsin Press, 1973).

10. "Of Queen's Gardens," *Sesame and Lilies* (London, 1864; New York: Metropolitan Publishing Co., 1871); the quotation is from an 1891 edition (pp. 136–37) in which Charles Eliot Norton states that this was still Ruskin's most popular book (p. v).

11. *National Builder* 1 (July 1885): 1.

12. Ibid. (September 1885): 1.

13. One of the early statements about poor-quality structures is Frederick Law Olmsted's account of the fire, "Chicago in Distress," *Nation* 13 (November 9, 1871): 302–5. Soon afterward, the *Chicago Architect and Building News* deplored the fact that "The dwelling house architecture of Chicago has always been far behind that of her business buildings" (1 [1876]: 111), cited in Jean F. Block, *Hyde Park Houses* (Chicago: University of Chicago Press, 1978), p. 35. The *Tribune* frequently printed similar diatribes. The *Times* quote is from "Our Suburbs," 4 May 1873, p. 4, cited in Andrew Jay King, "Law and Land Use in Chicago: A Prehistory of Modern Zoning" (Ph.D. diss., University of Wisconsin, 1976), p. 28.

14. *The Inter-State Exposition Souvenir* (Chicago: Van Arsdale & Massie, 1873–1891); *Sketch-Book of the Inter-State Exposition, Chicago, 1883,* ed. George M. Barbour (Chicago: Lakeside Press, 1883); Bessie Louise Pierce, *A History of Chicago* (Chicago: University of Chicago Press, 1937–57), vol. 3, *1871–1893,* p. 475; Helen Lefkowitz Horowitz, *Culture & the City: Cultural*

Philanthropy in Chicago from the 1880s to 1917 (Lexington: University of Kentucky Press, 1976), pp. 37–39; Perry R. Duis and Glen E. Holt, "Chicago's Lost Exposition," *Chicago* 26 (July 1977): 72–74, 190.

15. William Dean Howells, "A Sennight of the Centennial," *Atlantic Monthly* 38 (July 1876): 100. Also see *Harper's Weekly* 20 (1876): 344, 412, 876, 1041; Jackson, *American Space*, pp. 231–40; Lally Weymouth and Milton Glaser, *America in 1876: The Way We Were* (New York: Vintage Books, 1976), pp. 12–47.

16. *The House Beautiful: Essays on Beds and Tables, Stools and Candlesticks* (New York: Charles Scribner's Sons, 1878), p. 19.

17. Ibid., pp. 167, 49.

18. Ella Rodman Church, *How To Furnish a House* (New York: D. Appleton & Co., 1881), p. 7.

19. Harriet Prescott Spofford, *Art Decoration Applied to Furniture* (New York: Harper & Bros., 1878), p. 222.

20. *American Builder and Journal of Art* (1868–73); *American Builder; A Journal of Industrial Art* (1873–79); *Builder and Woodworker* (1880–93); *Architectural Era* (1893); *Builder and Woodworker* (1894), merged into *National Builder* (1895). Representative articles include "House Building" (taken from the January *Scribner's*), *American Builder* 12 (January 1876): 10–11; "English Art at the Centennial Exhibition," *American Builder* 12 (April 1876): 81–82; Catharine E. Beecher, "About Kitchens" (from the *Christian Century*), *American Builder* 12 (August 1876): 181–82. Beman's Woolsey house, a $1,200 cottage in Wyoming, New Jersey, appeared in September 1878; Margaret Hicks's "Workman's Cottage," (from the *American Architect*) in July 1883; suburban cottages by William Woollett and ready-made houses by Lyman Bridges & Co. of Chicago and by Colonel Derron of Patterson, New Jersey, appeared frequently.

21. On this interpretation of populism, see *American Populism*, ed. George McKenna (New York: G. P. Putnam's Sons, 1974); and Jack Newfield and Jeff Greenfield, *A Populist Manifesto: The Making of a New Majority* (New York: Praeger Publishers, 1972). On the theme of luxury, see Neil Harris, *The Artist in American Society: The Formative Years, 1790–1860* (New York: George Braziller, 1966).

22. "Rich Men's Houses," *Carpentry and Building* 5 (February 1883): 27; "Pedantic Architecture," *Carpentry and Building* 5 (February 1883): 26, both cited in Sadayoshi Omoto, "The Queen Anne Style and Architectural Criticism," *Journal of the Society of Architectural Historians* 23 (March 1964): 31.

23. Gilbert Bostwick Croff, *Progressive American Architecture* (New York: Orange Judd Co., 1875), n.p.

24. George and Charles Palliser, *Palliser's Model Homes for the People* (New York and Brooklyn: Palliser & Co., 1876); George Palliser, *Palliser's New Cottage Homes and Details* (New York: Palliser, Palliser & Co., 1887), n.p.

25. *Palliser's New Cottage Homes*, preface.

26. Cited in John Burchard and Albert Bush-Brown, *The Architecture of America: A Social and Cultural History* (Boston: Little, Brown, 1961), p. 179.

27. *Palliser's Model Homes,* p. 93.
28. *National Builder* 1 (November 1885): 4; see also "Improvement in Architecture," *Sanitary News* (Chicago) 1 (November 1882): 22.
29. Vaux, *Villas and Cottages,* p. 69.
30. Benjamin Ward Richardson, M.D., *Hygeia: A City of Health* (London: Macmillan, 1876), excerpts reprinted as "Modern Sanitary Science—A City of Health," in *Van Nostrand's Eclectic Engineering Magazine* 14 (January 1876): 31–42; also see Richardson's four-part series, "Health at Home," *Appleton's Journal: A Magazine of General Literature* 8–9 (April–October 1880); Henry Hartshorne, M.D., *Our Homes* (Philadelphia: P. Blakiston, 1880; American Health Primers #9).
31. William H. Cornfield, *Dwelling Houses: Their Sanitary Construction and Arrangement* (New York: Van Nostrand, 1880); George Preston Brown, *Sewer-Gas and Its Dangers* (Chicago: Jansen, McClurg and Co., 1881).
32. Henry Gradle, M.D., *Bacteria and the Germ Theory of Disease* (Chicago: W. T. Keener, 1883).
33. S. E. Gross and Co., advertising broadside, Chicago Historical Society.
34. Mrs. H. M. Plunkett, *Women, Plumbers, and Doctors; or, Household Sanitation* (New York: D. Appleton, 1885).
35. Cook, *The House Beautiful,* p. 117. Dr. Edward Youmans, a follower of Herbert Spencer, was editor of the *Popular Science Monthly,* where he promoted scientific principles for the reorganization of the home, programs which would substitute rational organization for what he described as archaic and romantic tradition.
36. John Pickering Putnam, *The Open Fire-Place in All Ages* (Boston: J. R. Osgood & Co., 1881). Frances Le Baron also extols the fireplace as the soul of the living room in "Mantels and Grates," *Inland Architect and News Record* (hereafter cited as *Inland Architect*) 3 (April 1884): 48, cited in Block, *Hyde Park Houses,* p. 36.
37. Mrs. C. S. Jones and Henry T. Williams, *Household Elegancies,* 5th ed. (New York: H. T. Williams, 1877); Julia McNair Wright, *The Complete Home: An Encyclopaedia of Domestic Life and Affairs* (Philadelphia and Chicago: J. C. McCurdy & Co., 1879), were among the most popular texts.
38. Pierce, *A History of Chicago,* 3:187; Polly Anne Earl, "Craftsmen and Machines: The Nineteenth Century Furniture Industry," *Technological Innovations and the Decorative Arts,* Winterthur Conference Report, 1973, ed. Ian M. G. Quimby and Polly Anne Earl (Charlottesville: University Press of Virginia, 1974), p. 315.
39. David M. Katzman, *Seven Days a Week: Women and Domestic Service* (New York: Oxford University Press, 1978), pp. 44–59, 66, 286. In 1880, with a population of 504,000, Chicago had 15,000 servants, although some families employed more than one servant.
40. *Homes, and How to Make Them* (Boston: J. R. Osgood & Co., 1874), p. 209.
41. On Beecher, see Dolores Hayden, "Catharine Beecher and the Politics of Housework," in *Women in American Architecture: A Historic and Contemporary Perspective,* ed. Susana Torre (New York: Whitney Library of Design,

Watson-Guptill Publications, 1977), pp. 39–49; and Kathryn Kish Sklar, *Catharine Beecher: A Study in American Domesticity* (New Haven, Conn.: Yale University Press, 1973). Beecher and Stowe's book was the basic text for the home economics department of the University of Illinois.

42. See, for instance, R[obert] W. Shoppell, ed., *Modern Houses; Beautiful Homes* (New York: Co-operative Building Plan Assn., ca. 1887), esp. "Warming the House," pp. 342–43, Maria Parloa, "A Model Kitchen," pp. 148–49; Charles F. Wingate, "The Removal of House Slops," pp. 274–76.

43. *Industrial Chicago* 4 vols. (Chicago: Goodspeed Publishing Co., 1891), 4:32–37; John J. Flinn, *Standard Guide to Chicago* (Chicago: Standard Guide Co., 1893), pp. 417–23; Caroline Kirkland and Joseph Kirkland, *The Story of Chicago*, 2 vols. (Chicago: Dibble Publishing Co., 1894), 2:369–72; Henry Justin Smith, *Chicago, A Portrait* (New York: The Century Company, 1831), pp. 203–4.

44. *Chicago Tribune*, January 19, 1890. (I would like to thank Jean F. Block for this reference.) See also Barbara M. Posadas, "A Home in the Country: Suburbanization in Jefferson Township, 1870–1889," *Chicago History* 7 (Fall 1978), 134–49.

Chapter 2

1. Arthur Clason Weatherhead, *The History of Collegiate Education in Architecture in the United States* (Los Angeles: Arthur Clason Weatherhead, 1941), pp. 3–7; Turpin C. Bannister, "Evolution and Achievement," in *The Architect at Mid-Century*, ed. Turpin C. Bannister (New York: Reinhold, 1954), p. 73; John William Ward, "The Politics of Design," *Red, White, and Blue: Men, Books, and Ideas in American Culture* (New York: Oxford University Press, 1969), pp. 283–88; Samuel Haber, "The Professions and Higher Education in America: A Historical View," Reprint no. 382 of the Institute of Industrial Relations, University of California, Berkeley, 1974 (reprinted in *Higher Education and the Labor Market*, ed. Margaret S. Gordon (New York: McGraw-Hill, 1974).

2. "Dangerous Architecture," *Scientific American* 35 (July 8, 1876): 17; *American Architect* 2 (August 18, 1877): 267. Conditions in Chicago were often discussed in Peter B. Wight's "Chicago Letter" in the *American Architect*. The Chicago chapter of the AIA did discipline several members for violations of ethics in accepting contractors' kickbacks.

3. George H. Ellwanger, *The Story of My House* (New York: D. Appleton & Co., 1890), p. 11; E[ugene] C[larence] Gardner, *Homes, and How to Make Them* (Boston: J. R. Osgood & Co., 1874), pp. 28–31; *Sanitary News* (Chicago) 2 (June 1, 1883): 27; *Industrial Chicago* 4 vols. (Chicago: Goodspeed Publishing Co., 1891, 1:507–8, 2:618; Frederick Bauman, "Relation of Architect to Contractor and Journeymen," *Inland Architect* 6 (November 1885): 60–61; E. F. Fassett, "The Modern Mechanic," *Inland Architect* 7 (March 1886): 22–23; Henry Hudson Holly, *Modern Dwellings for Town and Country, Adapted to American Wants and Climate* (New York: Harper & Bros., 1878), p. 43. For a

comparison with contemporary animosity against the legal profession, see Burton J. Bledstein, *The Culture of Professionalism: The Middle Class and the Development of Higher Education in America* (New York: W. W. Norton, 1976), pp. 184–87.

4. W. L. B. Jenney, "A Reform in Suburban Dwellings," *Inland Architect* 1 (February 1883): 2–3.

5. "Self-made Architects," *American Architect* 2 (December 8, 1877): 395. The unnamed author of this letter was responding to an earlier letter of November 17, in which a reader asks, "Would you drive the poor out of the profession, and close your doors against them," citing Ruskin on the value of learning at home from nature. Ware sided with the second letter's statement: "Nature simply obeys laws." Controversy over the name also related to the popularity of the American phrase "architects of their own fortune" throughout the nineteenth century among professionals and skilled craftsmen alike. (See Bledstein, *Culture of Professionalism,* p. 13; Lillian B. Miller, "Painting, Sculpture and the National Character, 1815–1860," *Journal of American History* 53 [March 1967]: 704; Stephen Thernstrom, *Poverty and Progress: Social Mobility in a Nineteenth Century City* [New York: Atheneum, 1969], pp. 64, 71.)

6. Cited in Joan Draper, "The Ecole des Beaux-Arts and the Architectural Profession in the United States: The Case of John Galen Howard," in *The Architect: Chapters in the History of the Profession* ed. Spiro Kostof (New York: Oxford University Press, 1977), p. 215.

7. "American Vernacular Architecture, II," *American Architect* 3 (May 25, 1878): 182; "American Architecture—With Precedent and Without," *American Architect* 4 (October 26, 1878): 138; see also "Evolution of the Builder," *Architectural Record,* special "Great American Architects" series (July 1896): 110–21.

8. "American Architecture—With Precedent and Without," p. 139.

9. "American Vernacular Architecture, II," p. 182.

10. "American Architecture—With Precedent and Without," p. 139.

11. "Archaeology and American Architecture," *American Architect* 4 (October 5, 1878): 115.

12. *Industrial Chicago,* 2:618.

13. For a history of the theories of the first house, see Joseph Rykwert, *On Adam's House in Paradise: The Idea of the Hut in Architectural History* (New York: Museum of Modern Art, 1972).

14. See Vincent Scully, *The Single Style and the Stick Style,* rev. ed. (New Haven and London: Yale University Press, 1971); "Sketch for House for Hon. P. T. Barnum, Black Rock Beach, Conn.," *American Architect* 1 (November 11, 1876), n.p.

15. Everett Chamberlin, *Chicago and Its Suburbs* (Chicago: T. A. Hungerford, 1874).

16. W. L. B. Jenney, "Country House," *American Architect* 1 (January 22, 1876), n.p.; Burnham and Root, "Design for House in Drexel Blvd., Chicago," *American Architect* 1 (October 7, 1876), n.p.; P[eter] B. Wight, "Residence at Rockford, Ill.," *American Architect* 2 (February 24, 1876), n.p.

17. John Ruskin, *The Seven Lamps of Architecture* (New York: John Wiley, 1849), pp. 15–17.

18. See Roger B. Stein, *John Ruskin and Aesthetic Thought in America, 1840–1890* (Cambridge: Harvard University Press, 1967) and Henry-Russell Hitchcock, "Ruskin and American Architecture, or Regeneration Long Delayed," in *Concerning Architecture: Essays Presented to Nikolaus Pevsner,* ed. John Summerson (Baltimore: Penguin, 1968), pp. 166–208. The AIA, the *Nation,* and even the *Journal of Speculative Philosophy* had debated the effect of Ruskin's influence in the 1850s and 1860s. One example of the pro-builder use of Ruskin's ideas is a letter to the *American Architect* 2 (November 17, 1877), p. 371, which cites Ruskin in support of those who study architecture on their own, claiming the profession closed its doors against these "self-made" artists. The editor firmly disputed that one could learn from nature in this manner.

19. On the functionalism of Viollet-le-Duc and its place in American architecture, see Donald Hoffman, "Frank Lloyd Wright and Viollet-le-Duc," *Journal of the Society of Architectural Historians* 28 (October 1969): 73–77; another perceptive essay is Colin Rowe, "Character and Composition; or, Some Vicissitudes of Architectural Vocabulary in the Nineteenth Century," in *The Mathematics of the Ideal Villa and Other Essays* (Cambridge: MIT Press, 1976), pp. 59–87. Excerpts from *The Habitations of Man in All Ages,* the *Dictionnaire,* and *Discourses on Architecture* also appeared in the *American Architect,* the *American Builder, Shoppell's Modern Houses, The Carpenter,* and other journals for architects and for builders. John Wellborn Root and Peter B. Wight were among the Chicago architects who recommended Viollet-le-Duc to readers of the *Inland Architect.*

20. "Architecture: Lectures Delivered at the University of Chicago," *Inland Architect* 1 (March 1883): 20.

21. P[eter] B. Wight, "Letter from Chicago," *American Architect* 1 (April 22, 1876): 134–35.

22. *Industrial Chicago,* 1:65; see also Wight, "Letter from Chicago," pp. 134–35.

23. Household Art. Co., Boston, Sheldon house, Chicago, *American Architect* 2 (August 11, 1877), n.p.; W. L. B. Jenney, "Chamber Furniture" and "Dining Room Furniture," *American Architect* 1 (September 2, 1876), n.p.; Julius Huber, "Sketch for a Suburban Cottage," *Inland Architect* 3 (April 1884): 41; "Details of Suburban Cottage," *Inland Architect* 3 (May 1884): 41.

24. Wight, "Letter from Chicago," pp. 134–35; "Interior Decoration," *American Architect* 3 (March 2, 1878): 77.

25. F. M. Whitehouse, "Design for Country Residence to Be Erected at the Seaside," *American Architect* 2 (September 29, 1877), n.p.; "French Architecture in America," *Inland Architect* 3 (April 1884): 38. On the Queen Anne in England and America, see Mark Girouard, *Sweetness and Light: The 'Queen Anne' Movement, 1860–1900* (New York: Oxford University Press, 1977) and Andrew Saint, *Richard Norman Shaw* (New Haven, Conn.: Yale University Press, 1976). A good description of the origins of the Queen Anne revival is also to be found in *Industrial Chicago,* 1:48–65.

26. Holly, "Modern Dwellings . . . Part I," *Harper's New Monthly Magazine* 52 (May 1876): 864. These articles were republished as *Modern Dwellings for Town and Country* in 1878. A condensation of the book, entitled "Country Homes," appeared in *Harper's Weekly* 22 (June 15, 1878): 469–70.

27. "Residence for B. F. Allen, Des Moines," *Inland Architect* 5 (August 1885), n.p.

28. Scully, *Shingle Style.*

29. Chicago architects worked in this style before the arrival of Joseph Silsbee. For examples of Shingle Style dwellings in the Chicago area, see W. A. Beman, "Sketch for a Cottage at Hyde Park," and Addison and Fielder, "Residences for W. J. Dodd and Mrs. A. J. Mereness, Lake View, Ill.," *Inland Architect* 6 (December 1885), n.p.; Joseph Silsbee, "Residence for J. L. Cochrane, Edgewater, Ill.," *Inland Architect* 11 (March 1888), n.p., reprinted in the *Building Budget* 3 (March 1888); the Chicago Architectural Club, "Eight-Room Frame House Competition," *Inland Architect* 12 (September 1888), n.p.

30. "Romanesque Architecture," translation of Edouard Corroyen, *L'Architecture romane,* by W. A. Otis, *Inland Architect* 13–15 (March 1889–March 1890).

31. See Wheelock and Clay, "Residence of S. B. Barker, Chicago," *Inland Architect* 9 (March 1887), n.p.; W. W. Clay, "Residence for W. A. Giles, Chicago," *Inland Architect* 10 (December 1887), n.p.; S. S. Beman, "Residence for S. S. Beman, Chicago," *Inland Architect* 10 (January 1888), n.p.—which is resolutely plain and Richardsonian—as well as photographs of Richardson's well-known MacVeagh house and Glessner house in Chicago, which often reappear. Characteristically, these were all city houses.

32. "Elegant Simplicity in Architecture," *National Builder* 30 (April 1900): 7. The article also singled out Sullivan and Adler's Auditorium as another local example that carpenters should take the time to study. On Richardson, also see Mariana Griswold Van Rensselaer's "Recent Architecture in America," which appeared in six installments in the *Century* magazine between May 1884 and March 1886, and "American Country Dwellings," which was featured between May 1886 and July 1886. Van Rensselaer's biography, *Henry Hobson Richardson and His Works* (New York: Houghton, Mifflin & Co., 1888) was adulatory. Henry-Russell Hitchcock presents an excellent study of the "Suburban Richardsonian" house in *The Architecture of H. H. Richardson and His Times* (Cambridge: MIT Press, 1966).

33. Alexander F. Oakey, *Building a Home* (New York: D. Appleton & Co., 1881); A[rnold] W. Brunner, ed. and comp., *Cottages; or, Hints on Economical Building* (New York: W. T. Comstock, 1884).

34. "Cottage Residence by T. T. Cramp," *Inland Architect* 2 (January 1884), n.p.; W. A. Arnold, "A $2,300 Cottage," *Inland Architect* 5 (January 1885).

35. *American Architect* 13 (March 3, 1883): 104. On aesthetic differences between the two journals, see Eileen Michels, "A Developmental Study of the Drawings Published in the *American Architect* and the *Inland Architect* through 1895," doctoral dissertation, University of Minnesota, 1971.

36. On Chicago life, including the influx of architects, during the 1870s, see

A[lfred] T[heodore] Andreas, *History of Chicago: From the Earliest Period to the Present Time,* 3 vols. (1884–86); Bessie Louise Pierce, *A History of Chicago* (Chicago: University of Chicago Press, 1937–57), vol. 3, *1871–1893; Industrial Chicago,* 2:593–643, 701–50; Harold M. Mayer and Richard C. Wade, *Chicago: Growth of a Metropolis* (Chicago: University of Chicago Press, 1969); H. W. S. Cleveland, *Landscape Architecture as Applied to the Needs of the West* (Chicago: Jansen, McClurg & Co., 1873); John Brinckerhoff Jackson, *American Space: The Centennial Years, 1865–1876* (New York: W. W. Norton, 1972, pp. 72–86.

37. Peter B. Wight, "Correspondence: Chicago," *American Architect* 1 (April 1, 1876): 111.

38. Peter B. Wight, "The Condition of Architecture in the Western States," *American Architect* 7 (March 13, 1880): 107–9; (March 20, 1880): 118–19, both reprinted from the *American Art Review.* John W[ellborn] Root, "The City House in the West," *Scribner's* 8 (October 1890): 416–34, reprinted in Russell Sturgis, John W. Root, Bruce Price et al., *Homes in City and Country* (New York: Charles Scribner's Sons, 1893), excerpts published in the *Chicago Tribune,* September 28, 1890; and Root (published anonymously), "Some Notes Upon Earlier Chicago Architects," *Inland Architect* 19 (May 1892): 47–48 (reprinted from *America,* November 1890).

39. *Industrial Chicago,* 1:72.

40. W. L. B. Jenney, "Architecture: Lectures Delivered at the University of Chicago," *Inland Architect* 1 (March–June 1883); John M. Van Osdel, "History of Chicago Architecture," *Inland Architect* 1–2 (March–August 1883); John W. Root, "Art of Pure Color," *Inland Architect* 1–2 (June–September 1883); "Development of Architectural Style," John W. Root, tr., from Gottfried Semper, *Der Stil in den Technischen und Tektonischen Kunsten,* 2 vols. (Munich, 1860–63); *Inland Architect* 14 (December 1889): 76–78, and 15 (February 1890): 5–6; Lulu Stoughton Beem, "Women in Architecture," *Inland Architect* 4 (October 1884): 40–41; through the 1880s, "Association Notes" carried synopses of the plumbers' and carpenters' association meetings, and occasionally prize-winning papers from them, as well as the proceedings of architects' and builders' groups.

41. Figures on journal circulation come from *N. W. Ayer & Son's American Newspaper Annual and Directory* (Philadelphia: N. W. Ayer & Son, yearly from 1880 to 1932).

42. *American Architect* 16 (November 22, 1884). Also see Barbara K. Silvergold, "Richard Morris Hunt and the Importation of Beaux-Arts Architecture to the United States" (Ph.D. diss., University of California, Berkeley, 1971), p. 177. With much opposition and the backing of Daniel Burnham and John Wellborn Root, the Western Association of Architects was merged with the American Institute of Architects in 1889.

43. "Official Report of the Second Annual Convention of Western Association of Architects, held at St. Louis, November 18, 19, and 20, 1885," *Inland Architect* 6 (November 1886): 71.

44. "Symposium: What Are the Present Tendencies of Architectural Design in America?" [an account of the Illinois State Association of Architects'

annual meeting, March 5, 1887], *Inland Architect* 9 (March 1887): 23–26; reprinted in Donald Hoffmann, ed., *The Meanings of Architecture: Buildings and Writings of John Wellborn Root* (New York: Horizon Press, 1967), pp. 206–17.

45. Ibid.; John W. Root, "The Dwelling, the Home," from "The Official Report of Proceedings of the Convention of Architects which met at Chicago, November 12, 13, and 14, 1884," *Inland Architect* 4 (November 1884): 2–12; B. W. S. Clark, "Needed Legislation to Protect Architects from Roguish Clients and to Protect the Public from Incapable Architects," *Inland Architect* 6 (November 1885): 63; E. F. Fassett, "The Modern Mechanic," *Inland Architect* 7 (March 1886): 22–23; Bauman, "Relation of Architect to Contractor," pp. 60–61.

46. The pages of *Inland Architect* and meetings of the Western Association of Architects were filled with references to a "democratic" architecture. Sullivan was especially fluent in such rhetoric. See *Kindergarten Chats on Architecture, Education and Democracy, and Other Writings* (New York: Wittenborn, Shultz, 1947), which included reprintes of articles from Cleveland's *Interstate Architect and Builder* (1900–1902), and Sherman Paul, *Louis Sullivan: An Architect in American Thought* (Englewood Cliffs, N.J.: Prentice-Hall, 1962). The talks and writings of Irving K. Pond were also deeply concerned with the issue of a democratic architecture that could meet the needs of an American "middle class."

47. "Three Houses for W. H. Burnet, Kenwood, Illinois," *Inland Architect* 9 (April 1887), n.p.

48. *A Holiday at Rosalie Villas* (Chicago: James P. Craig, 1888); cited in Jean F. Block, *Hyde Park Houses: An Informal History, 1856–1910* (Chicago: University of Chicago Press, 1978), pp. 42–43.

49. C. H. Blackall, "Notes of Travel: Chicago—IV," *American Architect* 23 (March 24, 1888): 140.

50. Richard Hofstadter, *The Age of Reform: From Bryan to F. D. R.* (New York: Vintage Books, 1955), pp. 91–93, 131–72; *Anti-Intellectualism in American Life* (New York: Knopf, 1963), pp. 145–96; John G. Sproat, *"The Best Men": Liberal Reformers in the Gilded Age* (New York: Oxford University Press, 1968).

Chapter 3

1. Charles N. Glaab and A. Theodore Brown, *A History of Urban America* (New York: Macmillan, 1967), p. 142. However, the importance of residential construction in the national economy began to fall in the late 1880s, with the major decline taking place between 1895 and 1900. The decline in relation to consumption, especially after the First World War, was steeper than that in relation to the GNP. See Leo Grebler, David M. Blank, and Louis Winnick, *Capital Formation in Residential Real Estate, Trends and Prospects* (Princeton, N.J.: Princeton University Press, 1956).

2. U.S. Bureau of the Census, *Historical Statistics of the United States* (Washington, D.C.: Government Printing Office, 1952), pp. 7, 14; Ray Ginger,

Altgeld's America: The Lincoln Ideal Versus Changing Realities (New York: New Viewpoints, 1973), p. 95; Bessie Louise Pierce, *A History of Chicago,* 3 vols. (Chicago: University of Chicago Press, 1937–57), vol. 3, *1871–1893,* pp. 146, 535.

3. Charles B. Spahr, *An Essay on the Present Distribution of Wealth in the United States* (New York: T. Y. Crowell & Co., 1896), pp. 50–70; Clarence Dickinson Long, *Wages and Earnings in the United States, 1860–1890* (Princeton, N.J.: Princeton University Press, 1960); Leila Houghteling, *The Income and Standard of Living of Unskilled Laborers in Chicago* (Chicago: University of Chicago Press, 1927); Stephen Thernstrom, *Poverty and Progress: Social Mobility in a Nineteenth Century City* (Cambridge: Harvard University Press, 1964), pp. 22, 80–85, 117–36; Sam Bass Warner, Jr., *Streetcar Suburbs: The Process of Growth in Boston, 1870–1900* (New York: Atheneum, 1970), pp. 52–56, 118–122; Charles Richmond Henderson, *Modern Methods of Charity* (New York: Macmillan, 1904), pp. 380–38.

4. U.S. Bureau of the Census, *Report on Farms and Homes: Proprietorship and Indebtedness in the United States at the Eleventh Census: 1890,* vol. 13 (Washington, D.C.: Government Printing Office, 1896), p. 32. In Chicago, the homes of 43 percent of the homeowners were encumbered with mortgages in 1890. (In the 28 largest U.S. cities, 38 percent of homeowners had encumbered houses.) Also see, Warner, *Streecar Suburbs,* pp. 118–29, and Roger D. Simon, "The City-Building Process: Housing and Services in the New Milwaukee Neighborhoods, 1880–1910," *Transactions of the American Philosophical Society, 1978,* vol. 68 (Philadelphia, 1978): 5–68, for other examples.

5. Henry George, *Progress and Poverty* (New York: L. W. Lovell Co., 1879).

6. "The Advantage of Being Middle Class," *Stories of the Streets and of the Town, from the Chicago Record, 1893–1900,* collected and ed. Franklin J. Meine (Chicago: The Caxton Club, 1941), p. 75.

7. Polly Anne Earl, "Craftsmen and Machines: The Nineteenth-Century Furniture Industry," *Technological Innovations and the Decorative Arts,* Wintherthur Conference Report, 1973, Ian M. G. Quimby and Polly Anne Earl, eds. (Charlottesville: University Press of Virginia, 1974), p. 315; "Wood-Working Machinery at Philadelphia," *American Builder* 12 (November, 1876): 253–55.

8. F. E. Kidder, *Building Construction and Superintendence,* 2 vols. (New York: William T. Comstock, 1896), 2:229.

9. Carroll D. Wright, *Thirteenth Annual Report of the Commissioner of Labor, 1898: Hand and Machine Labor,* 2 vols. (Washington, D.C.: Government Printing Office, 1899), 1:280; cited in Earle, "Craftsmen and Machines," p. 311. See also Charles Henry Cochrane, *The Wonders of Modern Mechanism* (Philadelphia: J. B. Lippincott Co., 1896), for a survey of these inventions.

10. *Industrial Chicago,* 4 vols. (Chicago: Goodspeed Publishing Co., 1891), 3:603–20; Pierce, *History of Chicago,* 3:12, 535; A[lfred] T[heodore] Andreas, *History of Chicago* 3 vols. (Chicago: A. T. Andreas, 1884–86), 3:4–84.

11. John W[ellborn] Root, "The City House in the West," *Scribner's* 8 (October 1890): 416–34; *Builder and Woodworker* 20 (September 1884): 161.

12. Kidder, *Building Construction,* 1:349. Portland cement, made of limestone and clay blended at high temperatures to yield a new compound, was introduced to America in 1869. The first American patent was extended to David Saylor in 1871, and his product received one of the highest awards at the Philadelphia Centennial. However, American-made cement was not widely used until the end of the century, with the impetus of government contracts for production during the Spanish-American War.

13. Bernard A. Weisberger, *The New Industrial Society* (New York: John Wiley & Sons, 1969), p. 16; also see Warren C. Scoville, *Revolution in Glassmaking* (Cambridge: Harvard University Press, 1948).

14. "Modern Plumbing," *Architectural Record* 8 ("Great American Architects" series, July 1898): 111–13; Siegfried Giedion, *Mechanization Takes Command* (New York: W. W. Norton, 1969), pp. 628–712; Lawrence Wright, *Clean and Decent: The Fascinating History of the Bathroom and the Water Closet* (Toronto and Buffalo: University of Toronto Press, 1967), pp. 188–238; Pierce, *History of Chicago,* 3:161; Chauncey M. Depew, ed., *One Hundred Years of American Commerce,* 2 vols. (New York: D. O. Haynes & Co., 1895), 2:364–70.

15. Homer Hoyt, *One Hundred Years of Land Values in Chicago* (Chicago: University of Chicago Press, 1933), pp. 103–4, 137; *The Autobiography of Richard Teller Crane* (Chicago: privately printed, 1927).

16. Everett Chamberlin, *Chicago and Its Suburbs* (Chicago: T. A. Hungerford, 1874), p. 188.

17. Pierce, *History of Chicago,* 3:52; Blue Island Land & Building Company, *Homes for the People* (Chicago, 1905).

18. Hoyt, *One Hundred Years,* pp. 134–95, 484; Pierce, *History of Chicago,* 3:327–33; Harold M. Mayer and Richard C. Wade, *Chicago: Growth of a Metropolis* (Chicago: University of Chicago Press, 1969), pp. 132–52. There were, however, almost no paved surfaces between cities or far outlying suburbs and cities until 1900.

19. George Gay, "The Furniture Trade," in Depew, *One Hundred Years of American Commerce,* 1:632; *Industrial Chicago,* 2:318–25.

20. *Building Budget: A Journal of Architecture and Kindred Arts* was published in Chicago by the Permanent Exhibition of Building Materials and Improvements Office between 1885 and 1890. It featured articles on fire prevention techniques, archaeology (the editor's "Rambles through England"), local real estate, available building stones, and, in 1890, more scholarly pieces on classical detailing.

21. The NAB proceedings were published in the *Inland Architect*. For instance, the second convention, which McLean himself attended, featured speeches against apprenticeship and a rising tone of concerted resistance to union demands. "Second Annual Convention of the National Association of Builders of the United States of America, Held at Cincinnati, February 7–8–9, 1886," *Inland Architect* 11 (February 1888): 21–27. A contemporary development was the emergence of the general contractor, who applied logistics to the work schedule and delivery of materials in order to erect buildings more cheaply and quickly than other contractors. In 1885, the first single-bid,

single-contract system was used in Chicago and, although the system was designed especially for skyscraper construction, the techniques were soon extended to large-scale residential developments. See Chad Wallin, *The Builders' Story: An Interpretive Record of the Builders' Association of Chicago* (Chicago: Builder's Association, 1966), p. 5. This picture contrasts sharply with that of the small builder of cautious, insecure taste in Warner's *Streetcar Suburbs,* pp. 126–32.

22. *Industrial Chicago,* 1:342–48, 588–92.

23. David W. King, ed., *Homes for Home-Builders* (New York: O. Judd Co., 1886), p. 12; George Preston Brown, *Sewer-Gas and Its Dangers* (Chicago: Jansen, McClurg & Co., 1881). The Chicago-based journal, *The Sanitary News,* edited by Brown, repeatedly stressed the need for skilled plumbers in house-building.

24. Plumbers held themselves responsible not only for the health of homes but for the sanitation of the entire city as well. See Alexander W. Murray, "The Sanitation of Cities. Essay Assigned to Chicago Master's Plumber's Association by the National Association," *Inland Architect* 3 (July 1884): 75–76.

25. Charles F. Wingate, "The Unsanitary Homes of the Rich," *North American Review* 137 (August 1883): 172–84; Clarence Cook, *The House Beautiful* (New York: Scribner, Armstrong & Co., 1878); idem., "Architecture in America," *North American Review* 135 (September 1882): 243–52; William Seale, *The Tasteful Interlude: American Interiors through the Camera's Eye, 1860–1917* (New York: Praeger, 1975), pp. 16–22.

26. The philosopher George Santayana used exactly this imagery in his 1911 speech, "The Genteel Tradition in American Philosophy," reprinted in *Winds of Doctrine: Studies in Contemporary Opinion* (New York: Charles Scribner's Sons, 1926), pp. 186–215.

27. Edward Westermarck, *The History of Human Marriage,* 3 vols. (New York: Macmillan, 1889). His work and that of C. S. Wake were polemics directed, in part, against the theories of Lewis Henry Morgan in *Ancient Society* (Chicago: Kerr and Co., 1877), which stated that monogamy was a social institution that had come into being only with property rights. A presentation similar to Westermarck's was that of amateur anthropologist Henry C. Wright, especially in his *The Empire of Mother over the Character and Destiny of the Race* (Boston: B. Marsch, 1870), although Wright emphasized the superiority of Anglo-Saxon family life. See George W. Stocking, *Race, Culture, and Evolution: Essays in the History of Anthropology* (New York: The Free Press, 1968). The recent literature on the history of the American family, particularly in the Victorian period, is voluminous. Among those I have found most helpful are Ann Douglas, *The Feminization of American Culture* (New York: Alfred A. Knopf, 1977); Aileen S. Kraditor, ed., *Up from the Pedestal* (Chicago: Quadrangle Books, 1968); Barbara Welter, "The Cult of True Womanhood, 1820–1860," *American Quarterly* 18 (Summer 1966): 151–74; Barbara Ehrenreich and Deirdre English, *For Her Own Good: 150 Years of the Experts' Advice to Women* (Garden City, N.Y.: Anchor Press, Doubleday, 1978); Sheila M. Rothman, *Woman's Proper Place: A History of Changing Ideas and Practices,*

1870 to the Present (New York: New Viewpoints, 1975); Eli Zaretsky, *Capitalism, the Family and Personal Life* (New York: Harper & Row, 1976). The classic study, still valuable, is Arthur W. Calhoun, *A Social History of the American Family from Colonial Times To the Present* (Cleveland: Arthur H. Clarke Co., 1919), vol. 3, *Since the Civil War.*

28. "A Further Notion or Two about Domestic Bliss," *Appleton's Journal of Popular Literature, Science, and Art* 3 (March 19, 1870): 328–29.

Chapter 4

1. Frances Willard, *How to Win: A Book for Girls* (New York: Funk & Wagnalls, 1886), p. 54. Also see Joseph R. Gusfield, *Symbolic Crusade: Status Politics and the American Temperance Movement* (Urbana: University of Illinois Press, 1963).

2. J[ohn] Pickering Putnam, *Architecture under Nationalism* (Boston: Nationalist Educational Association, 1890).

3. Historians take several conflicting positions regarding the progressive period and its leaders. The classic progressive historians placed the movement in the democratic reform tradition of Jefferson and Jackson. See Charles A. and Mary R. Beard, *The Rise of American Civilization,* 4 vols. (New York: Macmillan, 1927–57), and Vernon Louis Parrington, *Main Currents in American Thought,* 3 vols. (New York: Harcourt, Brace, 1927–30). Eric Goldman carried on this tradition with *Rendezvous with Destiny: A History of Modern American Reform* (New York: Vintage 1955), as did Russel B. Nye in *Midwestern Progressive Politics: A Historical Study of Its Origins and Development, 1870–1950* (East Lansing: Michigan State College Press, 1951). Richard Hofstadter, with *The Age of Reform: From Bryan to F. D. R.* (New York: Random House, Vintage Books, 1955), issued the strongest challenge, presenting the progressives as middle-class professionals concerned with their own status and sense of uselessness under urban capitalism, not as champions of the underprivileged, and labeling the movement a "status revolution." Samuel P. Hays went on to suggest that many of the reform measures were actually tactics of upper-class business interests to maintain an orderly labor force, in *The Response to Industrialism, 1885–1914* (Chicago: University of Chicago Press, 1957), an opinion carried further by James Weinstein, *The Corporate Ideal in the Liberal State, 1900–1918* (Boston: Beacon Press, 1968), and Gabriel Kolko, *The Triumph of Conservatism: A Re-interpretation of American History, 1900–1916* (New York: Free Press of Glencoe, 1963).

In a synthesis of these positions which allows for ambiguous and even unrecognized intentions, Robert Wiebe's *The Search for Order, 1877–1920* (New York: Hill and Wang, 1967), describes the concerns of a new middle class, often tied to corporate interests, which wished to stabilize and rationalize the economy and evolve principles for an unpredictable society. Both Wiebe and Hofstadter present an image of the progressives as longing for a world they assumed once existed in the American small town. However, it is those historians who probed more deeply into individuals in the movement who demonstrate this nostalgia most clearly. Daniel Aaron's *Men of Good Hope: A Story of American Progressives* (New York: Oxford University Press, 1961), while questioning his own enthusiasm of ten years before, shows a loss of this humanistic concern from the early progressives (among whom he includes the writers Bellamy, Lloyd, and Howells) to the latter-day, more rationalistic politicians (Wilson and Theodore Roosevelt). Christopher Lasch's study, "Jane Addams: The College Woman and the Family Claim," in *The New Radicalism in America, 1889–1963: The Intellectual as a Social Type* (New York: Alfred A. Knopf, 1965), pp. 3–37, offers a presentation of the reformer as motivated by personal needs and frustrations. Finally, Richard M. Abrams, *Conservatism in a Progressive Era: Massachusetts Politics, 1900–1912* (Cambridge: Harvard University Press, 1964), David W. Noble, *The Paradox of Progressive Thought* (Minneapolis: University of Minnesota Press, 1958), Arthur Mann, *Yankee Reformers in the Urban Age* (Cambridge: Belknap Press of Harvard University Press, 1954) and Morton G. White, *Social Thought in America: The Revolt Against Formalism* (New York: Viking Press, 1949) offer sensitive studies of major philosophical and political figures. My presentation of the "progressive movement" as a broad-based social reform movement of the 1890s, preceding the more defined Progressive party of 1912, follows from these texts.

4. Chester McArthur Destler, *Henry Demarest Lloyd and the Empire of Reform* (Philadelphia: University of Pennsylvania Press, 1963); *Speeches, Addresses, and Letters of Louise de Kouven Bown,* ed. Mary E. Humphrey, cited in Anthony M. Platt, *The Child Savers: The Invention of Delinquency* (Chicago: University of Chicago Press, 1969), p. 79. Also see John Higham, "The Reorientation of American Culture in the 1890's," in *Writing American History: Essays on Modern Scholarship* (Bloomington: Indiana University Press, 1970), pp. 73–102; Don S. Kirschner, "The Ambiguous Legacy: Social Control in the Progressive Era," *Historical Perspectives* 1 (Winter 1974): 69–88; and Paul Boyer, *Urban Masses and Moral Order in America, 1820–1920* (Cambridge: Harvard University Press, 1978) pp. 162–260.

5. Benjamin O. Flower in the *Arena,* cited in Nye, *Midwestern Progressive Politics,* p. 70. Flower left Chicago to edit the Boston journal between 1889 and 1896.

6. For example, in *Newest England* (1900), Henry Demarest Lloyd called for a society in which the middle class "is not to be exterminated, but is to absorb the other classes" (cited in Aaron, *Men of Good Hope,* p. 160).

7. Paul H. Douglas, *Real Wages in the United States, 1890–1926* (Boston and New York: Houghton Mifflin Co., 1930), pp. 110–12, demonstrates that real hourly wages remained almost stationary. On inequalities of wealth, see Charles B. Spahr, *An Essay on the Present Distribution of Wealth in the United States* (New York: Thomas Y. Crowell & Co., 1896), p. 69, where he states that seven-eighths of American families owned only one-eighth of the wealth, while 1 percent owned more than the remaining 95 percent. On the widening gap between different workers, see Albert Rees, *Real Wages in Manufacturing, 1890–1914* (Princeton: Princeton University Press, 1961). On the cost of living, see Frederic C. Howe, *The High Cost of Living* (New York: Charles

Scribner's Sons, 1917). The general point of the increasingly complicated definition of status is well made in David M. Potter's *People of Plenty: Economic Abundance and American Character* (Chicago: University of Chicago Press, 1954). On the depression as a whole, see Charles Hoffman, "The Depression of the Nineties," *Journal of Economic History* 16 (June 1956): 137–74, and Hoffman, *The Depression of the Nineties* (Westport, Conn.: Greenwood Pub. Co., 1970).

8. U.S. Bureau of the Census, *Housing Construction Statistics, 1889–1964* (Washington, D.C.: Government Printing Office, 1966), p. 19; Leo Grebler, David M. Blank, and Louis Winnick, *Capital Formation in Residential Real Estate, Trends and Prospects* (Princeton, N.J.: Princeton University Press, 1956), table B-1, p. 332, table K-1, pp. 428–30; Homer Hoyt, *One Hundred Years of Land Values in Chicago* (Chicago: University of Chicago Press, 1933), pp. 171–219; *Official Program and Catalogue of the First Annual Real Estate and Builders' Show* (Chicago, 1911), p. 15.

9. Harold M. Mayer and Richard C. Wade, *Chicago: Growth of a Metropolis* (Chicago: University of Chicago Press, 1969), p. 152; Goldman, *Rendezvous with Destiny,* p. 43; the term "city wilderness" was first used by M. A. De Wolfe Howe in the *Atlantic Monthly* in January 1896, who then suggested it to the Boston settlement-house worker Robert A. Woods for the title of his book, *The City Wilderness: A Settlement Study* (Boston: Houghton Mifflin & Co., 1898).

10. Henry Demarest Lloyd, *Wealth against Commonwealth* (New York: Harper & Bros., 1894).

11. Mel Scott, *American City Planning Since 1890* (Berkeley: University of California Press, 1969), p. 8; Hamlin Garland, *Crumbling Idols* (Chicago: Herbert S. Stone, 1894); Andrew Sorenson, "Lester Frank Ward: The 'American Aristotle' in Illinois," *Journal of the Illinois State Historical Society* 63 (Summer 1970): 158–66.

12. Thorstein Veblen, *The Theory of the Leisure Class* (New York: Macmillan, 1899; reprint ed., New York: Mentor, 1953), pp. 101, 110–11, 115, 226–27. For a suggestive comparison between Veblen and F. L. Wright, see Christopher Lasch, "The Moral and Intellectual Rehabilitation of the Ruling Class," *The World of Nations* (New York: Vintage, 1974), pp. 94–95.

13. Graham Taylor, *Chicago Commons through Forty Years* (Chicago: Chicago Commons Association, 1936), pp. 41–42; Isabel F. Hyams, "The Louisa M. Alcott Club," in *Proceedings of the Second Annual Conference on Home Economics* (Lake Placid, N.Y.: 1901), p. 18. On the programs and prejudices of Chicago settlement workers, see Thomas Lee Philpott, *The Slum and the Ghetto: Neighborhood Deterioration and Middle-Class Reform, Chicago, 1880–1930* (New York: Oxford University Press, 1978), and Allen F. Davis, *Spearheads for Reform: the Social Settlements and the Progressive Movement, 1890–1914* (New York: Oxford University Press, 1967). On Taylor, see Louise C. Wade, *Graham Taylor: Pioneer for Social Justice, 1851–1938* (Chicago: University of Chicago Press, 1969), and Taylor's *Chicago Commons Through Forty Years.*

14. Philpott, *The Slum and the Ghetto,* pp. 27–33, 37–41, 93–99. The Chicago

Architectural Club co-sponsored a Conference on the Improvement of Housing Conditions with the Chicago Improved Housing Association on March 20–26, 1900 (Philpott, p. 93).

15. Adna Ferrin Weber, *The Growth of Cities in the Nineteenth Century: A Study in Statistics* (1899; reprint ed., Ithaca, N.Y.: Cornell University Press, 1963), pp. 467–75; idem., "Suburban Annexations," *North American Review* 166 (May 1898): 612–17; Joseph Kirkland, *The Story of Chicago,* 2 vols. (Chicago: Dibble Publishing Co., 1892), 1:376, 448–50; for other social scientists praising suburban streetcars, see Joel Arthur Tarr, "From City to Suburb: The 'Moral' Influence of Transportation Technology," in *American Urban History,* 2d ed. Alexander B. Callow, Jr., ed. (New York: Oxford University Press, 2nd ed., 1973), pp. 202–12.

16. Weber, *The Growth of Cities,* p. 432.

17. C[harles] E[dward] A[mory] Winslow, *The Evolution and Significance of the Modern Public Health Campaign* (New Haven: Yale University Press, 1923), p. 36. However, as early as 1820, the *Journal of Health* noted that the "middle classes" were distinguishable by their considerable attention to matters affecting physical health (cited in Burton J. Bledstein, *The Culture of Professionalism* [New York: W. W. Norton, 1976], p. 155).

18. Dr. Henry Gradle, a student of Koch, published *Bacteria and the Germ Theory of Disease* (Chicago: W. T. Keener, 1883), the first text in English on germ theory. The book was based on his lectures at the Chicago Medical College.

19. "Books, Paper Money and Disease Germs," *Architects' and Builders' Magazine* 1 (December 1899): 95; Barbara Ehrenreich and Deirdre English, *For Her Own Good: 150 Years of the Experts' Advice to Women* (Garden City, N.Y.: Anchor Press, Doubleday, 1978), p. 142; see also Richard L. Schoenwald, "Training Urban Man: A Hypothesis about the Sanitary Movement," *The Victorian City: Images and Realities,* ed. H. J. Dyos and Michael Wolff (London and Boston: Routledge & Kegan Paul, 1973), pp. 669–92, for a more psychoanalytic interpretation of the sanitary reformers.

20. Bessie Louise Pierce, *A History of Chicago,* 3 vols. (Chicago: University of Chicago Press, 1937–57), vol. 3 *1871–1893,* p. 323.

21. *A Half Century of Public Health,* Mazyck P. Ravenal ed. (New York: American Public Health Association, 1921); and John Duffy, *A History of Public Health in New York City,* 2 vols. (New York: Russell Sage Foundation, 1968–74). The generally accepted idea that respiratory problems stemmed from people being poisoned by their own exhalations or from "sewer gas" was disproven scientifically in 1895. Laws requiring ventilation in every room, developed in the 1870s, which had resulted in narrow air shafts, were then seen to be ineffective, since it could be proven that they were, in fact, cultures for disease germs and prevented fresh air from circulating. Some physicians writing for a popular audience had made appeals for healthy housing, demanding improved architectural styles as one means, as early as the 1880s. Dr. Henry Hartshorne, in *Our Homes* (Philadelphia: Presley Blakiston, 1880), p. 15, had quoted Professor R. Barthomew's critique of the Cincinnati suburbs, in which he claimed that picturesque street curves obstructed surface drainage and

artificial lakes bred malaria. Such criticism had little effect in the 1880s, but with the increased fear of germs in the 1890s they reemerged. For instance, Helen Campbell's "Household Art and the Microbe," *The House Beautiful* 6 (October 1899): 218–21, railed against draperies, chromo-lithograph frames, and jigsawn furniture; Clarence A. Martin, a professor of architecture at Cornell, wrote a series, "How to Administer a Household," in which he condemned the practice of surrounding a house with trees and waterways as unhealthy ("The Selection of a Home," *Cosmopolitan* 34 [March 1903]: 545–52). Jonathon K. Allen specifically recommended that his readers buy homes in new neighborhoods, where they would find modern plumbing, simpler floor plans, better drainage, and open landscaping (*Sanitation in the Modern Home* [Chicago: Domestic Engineering, 1907]).

22. Hollis Godfrey, *The Health of the City* (Boston and New York: Houghton Mifflin Co., 1910), p. 15; his earlier articles in the *Atlantic Monthly* had spread these aesthetic ideas, calling for municipal services and legislation to control family health and homes; Lyman Abbott et al., *The House and Home: A Practical Book,* 2 vols. (New York: Charles Scribner's Sons, 1896); Agnes Bailey Ormsbee, *The House Comfortable* (New York: Harper & Bros., 1892); Isabel Bevier, "The Comfortable Home," *The House Beautiful* 15 (January 1904): 126–28; Birch Burdette Long, "Adaptation of an English Ingle-Nook," *The House Beautiful* 11 (March 1902): 275. The same point is made by Reyner Banham in *The Architecture of the Well-Tempered Environment* (Chicago: University of Chicago Press, 1969), p. 47.

23. Heidi Irmgard Hartman, "Capitalism and Women's Work in the Home, 1900–1930," (Ph.D. diss., Yale University, 1974; Ann Arbor, Mich.: University Microfilms), pp. 212–75; Edith Louise Allen, *American Housing as Affected by Social and Economic Conditions* (Peoria, Ill.: The Manual Arts Press, 1930), pp. 140–43, 188–208; Ruth Schwartz Cowan, "The Industrial Revolution in the Home: Household Technology and Social Change in the United States," *Technology and Culture* 17 (January 1876): 1–26.

24. Maury Klein and Harvey A. Kantor, *Prisoners of Progress: American Industrial Cities, 1850–1920* (New York: Macmillan, 1971), pp. 402–3; Richard Skolnick, "George Edwin Waring, Jr.," *New-York Historical Society Quarterly* 52 (1968), 354–78; Helen Campbell, *Household Economics* (New York: G. P. Putnam and Sons, 1897), p. 205, ties the event to the "municipal housekeeping" argument for women's professional roles and suffrage; on Chicago and Fox, see John J. Glessner, *The Commercial Club of Chicago* (Chicago: privately printed, 1910), pp. 159–67; William Hudson Harper, ed., *Chicago: A History and Forecast* (Chicago: Chicago Association of Commerce, 1921); Douglas Sutherland, *Fifty Years on the Civic Front, 1893–1943: A Report of the Civic Federation, Chicago* (Chicago: Civic Federation, 1943); Louis P. Cain, *Sanitation Strategy for a Lakefront Metropolis: The Case of Chicago* (De Kalb: Northern Illinois University Press, 1978).

25. Charles Richmond Henderson, *Social Elements, Institutions, Character, Progress* (New York: Charles Scribner's Sons, 1898); idem., *Practical Sociology in the Service of Social Ethics* (Chicago: University of Chicago Press, 1902); idem., *Modern Methods of Charity* (New York: Macmillan, 1904).

26. S. Maria Elliott, *Household Hygiene* (Chicago: American School Home Economics, 1905), p. 3.

27. Arthur W. Calhoun, *A Social History of the American Family,* 3 vols. (Cleveland: Arthur H. Clarke Co., 1919) 3:179–98. Mary P. Ryan, *Womanhood in America from Colonial Times to the Present* (New York: New Viewpoints, 1975), pp. 195–249; Ehrenreich and English, *For Her Own Good,* pp. 127–164.

28. Margaret Deland, "The Change in the Feminine Ideal," *Atlantic Monthly* 105 (March 1910): 290–91; Ella Wheeler Wilcox, "The Restlessness of the Modern Woman," *Cosmopolitan* 31 (July 1901): 315.

29. Olive Schreiner, "The Woman Question," *Cosmopolitan* 28 (November 1899): 45–54; Robert Grant, "The Art of Living," *Scribner's Magazine* 17–18 (January–October 1895), especially "The Dwelling" (February 1895), pp. 135–49; the articles were then reprinted as a book, *The Art of Living* (New York: Charles Scribner's Sons, 1899).

30. Most women would work for at least a part of the eight to ten years they would spend between leaving school and marrying. (And although few married women worked outside their homes, many earned incomes at home, taking in boarders or doing laundry, doing piecework or selling their own homemade products, according to their class.) The women working outside the home were also less likely to be concentrated in domestic service and a few industries, such as textiles, as had been the case earlier in the century; they were moving into more factory jobs and into white-collar positions that opened during the 1890s and were not yet sex-segregated. As business operations became more complex, requiring more extensive record-keeping, correspondence, and insurance services, and as department stores proliferated, women filled clerical and sales positions. Where in 1880, women had constituted only 4 percent of the clerical labor force, by 1890 they amounted to 21 percent. See Robert W. Smuts, *Women and Work in America* (New York: Schocken, 1971), pp. 14–24; Stanley Lebergott, *Manpower in Economic Growth: The American Record Since 1800* (New York: McGraw-Hill, 1964), table A-10, p. 519; Janet M. Hooks, *Women's Occupations Through Seven Decades* (Washington, D.C.: Government Printing Office, Women's Bureau Bulletin no. 218, 1947), table 11-AB.

31. The changes in Chicago were more striking for several reasons. The proportion of single people to married was rising rapidly, from 2:1 in 1870 to 3:1 in 1880 and 4:1 in 1890. The department stores for the Midwest and the mail-order houses for the country as a whole were concentrated in that city and hired many women. And industry was growing even more rapidly than the population, with the number of factories tripling between 1880 and 1890. Alfred T. Andreas, *History of Chicago* 3 vols. (Chicago: A. T. Andreas, 1886) 3:155; Ray Ginger, *Altgeld's America* (New York: Funk & Wagnalls, 1958), p. 244; Pierce, *History of Chicago,* 3:237–38. The information on the Illinois Federation was graciously supplied by Ruth B. Wiener.

32. However, this did not really take hold until the early 1900s, although it then dominated the housing articles. See, for example, Una Nixson Hopkins, "The Bachelor Girls' House," *Ladies' Home Journal* 26 (May 1909): 50; Charles E. White, Jr., "Three Girls Who Built on One Lot," *Ladies' Home*

Journal 27 (September 1, 1910): 25; Eulalie Andreas, "Apartments for Bachelor Girls," *The House Beautiful* 32 (November 1912): 168–70. Earlier articles had emphasized women staying at home: Edward Bok, "When Work Fits Women," *Ladies' Home Journal* 13 (February 1896): 14; "The Rush of American Women," *Ladies' Home Journal* 16 (January 1899): 14; "How Women Alone Have Saved for Homes," *Ladies' Home Journal* 20 (October 1903): 22–23.

33. "The American Woman in the Market Place, by an American Mother," *Ladies' Home Journal* 17 (April 1900): 19; Nellie M. S. Nearing and Scott Nearing, "Four Great Things a Woman Does at Home That Make Her the Greatest Power in America Today," *Ladies' Home Journal* 29 (May 1912): 12, 64–65; Laura Spencer Portor, "Where the Kindergarten Fails," *Ladies' Home Journal* 28 (March 1, 1911): 21, 57–58; Mary Ries Melendy, M.D., *Perfect Womanhood* (Chicago: K. T. Bland, 1903); [Augustus Moore], *The Domestic Blunders of Women, by a Mere Man* (New York: Funk & Wagnalls Co., 1900).

34. Day nurseries or crèches had increased rapidly in the cities during the 1880s, and the National Foundation of Day Nurseries was founded in 1898 to encourage working mothers to bring their children to supervised centers. Kindergarten associations during these years spread new ideas about professional early education, especially the Froebel Association. In 1885, Chicago had twenty-five kindergartens, all private or religious; in 1892, the city's public school system took them over and incorporated kindergarten classes in elementary schools. Although compulsory education laws had existed in Illinois since 1883 (resulting in an extensive school building campaign in the late 1880s), it was not until the passage of a state child labor law in 1891 that the education law began to be enforced. (In 1871 Chicago had 15 school buildings; in 1891–92, largely as a result of the improvements taken on with the 1889 annexations, there were 346.) During this same decade, junior high schools appeared, and the number of high schools increased dramatically. In the country as a whole, there were 10,000 high schools by 1910, compared with 500 in 1870. Furthermore, during the 1890s, the drive for "useful" instruction in everyday subjects, for vocational training and practical mathematics for the accounting clerk and the housewife, to be taught in the schools, was at a peak. Consequently, during this decade the schools became more standardized in their courses, in the age of students, and even in their environmental facilities. See Andreas, *History of Chicago,* 3:143–54; Pierce, *History of Chicago,* 3:324, 384–95; Helen Lefkowitz Horowitz, *Culture & the City: Cultural Philanthropy in Chicago from the 1880s to 1917* (Lexington: University of Kentucky Press, 1976), on the educational changes for the city as a whole; Richard Hofstadter, William Miller, and Daniel Aaron, *The United States: The History of a Republic* (Englewood Cliffs, N.J.: Prentice-Hall, 1967), p. 604.

35. Professor W. G. Sumner, "The First Steps Toward a Millennium," *Cosmopolitan* 5 (March 1888): 32; also see Jean B. Quandt, *From the Small Town to the Great Community: The Social Thought of Progressive Intellectuals* (New Brunswick, N.J.: Rutgers University Press, 1970).

36. Jane Addams, *Democracy and Social Ethics* (New York: Macmillan, 1902). The articles had originally appeared in the *Atlantic Monthly, The Ameri-*

can Journal of Sociology, and *The Commons*, and before that had been a course of lectures delivered at various colleges and university extension programs.

37. James Champlin Fernald, *The New Womanhood* (Boston: D. Lothrup Co., 1894), pp. 69, 365–66. Fernald was an American Baptist clergyman and dictionary editor.

38. "The Education of Women," *The House and Home* 2:347. See also Lyman Abbott, ed., *The Home Builder: Dealing Practically with the Modern Conditions of Home-Life, Self-Support, Education, Opportunities, and Every-Day Problems* (Boston: Houghton Mifflin Co., 1906). *The House and Home* was also published as *The Woman's Book*, again by Scribner's, in 1894.

39. Helen Churchill Candee, "House Building," *House and Home* 2:65–102.

40. Mary Gay Humphries, "House Decoration and Furnishings," *House and Home* 2:103–80, especially pp. 106 and 157.

41. Gillian Naylor, *The Arts and Crafts Movement: A Study of Its Sources, Ideals, and Influence on Design Theory* (London: Studio Vista, 1971; *The Arts and Crafts Movement in America, 1876–1916*, ed. Robert Judson Clark (Princeton, N.J.: Princeton University Press, 1972): Mabel Tuke Priestman, "History of the Arts and Crafts Movement in America," *The House Beautiful* 20 (October 1906): 15–16, (November 1906): 14–17; H. Allen Brooks, "Chicago Architecture: Its Debt to the Arts and Crafts," *Journal of the Society of Architectural Historians* 30 (December 1971), 312–17; Oscar Lovell Triggs, *Chapters in the History of the Arts and Crafts Movement* (Chicago: Bohemia Guild of the Industrial Art League, 1902); Rho Fisk Zueblin, "The Arts and Crafts Movement," *The Chautauquan* 37–38 (October 1902–June 1903); H. Allen Brooks, *The Prairie School: Frank Lloyd Wright and His Midwest Contemporaries* (New York: W. W. Norton, 1976), pp. 16–20; David Gebhard, "C. F. A.. Voysey—To and From America," *Journal of the Society of Architectural Historians* 30 (December 1971): 304–12.

42. The Chalk and Chisel Club of Minneapolis (later the Arts and Crafts Society) was founded in 1895; the Boston Society of Arts and Crafts in June 1896, four months before Chicago's.

43. Oscar Lovell Triggs, "The New Industrialism," *Craftsman* 3 (November 1902): 100. The list of society members is found in the *Annual of the Chicago Architectural Club, Being the Book of the Thirteenth Annual Exhibit, 1900*, p. 118.

44. Bertha Lynde Holden, "Tenement Furnishings," *The House Beautiful* 7 (April 1900): 307–13; George M. R. Twose, "A Statement Concerning the Arts and Crafts Exhibit," *Catalogue of the Eleventh Annual Exhibition*, pp. 104–8, which includes illustrations of model tenement rooms from New York and Chicago.

45. Sears, Roebuck and Company, *Modern Homes*, catalogue (Chicago: Sears Roebuck and Co., ca. 1905); for a general history, see Boris Emmet and John E. Jeuck, *Catalogues and Counters: A History of Sears, Roebuck and Company* (Chicago: University of Chicago Press, 1950).

46. H. Allen Brooks published two photographs of Wright's living room, one from 1895, in which the space was filled with a typical, if artistically arranged,

Victorian assortment of clutter, and the second from 1900, which suggests the effect of the Arts and Crafts Society on Wright himself ("Chicago Architecture," p. 16).

47. Frank Lloyd Wright, "The Art and Craft of the Machine," *Annual of the Fourteenth Annual Exhibit of the Chicago Architectural Club,* 1901; reprinted in *The New Industrialism,* ed. Oscar L. Triggs (Chicago: The Bohemia Guild of the National League of Industrial Art, 1902), p. 111.

48. William D. Kempton, "A Social Want," *Cosmopolitan* 24 (February 1898): 392–94. Charlotte Perkins Gilman, *Women and Economics* (1898; reprint ed., New York: Harper and Row, 1966); idem., *The Home: Its Work and Influence* (1903; reprint ed., Urbana and Chicago: University of Illinois Press, 1972); idem., "The Passing of the Home in Great American Cities," *Cosmopolitan* 38 (December 1904): 137–47; idem., "The Beauty of a Block," *Independent* (July 14, 1904): 67–72; Mary Hinman Abel, "Recent Phases of Co-operation among Women," *The House Beautiful* 13 (March–June 1903); Jane Addams, *Twenty Years at Hull House* (New York: Macmillan, 1925), p. 177.

49. "For Best Ideas on Organization of a Home, $500," *Cosmopolitan* 26 (February 1899): 419; "The Ideal and Practical Organization of a Home," *Cosmopolitan,* essays by Edith Elmer Wood (26 [April 1899]: 659–64), Van Buren Denslow (27 [May 1899]: 49–54). and ". . . Fifty Young Women, Compiled by a Committee" (27 [June 1899]: 167–71).

50. Ignatius Donnelly [Edmund Boisgilbert], *Caesar's Column* (Chicago: F. J. Schulte & Co., 1890); Charles M. Sheldon, *In His Steps: What Would Jesus Do?* (Chicago: Thompson and Thomas, 1897); John Burroughs, "The Vanity of Big Houses," *Cosmopolitan* 41 (May 1906): 89.

51. Edward Bok, *The Americanization of Edward Bok* (New York: Charles Scribner's Sons, 1924), pp. 240–43; "The Morals of the Bathtub," *Ladies' Home Journal* 13 (November 1896): 14; "Some of the Coziest Homes in America," *Ladies' Home Journal* 16 (April 1899): 18–19. Bok also quoted Theodore Roosevelt: "Bok is the only man I ever heard of who changed, for the better, the architecture of an entire nation, and he did it so quickly and yet so effectively that we didn't know it was begun before it was finished" (*Americanization,* pp. 249–50).

52. W[illiam] L. Price, "A $3400 Suburban House," *Ladies' Home Journal* 12 (December 1895): 37; Ralph Adams Cram, "A $5,000 Colonial House," *Ladies' Home Journal* 13 (February 1896): 17; Edward T. Hapgood, "A $4,500 Shingle House," *Ladies' Home Journal* 13 (March 1896): 19; Bruce Price, "A Georgian House for Seven Thousand Dollars," *Ladies' Home Journal* 17 (October 1900): 15; Joy Wheeler Dow, "Some Artistic Little Homes," *Ladies' Home Journal* 18 (April 1901): 5; Arthur Little, "A Successful House at Manchester-by-the-Sea," *Ladies' Home Journal* 18 (August 1901): 9.

53. For one survey of these Prairie School houses, see "Good-Taste Homes of Chicago Folks," *Ladies' Home Journal* 27 (August 1910): 28–29.

54. Frank Lloyd Wright, "A Small House with 'Lots of Room in It,'" *Ladies' Home Journal* 18 (July 1901): 15. Bok, a friend of the Chicago journalist Eugene Field and the evangelist Dwight Moody, had visited the city in

his search for American architects to design model houses and had probably met Wright through such a visit (Bok, *Americanization,* pp. 182–90.). On the early Prairie houses, see Henry-Russell Hitchcock, *In the Nature of Materials: The Buildings of Frank Lloyd Wright, 1887–1941* (New York: Da Capo Press, 1975), pp. 23–55, and Grant C. Manson, *Frank Lloyd Wright to 1910* (New York: Reinhold Publishing Corp., 1958).

55. *National Builder* 40 (October 1905): 29; 43 (December 1906): 35. Hodgson described the Fricke house as having "a massive look and is somewhat unique in style, but withal quite pleasing."

56. On Wright's Broadacre City, an elaboration of this quadruple block plan, see Wright's *When Democracy Builds* (Chicago: University of Chicago Press, 1945), *The Living City* (New York: Horizon Press, 1958), and "Broadacre City, A New Community Plan," *Architectural Record* 77 (April 1935), 243–44; Robert Fishman, *Urban Utopias in the Twentieth Century* (New York: Basic Books, 1977), pp. 122–60; Robert C. Twombley, *Frank Lloyd Wright: An Interpretive Biography* (New York: Harper & Row, 1973); and Norris Kelly Smith, *Frank Lloyd Wright: A Study in Architectural Content* (Englewood Cliffs, N.J.: Prentice-Hall, 1966). In 1901, the average cost for a three- or four-bedroom middle-class house in the suburbs of a large city was $2,000–$6,000; the average size of the plot of land for such a house was 50′ × 75′, or twelve houses to the acre.

57. John Freeman, *The Forgotten Rebel: Gustav Stickley and His Craftsman Mission Furniture* (Watkins Glen, N.Y.: Century House, 1966); Oscar L. Triggs, "The Workshop and School," *The Craftsman* 3 (October 1902): 20–32; Warren H. Manning, "The History of Village Improvement in the United States," *The Craftsman* 5 (February 1904): 423–32; L. M. McCauley, "Municipal Art in Chicago: A Civic Renaissance Planned for the Western Metropolis," *The Craftsman* 9 (December 1905): 321–40; C. Valentine Kirby, "Craftsmanship as a Preventive of Crime," *The Craftsman* 8 (May 1905): 150–70; A. D. F. Hamlin, "Style in Architecture," *The Craftsman* 8 (June 1905): 325–31; Louis H. Sullivan, "Reply to Mr. Frederick Stymetz Lamb on 'Modern Use of the Gothic; The Possibility of New Architectural Style,'" *The Craftsman* 8 (June 1905): 336–38; idem., "What Is Architecture: A Study of the American People," *The Craftsman* 10 (May–July, 1906): 143–49, 352–58, 507–13 (originally published in *The American Contractor,* January 1906). The influence of this journal is suggested by the number of clippings that appeared in the volume "City Planning, United States, 1903–1912," compiled by George Hooker of the City Club and Hull House. H. Allen Brooks comments upon the importance of homemaker magazines in *The Prairie School* (pp. 8–11), although he contends that the average reader was a passive recipient of architects' ideas and "largely unaware of what he was getting." For reprints of many of these articles and designs, see Barry Sanders, ed., *"The Craftsman": An Anthology* (New York: Peregrine Smith, 1978).

58. "The Craftsman House," designed by E. G. W. Dietrich and Gustav Stickley, *The Craftsman* 4 (May 1903): 84–92. Stickley also published a pattern book, *Craftsman Homes,* in 1909, and a second, *More Craftsman Homes,* in 1912.

59. Robert Louis Stevenson, "The House Beautiful," *The House Beautiful* 15 (December 1903): 2–3; Herbert E. Fleming, "The Literary Interests of Chicago—IV," *American Journal of Sociology* 11 (May 1906): 803–4; Frank Luther Mott, *A History of American Magazines,* 5 vols. (Cambridge: Harvard University Press, 1957), 5:154–65. A venture in many ways comparable but one more interested in promoting the Arts and Crafts aesthetic than a social or political aspect of architecture, was Philadelphia's *House and Garden,* edited by architect Wilson Eyre together with Frank Miles Day and Herbert C. Wise, from 1901.

60. Stone was a strong editorial force. In 1900 the journal had 3,000 subscribers and 4,000 newsstand sales; by 1905 it claimed 40,000 (Fleming, p. 804).

61. Ellen M. Henrotin's "The Woman's Forum" ran from 1903 to 1904; it was dedicated to the perpetuation of the "city beautiful" and women's involvement in civic affairs. See, for instance, Henrotin, "Woman in Modern Industry," *The House Beautiful* 15 (May 1904): 351–53; and Mrs. Frank Asbury Johnson, "Neighborhood Improvement Associations," *The House Beautiful* 15 (December 1903): 46–47; (January 1904): 115–17.

62. Grace Van Everen Stoughton, "Popular Indifference to House Sanitation," *The House Beautiful* 15 (May 1904): 386–88; Herbert S. Stone, editorial "Notes," *The House Beautiful* 3 (February 1898): 101–2.

63. Virginia Robie, "A House Designed by a Woman: Another Home-Made Home," *The House Beautiful* 16 (October 1904): 7–10; Kinney's series ran from 1899 to 1901.

64. "Model Houses in England," *The House Beautiful* 8 (June 1900): 407–10; Edward W.Gregory, "Architects of the Modern English Home, I—The Work of Mr. H. H. Baillie Scott," *The House Beautiful* 30 (August 1911): 66–71; idem., "II—The Work of Mr. R. Barry Parker," *The House Beautiful* 30 (September 1911): 116–23; Edward W. Gregory, "The Garden Cities of England," *The House Beautiful* 31 (May 1912): 161–66, 182.

65. Dwight Perkins, "Notes," *The House Beautiful* 6 (June 1899): 40–41; Alfred H. Granger, "An Architect's Studio," (on Frank Lloyd Wright), *The House Beautiful* 7 (December 1899): 36–45; Robert C. Spencer, Jr., "Half-Timbers and Casements," *The House Beautiful* 11 (December 1901): 12–19; idem., "The Window Problem," *The House Beautiful* 13 (May 1902): 367–68; "Recent Work of Tallmadge and Watson," *The House Beautiful* 29 (April 1911): 158–59, are among the works that make this point.

66. "The Poor Taste of the Rich," *The House Beautiful* 16–17 (December 1904): 20–23; (January 1905): 14–15; (February 1905): 18–21; (March 1905): 26–28.

67. Lloyd, *Wealth against Commonwealth,* p. 510.

68. *Proceedings of the Fourth Annual Conference on Home Economics, Lake Placid, New York, 1902,* p. 36.

Chapter 5

1. "The Ballot for the Householder," Suffrage Hearing, Springfield, Mass., April 14, 1909 (Talbot Papers, University of Chicago, Box VI, Folder 6). On

women in Chicago, a useful source is Adade Mitchell Wheeler and Marlene Stein Wortman, *The Roads They Made: Women in Illinois History* (Chicago: Charles H. Kerr Publishing Co., 1977).

2. The 1870s were a period of notable advances in education for women, and training in domestic science must be considered part of this. Three midwestern universities pioneered departments in household science: Kansas (1873) and Iowa (1874) state universities and the University of Illinois (1874). Even earlier, Vassar (1865) had introduced some household arts courses, training women for public work in nutrition, sanitation, and social services. The main movement for training in the cities came from the cooking schools, in which the emphasis was on scientific cooking techniques and collective research by women. The New York School was established in 1874. The real innovations, however, took place in Boston. The Women's Educational Association had been formed in 1872, and, with Elizabeth Peabody's early kindergarten experiments, promoted manual training in household arts for young girls. Maria Parloa's school in New London, Connecticut (1876) led to the founding of the Boston Cooking School in 1879. Parloa also began to lecture on the Chautauqua circuit about techniques for modern, standardized, economical, and healthful cooking. A parallel development was the Kitchen Garden Associations, the first incorporated in New York in 1880, which sought to teach young children about household tasks through play. In 1884, the New York Association became the Industrial Education Association, from which, in 1888, was organized the College for the Training of Teachers. These associations, however, as well as the occasional high school curricula (e.g., in San Francisco, 1885) and the home economics courses at Pratt Institute, New York (founded 1887), were limited to cooking lessons for future housewives and servants. (For histories of the movement, see Isabel Bevier and Susannah Usher, *The Home Economics Movement* [Boston: Whitcomb and Barrows, 1906], Isabel Bevier, *Home Economics in Education* [Philadelphia: J. B. Lippincott, 1924], Paul V. Betters, *The Bureau of Home Economics: Its History, Activities and Organization* [Washington, D.C.: The Brookings Institution, 1930], and Helen Campbell, "Household Economics as a University Movement," *American Review of Reviews* 13 [March 1896]: 294–99 [from *The American Kitchen* of November 1894].)

3. Marion Talbot and Lois Kimball Mathews Rosenberry, *The History of the American Association of University Women, 1881–1931* (Boston: Houghton Mifflin, 1931). The sixty-five charter members of the AAUW included Richards, Marion Talbot, Lucy Stone, Alice Freeman Palmer, and the architect Margaret Hicks.

4. *Journal of Home Economics* (Baltimore) 1 (April 1909): 185; cited in Bevier and Usher, *Home Economics Movement*, p. 145. Mrs. John Wilkinson was the president of the NHEA and Ellen M. Henrotin was the honorary president; both women were prominent in the Chicago Club and the National Federation of Women's Clubs.

5. Jeanne Madeline Weimann, "A Temple to Women's Genius: The Woman's Building of 1893," *Chicago History* 6 (April 1977): 23–33; Judith Paine, "Pioneer Women Architects," in *Women in American Architecture: A Historic*

and Contemporary Perspective, ed. Susana Torre (New York: Watson-Guptill Publications: Whitney Library of Design, 1977), pp. 57–60. Horace Morgan, in *The Historical World's Columbian Exposition and Chicago Guide* (St. Louis, Mo.: The Pacific Publishing Co., 1892), p. 81, noted that of the inventions patented by women between 1809 and 1889, only 42 percent were for the household.

6. Major Ben. C. Truman, *History of the World's Fair* (Chicago, 1893), p. 189; *Condensed Official Catalogue of Interesting Exhibits with Their Locations in the World's Columbian Exposition,* ed. M. P. Handy (Chicago: W. B. Conkey Co., 1893). On the cooperative housekeeping movement, see Dolores Hayden, "Two Utopian Feminists and Their Campaigns for Kitchenless Houses," *Signs* 4 (Winter 1978), 274–90; and her forthcoming book (Cambridge: MIT Press, 1980) on feminism and housing reform, 1860–1940.

7. The Rumford Kitchen was based upon the New England Kitchen experiment that Richards had carried out in Boston, on Pleasant Street, with Edward Atkinson, the inventor of the Alladin oven, in 1890. They set up a kitchen-dining room-demonstration area in which they hoped to teach the poor about scientific cooking. The Boston project, however, received little response and soon failed. Richards also approached these problems with the Household Aid Company, organized under the auspices of the Woman's Educational Association of Boston. In this experiment, she tried to teach young working girls scientific cooking to be used in their own homes and in others, where they would be servants. This more individualized experiment was also abandoned. The Chicago Rumford Kitchen was less "educational" and was more successfully received. One visitor apparently commented, upon leaving the workingman's cottage display, "It takes a $5,000 wife to live on $500 a year" (*Report of the Commission on the Cost of Living* [Boston: Wright & Potter, 1910], p. 255).

8. Betters, *Bureau of Home Economics,* p. 5; Bevier and Usher, *Home Economics Movement,* pp. 34–36. Most of these schools were in the South, West, and Midwest.

9. "Woman's Most Vexing Problem," *Ladies' Home Journal* 14 (April 1897): 14.

10. The centers of industrial training programs were the Carnegie School of Pittsburgh, Pratt Institute in Brooklyn, Boston's Simmons College, and the Armour Institute of Technology's School of Domestic Arts and Science in Chicago. The emphasis in these schools was on training girls technically for housekeeping and for self-support as cooks, waitresses, domestic servants, as well as for managerial positions in nutrition, institutional work, and so on. The schools also set up "housekeeping stations" in immigrant neighborhoods. (See Ruby Ross Goodnow, "The New Housekeeping," in Mary Virginia [Hawes] Terhune [Marion Harland], ed., *Home Making* [Boston: Hall & Locke Co., 1911], pp. 331–40; and Marion Talbot, "The Education of the Housekeeper," *The House Beautiful* 15 [March 1904]: 243–46.) The Lake Placid Conferences describe the work of settlement houses. G. W. W. Hanger, *Housing of the Working People in the United States by Employers* (Washington, D.C.: Bulletin of the Bureau of Labor no. 54, 1904), and Winthrop A. Hamlin, *Low-Cost*

Cottage Construction in America (Cambridge: Harvard University Department of Social Ethics, 1917) outline the programs instituted in model houses of planned company towns. On Chicago's Business Woman's Exchange and School of Domestic Arts and Sciences (which replaced the Armour Institute's Domestic Science Program in 1901), see Stella V. Remiasz, "The History of the School of Domestic Arts and Science of Chicago from 1901–1944" (Collection of Chicago Historical Society).

11. Margaret E. Sangster, "Queen of One's Own Kitchen" *The Little Kingdom of Home* (New York: J. F. Tayler & Co., 1904), pp. 64–70; Catharine Beecher and Harriet Beecher Stowe, *The American Woman's Home* (1889; reprint ed., New York: Arno Press and the New York Times, 1971); and Lucy Maynard Salmon's book, *Domestic Service* (New York: Macmillan, 1897), derived from the courses she taught in economics at Vassar. Working-class girls increasingly found employment in other areas, whether factory work or clerical work, more socially satisfying and often more remunerative as well. The number of servants per 1,000 families remained at about 93 or 94 between 1890 and 1910, while the population as a whole increased by half. Other critics of the "servant problem" were Jane Addams, *Democracy and Social Ethics* (New York: Macmillan, 1902); Carl Bucher, *Industrial Evolution* (New York: Henry Holt, 1901); Lilian Pettingill, *Toilers of the Home* (New York: Doubleday, Page & Co., 1902).

12. Betters, *Bureau of Home Economics,* p. 9; Barbara Ehreinreich and Deirdre English, *For Her Own Good: 150 Years of the Experts' Advice to Women* (Garden City, N.J.: Anchor Press, Doubleday, 1978), pp. 127–64.

13. Clarence Elmer Rainwater, *The Play Movement in the United States* (Chicago: University of Chicago Press, 1922); William L. Hard, *The Women of Tomorrow* (New York: Baker & Taylor, 1911), p. 128; the Woman's Building was a three-story U-shaped structure in Colonial revival style, with a porticoed front facade.

14. *Proceedings of the Sixth Annual Lake Placid Conference on Home Economics,* 1904, p. 31; Richards, *The Cost of Living as Modified by Sanitary Science* (New York: John Wiley, 1899); and "The Creative and Vital Interest of Home Economics" in Talbot's "Home Economics" department in *The House Beautiful* 13 (April 1903): 303–4, makes these points as well. There was also an awareness of the limitations of technological progress at this stage in the home economics movement. Mrs. W. N. Shaw's article on "Science in the Household," in Alice Ravenhill and Catherine J. Schiff, eds., *Household Administration: Its Place in the Higher Education of Women* (New York: Henry Holt & Co., 1911), had declared, "It is a paradox that one of the difficulties with which the modern mistress has to contend is the fact that her house is 'replete with every modern convenience.' Every labour-saving contrivance, every mechanical convenience, calls for vigilance to ensure its proper use, and for knowledge as to the ways in which it may fail, and of the method of readjustment should it happen to do so" (p. 74).

15. Gilman's best-known works recognized the importance of the home, as an environment and as an ideology, for women's roles in the world. *Women and Economics* (1898; reprint ed., New York: Harper & Row, 1966), and *The*

Home: Its Work and Influence (1903; reprint ed., Urbana: University of Illinois Press, 1972), demanded change. "The Passing of the Home in Great American Cities," *Cosmopolitan* 38 (December 1904): 137–47, described the benefits of apartment hotels and offered numerous illustrations of luxurious existing ones. *What Diantha Did* was a popular novel describing cooperative housekeeping (New York: Charleton Co., 1910), often cited by the home economists. One later tract, *The Man-Made World; or, Our Androcentric Culture* (New York: Charlton Co., 1911), was even more emphatically critical of existing housing prototypes, asserting that "A house life is not good for man, woman, or child" (p. 65) but offering no specific alternatives.

16. W[alter] L[ionel] George, *Woman and To-Morrow* (New York: D. Appleton & Co., 1913), pp. 57–58.

17. Ibid., pp. 83–87.

18. Richards, *The Cost of Living;* Helen Campbell, "Household Furnishings," *Architectural Record* 6 (October–December 1896): 102–3; Marion Talbot and Sophonisba Preston Breckinridge, *The Modern Household* (Boston: Whitcomb and Barrow, 1912); Ethelda Morrison, "Household Industries in the Home: I. Reasons for Their Retention," in Marion Talbot's "Domestic Science" column, *The House Beautiful* 16 (November 1904): 32–33.

19. Richards, *The Cost of Living*, pp. 8, 14.

20. Ellen H. Richards, *The Cost of Shelter* (New York: John Wiley & Sons, 1905), pp. 6, 20–30, 75–78; Talbot and Breckinridge, *Modern Household*, pp. 10–17.

21. Talbot and Rosenberry, *The History of the American Association of University Women; Home Sanitation: A Manual for Housekeepers*, ed. Ellen Richards and Marion Talbot (Boston: Ticknor & Co., 1887).

22. Talbot's orientation toward reform came early in life. Her father, Israel Tisdale Talbot, served as dean of the medical school of Boston University and was active in public health. Her mother, Emily Fairbanks Talbot, campaigned for women's higher education. In her crusade for sanitary science, Marion combined the interests of both parents and her strong Unitarian upbringing. She was actually appointed to the university faculty at the request of Alice Freeman Palmer, then president of Wellesley, where Talbot had been teaching, when Harper asked Palmer to become professor of history and dean of women. For a history of the early years of the sociology department, see Steven J. Diner, "The Beginnings of Sociology at Chicago, 1892–1919: An Institutional and Intellectual History," in the Special Collections of the University of Chicago's Regenstein Library. The period for which the department is perhaps best known is the 1920s, when Robert Park and Ernest W. Burgess carried out seminal studies in urban form and social life, and George Herbert Mead, a professor of philosophy, gave an important theoretical framework with his "symbolic interactionism." See also Talbot's autobiography, *More than Lore* (Chicago: University of Chicago Press, 1934), and Marie Dye, *History of the Department of Home Economics, University of Chicago* (Chicago: Home Economics Alumni Assoication, 1972).

23. "Sanitary Science and Its Place in the University," *University Record* 1 (December 4, 1896): 457.

24. Marion Talbot, "Sanitation and Sociology," *American Journal of Sociology* 2 (July 1896): 74–81; Caroline Louisa Hunt, *The Italians in Chicago: A Social and Economic Study* (Washington, D.C.: Government Printing Office, 1897), and "The Home: Its Relation to the Problem of More Life for All: Home Problems from a New Standpoint," *The Chautauquan* 36–37 (October 1902–June 1903).

25. Sophonisba P. Breckinridge and Edith Abbott, "The Housing Problem in Chicago," *American Journal of Sociology* 16–17 (September 1910–September 1911), reprinted by the University of Chicago Press, 1910–15. Other works by Breckinridge include *The Child in the City*, Chicago Child Welfare Exhibit lectures (Chicago: Hollister Press, 1912); *The Delinquent Child and the Home*, with Edith Abbott (New York: Charities Publication Committee, 1912); *The Family and the Law* (New York: American Social Hygiene Association, 1925); *The Tenements of Chicago, 1908–1935*, with Edith Abbott (Chicago: University of Chicago Press, 1936); *Women in the Twentieth Century: A Study of Their Political, Social and Economic Activities* (New York: McGraw-Hill, 1933).

26. John Dewey, *The School and Society* (Chicago: University of Chicago Press, 1899).

27. Charles Richmond Henderson, *Practical Sociology in the Service of Social Ethics*, reprinted from vol. 3 of the Decennial Publications of the University of Chicago (Chicago: University of Chicago Press, 1902); see also above, chap. 4, n. 25.

28. "The House as a Unit of Health," *The House Beautiful* 12 (September 1902): 256.

29. Mary Hinman Abel, "Recent Phases of Cooperation among Women," *The House Beautiful* 13 (March–June, 1903); Marion Talbot, "The Housekeeper and Her Opportunity," *The House Beautiful* 12 (June 1904): 121, praises Abel's project.

30. Ethel Glover Halfield, "Flatland," *The House Beautiful* 12 (August 1902): 189.

31. "Housekeeping in Relation to Social Progress: Influence of the Development of Science upon a Progressive Housewife," delivered before the Farmers' Institute in 1899 (Talbot Papers, University of Chicago, Box 6), reprinted in *The House Beautiful* 14 (July 1903): 119–21.

32. Marion Talbot, "Instruction in Domestic Science in Chicago," *The House Beautiful* 16 (Auguest 1904): 28–29; Stella V. Remiasz, "The History of the School of Domestic Arts and Sciences of Chicago from 1901–1944," collection of the Chicago Historical Society.

33. Helen Campbell, *Household Economics: A Course of Lectures in the School of Economics of the University of Wisconsin* (New York: G. P. Putnam's Sons, 1896), p. 35.

34. Isabel Bevier, *The House: Its Plan, Decoration, and Care* (Chicago: American School of Home Economics, 1904; title varies slightly in later editions).

35. *Syllabus of Home Economics* (Baltimore: American Home Economics Association, 1913), pp. 40–46.

36. Talbot, "Housekeeping in Relation to Social Progress," p. 119; "Domestic Science in the Colleges," *Table Talk* 10 (September 1895): 4.

37. Isabel Bevier, "The Comfortable House," *The House Beautiful* 15 (January 1904): 128; Campbell, *Household Economics*, pp. 93–94; Richards, *The Cost of Shelter*, p. 78.

38. Cited in Madeleine Stern, *We the Women: Career Firsts of Nineteenth-Century America* (New York: Shulte Publishing Co., 1963), p. 140.

39. Campbell, "Household Furnishings," p. 101.

40. Campbell, *Household Economics*, p. 57.

41. Campbell, *Household Economics*, pp. 98–105; Bevier, *The House: The Handbook of Housekeeping* (1912).

42. Campbell, "Household Furnishings," p. 101.

43. Richards, *The Cost of Shelter*, p. 81; idem., *Euthenics: The Science of Controllable Environment* (Boston: Whitcomb & Barrows, 1910). Also see Christopher Lasch, "Politics as Social Control," in *The New Radicalism in America* (New York: Alfred A. Knopf, 1965), pp. 141–80; and Emma Siefril Weigley, "It Might Have Been Eugenics: The Lake Placid Conference and the Home Economics Movement," *American Quarterly* 26 (March 1974): 79–96. On scientism in general during this period, see Samuel Haber, *Efficiency and Uplift: Scientific Management in the Progressive Era, 1890–1920* (Chicago: University of Chicago Press, 1964).

Chapter 6

1. *National Builder* 33 (October 1901): 7; *Architects' and Builders' Magazine* n.s., 4 (July 1903): 573.

2. William H. Jordy notes that the Craftsman movement actually implied more responsibility for the architect, since the designer of a house was now also the furniture designer and interior decorator. His portrayals of the "Craftsmanship" aesthetic of the Greenes, Gill, and Maybeck emphasize the control each architect was able to achieve over his buildings. See Jordy's *American Buildings and Their Architects: Progressive and Academic Ideals at the Turn of the Twentieth Century* (Garden City, N.J.: Doubleday, 1972), pp. 217–20.

3. "The Workman Again," *American Architect* 1 (February 12, 1876): 50–51. Ruskin said of architecture, "In no art is there closer connection between our delight in the work and our admiration of the workman's mind, and yet we rarely ask for a builder's name" (*The Stones of Venice* [New York: John Wiley, 1860], p. 42.) Also see Daniel T. Rodgers, *The Work Ethic in Industrial America, 1850–1920* (Chicago: University of Chicago Press, 1977), pp. 32–40.

4. Henry Ericsson, *Sixty Years a Builder: The Autobiography of Henry Ericsson* (Chicago: A. Kroch & Son, 1942), p. 222. Robert A. Christie, *Empire in Wood: A History of the Carpenter's Union* (Ithaca, N.Y.: Cornell University Press, 1956), pp. 7–40; Wellington Roe, *Juggernaut: American Labor in Action* (Philadelphia: J. B. Lippincott, 1948), pp. 24–43. Philip S. Foner, *History of the Labor Movement in the United States* (New York: International Publica-

tions, 1964), vol. 3, *The Policies and Practices of the American Federation of Labor, 1900–1909,* pp. 185–86.

5. Christie, *Empire in Wood,* p. 63.

6. Foner, *Labor Movement,* 3:185–92. An example is the National Window Glass Worker's Union, organized in 1880, which controlled almost every shop in the country by 1910. But since this union refused to accept the new machinery and chemistry introduced in 1902 or to allow anyone who worked in a machine shop to join, it quickly declined and went out of existence in 1928.

7. *Selected Readings for Industrial Arts,* ed. Rex Miller and Lee H. Smalley (Bloomington, Ill.: McKnight and McKnight, 1963); Charles A. Bennett, *History of Manual and Industrial Education, 1870 to 1917* (Peoria, Ill.: The Manual Arts Press, 1937); *American Education and Vocationalism: A Documentary History, 1870–1970,* ed. Marvin Lazerson and W. Norton Grubb (New York: Teachers College Press, Columbia University, 1974); A. Theodore Andreas, *History of Chicago,* 3 vols. (Chicago: A. T. Andreas, 1886) 3:143–53.

8. *Industrial Chicago,* 4 vols. (Chicago: Goodspeed Publishing Co., 1891), 1:550–5, 2:322–4.

9. *Carpentry and Building* 27 (March 1905): 59; "The Trade School," editorial, *National Builder* 25 (October 1897): 8, makes the same point. See "Trade Unions' Hostility to Trade Schools," *American Architect* 21 (April 16, 1887): 181, for an attack on this resistance.

10. "Trades vs. Profession," *National Builder* 25 (March 1897): 11.

11. *Industrial Chicago,* 1:550–54.

12. Ibid., p. 553, from an article by Cyrus Kehr, "Mistakes of Employes," *Inland Architect* 16 (December 1890): 79–80.

13. Homer Hoyt, *One Hundred Years of Land Values in Chicago* (Chicago: University of Chicago Press, 1933), pp. 122–23; Samuel Henry Wright, "A Local Phase of Labor Combination," paper read before the Chicago Literary Club, November 27, 1889, published by the Literary Club (Collection of Chicago Historical Society); Frank Harris's *The Bomb* (1909) and Carlotte Teller's *The Cage* were novels describing these tensions; also see Joseph Kirkland, *The Story of Chicago,* 2 vols. (Chicago: Dibble Publishing Company, 1892), 1: 376–87.

14. Royal E. Montgomery, *Industrial Relations in the Chicago Building Trades* (Chicago: University of Chicago Press, 1927), p. 18.

15. *American Architect* 38 (December 10, 1892): 157; Sidney Smith, "Skilled and Unskilled Labor," *Building Budget* 4 (January 1888): 6–7, was an early lament, but Smith still held to Ruskin and the need for general trade skills.

16. Ray Ginger, *Altgeld's America* (New York: New Viewpoints, 1973), p. 92.

17. Montgomery, *Industrial Relations,* p. 18.

18. "History of Chicago's Building Troubles," *Carpentry and Building* 23 (March 1901): 75.

19. *National Builder* 30 (March 1900): 7.

20. Hoyt, *Land Values,* p. 207; U.S. Bureau of the Census, *Housing Construction Statistics, 1889–1964* (Washington, D.C.: Government Printing Office, 1966), pp. 18–19.

21. Montgomery, *Industrial Relations*, pp. 28–30; John Hutchinson, *The Imperfect Union: A History of Corruption in American Trade Unions* (New York: E. P. Dutton, 1972), pp. 25–28, 53–61.

22. Eugene Staley, *History of the Illinois State Federation of Labor* (Chicago: University of Chicago Press, 1930), pp. 140–75.

23. U.S. Bureau of the Census, *Eleventh Census of the United States, 1890, Chicago* (Washington, D.C.: Government Printing Office, 1891), vol. 1, table XXVI, p. 933; idem., *Twelfth Census of the United States, 1900, Chicago* (Washington, D.C., Government Printing Office, 1901) vol. 1, table XXVI, p. xxiv; vol. s, table CIV, p. 642.

24. Staly, *History of the Illinois State Federation of Labor*, pp. 108–11; quotation is from a letter of Michael H. Madden, secretary of the federation, printed in the *Chicago Labor Gazette* (n.d.).

25. *N.W. Ayer & Son's American Newspaper Annual and Directory* (Philadelphia: N. W. Ayer & Son, 1900, 1910).

26. *The Carpenter* 11 (September 1891): 11; cited in Christie, *Empire in Wood*, p. 69.

27. Fred T. Hodgson, "Carpentry under Modern Conditions," *Architects' and Builders' Magazine* 32 (October 1899): 25–28.

28. Fred T. Hodgson, *The Builder's Guide and Estimator's Price Book* (New York: Industrial Publication Co., 1882); *Modern Carpentry*, 2 vols. (Chicago: F. J. Drake & Co., 1902–17); Sears commissioned such texts as *Builders' Reliable Estimator and Contractors' Guide* (Chicago: F. J. Drake & Co., 1911), *The Carpenter's Cyclopedia* (Chicago: F. J. Drake & Co., 1913), and *Cyclopedia of Bricklaying, Stone Masonry, Concretes, Stuccos and Plasters* (Chicago: F. J. Drake & Co., 1913).

29. Fred T. Hodgson, *Easy Steps to Architecture and Archtecture of Antiquity, for Home Study* (Chicago: F. J. Drake & Co., 1907); *A Treatise on the Five Orders of Architecture, Compiled from the Works of Sir Willlam Chambers, Palladio, Vignola, Gwilt and Others* (Chicago: F. J. Drake & Co., 1910). In a similar effort to encourage general education, McGuire offered special discounts in *The Carpenter* on the works of Plato and Ruskin and on sets of world history volumes.

30. Houses by Wright, Tallmadge and Watson, and E. E. Roberts appeared in "Exterior Plastering," *National Builder* 55 (April 1913): 80–83; houses by Richard Schmidt, George Maher, Frank Lloyd Wright, and Howard V. D. Shaw appeared in the following issues of *National Builder*—40 (August 1905): 22; 40 (September 1905): 30; 40 (October 1905): 29; an Arthur Heineman bungalow court appears in "A View of Bungalow Land, Southern California," April 1911, p. 53; others by Hunt & Eager and Helen Lukens Gaut appear from 1903 until 1915. Of these, Hodgson wrote, "The new type of home, now so popular, has utility for its fundamental principle. It aims to eliminate all that is superfluous, and to embody all modern improvements" (*National Builder* 55 [January 1913]: 51).

31. "A Cozy Corner," *National Builder* 21 (October 1896): 258; "Styles of Furniture and Fitments," *National Builder* 39 (July 1904): 24; "Interior of the Ducal Palace at Darmstadt and Other 'New Art' Furniture," *National Builder*

37 (July 1903): 23; "Two New Interior Styles," *National Builder* 37 (December 1903): 21.

32. Herbert G. Gutman, *Work, Culture and Society in Industrializing America* (New York: Alfred A. Knopf, 1976) and "The Worker's Search for Power," in *The Gilded Age*, ed. H. Wayne Morgan (Syracuse: Syracuse University Press, 1963), pp. 31–54.

33. "Domestic Architecture," *Builder and Woodworker* 20 (January 1884): 20.

34. "Hints to Young Workmen," *American Builder* 12 (January 1876): 8; "Trades vs. Profession," *National Builder* 24 (March 1897): 11; "Women in Architecture," *Builder and Woodworker* 20 (July 1884): 122; "Department of Interior Decoration and Furniture," *National Builder* 19 (July 1895): 198; "Women Architects," *National Builder* 24 (May 1897): 8. In 1899 the National Building Trades Council and the International Union of Bricklayers and Stonemasons adopted resolutions demanding women's suffrage.

35. "The Building Situation," editorial, *National Builder* 20 (June 1896): 158; see also "The Building Situation," *National Builder* 21 (August 1896): 212. The editorials (e.g., *National Builder* 21 [November 1896] 269) address the populist movement and the free silver issue. A poem by an anonymous reader (October 1896, p. 249) catches Hodgson's "progressive" spirit and urges builders to "Read, read, read."

36. Allan R. Pred, *The Spatial Dynamics of U.S. Urban-Industrial Growth, 1800–1914* (Cambridge: MIT Press, 1966), p. 61; Adna Ferrin Weber, *The Growth of Cities in the Nineteenth Century* (1899; reprint ed., Ithaca, N.Y.: Cornell University Press, 1965), p. 188.

37. Bernard A. Weisberger, *The New Industrial Society* (New York: John Wiley & Sons, 1969), p. 18. Gabriel Kolko, *The Triumph of Conservatism* (Chicago: Quadrangle Books, 1963), pp. 30–34.

38. Koklo, *The Trimph of Conservatism*, pp. 11–17; *American Architect* 9 (February 12, 1881): 78; Sidney Fine, *Laissez Faire and the General-Welfare State* (Ann Arbor: University of Michigan Press, 1969), pp. 335–40.

39. *Industrial Chicago* 2:330; *American Architect* 9 (March 26, 1881): 146; Harry W. Laidler, *Concentration of Control in American Industry* (New York: Thomas Y. Crowell, 1931), pp. 76–82; Ralph W. Hidy, Frank Ernest Hill, and Allan Nevins, *Timber and Men: The Weyerhaeuser Story* (New York: Macmillan, 1963).

40. Sam L. Leffinwell, "Trusts and Combines—Of What Constituted and Remedy Therof," *The Carpenter* 21 (April 1901): 8; Fred T. Hodgson, editorial, *National Builder* 30 (May 1900): 7.

41. "Architects' Fees," *National Builder* 21 (October 1896): 248.

42. "Simple Elegance," *National Builder* 20 (July 1896): 194; "Houses for Homes," *National Builder* 25 (May 1897): 14–15; editorial, *National Builder* 33 (September 1901): 7.

43. George O. Garnsey, "Crescent Cottage," *National Builder* 24 (February 1897) 8; Robert Rae, "Colonial Cottage," *National Builder* 25 (November 1897) 15, 26; "Block of Stone City Residences," *National Builder* 25 (August 1897): 11; "Workingman's Cottage," *National Builder* 16 (February 1894): 23.

44. Fred T. Hodgson, ed., *Practical Bungalows and Cottages for Town and Country* (Chicago: F. J. Drake & Co., 1906); idem, *Hodgson's Low Cost American Homes* (Chicago: F. J. Drake & Co., 1904); idem, *Hodgson's Modern House Building* (Chicago: F. J. Drake & Co., 1905).

45. "German House Building," *National Builder* 20 (September 1896): 230; "Some Interior Decorations from Many Sources," 30 (June 1900): 10–11; "Cabinet-Making Schools in Germany," 30 (September 1900): 12.

46. Series by Ben Johnson, *National Builder* 43–44 (September 1906–January 1907), with commentary and lessons by Fred T. Hodgson.

Chapter 7

1. John Calvin Stevens and Albert Winslow Cobb, *Examples of American Domestic Architecture* (New York: W. T. Comstock, 1889), p. 9.

2. Ibid., p. 10.

3. *Inland Architect and News Record* 15 (February 1890): 27.

4. This same attitude had existed in the previous decade. See above, chap. 2, n. 51.

5. Herbert Croly, editor of the *Architectural Record* from 1901 to 1907, would make this point many times. In *The Age of Reform* (New York: Random House, Vintage Books, 1955), p. 153, Richard Hofstadter also comments upon the strength of this tie from the 1890s. He cites F. W. Fitzpatrick, "The Architects," in *Inland Architect* 39 (June 1902): 38–39, complaining of a loss of status for his profession. In his youth, Fitzpatrick mused, "an architect was somebody . . . He ranked with the judge, the leading lawyer, the eminent physician—several pegs higher in the social rank than the merely successful merchant or broker." But as Hofstadter points out, this was a false impression. The development of urban capitalism had brought the architect wealthy clients. Hofstadter speculates that it was the architect's sense of inferiority vis-à-vis this powerful "reference group" of wealthy businessmen that was responsible for the feelings of a loss of standing and value.

6. Nationally the number of architects listed in the census rose between 1890 and 1900; however, in proportion to the national population the number dropped. The tendency in the Chicago area was parallel, even slightly more exaggerated. Richard Levy, "The Architect and Civil Engineer, 1890: A Discussion of Professionalization in America," paper presented at the Annual Conference of the Society of Architectural Historians, February 4, 1977, Los Angeles, California; Turpin C. Bannister, ed., *The Architect at Mid-Century: Evolution and Achievement* (New York: Reinhold Publishing Corp., 1954), table 54.

7. "A Long-Felt Want," *Architectural Record* 7 (July–September 1897): 118.

8. Walter Blackburn Harte, "The Back Bay, Boston's Throne of Wealth," *Arena* 10 (June 1893): 6; cited in Arthur Mann, *Yankee Reformers in an Urban Age* (Cambridge: Harvard University Press, 1954), p. 5. Also see Paul Boyer, *Urban Masses and Moral Order in America, 1820–1920* (Cambridge: Harvard University Press, 1978), pp. 175–87.

9. A Long-Felt Want," pp. 118–19.

10. Ibid., p. 118.

11. Frank Lloyd Wright referred to offices of the late 1890s as "plan-factories" in *A Testament* (New York: Horizon Press, 1957), p. 33; also see Bernard Michael Boyle, "Architectural Practice in America, 1865–1965—Ideal and Reality," in *The Architect: Chapters in the History of the Profession,* ed. Spiro Kostof (New York: Oxford University Press, 1977), pp. 309–19, and Barbara K. Silvergold, "Richard Morris Hunt and the Importation of Beaux-Arts Architecture to the United States" (Ph.D. diss., University of California, Berkeley, 1974). William H. Jordy also comments on the ties between the rise of the Beaux-Arts method and the corporate architectural office in *American Buildings and Their Architects,* vol. 3: *Progressive and Academic Ideals at the Turn of the Twentieth Century* (Garden City, N.Y.: Doubleday, 1972), pp. 344–49. One of the reasons for larger offices in Chicago was the sudden passage of a law in 1893 (amended several times, but in effect until the 1920s) that limited the height of buildings to 130 feet. Once offices and businessesmen got wind of the move, they proceeded to put up as many tall buildings as possible before the prohibition went into effect. (Chad Wallin, *The Builders' Story: An Interpretive Record of the Builders' Association of Chicago, Inc.* [Chicago: Builders' Association, 1966], p. 8.)

12. Louis H. Sullivan, *The Autobiography of an Idea* (New York: Dover Publications, 1956), pp. 285–86.

13. John W. Root, "The City House in the West," *Scribner's* 8 (October 1890): 426.

14. William P. P. Longfellow, "The Architect's Point of View," *Scribner's* 9 (January 1891): 119–20.

15. C. E. Jenkins, "Style in Residential Architecture," *Inland Architect* 27 (August 1896): 5.

16. Henry-Russell Hitchcock, "Frank Lloyd Wright and the 'Academic Tradition' of the Early Eighteen-Nineties," *Journal of the Warburg and Courtauld Institutes* 7 (1944): 46–63. Wright was even offered the chance to study at the Ecole and then in Rome, he so excelled at academic architecture; he refused. Wright's other commissions of the mid-1890s included the Roloson rowhouses (1894), Francis Apartments, Francisco Terrace, and Edward C. Waller Apartments (1895), all in Chicago. Charles Roberts also proposed carrying out Wright's quadruple block plan for a small development in Oak Park, but the citizens of the town protested. Wright also designed Waller Estates, several low-cost dwelling prototypes, for Edward C. Waller around 1897. See Grant Carpenter Manson, *Frank Lloyd Wright to 1910: The First Golden Age* (New York: Reinhold Publishing Corp., 1958), pp. 203–7; Henry-Russell Hitchcock, *In the Nature of Materials: The Buildings of Frank Lloyd Wright, 1887–1941* (New York: Da Capo Press, 1975), pp. 23–35.

17. *Kindergarten Chats and Other Writings* (published in the *Interstate Architect and Builder* [Cleveland] 2–3 [February 16, 1901–February 8, 1902]; reprinted as a book, New York: Wittenborn, Shultz, 1947), pp. 130, 139, 150–53. For discussions of Sullivan's political vision, see Sherman Paul, *Louis Sullivan: An Architect in American Thought* (Englewood Cliffs, N.J.: Prentice

Hall, 1962), and Donald Drew Egbert, "The Idea of Organic Expression and American Architecture," in *Evolutionary Thought in America,* ed. Stow Persons (New York: G. Braziller, 1956), pp. 336–96.

18. Review of Carl Pfeiffer's *American Mansions and Cottages* (1890), *Inland Architect* 15 (July 1890): 89. Another example of this attitude is the article "Cottage Homes," *Inland Architect* 43 (July 1904): 19–21, a reprint from *The Builder.* (The author describes his low-cost English housing [$800–$3,000] and notes that American architects rarely designed houses costing less than $3,000. Even if McLean did publish the piece, he did not bother to give the architect's name or the citation from the English magazine.) "The Architecture of the People," *Architecture and Building* 30 (January 21, 1899): 17–18. In an article on "Cottages," Hobart A. Walker ridiculed the advertising rhetoric of charm and homeyness builders used to promote small dwellings. His tone suggests that the lavish praise for the "Queen Anne Cottage, All Modern Improvements" was a speculator's ploy. However, he does not suggest how the architect could do anything but distance himself from this moderate-cost housing, using every tactic, including ridicule. (*The Art Interchange* [August 1895]: 50, cited in Sadayoshi Omoto, "The Queen Anne Style and Architectural Criticism," *Journal of the Society of Architectural Historians* 23 (March 1964): 34.

19. Jenkins, "Style in Residential Architecture," p. 5.

20. Charles Zueblin, *A Decade of Civic Development* (Chicago: University of Chicago Press, 1905), pp. 60–61 (the articles making up the book had first appeared as a series entitled "Civic Progress" in *The Chautauquan* 36–37 (September 1902–June 1903); Richard Watson Gilder, "The Vanishing City," *Century* 46 (October 1893): 868–69 (cited in Boyer, *Urban Masses,* p. 270); William T. Stead, *If Christ Came to Chicago* (Chicago, 1894; reissued, New York: Living Books, 1964), pp. 409–28; William Dean Howells, *Letters of an Altrurian Traveler* (originally in *Cosmopolitan* 22–24 [November 1892–September 1894]), reprinted by Scholars' Facsimiles and Reprints (Gainesville, Fla., 1961); Henry Demarest Lloyd, "No Mean City," *Mazzini and Other Essays* (New York: G. P. Putnam's Sons, 1910), pp. 210–32. Among the many articles trumpeting the positive effects of the exposition were Alice Freeman Palmer, "Some Lasting Results of the World's Fair," *Forum* 16 (1893–94): 517–23; and Henry B[lake] Fuller, "The Upward Movement in Chicago," *Atlantic Monthly* 80 (October 1897): 534–47. Interesting comparisons are in Boyer, *Urban Masses,* pp. 182–87, and William A. Coles and Henry Hope Reed, eds., *Architecture in America: A Battle of Styles* (New York: Appleton-Century-Crofts, 1961), pp. 137–212.

21. Letter to Daniel H. Burnham, March 26, 1895 (Lloyd Papers, Wisconsin State Historical Society, Madison, Wis.), cited in Thomas S. Hines, *Burnham of Chicago: Architect and Planner* (New York: Oxford University Press, 1974), p. 120.

22. Louis Sullivan, *Autobiography of an Idea,* pp. 317–25; Henry Adams, *The Education of Henry Adams* (New York: Modern Library, 1931), p. 341.

23. Montgomery Schuyler, "Last Words About the World's Fair," *Architectural Record* 3 (January–March 1894): 291–301.

24. Henry Van Brunt, "Architecture at the World's Columbian Exposition," *Century* 44 (May 1892): 88, cited in Hines, *Burnham,* p. 121.

25. Cited in Wayne Andrews, *Battle for Chicago* (New York: Harcourt, Brace & Co., 1946), p. 161; see also Michael P. McCarthy, "Chicago Businessmen and the Burnham Plan," *Journal of the Illinois State Historical Society* 63 (August 1970): 228–56; and Boyer, *Urban Masses,* pp. 261–76.

26. Letter from the board of the University of Chicago Settlement House to the City Plan Commission, October 5, 1910; cited by Helen Lefkowitz Horowitz, *Culture & the City: Cultural Philanthropy in Chicago from the 1880s to 1917* (Lexington: University Press of Kentucky, 1976), pp. 224; Howard E. Wilson, *Mary McDowell: Neighbor* (Chicago: University of Chicago Press, 1928); Richard T. Crane, letter to the *Chicago Tribune,* December 29, 1907; cited by Mel Scott, *American City Planning since 1893* (Berkeley and Los Angeles: University of California Press, 1969), p. 79.

27. Daniel H[udson] Burnham and Edward H. Bennett, *Plan of Chicago,* ed. Charles Moore (Chicago: Commercial Club, 1909), p. 108.

28. Bannister, *The Architect,* p. 356; D. H. Burnham, "What an Architectural Association Should Be," *Inland Architect* 5 (March 1885): 20–21; 6 (November 1885): 72, 82–83; 6 (January 1886): 127–29; *American Architect* 57 (August 7, 1898): 49.

29. "Illinois Architects' License Bill," *Inland Architect* 29 (April 1897): 27–28; Bannister, *Architect at Mid-Century,* p. 356; Wallin, *Builders' Story* p. 14, notes that Adler wrote the definition and the tests.

30. "The New License Law in Force," *American Architect* 57 (August 7, 1897): 49. An earlier effort to pass legislation had been the proposed "Architects' Protective Association," drawn up by Louis Sullivan and approved by the Illinois State Association of Architects in 1888. The plan called for measures to prevent "men not worthy to be called architects" from taking on commissions worth over $3000 and specified limits on the architect's liability to "roguish clients" who had a "perverse and far-fetched insistence upon minute and abstract fulfillment of the duties of architectural services." The plan, as such, never passed the state legislature, but the provisions for defining the professional architect as one who took large commissions and who dealt with the spirit rather than the letter of a program would form part of the definition used by the licensing board. The important point, for the present discussion, is the price range and the elite attitude toward ordinary building. (B. W. S. Clark, "Needed Legislation to Protect Architects from Roguish Clients and to Protect the Public from Incapable Architects," *Inland Architect* [November 1885]: 63).

31. John Beverly Robinson, "The Proposal to License Architects," *The Engineering Magazine* 9 (May 1895): 197–203; Fred T. Hodgson, "Chicago Architects May Combine," *National Builder* 25 (August 1897): 7.

32. George Maher, "House for J. L. Cochran, North Edgewater, Chicago," *Inland Architect* 25 (June 1895), n.p.; George Maher, "Residence of Mrs. A. D. Wheeler, Edgewater, Ill., *Inland Architect* 24 (December 1894), n.p.; W. W. Boyington, "Views of 'Ravine Lodge,' Residence of S. M. Millard, Highland Park [Ill.]" *Inland Architect* 20 (November 1892) n.p.; George W.

Maher, "Residence of J. MacMeans, North Edgewater, Chicago," *Inland Architect* 27 (February 1896), n.p.

33. W. L. B. Jenney, "Designs for Houses to Be Erected at Buena Park, Ill., for R. A. Waller," *Inland Architect* 15 (February 1890), n.p.

34. Henry Ives Cobb, "Residence of Dr. J. A. McGill, Chicago," *Inland Architect* 20 (August 1892), n.p.; "Design by F. G. Meuller, of Architectural Class, Art Institute, Chicago," *Inland Architect* 27 (July 1896), n.p. For a critique of the school's program, see P[eter] B. Wight, "Architecture and Decorative Art at the Art Institute of Chicago," *Inland Architect* 27 (July 1896): 52–53.

35. *Catalogue of the Seventh Annual Exhibition of the Chicago Architectural Sketch Club, 1894;* ibid., *1895, 1897* (titles change slightly).

36. *The Chicago Architectural Club, Book of the Exhibition of 1900;* see also H. Allen Brooks, *The Prairie School* (New York: W. W. Norton, 1972), pp. 18, 27–28.

37. Bannister, *Architect at Mid-Century,* p. 99; Horowitz, *Culture & the City,* pp. 220–21.

38. *Circular of Instruction of the School of Drawing, Painting, Modelling, Decorative Designing and Architecture, 1900–1901* (Chicago: Chicago Art Institute, 1900), p. 46.

39. Wight, "Architecture and Decorative Art," p. 52; Arthur Clason Weatherhead, *The History of Collegiate Education in Architecture in the United States* (Los Angeles: Arthur Clason Weatherhead, 1941), pp. 62–71.

40. "Architectural Education for America," Arthur Rotch, "I. The Ecole des Beaux-Arts", Robert D. Andrews, "II. A Practical Training," *Inland Architect* 23 (May 1894): 41–43; reprinted from *Engineering Magazine* (April 1894).

41. Nathan Ricker's one-year builders' course at the University of Illinois Architecture School, modeled on similar German programs for carpenters and mechanics, began in 1875. Winton U. Solberg, *The University of Illinois, 1867–1894: An Intellectual and Cultural History* (Urbana: University of Illinois Press, 1968), pp. 261–63.

42. Francis S. Swales, "The Small English House as a Place to Live In—Its Seamy Side," *Architectural Record* 25 (June 1904): 400–403; H. Langford Warren, "Recent Domestic Architecture in England," *Architectural Review* (Boston) 11 (January 1904): 5–12; H. W. Frohne, "Recent English Domestic Architecture," *Architectural Record* 25 (April 1909): 259–70; Robert C. Spencer, Jr., "The Chicago School of Architecture," paper presented to the Illinois Society of Architects, November 28, 1938 (Collection, Chicago Historical Society); H. Allen Brooks, "Chicago Architecture: Its Debt to the Arts and Crafts," *Journal of the Society of Architectural Historians* 30 (December 1971): 312–13. It was not until Morris's death in 1896 that American arts and crafts societies gained credibility. On Voysey, see David Gebhard's introduction to a catalogue of his work, *Charles F. A. Voysey, Architect* (Santa Barbara: University of California at Santa Barbara Art Galleries, 1970), and his "C. F. A. Voysey—To and From America," *Journal of the Society of Architectural Historians* 30 (December 1971): 304–12.

43. Herbert Croly, "The New World and the New Art," *Architectural Record* 12 (June 1902): 137. Other anti-Art Nouveau articles include "The Art Nouveau," *Inland Architect* 40 (December 1902): 40; Claude Bragdon, "L'Art Nouveau in American Architecture," *Inland Architect* 42 (October 1903): 19–21.

44. Irving K. Pond, "German Arts and Crafts at St. Louis," *Architectural Record* 17 (February 1905): 119–25; Gustav Stickley, "The German Exhibit at the Louisiana Purchase Exposition," *The Craftsman* 6 (August 1904): 489–506. There were loose ties between the Vienna leaders of the movement and the Chicago profession. Adolph Loos himself had lived in the U.S. from 1893 to 1897 and spent much of that time studying the innovations in commercial architecture in Chicago. More important for local architects was the attention Nathan Ricker placed on Otto Wagner. In 1894, Wagner had introduced his text, *Moderne Architektur,* conceived as an alternative to the Beaux-Arts philosophy of formal composition and historical precedent, especially as defined by Gaudet, who began teaching at the Ecole that year; Wagner preached the need to respond to new materials in totally new ways. Ricker, who had also given his students at Illinois his own hand-written translations of other German architectural theorists, began to translate Wagner.

45. Among the historians who draw a parallel between Wright, Gill, and the Greenes in California, Voysey, Scott, Mackintosh, and Ashbee in England, and Olbrich, Hoffmann, Loos, and Behrens on the Continent, are Henry-Russell Hitchcock, *Architecture: Nineteenth and Twentieth Centuries* (Baltimore: Penguin Books, 1958); Esther McCoy, *Five California Architects* (New York: Praeger Publishers, 1975); James D. Kornwolf, *M. H. Baillie Scott and the Arts and Crafts Movement* (Baltimore: Johns Hopkins Press, 1972); Brooks, *Prairie School;* Reyner Banham, *The Architecture of the Well-Tempered Environment* (Chicago: University of Chicago Press, 1969); and David Gebhard, "Louis Sullivan and George Grant Elmslie," *Journal of the Society of Architectural Historians* 19 (May 1960): 62–68; idem., "William Gray Purcell and George Grant Elmslie and the Early Progressive Movement in American Architecture from 1900 to 1920" (Ph.D., diss., University of Minnesota, 1957); and idem., *The Work of Purcell and Elmslie, Architects* (Park Forest, Ill.: Prairie School Press, 1965). Thus, for example, when American architects demanded a moratorium on architectural ornament, as in Sullivan's case, it was a pragmatic experiment, to see what would happen ("Ornament in Architecture," *Engineering Magazine* 3 [August 1892]: 633–44; reprinted in *Kindergarten Chats,* pp. 187–90).

46. Henry A. Goetz, "Architecture and Its Effect on Insurance," *Inland Architect* 20 (August 1892): 4–5; editorial, "Chicago Building Law a Dead Letter," *Inland Architect* 25 (April 1895): 26.

47. James Clinton Peebles, "A History of the Armour Institute of Technology, 1896–1940" (manuscript in Chicago Historical Society), p. 53; *Industrial Chicago* 4 vols. (Chicago: Goodspeed Publishing Co., 1891), 1:293–309, 2:304–7.

48. John H. Jones and Fred A. Britten, eds., *A Half Century of Chicago*

Building (Chicago: n.p. 1910); *Revised Ordinances of the City of Chicago, with Amendments and Additions,* December 5, 1910; F. W. Fitzpatrick, *Building Code* (Chicago: American School of Correspondence, 1911); *Industrial Chicago,* 2:481–539.

49. Candace Wheeler, "Art and Its Relation to Commerce and Manufacture," lecture delivered to the Chicago CAA, February 25, 1898; Louis and Emily Gilbert Gibson, "Architectural Study Course," September 1897–March 1898; George R. Dean, "Department of Architecture," *Arts for America* 8 (December 15, 1898): 165–66. (Earlier known as *The Arts,* this was the publication of the Central Art Association. See also Thomas James Riley, *The Higher Life in Chicago* (Chicago: University of Chicago Press, 1905), pp. 96–102; and Horowitz, *Culture & the City,* pp. 171–82.

50. Frank Lloyd Wright, "Art in the Home," *Arts for America* 7 (June 1898): 579–88 (Paper read before the Home Decorating and Furnishing Department Congress of the CAA; the quotations are from pp. 581 and 582).

51. Dwight Perkins, "Criticism of Architecture by the Public," *Arts for America* 7 (June 1898): 573–74.

52. Robert G. Spencer, Jr., "Is There an American Style of Architecture?" *Arts for America* 7 (June 1898): 569–72.

53. Kenyon Cox praised the unique "friendly and familiar cooperation of artist and layman" in such Chicago clubs and organizations, "Art: An Example from Chicago," *Nation* 92 (May 4, 1911): 455–56; cited in Horowitz, *Culture & the City,* p. 169.

54. The lot, on Lexington (now University Avenue) between 57th and 58th streets, was the gift of a friend's father in the spring of 1899. Gardner was hired later that year, but it was not until late in 1902 that the house was ready for occupancy, and Herrick was greatly angered by the delays, convinced that the contractors were dishonest. He sold the house in 1907. See Blake Nevius, *Robert Herrick: The Development of a Novelist* (Berkeley and Los Angeles: University of California Press, 1962), pp. 103–4.

55. See *The City Club Bulletin* and John A. Glessner, *The Commercial Club of Chicago* (Chicago: privately printed, 1910).

56. Interview with Barry Byrne by H. Allen Brooks, cited in Brooks, *Prairie School,* p. 79; Brooks, "Steinway Hall, Architects and Dreams," *Journal of the Society of Architectural Historians* 22 (October 1963): 171–75.

57. *Twelfth Annual Exhibition of the Chicago Architectural Club, Catalogue,* Chicago 1899, p. 141.

58. "The Modern Phase of Architecture" was later published in *The Architectural Annual,* ed. Albert Kelsey (Philadelphia, 1900), p. 27; see Brooks, *Prairie School,* p. 38.

59. "Second Annual Convention of the Architectural League of America," *American Architect* 68 (June 16, 1900): 87; Brooks, *Prairie School,* pp. 37–42. The Chicago delegation was dominated by Frank Lloyd Wright, Robert Spencer, Hugh Garden, Emil Lorch, Richard Schmidt, Henry Webster Tomlinson, Dwight Perkins, Joseph C. Llewellyn, and, in spirit, Louis Sullivan.

Chapter 8

1. Oliver R. Williamson, "Choosing a Place to Live," in *The Complete Home,* Sarah C. Laughlin, ed. (New York: D. Appleton & Co., 1907), p. 19.

2. Katherine G. Busbey, *Home Life in America* (New York: Macmillan, 1910), p. 369.

3. Robert C. Spencer, Jr., "Brick Architecture in and about Chicago, Ill.," *Brickbuilder* 12 (November 1903): 222. He cited, in particular, Pond and Pond, Schmidt, and Wright.

4. Robert C. Spencer, Jr., "Planning the House: Economical Floor Plans," *The House Beautiful* 18 (June 1905): 22–23. This was one of the twenty-four articles Spencer published in this journal between 1905 and 1910.

5. The most vehement critics were Joy Wheeler Dow in *American Renaissance: A Review of Domestic Architecture* (New York: William T. Comstock, 1904), and Frank E. Wallis in *How To Know Architecture: the Human Elements in the Evolution of Styles* (New York: Harper & Bros., 1900).

6. "The Contemporary Suburban Residence," *Architectural Record* 11 (January 1902): 79.

7. *Architect's Journal* (London, 1936); reprinted in Frank Lloyd Wright, *The Natural House* (New York: Horizon Press, 1954), p. 27. Wilhelm Miller was the first to speak of a "Prairie style" among those architects and landscape architects who emphasized horizontality in their work (*The Prairie Spirit in Landscape Gardening* [Urbana: University of Illinois Press, 1915], p. 5). However, there had been talk of a "Chicago School," a "Wright-school," and a "New School of the Middle West" since 1904. See H. Allen Brooks, *The Prairie School: Frank Lloyd Wright and His Midwest Contemporaries* W. W. Norton, 1972), pp. 3–13; Mark L. Peisch, *The Chicago School of Architecture: Early Followers of Sullivan and Wright* (New York: Random House, 1964); H. Allen Brooks, "'Chicago School': Metamorphosis of a Term," *Journal of the Society of Architectural Historians* 25 (May 1966): 115–18; Titus M. Karlowicz, "The Term Chicago School: Hallmark of a Growing Tradition," *Prairie School Review* 4 (1967): 26–30; Carl W. Condit, *The Chicago School of Architecture: A History of Commercial and Public Building in the Chicago Area, 1875–1925* (Chicago: University of Chicago Press, 1964).

8. Busbey, *Home Life in America,* p. 373.

9. These same tenets of a modern architecture were also laid out by Frank Lloyd Wright ("In the Cause of Architecture," *Architectural Record* 24 [March 1908]: 155–65; and 35 [May 1914]: 405–13). It is clear that the changes he advocated—reducing the number of rooms and the amount of ornament, building appliances into the house, opening up the space—were widely accepted. Wright, however, emphasized individualized design, commenting that there should be as many house designs as families.

10. Henry Demarest Lloyd, "In New Applications of Democracy," *Congregationalist* (January 5, 1901). (The reference is from the bound volume, "City Planning, United States, 1893–1912," containing the clippings assembled by

George E. Hooker for the collection of the Chicago City Club, now in the University of Chicago library.)

11. "The Suburban House and Suburban Life," *The House Beautiful* 14 (July 1903): 113 (reprinted from *Building Monthly*).

12. Helen Campbell, *Household Economics* (New York: G. P. Putnam & Sons, 1897), pp. 75–77; Heidi Irmgard Hargman, "Capitalism and Women's Work in the Home" (Ph.D. diss., Yale University, 1974), p. 149.

13. Fred T. Hodgson, *Hodgson's Low Cost American Homes* (Chicago: F. J. Drake, 1904), p. 17; Sears, Roebuck and Co., *Modern Plumbing* (Chicago: Sears, Roebuck and Co., ca. 1905). (Despite these standards, most working-class homes and certainly most urban tenements did not have indoor toilets and running water.)

14. Edith Louise Allen, *Mechanical Devices in the Home* (Peoria, Ill.: Manual Arts Press, 1929); George R. Steward, *American Ways of Life* (Garden City, N.Y.: Doubleday, 1954); Mark Sullivan, *Our Times,* vol. 1: *The Turn of the Century, 1900–1904* (New York: Charles Scribner's Sons, 1926).

15. The pioneer cement journal was *Cement and Engineering News* (1896–1924), founded by William Seafert in Chicago; *Cement Era* was also published there between 1903 and 1917. Also see George Hill, "Reenforced Concrete Construction: American Methods," *Architectural Record* 12 (September 1902): 393–412; Frank Lloyd Wright, "A Fireproof House for $5,000," *Ladies' Home Journal* 24 (April 1907): 24; Oswald C. Hering, *Concrete and Stucco Houses* (New York: McBridge, Nast & Co., 1912); Maurice M. Sloan, *The Concrete House and Its Construction* (Philadelphia: Association of American Portland Cement Manufacturers, 1912); *Cement Houses and Private Garages* (New York: David Williams Company, 1912). The construction of the Panama Canal gave a great impetus to the concrete business in 1908 (Russell Lynes, *The Tastemakers* [New York: Grosset & Dunlap, 1954], p. 193).

16. Ellen H. Richards, *The Cost of Shelter* (New York: John Wiley and Sons, 1905), p. 84.

17. The cost of building increased between 40 and 60 percent in the first five years of the decade (according to how one defined the average house). If one looks back (as people certainly did) to the years before the depression of 1893–1900, the differences are even more startling. Some economists estimate that the average expenditure per dwelling increased 130 percent between the decade of 1890–99 and 1920 (from $2,194 to $5,137). (Leo Grebler, David M. Blank, and Louis Winnick, *Capital Formation in Residential Real Estate* [Princeton, N.J.: Princeton University Press, 1956], pp. 106–7.) Whereas earlier construction costs had gone toward space in which to do housekeeping, it was now being invested in equipment with which to meet higher standards of housekeeping. Most writers put the size of the modern $3,000 house of 1905 at 1,000 to 1,500 square feet, compared to 2,000 to 2,500 square feet for a comparable house of the 1880s. The biggest expense in the new dwelling was for plumbing. By 1904, each bathroom for a relatively inexpensive $2,000 house cost between $150 and $300. More elaborate fittings and more than one bathroom (the tendency was toward several small ones rather than one large and luxuri-

ous room) might cost from $2,000 to $4,000. A hot-water heating system for a moderate-sized and square-shaped house cost at the least $400, with $40 for each register or radiator. As Ellen Richards figured the cost, the finish and fittings now found in the best houses doubled the additional cost for plumbing again, so a house that would have cost $5,000 and met the needs of the day in 1850 would cost $20,000 by 1905. (Richards, *Cost of Shelter,* p. 84; Grebler et al., *Capital Formation,* pp. 114–19, 426; Burnham Kelley, *Design and the Production of Houses* [New York: McGraw-Hill, 1959], pp. 51, 382; Frank Chouteau Brown, "The Cost of Building," in Isabel Bevier, *The House* [Chicago: American School of Home Economics, 1911], pp. 189–216; Jonathon Kermott Allen, *Sanitation in the Modern Home* [Chicago: Domestic Engineering, 1907]).

18. U.S. Bureau of the Census, *Housing Construction Statistics: 1889 to 1964* (Washington, D.C.: Government Printing Office, 1966), table A-1, p. 18–19. (These figures were for 328,000 units, 507,000 units, and 387,000 units, respectively.) One crucial issue in this pressure on the housing market was the ratio of actual supply to population. Nationally, there was actually a decline in total housing stock during the 1890s, amounting to some 670,000 units, mostly because of demolition combined with the slow-down in construction (Grebler et al. *Capital Formation,* pp. 64–65, 85–89). The year 1900 was the lowest point in residential construction between 1880 and 1918. And this was after a decade when the national population had increased from 63 to 76 million, and Chicago's from just under a million to 1.7 million. There were also noticeable changes when building did recover. As Hoyt reports, annual residential construction volume in Chicago more than tripled between 1900 and 1916. But there was more caution about real estate speculation on the part of the general public. Most of the increase was accounted for by builders and developers, eager to find ways to keep their costs per unit down. Not only was construction rationalized, but standards were lowered, houses made smaller, detailing cut. Furthermore, the size of the average plot of land for a house decreased. More money went into municipal services, and, for the individual consumer, into other kinds of consumption, such as transportation. On the whole, however, the situation in residential building was unsteady: undercapitalized, inefficient, and still, for the most part, based on small business (Homer Hoyt, *One Hundred Years of Land Values in Chicago* [Chicago: University of Chicago Press, 1933], p. 206; see also Kelley, *Design,* pp. 51–65).

19. Allen, *Sanitation in the Modern Home,* p. 52.

20. Robert E. Thompson, "The Future of the Dwelling-House," *Indoors and Out* 1 (October 1905): 16–19; idem, *The History of the Dwelling-House and Its Future* (Philadelphia: J. B. Lippincott, 1914). Thompson also wrote numerous texts on political economy and religious history and edited a journal, *The American,* in Philadelphia (1880–1900). For a critique of Thompson's reliance on expertise, see "The Household," *American Homes and Gardens* 1 (July 1905): 45.

21. George Harvey, "Housework and Machinery," *Harper's Weekly* 49 (August 5, 1905): 1113.

22. Nina C. Kinney, "The Kitchen of the Present Day," *Carpentry and*

Building 22 (August 1900): 224–25; Esther Stone, "The Modern Kitchen," *Indoors and Out* 1 (February and March 1906): 218–23, 298–301; Isabel McDougall, "An Ideal Kitchen," *The House Beautiful* 13 (December 1902): 27; George E. Walsh, "Scientifically Designed Kitchens," *The House Beautiful* 30 (November 1911): 183–84; James Thomson, "The Ideal Kitchen," *Ladies' Home Journal* 12 (December 1895): 36.

23. Oliver Coleman [Eugene Klapp], *Successful Houses* (Chicago: Herbert S. Stone & Co., 1899). The book had originated in a series of articles Klapp published in *The House Beautiful* in its first issues, while he was editor.

24. Edith Louise Allen estimated that the average size of a kitchen had been 148 square feet in 1884, 130 in 1900, and 120 in 1920 (*American Housing* [Peoria, Ill.: Manual Arts Press, 1930], pp. 155–56).

25. A few examples are John Henry Newson, *Homes of Character*, 2d ed. (Cleveland, Ohio: John Henry Newson Co., 1913), pp. 87–92, on the pantry-ette; Margaret Greenleaf, "Three Meals a Day: Kitchens and Kitchenettes," *Good Housekeeping* 53 (November 1911): 682–88; Charles E. White, Jr., "The Sunshine Cottages," *The House Beautiful* 27 (April 1910): 135–36; idem., "Three Girls Who Built on One Lot: A Group of Low-Cost Cottages Designed Especially for Business Girls," *Ladies' Home Journal* 27 (September 1, 1910): 25; "An Ingenious Kitchenette," *American Homes and Gardens* 11 (October 1914): 356–57.

26. *The History of the Dwelling-House*, pp. 105–20, 152. Thompson instead defended cooperative housekeeping and communal kitchens (pp. 135–36). The apartment boom had begun in the late 1880s and by the early twentieth century was seriously competing in the market for single-family and two-family houses. (Nationally, in 1900, 65 percent of housing starts were single-family, 16 percent two-family, 19 percent multiple.) Chicago, like other large cities, had been constructing luxury apartment buildings and some moderate-cost flats since the 1871 fire, but these, until the 1890s, had been only three to five stories high. But there was a "flat-fever," observers noted, since the 1880s. (In 1883 alone, over 1,100 flat buildings went into construction.) Duirng the depression years, the trend became stronger. The lowered cost of elevator service, with the use of electric current from street conduits in the late 1890s, sent the buildings up higher. Improvements in construction techniques (especially in concrete technology and steel framing), stiffer regulations governing fire-resistant materials and requiring fire escapes, better-planned internal layouts and services for the families in an apartment or an "apartment-hotel" reinforced a new kind of urban living. Social and family life, as well as aesthetics, were more anonymous there and less self-sufficient, seemingly, than in the suburbs. (See *The Apartment House*, published monthly in Chicago, 1911–12; also, Harold M. Mayer and Richard C. Wade, *Chicago: Growth of a Metropolis* [Chicago: University of Chicago Press, 1969], p. 144; Bessie Louise Pierce, *A History of Chicago*, 3 vols. [Chicago: University of Chicago Press, 1937–57], 3:57; Hoyt, *One Hundred Years*, p. 208.)

27. Wallis, *How to Know Architecture*, p. 295.

28. "The Hall and the Stairs," *Architectural Record* 16 (October 1904): 310–32. The same illustration also appeared in Virginia Robie's article on the

Healy house, "An Inexpensive Suburban Residence," *The House Beautiful* 17 (March 1905): 21–25. For other articles on change, see "Before and After," *The House Beautiful* 17 (February 1905): 29. Una Nixson Hopkins, "Small Houses and Their Decoration," *The House Beautiful* (April 1904): 269–72.

29. "How To Make Plumbing Ornamental," *Domestic Engineering* 20 (October 15, 1900): 25–26; Charles E. White, Jr., "Built-in Furniture," *The House Beautiful* (1911–12).

30. John Sparrowhawk, "Divans and Cozy Corners," *Ladies' Home Journal* 13 (October 1896): 17; *National Builder* 32 (April 1901): 14–15.

31. Annie Howes Barus, "Order and Disorder in the Home," *The House Beautiful* 14 (June 1903): 53.

32. All the popular women's magazines began regular series on "The Little House Home," as Stone called the new section in *The House Beautiful.* Also see, for example, Hopkins, "Small Houses and Their Decoration"; Spencer, "Economical Floor Plans"; or Spencer's seven-part series, "Building the House of Moderate Cost," in the *Architectural Record* 31–33 (June 1912–April 1913).

33. See, among others, Campbell, *Household Economics;* Richards, *The Cost of Shelter;* Marion Talbot and Sophonisba Preston Breckinridge, *The Modern Household* (Boston: Whitcomb & Barrows, 1912); Charles E. White, Jr. *Successful Houses and How to Build Them* (New York: Macmillan, 1912); and P[eter] B. Wight, "Studies of Design without Ornament: Recent Demonstrations of the Intelligent Use of Economical Materials," *Architectural Record* 29 (February 1911): 167–76.

34. "The Tendency in Home Architecture," *Carpentry and Building* 22 (June 1900): 165.

35. The same themes now dominated *The House Beautiful;* see Charles E. White, Jr., "House Design: Good Taste and Poor Taste," *The House Beautiful* 30 (October 1911): 129–33.

36. Fred T. Hodgson, *Hodgson's Modern House Building* (Chicago: F. T. Drake, 1905), design no. 2140.

37. Von Holst, *Modern American Homes.*

38. "The Unusual House: Helps to Home Building," *American Homes and Gardens* 2 (January 1906): 28; *The Radford American Homes* (Chicago: Radford Architectural Co., 1903), p. 3.

39. Wallis, *How to Know Architecture,* pp. 298, 318.

40. Charles Mulford Robinson, *City Planning, with Special Reference to the Planning of Streets and Lots* (New York: G. P. Putnam's Sons, 1916), p. 60. Robinson had made the same point, but less forcefully, in his widely read *The Improvement of Towns and Cities; or, the Practical Basis of Civic Aesthetics* (New York: G. P. Putnam's Sons, 1901).

41. Brooks's *The Prairie School* and Peisch's *The Chicago School of Architecture* present insightful and scholarly accounts of this group of architects. (See n. 7, above, for references to the appropriate name for the group.)

42. "Three Houses by Mr. Robert C. Spencer, Jr.," *Architectural Record* 18 (July 1905): 40–50. This house was also an illustration in a book by the *Record*'s editors, Harry W. Desmond and Herbert Croly, *Stately Homes in America:*

From Colonial Times to the Present Day (New York: D. Appleton & Co., 1903).

43. Elizabeth Helsing Dull, "The Domestic Architecture of Oak Park, Illinois: 1900–1930" (Ph.D. diss., Northwestern University, 1973); Wilbert R. Hasbrouck and Paul Sprague, *A Survey of Historic Architecture of the Village of Oak Park, Illinois* (Oak Park, Ill.: Landmarks Commission, 1974); Paul E. Sprague, *Guide to Frank Lloyd Wright and Prairie School Architecture in Oak Park* (Oak Park, Ill.: Landmarks Commission, 1976). The Austin house appeared in the *Architectural Review* 2 (October 1913): 256.

44. On the evolution of the American bungalow, see Clay Lancaster, "The American Bungalow," *Art Bulletin* 40 (September 1959): 239–53; and Brooks, *Prairie School,* pp. 20–22. For examples, See W. A. Borden, "Bungalows: Summer Homes for the North, Winter Homes for the South," *The House Beautiful* 18 (June 1905): 14–17; *Journal Bungalows* (Philadelphia: *Ladies' Home Journal,* n.d.); William T. Comstock, *Bungalows, Camps and Mountain Homes* (New York: William T. Comstock, 1908); *The Bungalow Book* (Los Angeles: Henry L. Wilson, 1908); Max L. Keith, *Bungalows and Cottages* (Minneapolis: M. L. Keith, 1908); Henry H. Saylor, *Bungalows* (New York: McBridge, Winston & Co., 1911): and Charles E. White, Jr., *The Bungalow Book* (New York: Macmillan, 1923), which features numerous earlier designs.

45. Dow, *American Renaissance,* p. 41.

46. "The Tendency in Home Architecture," p. 165.

Chapter 9

1. Martha Bensley and Robert W. Bruère, *Increasing Home Efficiency* (New York: Macmillan, 1916, p. 10). Martha Bensley Bruère was a New-York-based home economist, and Robert W. Bruère was a Taylorite who had earlier been director of social welfare at the McCormick works in Chicago.

2. "'Domestic' Architecture," *Nation* 91 (September 29, 1910): 284–85.

3. Frederic C. Howe, "The American City of To-Morrow: Progress Already Made and Plans Now Being Perfected to Remake Scientifically Our Cities," *Hampton's Magazine* 26 (May 1911): 573–84.

4. Emile Siedel, "Municipal Socialism," *Case and Comment* 34 (December 1911): 378–84. See also Ernst C. Meyer, "Helping Cities to Help Themselves: How the State University, through its Extension Division, Is Placing the Practical Assistance of Experts at the Disposal of Wisconsin Cities," *La Follette's Weekly Magazine* 1 (September 1909): 8–11. All of the above articles were found in the volume of clippings and brochures collected by George E. Hooker of the City Club and Hull House as "City Planning, United States, 1908–1910," now in the collection of Regenstein Library of the University of Chicago.

5. Frederic C. Howe, *The City: The Hope of Deomocracy* (1905); reprint ed., Seattle: University of Washington Press, 1967), pp. 131, 204.

6. Ibid., pp. 47, 239, 205.

7. H. G. Wells, *The Future in America, a Search after Realities* (New York: Harper & Bros., 1906), p. 78.

8. *Revised Building Ordinances of the City of Chicago, Passed December 5,*

1910, Article VI, Class III. Residences over 90 feet in height had to be entirely fireproof; those 50 to 90 feet, of slow-burning construction; those less than 50 feet could be of conventional wood-frame construction—that is, unless the residence was within the fire limits, where fireproof standards applied in all cases of new construction. Fireproof materials at this time included burnt brick, burnt brick tiles, cement, concrete, and terra-cotta. Skylights also had to be fireproof, and any bay windows more than 12 feet wide. Regulations already specified that porches had to be of noncombustible material. Outside walls, roofs, and soffits of any extension now had to be covered with sheet metal. Regulations governing foundations and wall thickness, size of studs, and fire-stops were also more stringent. This, too, discouraged the builder who was putting up a moderate-cost house from introducing breaks and jags in the outline. While Chicago had had earlier building codes, they had really only been enforced with any rigor since 1907, when Charles Ball was appointed head of the Sanitary Bureau and inaugurated thorough inspection procedures in all departments. On the codes, see F. W. Fitzpatrick, *Building Codes* (Chicago: American School of Correspondence, 1911), and *A Half Century of Chicago Building, A Practical Guide*, [Aldermen] John H. Jones and Fred A. Britten, eds. (Chicago: n.p., 1910).

9. Andrew Jay King, "Law and Land Use in Chicago: A Prehistory of Modern Zoning" (Ph.D. diss., University of Wisconsin, 1976), pp. 257, 322, 327.

10. Ibid.

11. Frank Chapin Bray, "Co-Operation of Civic Societies," *Chautauquan* 37 (August 1903): 441–42; also see Charles M. Robinson, *The Improvement of Towns and Cities* (New York: G. P. Putnam's Sons, 1901).

12. The School of Civics had begun with a special University of Chicago extension course taught by Graham Taylor and Lathrop at Hull House; Breckinridge and the Abbotts were also on the staff. In 1920 it became the University of Chicago School of Social Work (now the University of Chicago School of Social Service Administration). On the professionalization of social work, see Roy Lubove, *The Professional Altruist: The Emergence of Social Work as a Career, 1880–1930* (New York: Atheneum, 1973). On Merriam, see Barry D. Karl, *Charles E. Merriam and the Study of Politics* (Chicago: University of Chicago Press, 1974).

13. "Efficiency in City Planning," *American City* 8 (February 1913): 139; cited in Mel Scott, *American City Planning since 1890* (Berkeley and Los Angeles: University of California Press, 1971), p. 122. On scientific management, see Samuel Haber, *Efficiency and Uplift: Scientific Management in the Progressive Era, 1890–1920* (Chicago: University of Chicago Press, 1964). Chicago, in fact, became so enthralled with rational planning that a municipal Bureau of Public Efficiency, instituted by Charles Merriam and the City Club in 1910, was empowered to oversee accounting and bureaucratic procedures in all city offices.

14. George B. Ford, "The City Scientific," *Proceedings of the Fifth National Conference on City Planning* (1913), pp. 31–41.

15. *The City Club Bulletin* 2 (March 17, 1909): 327–37. The same article had been published in *Charities* 19 (February 1, 1908).

16. *The City Club Bulletin* 3 (June 29, 1910): 325–34, had Hooker's report on the Second National Conference on City Planning. The *Chicago Post* of August 18, 1910, carried an article, "Hooker Brings Ideas to Benefit the City," on his response to the Berlin exhibit and his plans for Chicago. (This clipping is prominently featured in the bound volume "City Planning, United States, 1893–1912.")

17. Jens Jensen, "Regulating City Building," *The Survey* (November 18, 1911): 12–14. On Jensen, see Leonard K. Eaton, *Landscape Artist in America: The Life and Work of Jens Jensen* (Chicago: University of Chicago Press, 1964); and Jensen, "Designs for a Neighborhood Center: Chicago City Club Competition," *Architectural Record* 46 (July 1919): 44–45, which he carried out with Wilhelm Bernhard. A similar argument for "independence" was voiced by the literary historian Vernon Louis Parrington in "On the Lack of Privacy in American Village Homes," *The House Beautiful* 13 (January 1903): 109–12; and by Henry S. Curtis, "The Neighborhood Center," *American City* 7 (July 1912): 14–17. On neighborhood centers, see Don S. Kirschner, "The Ambiguous Legacy: Social Justice and Social Control in the Progressive Era," *Historical Perspectives* 1 (Winter 1974): 69–88.

18. Jensen, "Regulating City Building," p. 15.

19. See Thomas Lee Philpott, *The Slum and the Ghetto: Neighborhood Deterioration and Middle-Class Reform. Chicago, 1880–1930* (New York: Oxford University Press, 1978), pp. 62–109; and Allen F. Davis, *Spearheads for Reform: The Social Settlements and the Progressive Movement, 1890–1914* (New York: Oxford University Press, 1967).

20. *Classic Essays on the Culture of Cities*, ed. Richard Sennett (New York: Meredith Corp., 1960); Robert E. Park and Ernest W. Burgess, *The City* (Chicago: University of Chicago Press, 1925); Louis Wirth, *On Cities and Social Life*, ed. with an introduction by Albert R. Reiss (Chicago: University of Chicago Press, 1964).

21. Edward Alsworth Ross, *Social Control: A Survey of the Foundations of Order* (1901; reprint ed., New York: Macmillan, 1954), pp. 263–64, cited in Paul Boyer, *Urban Masses and Moral Order in America, 1820–1920* (Cambridge: Harvard University Press, 1978), p. 226.

22. Luther Lee Bernard, "The Transition to an Objective Standard of Social Control," *American Journal of Sociology* 16 (1911): 523, cited in Boyer, *Urban Masses*, p. 231.

23. *Hull-House Maps and Papers, A Presentation of Nationalities and Wages in a Congested District of Chicago* (New York: Arno, 1970; originally published 1895): William I. Thomas and Florian Znaniecki, *The Polish Peasant in Europe and America*, 2 vols. (1918; reprint ed., New York: Dover Publications, 1958).

24. Graham Romeyn Taylor, *Satellite Cities: A Study of Industrial Suburbs* (New York: D. Appleton, 1915).

25. Louise de Kouven Bowen, quoted by Barbara Spackman in "The Woman's City Club of Chicago" (Master's thesis, University of Chicago, 1930), p. 6.

26. On the exhibit, see Spackman, "The Woman's City Club," and also Anna E. Nicholes, "How Women Can Help in the Administration of a City,"

in *The Woman Citizen's Library* ed. Shailer Mathews, vol. 10, *Women and the Larger Citizenship: City Housekeeping* (Chicago: The Civics Society, 1914), pp. 2123–42. Also see comments by Edith Abbott and Sophonisba Breckinridge on women and the housing problem at the Third National Conference on Housing, reprinted in *The City Club Bulletin* 7 (January 12, 1914): 2–12.

27. Charles Zueblin, "The Twentieth Century City," *Proceedings of the Annual Convention, 1901, of the American League for Civic Improvement* (Springfield, Ohio: n.p.), p. 66.

28. Folder on the Municipal Museum, Chicago Historical Society; Frederick Stymetz Lamb and Charles Zueblin, "The Municipal Museum of Chicago," speech before the Commercial Club, February 25, 1905; Professor H. M. Scott, "Social Museums," *Charities and the Commons* 8 (July 1903): 3–4.

29. Walter D. Moody, *Wacker's Manual of the Plan of Chicago: Municipal Economy* (Chicago: H. C. Sherman & Co., for the Chicago Plan Commission, 1912), p. 17. The book was inspired by and named for Charles Henry Wacker, chairman of the Chicago Plan Commission. Moody was the commission's managing director.

30. Oscar L[ovell] Triggs, "The Philosophy of the Betterment Movement," *Chautauquan* 37 (August 1903): 464.

31. Ibid., p. 463.

32. "A Craftsman House That Shows the Development of a New Idea," *The Craftsman* 17 (January 1910): 430; "The Cost of The Craftsman House: Why These Designs Do Not Lend themselves to What Is Called 'Cheap Building,'" *The Craftsman* 17 (March 1910): 680–88. Also see H. Allen Brooks, *The Prairie School: Frank Lloyd Wright and His Midwest Contemporaries* (New York: W. W. Norton, 1972, p. 196.

33. Gilbreth had been a New York contractor. See his *Concrete System* (New York: Engineering News Publishing Co., 1908), *Bricklaying System* (New York: M. C. Clark Publishing Co., 1909), and *Field System* (New York: M. C. Clark Publishing Co., 1908), which referred specifically to Taylor; editorial, *National Builder* 50 (June 1910): 31. See also Haber, *Efficiency and Uplift*, pp. 37–38.

34. Frank Wallis, *How to Know Architecture*, cited in Herbert S. Stone's "Trade and Art," *The House Beautiful* 19 (November 1911): 178.

35. Spackman, "The Woman's City Club," p. 6.

36. Candance [Thurber] Wheeler, *Principles of Home Decoration with Practical Examples* (New York: Doubleday, Page & Co., 1903), pp. 13–14; see also Wheeler, "Interior Decoration as a Profession for Women," *Outlook* (April 6, 1895, and February 15, 1896); Elsie de Wolfe, *The House in Good Taste* (New York: Century Co., 1913); George Davis, "The Future of House Decoration," *The House Beautiful* 6 (May 1899): 260–66; Isabel Gordon Curtis, "The Creation of the New Calling," *The House Beautiful* 19 (April 1906): 29–30, all of which discuss the emergence of the professional interior decorator, usually a young woman with training in either architecture, art, or decorative art, who now worked for department stores, private firms, or even, according to Curtis, real estate developers. (The best-known male decorator in

Chicago was Joseph Twyman of the Tobey Furniture Company, an ardent follower of William Morris.)

37. See Christine [McGaffey] Frederick, *The New Housekeeping: Efficiency Studies in Home Management* (Garden City, N.Y.,: Doubleday, Page & Co., 1913), which had appeared in a popular series of articles in the *Ladies' Home Journal* the previous year; idem, *Household Engineering: Scientific Management in the Home* (Chicago: American School of Home Economics, 1915); and idem, "Putting the American Woman and Her Home on a Business Basis," *American Review of Reviews* 49 (February 1914): 199–208; Mary [Green] Pattison, *Principles of Domestic Engineering* (New York: Trow Press, 1915) and "Domestic Engineering: The Housekeeping Experiment Station at Colonia, N.J.," *Scientific American* 106 (August 13, 1912): 330–31. Other articles professing the same philosophy include Mary Urie Watson, "Scientific Housecleaning," *The Craftsman* 23 (December 1912): 353–55; Frank B. Gilbreth, "Scientific Management in the Household," *Journal of Home Economics* 4 (December 1912): 438–47; idem., "Motion Study in the Household," *Scientific American* 106 (April 13, 1912): 328, 342; and F. A. Pattison, "Scientific Management in Home-Making," *Annals of the American Academy of Political and Social Science* 48 (July 1913): 96.

38. "Forewords," *The Principles of Domestic Engineering,* p. 17.

39. *Household Engineering,* pp. 449–59; also see Gwendolyn Wright, "The Model Domestic Environment: Icon or Option?" in *Women in American Architecture,* ed. Susana Torre (New York: Whitney Library of Design, 1977), pp. 20–21.

40. Helen Binkerd Young, "The Modern House," in *A Manual of Home-Making,* comp. Martha Van Rensslaer, Flora Rose, and Helen Canon (New York: Macmillan, 1919), p. 1. See also Barbara Ehrenreich and Deirdre English, *For Her Own Good: 150 Years of the Experts' Advice to Women* (Garden City, N.Y.: Anchor Press, Doubleday, 1978); and David P. Handlin, "Efficiency and the American Home," *Architectural Association Quarterly* 5 (October–December 1973): 50–54.

41. See above, chap. 7; Brooks, *Prairie School;* Esther McCoy, *Five California Architects* (New York: Praeger Publications, 1960). Henry-Russell Hitchcock offers an interesting comparison of American and European avant-garde architect-client relations in *Architecture: Nineteenth and Twentieth Centuries* (Baltimore: Penguin Books, 1969).

42. Robert C. Spencer, Jr., "Planning the House: Economical Floor Plans," *The House Beautiful* 18 (June 1905): 22–23.

43. "Building the House of Moderate Price," *Architectural Record* 32 (August 1912): 109.

44. Herbert Croly, "American Artists and Their Public," *Architectural Record* 10 (January 1901): 257.

45. White's correspondence with Walter Willcox, a former employer and then dean of the College of Architecture at the University of Oregon, traces White's growing interest in architecture as a business. See, in particular, Charles E. White, Jr., to Walter Willcox, March 28, 1907; May 31, 1910 (from the Collection of the Library of the University of Oregon, Eugene, Oregon);

and Charles E. White, Jr., "The Contractor—Himself and His Office," *National Builder* 55 (February 1913): 68–73 (originally published in *Building Progress*, 1912). White took over Spencer's post on the staf of *The House Beautiful* in 1910 and published some twenty articles over the next five years, illustrating them with the work of his Prairie school colleagues and drawing his readers' attention to the complexities of modern architectural decision-making. He also published pieces in the *Ladies' Home Journal, Pictorial Review* (including an article on his own simple Colonial Revival house, written under the pseudonym of William R. Safford, "The House I Built My Wife for $5000," *Pictorial Review* [March 1914]: 18), and other magazines.

46. Brooks, *Prairie School*, p. 25.

47. William Herbert [Herbert Croly], *Houses for Town or Country* (New York: Architectural Record Co., 1903), p. 5; also see Croly's "The New World and the New Art," *Architectural Record* 12 (June 1902): 134–53, "Civic Improvements," *Architectural Record* 21 (May 1907): 347–52, and, written with Harry W. Desmond, *Stately Homes in America from Colonial Times to the Present Day* (New York: D. Appleton & Co., 1903). It is worth noting that Croly's mother, Jane Cunningham Croly, was an active feminist who edited *The Home-Maker* between 1890 and 1892 and published *The History of the Woman's Club Movement in America* (New York: H. G. Allen & Co., 1898), under the pseudonym of Jenny June.

48. "The Contemporary Suburban Residence," *Architectural Record* 11 (January 1902): 70.

49. "The New World and the New Art," p. 153; Croly, *Houses for Town or Country*, p. 4. In "New York as the American Metropolis," *Architectural Record* 13 (March 1903): 199, Croly praises "[t]he homogeneity so characteristic of American democracy at its best"; see also his "Rich Men and Their Houses," *Architectural Record* 12 (May 1902): 27–32.

50. *The Promise of American Life* (New York: Macmillan, 1909), p. 446, states that "The case of the statesman, the man of letters, the philanthropist, or the reformer does not differ essentially from that of the architect." That is, he went on, every field of service was moving toward a higher degree of specialization and expertise in order to provide a beneficent "strong state," overseen by people of professional skills—in other words, the welfare state. After reading the book, Dorothy and Michael Straight gave Croly the money to found a magazine of political commentary; the *New Republic*, edited by Croly, first appeared in 1914.

51. See, for example, the Heineman bungalow court in "A View in Bungalow Land, Southern California," *National Builder* 52 (April 1911): 53.

52. Herbert Croly, "Some Recent Work of Mr. Howard Shaw," *Architectural Record* 22 (December 1907): 422. Also see Croly and C. Matlack Price, "The Recent Work of Howard Shaw," *Architectural Record* 33 (April 1913): 285–307. Considering this strong endorsement by the *Record*, the contentions of Leonard Eaton, H. Allen Brooke, and Thomas Tallmadge that it was the growing influence of women in the society which brought about Shaw's prominence and the rise of revival styles over Prairie style architecture seem a particularly erroneous interpretation. (See Leonard K. Eaton, *Two Chicago*

Architects and Their Clients: Frank Lloyd Wright and Howard Van Doren Shaw [Cambridge: MIT Press, 1969], and Thomas E[ddy] Talmadge, "The Thirteenth Annual Architectural Exhibit in Chicago," *Western Architect* 25 [April 1917]: 27, citd in Brooks, *Prairie School*, p. 338.) The fact that George E. Hooker's collection of clippings, "City Planning, United States, 1903–1912," included many items from the *Architectural Record* testifies to that journal's wide audience and authority.

53. Six of Griffin's subdivisions were published in the *Western Architect* 20 (August 1913): 62–79. See also Thomas A. Heinz, "Walter Burley Griffin: Comprehensive Subdivision Planning in the Midwest" (thesis project, University of Illinois, Department of Architecture, 1972, in the collection of the Oak Park Library); Mark L. Peisch, *The Chicago School of Architecture: Early Followers of Sullivan and Wright* (New York: Random House, 1964); James Birrell, *Walter Burley Griffin* (Brisbane, Australia: University of Queensland Press, 1964); D. Van Zanten, *Walter Burley Griffin: Selected Designs* (Palos Park, Ill.: Prairie School Press, 1970).

54. "The Third National Conference on Housing," *The City Club Bulletin* 7 (January 12, 1914), p. 4.

55. The jury included John C. Kennedy (a housing expert), John W. Alvord (an engineer), Jens Jensen, George Maher, A. W. Woltersdorf (also an architect), with special consultants Edward H. Boulton (director of Olmsted's Roland Park suburb outside Baltimore), Albert Kelsey, Irving K. Pond, and Carol Aronovici.

56. Alfred B. Yeomans, ed., *City Residential Land Development, Studies in Planning: Competitive Plans for Subdividing a Typical Quarter Section of Land in the Outskirts of Chicago* (Chicago: University of Chicago Press, 1916), p. 16.

57. Ibid., pp. 37–44. On Drummond, see also Suzanne Ganschinietz, "William Drummond: I. Talent and Sensitivity," *The Prairie School Review* 6 (1969): 5–19.

58. *City Residential Land Development*, pp. 66–72.

59. Ibid., pp. 61–66, 56–57.

60. Ibid., pp. 84–86, 45–47.

61. Ibid., p. 43.

62. Ibid., pp. 10–12.

63. Ibid., pp. 45–57, 84–86.

64. Ibid., p. 70.

65. Ibid., pp. 105–6.

66. Ibid., p. 106.

67. Ibid., pp. 117–22.

68. Ibid., p. 14.

69. Howe, *The City*, p. 294.

BIBLIOGRAPHY

Journals

American Architect and Building News. Boston, 1876–1938.
American Builder. New York and Chicago, 1868–95.
American City. New York, 1909–20.
American Homes. Knoxville, Tenn., 1895–1904.
American Kitchen, later *Everyday Housekeeping.* Boston, 1894–1908.
Appleton's Journal of Literature, Science and Art. New York, 1869–81.
Architects' and Builders' Edition of the Scientific American, later *Scientific American Building Monthly,* later *American Homes and Gardens.* New York, 1885–1915.
Architecture and Building, a Magazine Devoted to Architecture, Archaeology, Engineering and Decoration, later *Architects' and Builders' Magazine.* New York, 1882–1911.
Architectural Record. New York, 1891–current.
Arts, later *Arts for America.* Chicago, 1899–1919.
Building Budget. Chicago, 1885–90.
Brickbuilder, later the *Architectural Forum.* New York, 1892–current.
The Builder. Holyoke, Mass., 1883–86.
Builder and Woodworker. Chicago and New York, 1868–95.
Builder, Decorator and Furnisher, later *House and Home.* New York, 1883–1905.
The Carpenter. Philadelphia, 1881–1902.
Carpentry and Building, later *Building Age.* New York, 1870–95.
The Chautauquan. Chautauqua, N.Y., 1880–1914.
Charities and The Commons, later the *Survey.* Chicago and New York, 1894–1909.

Construction News. Chicago, 1895–1916.
Cosmopolitan. New York, 1886–1925.
The Craftsman. Eastwood, N.Y., 1901–16.
The Delineator. New York, 1873–1937.
Engineering Magazine. New York, 1891–1916.
Fine Arts Journal. Chicago, 1899–1919.
Godey's Lady's Magazine. Philadelphia, 1827–98.
Good Housekeeping. Holyoke, Mass., and New York, 1885–current.
House and Garden. New York and Philadelphia, 1901–current.
The House Beautiful. Chicago and New York, 1896–current.
Inland Architect and News Record. Chicago, 1883–1908.
Ladies' Home Journal. Philadelphia, 1884–current.
National Builder. Chicago, 1885–1924.
Northwestern Lumberman. Chicago, 1873–98.
Sanitary News. Chicago, 1882–92.
Shoppell's Modern Homes. New York, 1884–94.
Western Architect. Minneapolis, 1901–31.

American Housing Guides, 1870—1893

For an invaluable chronicle of architectural texts of this period, see Henry-Russell Hitchcock, *American Architectural Books, a List of Books, Portfolios, and Pamphlets on Architecture and Related Subjects Published in America Before 1895*. Minneapolis: University of Minnesota, 1962.

Allen Frank P. *Artistic Dwellings . . . from $700.00 Upwards*. Grand Rapids, Mich.: F. P. Allen, 1891.

Appleton, D. *Artistic Homes: Being a Series of Interior Views of a Number of the Most Beautiful Homes in the United States* New York: D. Appleton, 1883–84.

The Architect's Second Builder's Reference Book. Chicago: Mercantile Publishing, 1889.

Baumann, Frederick. *Thoughts on Style: A Lecture Prepared for Delivery before the American Institute of Architects at the Meeting in Chicago, 1892*. Privately printed, collection of the Newberry Library.

Bicknell, Amos J. *Wooden and Brick Buildings*. New York: A. J. Bicknell, 1875.

Brown, George Preston. *Sewer-Gas and Its Dangers*. Chicago: Jansen, McClurg, 1881.

Brunner, A. W., ed. *Cottages; or, Hints on Economical Building*. New York: W. T. Comstock, 1884.

Brunner, A. W., and Thomas Tryon. *Interior Decoration.* New York: W. T. Comstock, 1887.
Bunce, Oliver. *My House: An Ideal.* New York: Charles Scribner's Sons, 1884.
Bunner, Henry Cuyler. *The Story of a New York House.* New York: Charles Scribner's Sons, 1887.
Carpenter, James H. *The Complete House Builder.* Chicago: Donohue, Henberry & Co., 1890.
———. *Hints on Building.* Hartford, Conn.: Press of the Case, Lockwood & Brainard Co., 1883.
Chamberlin, Everett. *Chicago and Its Suburbs.* Chicago: T. A. Hungerford & Co., 1874.
Chandler, Francis Ward. *The Colonial Architecture of Maryland, Pennsylvania and Virginia.* Boston: Bates, Kimball & Guild, 1892.
Child, Henry T. *Colonial Houses for Modern Homes: For People Who Wish Their Dwellings To Be Distinctive, Tasteful and Characteristic.* New York: E. S. Child, 1890.
Church, Ella Rodman. *How To Furnish a Home.* New York: D. Appleton, 1881.
Clark, Alfred C., *The Architect, Decorator and Furnisher.* Chicago: Cowdrey Clark & Co., 1884.
Cleveland, H. W. S. *Landscape Architecture as Applied to the Wants of the West.* Chicago: Jansen, McClurg, 1873.
Comstock, William T. *Illustrated Catalogue of Practical Books on Architecture, Building, Carpentry, Drawing, Painting, Decoration and Ornament.* New York: W. T. Comstock, 1891.
———. *Modern Architectural Designs and Details.* New York: W. T. Comstock, 1881.
———. *Selected Details of Interior and Exterior Finish for Architects, Carpenters, and Builders.* New York: W. T. Comstock, 1890.
———. *Suburban and Country Houses.* New York: W. T. Comstock, 1893.
Cook, Clarence. *The House Beautiful.* New York: Scribner, Armstrong, 1878.
———. *What Shall We Do with Our Walls?* New York: Warren, Fuller, 1881.
Cooper, H. J. *The Art of Furnishing on Rational and Aesthetic Principles.* New York: Henry Holt, 1881.
Cornfield, Prof. William Henry. *Dwelling Houses: Their Sanitary Construction and Arrangements.* New York: Van Nostrand, 1880.
Corner, James M., and Eric Ellis Soderholtz. *Examples of Domestic Colonial Architecture in Maryland and Virginia.* Boston: Boston Architectural Club, 1892.

———. *Examples of Domestic Colonial Architecture in New England.* Boston: Boston Architectural Club, 1891.
Croff, Gilbert Bostwick. *Modern Suburban Architecture, Embodying Designs for Moderate Price, from $1,400 to $5,000.* New York: Roby & O'Neill, 1870.
———. *Progressive American Architecture.* New York: Orange Judd Co., 1875.
De Forest, Lockwood. *Indian Architecture and Ornament.* Boston: George H. Polley & Co., 1887.
———. *Indian Domestic Architecture.* Boston: Heliotype Printing Co., 1885.
Dehli, Arne. *Selections of Byzantine Ornament.* New York: William Helburn, 1890.
Downing, Andrew Jackson. *The Architecture of Country Houses.* New York: D. Appleton, 1850.
———. *Cottage Residences.* New York: G. P. Putnam, 1842.
Dwyer, Charles P. *The Immigrant Builder.* Philadelphia: Claxton, Remsen & Haffelfinger, 1872.
Eassie, William. *Healthy Homes.* New York: D. Appleton, 1872.
Eastlake, Charles Locke. *Hints on Household Taste in Furniture, Upholstery and Other Details.* Boston: James R. Osgood, 1872.
Ellwanger, George Herman. *The Story of My House.* New York: D. Appleton, 1890.
Feathergill, J. Milner, M.D., with an introduction by B. W. Richardson, M.D. *The Town Dweller: His Wants and Needs.* New York: D. Appleton, 1889.
Fuller, Albert W. *Artistic Homes in City and Country.* Boston: James R. Osgood, 1882.
———, and William Arthur Wheeler. *Artistic Homes in City and Country.* Rev. and enlarged ed. Boston: Ticknor & Co., 1886.
Gardner, Eugene Clarence. *Home Interiors: Leaves from an Architect's Diary.* Boston: James R. Osgood, 1878.
———. *Homes, and All About Them.* Boston: James R. Osgood, 1885.
———. *Homes, and How to Make Them.* Boston: James R. Osgood, 1874.
———. *The House That Jill Built, After Jack's Had Proved a Failure.* New York: Fords, Howard & Hulbert, 1882.
———. *Illustrated Homes: A Series of Papers Describing Real Houses and Real People.* Boston: James R. Osgood, 1875.
Garnsey, George O. *The American Glossary of Architectural Terms.* Chicago: Clark & Langley, 1887.
———. *The National Builder's Album of Beautiful Homes, Villas,*

Residences, and Cottages. Chicago: National Builder Publishing Co., 1891.
Gibson, Louis. *Convenient Houses, with Fifty Plans for the Housekeeper*. New York: Thomas Y. Crowell, 1889.
Hartshorne, Henry, M.D. *Our Homes*. Philadelphia: P. Blakiston, 1880.
Hobbs, Isaac H., and Son. *Hobbs's Architecture*. Philadelphia: J. B. Lippincott, 1873.
A Holiday at Rosalie Villas. Chicago: James P. Craig, 1884.
Holly, Henry Hudson. *Modern Dwellings in Town and Country, Adapted to American Wants and Climate*. New York: Harper & Bros., 1878.
Hopkins, David S. *Cottage Portfolio. 12 Designs of Low Cost Homes*. New York: F. A. Hodgson, 1886.
———. *Houses and Cottages*. Grand Rapids, Michigan: D. S. Hopkins, 1889.
The House and Its Surroundings. New York: D. Appleton, 1879.
Hussey, Elisha Charles. *Home Building*. New York: Leader & Van Hoesen, 1876.
———. *Hussey's National Cottage Architecture; or, Homes for Everybody*. New York: George E. Woodward, 1874.
Jenkins, Fleming. *Healthy Houses. Adapted to American Conditions*. New York: Harper & Bros., 1879.
King, David W., ed. *Homes for Home-Builders*. New York: Orange Judd, 1886.
Lamb, Martha J. *The Homes of America*. New York: D. Appleton, 1879.
Little, Arthur. *Early New England Interiors*. Boston: A. Williams, 1876.
Mayer, I. H., M.D. *Domestic Economy*. Lancaster, Pa.: I. H. Mayer, 1893.
Morse, Edward Sylvester. *Japanese Homes and Their Surroundings*. Boston: Ticknor & Co., 1886.
National Architects' Union. *Artistic One-Story Houses*. New York and Philadelphia: National Architects' Union, 1893.
———. *Modern Homes*. Philadelphia: National Architects' Union, 1889.
———. *Sensible Low-Cost Houses*. Philadelphia: National Architects' Union, 1889.
Oakey, Alexander F. *Building A Home*. New York: D. Appleton, 1881.
———. *My House Is My Castle*. San Francisco: Pacific States Savings,

Loan and Building Co., 1891.
Ogilvie, George W. *Architecture Simplified: or, How to Build a House*. Chicago: G. W. Ogilvie, 1885.
Osborne, C. Francis. *Notes on the Art of House-Planning*. New York: W. T. Comstock, 1888.
Page, Harvey L. *Architectural Designs*. Washington: Gibson Bros., 1886.
———. *Houses of Moderate Cost*. Washington: Gibson Bros., 1889.
Palliser, George, and Charles Palliser. *Palliser's American Architecture; or, Every Man a Complete Builder*. Bridgeport, Conn.: Palliser & Co., 1888.
———. *Palliser's American Cottage Homes*. Bridgeport, Conn., and New York: Palliser & Co., 1878.
———. *Palliser's Model Dwellings*. New York: J. S. Ogilvie, 1893.
———. *Palliser's Model Homes for the People*. Bridgeport, Conn., and New York: Palliser & Co., 1876.
———. *Palliser's New Cottage Homes and Details*. New York: Palliser, Palliser & Co., 1887.
Pelton, John Cotter. *Cheap Dwellings*. San Francisco: San Francisco Bulletin Co., 1882.
Plunkett, Mrs. H. M. *Women, Plumbers and Doctors; or, Household Sanitation*. New York: D. Appleton, 1885.
Putnam, John Pickering. *Architecture under Nationalism*. Boston: Nationalist Educational Assn., 1890.
———. *The Open Fire-Place in All Ages*. Boston: James R. Osgood, 1881.
Reed, Samuel Burrage. *Cottage Houses for Village and Country Homes*. New York: Orange Judd, 1883.
———. *Dwellings for Village and Country*. New York: S. B. Reed, 1885.
———. *House Plans for Everybody*. New York: Orange Judd, 1878.
Shoppell, Robert W., and the Co-Operative Building Plan Association, *Artistic Modern Homes of Low-Cost*. New York: Co-Operative Building Plan Association, 1881.
———. *Building Designs: Shoppell's Modern Houses*. 6 vols. New York: Co-Operative Building Plan Association, n.d.
———. *How to Build, Furnish and Decorate*. New York: Co-Operative Building Plan Association, 1883.
———. *How to Build a House*. New York: Co-Operative Building Plan Association, 1883.
———. *Modern Houses, Beautiful Homes*. New York: Co-Operative Building Plan Association, 1887.
———. *Shoppell's Building Plans for Modern Low-Cost Houses*. New

York: Co-Operative Building Plan Association, 1884.
———. *Shoppell's Model Houses*. New York: Co-Operative Building Plan Association, 1890.
Silsbee, E. A. *An Informal Talk on Architectural and Art Topics*. Salem: Essex Institute, 1880.
Smith, F. D. *A Cozy Home: How It Was Built*. Boston: F. L. Smith, 1887.
———. *Homes of To-Day; or, Modern Examples of Moderate Cost Houses*. Boston: F. L. Smith, 1888.
Soderholtz, Eric Ellis, and Edward Andrew Crane. *Examples of Colonial Architecture in Charleston, S.C. and Savannah, Ga*. Boston: Boston Architectural Club, 1895.
Spofford, Harriet P. *Art Decoration Applied to Furniture*. New York: Harper & Bros., 1878.
———. *House and Hearth*. New York: Dodd, Mead & Co., 1891.
Stevens, John Calvin, and Albert Winslow Cobb. *Examples of American Domestic Architecture*. New York: W. T. Comstock, 1889.
Sturgis, Russell, ed. *Homes in City, Suburbs and Country*. New York: Charles Scribner's Sons, 1893.
Tabor, Clarence. *Tabor's Modern Homes*. Chicago: Building Plan Co., 1889.
Varney, Almon Clothier. *Our Homes and Their Adornments*. Detroit: J. C. Chilton & Co., 1882.
Wallis, Frank Edwin. *Old Colonial Architecture and Furniture*. Boston: George H. Polley & Co., 1887.
Woodward, George Evertson. *Woodward's National Architect*. New York: G. E. Woodward, 1868.
Woollett, William M. *Old Homes Made New*. New York: A. J. Bicknell, 1878.
———. *Villas and Cottages; or, Homes for All*. New York: A. J. Bicknell, 1876.

American Housing Guides, 1894–1916

Abbott, Lyman, et al. *The Home Builder*. Boston: Houghton Mifflin, 1906.
———, ed. *The House and Home: A Practical Book*. 2 vols. New York: Charles Scribner's Sons, 1896.
Adler, Hazel H. *The New Interior: Modern Decorations for the Modern Home*. New York: Century, 1916.
Allen, Jonathan Kermott. *Sanitation in the Modern Home*. Chicago: Domestic Engineering, 1907.

Editor of the *Architects' and Builders' Magazine*. *Two Family and Twin Houses*. New York: W. T. Comstock, 1908.
Benoit-Lévy, Georges. *Cités-Jardins d'Amérique*. Paris: Henri Jouvé, 1905.
Blue Island Land and Building Company. *Homes for the People*. Chicago, ca. 1905.
The Book of a Hundred Houses. Chicago: Herbert S. Stone & Co., 1902.
The Book of Little Houses. New York: Macmillan, 1915.
Building Brick Association of America. *A House of Brick of Moderate Cost*. Boston: Rogers & Manson, 1910.
———. *One Hundred Bungalows*. Boston: Rogers & Manson, 1912.
Building Economics Correspondence School. *Economics of Home Building*. Far Rockaway, N.Y.: B.E.C.S., 1914.
The Bungalow Book. Los Angeles: Henry L. Wilson, 1908.
Butterfield, W. H. and H. W. Tuttle. *A Book of House Plans*, New York: McBride, Nast & Co., 1912.
Calkins, Charlotte Wait. *A Course in House Planning and Furnishing*. Chicago: Scott, Foresman & Co., 1916.
Chapin, Henry Sterling. *A Revolution in Building Materials*. New York: Building Brick Association of America, 1911.
Chicago Millwork Supply Company. *Plans for Modern Homes*. Chicago, 1912.
Child, Edward Southwick. *Colonial Houses for Modern Homes, for Admirers of the Grand Old Houses Our Ancestors Built*. New York: Child & de Goll, 1896–99.
Chivers, Herbert C. *Artistic Houses*. St. Louis: H. C. Chivers, 1907.
Coleman, Oliver [Eugene Klapp]. *Successful Houses*. Chicago: Herbert S. Stone & Co., 1898.
Comstock, William T. *Bungalows, Camps and Mountain Houses*. New York: W. T. Comstock, 1908.
Croly, Herbert. *Houses for Town or Country*. New York: Architectural Record Co., 1903.
Daniels, Fred Hamilton. *The Furnishing of a Modest Home*. New York and Chicago: Atkinson, Mentzer & Grover, 1908.
Davis, Francis P., et al. *Ideal Homes in Garden Communiites: A Book of Stock Plans*. New York: Robert M. McBride, 1915.
The Delineator's Prize $3,000 Houses. New York: B. W. Dodge, 1909.
Desmond, Harry W., and H. W. Frohne. *Building a Home; Book of Fundamental Advice for the Layman about to Build*. New York: Baker & Taylor, 1908.
Desmond, Harry W., and Herbert Croly. *Stately Homes in America*

from Colonial Times to the Present Day. New York: D. Appleton, 1903.
Detached Dwellings, Country and Suburb. New York: Swetland, 1909.
Dow, Joy Wheeler. *American Renaissance: A Review of Domestic Architecture*. New York: W. T. Comstock, 1904.
Ford, James. *American Country Houses of Today*. New York: Architectural Book Publishing Co., 1912–15.
French, Lillie. *The House Dignified*. New York: G. P. Putnam's Sons, 1908.
Gannett, W. C. *The House Beautiful, in a setting designed and printed by hand by William Hermann Winslow and Frank Lloyd Wright*. River Forest, Ill.: Auvergne Press, 1896–97.
Gibson, Louis H. *Beautiful Houses*. New York: Thomas Y. Crowell, 1895.
Godfrey, Hollis, *The Health of the City*. Boston: Houghton Mifflin, 1910.
Goodnow, Ruby Ross. *The Honest House*. New York: Century, 1914.
Gowing, Frederick Henry. *Building Plans for Modern Homes*. Boston: F. H. Gowing, 1911.
Grant, Robert. *The Art of Living*. New York: Charles Scribner's Sons, 1899.
Hering, Oswald C. *Concrete and Stucco Houses*. New York: McBride, Nast, 1912.
Hodgson, Frederick Thomas. *The Carpenter's Cyclopedia*. Chicago: F. J. Drake, 1913.
———, *Cyclopedia of Bricklaying, Stone Masonry, Cements, Stuccos and Plasters*. Chicago: F. J. Drake, 1913.
———. *Hodgson's Low Cost American Homes*. Chicago: F. J. Drake, 1905.
———. *Hodgson's Modern House Building*. Chicago: F. J. Drake, 1905.
———. *Practical Bungalows and Cottages for Town and Country*. Chicago: F. J. Drake, 1906.
———, ed. *Cyclopedia of the Building Trades*. 6 vols. Chicago: American Building Trades School, 1907.
von Holst, Hermann Valentin. *Modern American Homes*. Chicago: American School of Correspondence, 1912.
Hopkins, David S. *Cottage Residences*. New York: F. A. Hodgson, 1896.
Editors of *House and Garden*. *Low-Cost Suburban Homes*. Philadelphia: John C. Winston, 1908.
House and Town Planning. Philadelphia: American Academy of Politi-

cal and Social Science, 1914.
Johnson, William Martin. *Inside of One Hundred Houses*. New York: Curtis, 1897.
Keeler, Charles. *The Simple House*. San Francisco: P. Elder, 1904.
Keith, Max L. *Bungalows and Cottages*. Minneapolis: M. L. Keith, 1909.
Klein, Frederic J. *The House Book*. Peoria, Ill.: J. W. Franks & Sons, 1903.
Ladies' Home Journal. Journal Bungalows. Philadelphia, n.d.
Laughlin, Sarah C., ed. *The Complete Home*. New York: D. Appleton, 1907.
Modern Dwellings with Constructive Details. New York: David Williams, 1907.
Editors of the *National Builder*. *National Builder* catalogue of *Building Designs*. Chicago: Porter, Taylor, 1899.
Newson, John Henry. *Homes of Character*. Cleveland: J. H. Newson, 1913.
Osborne, Charles Francis. *The Family House*. Philadelphia: The Penn Publishing Co., 1910.
The Portfolio of House-Building. Harrisburg and New York: The Suburban Press, 1915.
Price, Charles Matlack. *The Practical Book of Architecture*. Philadelphia: J. B. Lippincott, 1915.
Price, William L., and Frank L. Guild. *Model Homes for Little Money*. Philadelphia: Curtis, 1895.
Priestman, Mabel Tuke. *Art and Economy in Home Decoration*. New York: John Lane, 1908.
———. *Home Decoration*. Philadelphia: The Pennsylvania Publishing Co., 1909.
Quin, Charles William. *The Complete House Builder*. Chicago: M. A. Donohue, ca. 1904.
Quinn, Mary J. *Planning and Furnishing the Home*. New York: Harper's, 1914.
Radford Architectural Company, *The Radford American Homes: 100 House Plans*. New York: Industrial Publication Co., 1903.
———. *The Radford Ideal Homes: 100 House Plans*. Chicago: Radford Architectural Company, 1905.
Reed, Samuel Burrage. *Modern House Plans for Everybody*. New York: Orange Judd, 1900.
Saylor, Henry H. *Bungalows*. New York: McBridge Winston, 1911.
———. *Distinctive Homes of Moderatè Cost*. New York: McBridge, Winston, 1910.

———. *Inexpensive Homes of Individuality*. New York: McBride, Nast, 1912.

Schofield, Alfred Taylor. *The Home Life in Order*. New York: Funk & Wagnalls, 1909.

Editors of *Scientific American*. *Inexpensive American Homes*. New York: 1897.

Shackleton, Robert, and Elizabeth. *Adventures in Home-Making*. Philadelphia: Curtis, 1909.

Sherwin-Williams Paint Company. *Your Home and Its Decoration*. New York: John Lane, 1912.

Sloan, Maurice M. *The Concrete House and Its Construction*. Philadelphia: Association of American Portland Cement Manufacturers, 1912.

Statham, Henry Heathcoate. *Modern Architecture: A Book for Architects and the Public*. New York: Charles Scribner's Sons, 1898.

Stickley, Gustav, *Craftsman Homes*. New York: Craftsman Publishing Co., 1909.

———. *More Craftsman Homes*. New York: Craftsman Publishing Co., 1912.

Suburban Homes with Constructive Details. New York: David Williams Co., 1912.

Taylor, Graham. *Satellite Cities: A Study of Industrial Suburbs*. New York: D. Appleton, 1915.

Thompson, Robert Ellis. *The History of the Dwelling-House and Its Future*. Philadelphia: J. B. Lippincott, 1914.

Vogel, F. Rud. *Das Amerikanische Haus*. Berlin: Verlagbei Ernst Wasmuth, 1910.

Wallick, Ekin. *The Small House for a Moderate Income*. New York: Hearst's International Library Co., 1915.

Wallis, Frank Edwin. *How To Know Architecture: The Human Elements in the Evolution of Styles*. New York: Harper & Bros., 1900.

Ward, Montgomery & Co. *Building Plans of Modern Homes*. Chicago, n.d. [ca. 1912].

Wharton, Edith, and Ogden Codman, Jr., *The Decoration of Houses*. New York: Charles Scribner's Sons, 1897.

Wheeler, Candace. *Principles of Home Decoration, with Practical Examples*. New York: Doubleday, Page, 1903.

White, Charles E., Jr. *Some Western Houses: How to Build a Little House*. Philadelphia: Curtis, 1921.

———. *Successful Houses and How to Build Them*. New York: Macmillan, 1912.

White, Marian A. *Book of the North Shore*. Chicago: J. Harrison

White, 1910.
———. *Second Book of the North Shore*. Chicago: J. Harrison White, 1911.
———. *Book of the Western Suburbs*. Chicago: J. Harrison White, 1912.
Williams, David. *Cement Houses and Private Garages*. New York: David Williams Co., 1912.
de Wolfe, Elsie. *The House in Good Taste*. New York: Century, 1913

Chicago Guidebooks and Histories

Andreas, Alfred Theodore. *History of Chicago*. 3 vols. Chicago: A. T. Andreas, 1884–46.
———. *History of Cook County, Illinois*. Chicago: A. T. Andreas, 1884.
Andrews, Wayne. *Battle for Chicago*. New York: Harcourt, Brace & Co., 1946.
Annals of the Chicago Woman's Club for the First Forty Years of Its Organization, 1876–1916. Chicago: Chicago Woman's Club, 1916.
The Book of Chicago, 1911. Chicago: *Chicago Evening Post*, 1911.
Cain, Louis P. *Sanitation Strategy for a Lakefront Metropolis: The Case of Chicago*. DeKalb, Ill.: Northern Illinois University Press, 1978.
Chamberlin, Everett. *Chicago and Its Suburbs*. Chicago: T. A. Hungerford, 1874.
Chicago Public Works: A History. Chicago: Rand McNally & Co., 1973.
Clark, Herma. *The Elegant Eighties*. Chicago: A. C. McClurg & Co., 1941.
Condit, Carl W. *Chicago, 1910–29: Building, Planning, and Urban Technology*. Chicago: University of Chicago Press, 1973.
Currey, J. Seymour. *Chicago: Its History and Its Builders*. Chicago: S. J. Clarke, 1912.
Destler, Chester McArthur. *Henry Demarest Lloyd and the Empire of Reform*. Philadelphia: University of Pennsylvania Press, 1963.
Duffey, Bernard. *The Chicago Renaissance in American Letters*. East Lansing: Michigan State College Press, 1954.
Duis, Perry R. *Chicago: Creating New Traditions*. Chicago: Chicago Historical Society, 1976.
Duncan, Dalziel Hugh. *Culture and Democracy: The Struggle for Form in Society and Architecture in Chicago and the Middle West during the Life and Times of Louis Sullivan*. Totowa, N.J.: Bedminster Press, 1965.

———. *The Rise of Chicago as a Literary Center from 1885 to 1920.* Totowa, N.J.: Bedminster Press, 1964.

Elazar, Daniel J. *Cities of the Prairie.* New York: Basic Books, 1970.

Ericsson, Henry, in collaboration with Lewis E. Meyers. *Sixty Years a Builder: The Autobiography of Henry Ericsson.* Chicago: A. Kroch & Son, 1942.

Flinn, John J. *Chicago, the Marvelous City of the West.* Chicago: Flinn and Sheppard, 1891.

———. *Standard Guide to Chicago.* Chicago: Standard Guide Co., 1893.

Flower, Benjamin Orange. *Progressive Men, Women, and Movements of the Past Twenty-Five Years.* Boston: New Arena, 1914.

Ginger, Ray. *Altgeld's America: The Lincoln Ideal versus Changing Realities.* New York: Funk & Wagnalls, 1958.

Goodspeed, Thomas Wakefield, *A History of the University of Chicago* Chicago: University of Chicago Press, 1916, 1972.

Hamilton, Henry R. *The Epic of Chicago.* Chicago: Willett, Clark & Co., 1932.

Harper, William Hudson, ed. *Chicago: A History and a Forecast.* Chicago: Chicago Association of Commerce, 1921.

Hayes, Dorsha B., *Chicago: Crossroads of American Enterprise.* New York: Julian Messner, 1944.

Hillman, Arthur, and Robert J. Casey. *Tomorrow's Chicago.* Chicago: University of Chicago Press, 1953.

Historic City: The Settlement of Chicago. Chicago: Department of Development and Planning, 1976.

Horowitz, Helen Lefkowitz. *Culture & the City: Cultural Philanthropy in Chicago from the 1880s to 1917.* Lexington: University Press of Kentucky, 1976.

Hoyt, Homer. *One Hundred Years of Land Values in Chicago.* Chicago: University of Chicago Press, 1933.

Hughes, Everett C. *The Growth of an Institution, the Chicago Real Estate Board.* Chicago: Society for Social Research of the University of Chicago, 1931.

Industrial Chicago. 4 vols. Chicago: Goodspeed Publishing Co., 1891.

Jones, John H., and Fred A. Britten. *A Half Century of Chicago Building.* Chicago: 1910.

Just as God Made Nature: A Story of the North Shore. Chicago: McGuire & Orr, 1911.

Karl, Barry D. *Charles E. Merriam and the Study of Politics.* Chicago: University of Chicago Press, 1977.

King, Andrew J. "Law and Land Use in Chicago: A Pre-history of Modern Zoning." Ph.D. diss., University of Wisconsin, 1976.

Kirkland, Joseph, and Caroline. *The Story of Chicago*. 2 vols. Chicago: Dibble Publishing Co., 1892.
Kleppner, Paul J. *The Cross of Culture: A Social Analysis of Midwestern Politics, 1850–1900*. New York: The Free Press, 1970.
Kogan, Herman, and Lloyd Wendt. *Chicago: A Pictorial History*. New York: E. P. Dutton, 1958.
Mayer, Harold M., and Richard C. Wade. *Chicago: Growth of a Metropolis*. Chicago: University of Chicago Press, 1969.
Monchow, Helen C. *Seventy Years of Real Estate Subdividing in the Region of Chicago*. Studies in the Social Sciences, no. 3. Evanston: Northwestern University Press, 1939.
Montgomery, Royal. *Industrial Relations in the Chicago Building Trades*. Chicago: University of Chicago Press, 1927.
Moses, Hon. John, and Maj. Joseph Kirkland. *The History of Chicago, Illinois*. 2 vols. Chicago and New York: Munsell & Co., 1895.
Nye, Russell B. *Midwestern Progressive Politics: A Historical Study of Its Origins and Development*. East Lansing: Michigan State College Press, 1951.
Philpott, Thomas Lee. *The Slum and the Ghetto: Neighborhood Deterioration and Middle-Class Reform, Chicago 1880–1930*. New York: Oxford University Press, 1978.
Pierce, Bessie Louise. *A History of Chicago*. 3 vols. Chicago: University of Chicago Press, 1937–57.
———, ed. *As Others See Chicago: Impressions of Visitors, 1673–1933*. Chicago: University of Chicago Press, 1933.
Poole, Ernest. *Giants Gone: Men Who Made Chicago*. New York: Whittlesey House, McGraw-Hill, 1943.
Powers, Dorothy E. "History of the Chicago Woman's Club." Ph.D. diss., University of Chicago, 1939.
Ralph, Julian E. *Harper's Chicago and the World's Fair*. New York: Harper & Bros., 1893.
———. *Our Great West*. New York: Harper & Bros., 1893.
Rand, McNally & Co.'s Handy Guide to Chicago. Chicago: 1893.
Randall, Frank. *History of the Development of Building Construction in Chicago*. Urbana: University of Illinois Press, 1949.
Riley, Thomas James. *The Higher Life of Chicago*. Chicago: University of Chicago Press, 1905.
Seeger, Eugen. *Chicago, the Wonder City*. Chicago: G. Godfrey, 1893.
Sennett, Richard. *Families Against the City: Middle-Class Homes of Industrial Chicago, 1872–1890*. New York: Vintage Books, 1970.
Smith, Henry Justin. *Chicago's Great Century, 1833*.
———. *Chicago: A Portrait*. New York: Century, 1931.

Spackman, Barbara Spencer. "The Woman's City Club of Chicago: A Civic Group." Master's thesis, University of Chicago, 1930.
Staley, Eugene. *History of the Illinois State Federation of Labor.* Chicago: University of Chicago Press, 1930.
Storr, Richard J. *Harper's University: The Beginnings.* Chicago: University of Chicago Press, 1966.
Tarr, Joel. *A Study in Boss Politics: William Lorimer of Chicago.* Urbana, Ill., Chicago, and London: University of Illinois Press, 1971.
Wallin, Chad. *The Builders' Story: an Interpretive Record of the Builders' Association of Chicago, Inc.* Chicago: Builders' Association, 1966.
Wheeler, Adele Mitchell, with Marlene Stein Wortman. *The Roads They Made: Women in Illinois History.* Chicago: Charles H. Kerr, 1977.
Winchell, S. R. *A Civic Manual for Chicago, Cook County, and Illinois.* Chicago: A. Flanagan Co., 1910.
Zorbaugh, Harvey Warren. *The Gold Coast and the Slum: A Sociological Study of Chicago's Near North Side.* Chicago: University of Chicago Press, 1929.

Architectural Histories of Chicago

Andrews, Wayne. *Architecture in Chicago and Mid-America.* New York: Harper & Row, 1968.
Block, Jean F. *Hyde Park Houses: An Informal History, 1865–1919.* Chicago: University of Chicago Press, 1978.
Brooks, H. Allen. *The Prairie School: Frank Lloyd Wright and His Midwest Contemporaries.* New York: W. W. Norton, 1976.
———. *Prairie School Architecture: Studies from "The Western Architect."* Toronto: University of Toronto Press, 1975.
Birrell, James. *Walter Burley Griffin.* Brisbane: University of Queensland Press, 1964.
Coles, William A., ed. *Architecture and Society: Selected Essays of Henry Van Brunt.* Cambridge: Harvard University Press, 1969.
Condit, Carl W. *The Chicago School of Architecture: A History of Commercial and Public Building in the Chicago Area, 1875–1925.* Chicago: University of Chicago Press, 1964.
Drury, John. *Old Chicago Houses.* Chicago: University of Chicago Press, 1941, 1975.
Dull, Elizabeth Helsing. "The Architecture of Oak Park, Illinois: 1900–1930." Ph.D. diss. Northwestern University, 1973.

Eaton, Leonard K. *Landscape Artist in America: The Life and Work of Jens Jensen*. Chicago: University of Chicago Press, 1964.

———. *Two Chicago Architects and Their Clients: Frank Lloyd Wright and Howard Van Doren Shaw*. Cambridge: MIT Press, 1969.

Hasbrouck, W. R., ed. *Architectural Essays from the Chicago School, 1900–1909*. Park Forest, Ill.: Prairie School Press, 1967.

———, and Paul Sprague. *A Survey of Historic Architecture of the Village of Oak Park, Illinois*. Oak Park: Landmarks Commission, 1974.

Hines, Thomas S. *Burnham of Chicago: Architect and Planner*. New York: Oxford University Press, 1974.

Hitchcock, Henry-Russell. *In the Nature of Materials: The Buildings of Frank Lloyd Wright, 1887–1941*. New York: Da Capo Press, 1975.

Hoffman, Donald. *The Architecture of John Wellborn Root*. Baltimore: Johns Hopkins University Press, 1973.

———. *The Meanings of Architecture: Buildings and Writings of John Wellborn Root*. New York: Horizon, 1967.

Leonard, Herbert Stewart. "The History of Architecture in Chicago." Master's thesis. University of Chicago, 1934.

Manson, Grant C. *Frank Lloyd Wright to 1910: The First Golden Age*. New York: Reinhold Publishing Co., 1958.

Monroe, Harriet. *John Wellborn Root*. New York and Boston: Houghton, Mifflin, 1896.

Moore, Charles. *Daniel Burnham: Architect-Planner of Cities*. 2 vols. Boston: Houghton-Mifflin, 1921.

Paul, Sherman. *Louis Sullivan: An Architect in American Thought*. Englewood Cliffs, N.J.: Prentice-Hall, 1962.

Peisch, Mark L. *The Chicago School: Early Followers of Sullivan and Wright*. New York: Random House, 1964.

Schuyler, Montgomery. *American Architecture and Other Writings*, ed. William H. Jordy and Ralph Coe. Cambridge: Harvard University Press, 1961.

Sprague, Paul E. *Guide to Frank Lloyd Wright and Prairie School Architecture in Oak Park*. Oak Park, Ill.: Landmarks Commission, 1976.

Tallmadge, Thomas. *Architecture in Old Chicago*. Chicago: University of Chicago Press, 1942.

Twombley, Robert C. *Frank Lloyd Wright: An Interpretive Biography*. New York: Harper & Row, 1973.

Wacker, Charles Henry, and W. D. Moody. *Wacker's Manual for the Plan of Chicago. Municipal Economy*. Chicago: Chicago Plan Commission, 1912.

Wright, Frank Lloyd. *An Autobiography*. New York: Horizon Press, 1977.
———. *A Testament*. New York: Horizon Press, 1957.

Domestic Guides and Domestic Science Texts

Abel, Mary Hinman. *Successful Family Life on the Moderate Income*. Philadelphia: J. B. Lippincott, 1921.
Addams, Jane, et al. *The Child in the City*. Chicago: Blakely Publishing Co., 1911.
Barker, C. Hélène. *Wanted: A Young Woman to Do Housework. Business Principles Applied to Housework*. New York: Moffat, Yard & Co., 1917.
Barnett, Edith A., and H. C. O'Neill. *Primer of Domestic Economy*. New York: Macmillan, 1894.
Beecher, Catharine, and Harriet Beecher Stowe. *The American Woman's Home*. New York: J. B. Ford & Co., 1869.
Beecher, Mrs. Henry Ward. *The Home: How to Make and Keep It*. Minneapolis: Buckeye Publishing Co., 1885.
Bennett, Helen Christine. *American Women in Civic Work*. New York: Dodd, Mead & Co., 1915.
Bevier, Isabel. *The House: Its Plan, Decor and Care* [title varies in succeeding editions]. Chicago: American School of Home Economics, 1904.
———, and Susannah Usher. *The Home Economics Movement*. Boston: Whitcomb & Barrows, 1906.
Bruère, Martha B., and Robert W. *Increasing Home Efficiency*. New York: Macmillan, 1912.
Burbank, Emily. *Woman as Decoration*. New York: Dodd, Mead & Co., 1917.
Busbey, Katherine G. *Home Life in America*. New York: Macmillan, 1910.
Campbell, Helen. *Household Economics: A Course of Lectures in the School of Economics of the University of Wisconsin*. New York: G. P. Putnam's Sons, 1897.
Chavasse, Pye Henry. *Advice to a Mother on the Management of Her Children*. Chicago: Belford, Clark & Co., 1878.
———. *Woman as a Wife and Mother*. Philadelphia: William B. Evans, 1871.
Coolidge, Mary Roberts, *Why Women Are So*. New York: Henry Holt, 1912.
Croly, Jane Cunningham. *The History of the Woman's Club Movement*

in America. New York: H. G. Allen & Co., 1898.
Diaz, Mrs. A. M. *Domestic Problems: Work and Culture in the Household*. Boston: D. Lothrop, 1884.
Dodd, Helen. *The Healthful Farmhouse, by a Farmer's Wife*. Boston: Whitcomb & Barrows, 1911.
Donham, S. Agnes. *Marketing and Housework Manual*. Boston: Little, Brown, 1917.
Eliot, William G., Jr. *Lectures to Young Women*. Boston: Crosby, Nichols & Co., 1880.
Elliott, S. Maria. *Household Hygiene*. Chicago: American School of Home Economics, 1905.
Fernald, James C. *The New Womanhood*. Boston: D. Lothrop, 1891.
Frederick, Christine. *Household Engineering: Scientific Management in the Home*. Chicago: New School of Home Economics, 1915.
———. *The New Housekeeping: Efficiency Studies in Home Management*. New York: Doubleday, 1912.
George, Walter Lionel. *Woman and To-Morrow*. New York: D. Appleton & Co., 1913.
Gilman, Charlotte Perkins. *The Home: Its Work and Influence* . Boston: McClure, Phillips & Co., 1903.
———. *The Man-Made World; or, Our Androcentric Culture*. New York: Charlton Co., 1911.
———. *Women and Economics*. Boston: Small, Maynard, 1898.
Goodnow, Ruby. *The Honest House, Presenting Examples of the Usual*. Philadelphia: *Ladies' Home Journal*, 1914.
Grant, Robert. *Law and the Family*. New York: Charles Scribner's Sons, 1916.
Hard, William. *The Women of Tomorrow*. New York: Baker & Taylor Co., 1911.
Harland, Marion [Mary Virginia Hawes Terhune], ed. *Home Making*. Boston: Hall & Locke, 1911.
———, et al. *Ideal Home Life*. New York: The University Society, 1910.
———, ed. *Some Colonial Homesteads and Their Stories*. New York: G. P. Putnam's Sons, 1897.
———, ed. *Talks upon Practical Subjects*. Chicago and New York: Warner Bros., 1895.
Herrick, Christine Terhune. *Housekeeping Made Easy*. New York: Harper & Bros., 1888.
———. *In City Tents: How to Find, Furnish and Keep a Small Home on Slender Means*. New York: G. P. Putnam's Sons, 1902.
Hewitt, Emma C. *Queen of the Home*. Philadelphia and Chicago: International Publishing Co., 1892.

Hunt, Caroline Louisa. *The Life of Ellen Richards*. Boston: Whitcomb & Barrows, 1912.
Jones, Mrs. C. S., and Henry T. Williams. *Household Elegancies*. New York: Henry T. Williams, 1875.
Kittredge, Mabel. *Housekeeping Notes: How to Keep a Tenement*. New York: Century, 1911.
———. *Practical Homemaking: A Textbook for Young Housekeepers*. New York: Century, 1914.
[Lancaster, Maud]. *Electric Cooking, Heating, Cleaning, etc*. London: Constable & Co., 1914.
Logan, Mrs. John A. *The Home Manual: Everybody's Guide in Social, Domestic, and Business Life*. Boston: A. M. Thayer, 1889.
Marden, Orison Swett. *Woman and Home*. New York: Thomas Y. Crowell, 1915.
Mathews, Shailer, ed. *The Woman Citizen's Library*. 10 vols. Chicago: The Civics Society, 1912–14.
McCracken, Elizabeth. *The Women of America*. New York: Macmillan, 1903.
Melendy, Mary Ries, M.D. *Perfect Womanhood*. Chicago: K. T. Boland, 1903.
———. *Vivilore*. W. R. Vansant, 1904.
[Moore, Augustus]. *The Domestic Blunders of Women, by a Mere Man*. New York: Funk & Wagnalls Co., 1900.
Nearing, Scott, and Nellie. *Woman and Social Progress*. New York: Macmillan, 1912.
Ormsbee, Agnes Bailey. *The House Comfortable*. New York: Harper & Bros., 1892.
Owen, Catherine. *Progressive Housekeeping*. Boston and New York: Houghton Mifflin, 1889.
Parloa, Maria. *Home Economics: A Practical Guide in Every Branch of Housekeeping*. New York: Century, 1898.
———. *Miss Parloa's Kitchen Companion*. Boston: Estes & Lauriat, 1887.
Pattison, Mary [Green]. *The Business of Home Management*. New York: Robert M. McBride & Co., 1918.
———. *The Principles of Domestic Engineering*. New York: Trow Press, 1915.
Paul, F. T. *Domestic Economy*. New York: Longman's, Green, 1894.
Pennell, Elizabeth Robins. *Our House and the People in It*. Boston: Houghton Mifflin, 1910.
Priestman, Mabel Tuke. *Artistic Houses*. Chicago: A. C. McClurg, 1910.
Ravenhill, Alice, and Catherine Schiff, eds. *Household Administra-*

tion: Its Place in the Higher Education of Women. New York: Henry Holt & Co., 1911.
Richards, Ellen H. [Swallow]. *The Art of Right Living*. Boston: Whitcomb & Barrows, 1904.
———. *The Cost of Cleanness*. New York: John Wiley & Sons, 1908.
———. *The Cost of Living as Modified by Sanitary Science*. New York: John Wiley & Sons, 1899.
———. *The Cost of Shelter*. New York: John Wiley & Sons, 1905.
———. *Euthenics, the Science of a Controllable Environment*. Boston: Whitcomb & Barrows, 1910.
———. *Sanitary Science in the Home*. Philadelphia: Journal of the Franklin Institute, 1888.
———. *Sanitation in Daily Life*. Boston: Whitcomb & Barrows, 1910.
———, and Marion Talbot, eds. *Home Sanitation*. Boston: Home Science Publishing Co., 1887.
Richardson, Bertha June. *The Woman Who Spends: A Study of Her Economic Function*. Boston: Whitcomb & Barrows, 1904.
Saleeby, C. W. *Woman and Womanhood: A Serach for Principles*. New York: Mitchell Kennerley, 1911.
Salmon, Lucy Maynard. *Domestic Science*. New York: Macmillan, 1897.
———. *Progress in the Household*. Boston: Houghton Mifflin, 1906.
Sargent, C. E. *Our Home; or, The Key to a Nobler Life*. Springfield, Mass.: W. C. King & Co., 1883.
Sherwood, Mary Elizabeth. *Amenities of Home*. New York: D. Appleton & Co., 1882.
Slattery, Margaret. *The American Girl and Her Community*. Boston and Chicago: Pilgrim Press, 1918.
Taber, C. W. *The Business of the Household*. Philadelphia: J. B. Lippincott, 1918.
Talbot, Marion, and Sophonisba Preston Breckinridge. *The Modern Household*. Boston: Whitcomb & Barrows, 1912.
Terrill, Bertha M. *Household Management*. Chicago: American School of Home Economics, 1907.
———, ed. *The Profession of Home Making: A Condensed Home-Study Course*. Chicago: American School of Home Economics, 1911.
Thomas, William I. *Sex and Society: Studies in the Social Psychology of Sex*. Chicago: University of Chicago Press, 1907.
Editorial Board of the University Society. *The Child Welfare Manual: A Handbook of Child Nature and Nurture for Parents and Teachers*. 2 vols. New York: University Society, 1915.

Van Rensselaer, Martha, Flora Rose, and Helen Canon, eds. *A Manual of Home-Making*. New York: Macmillan, 1919.

Van de Water, Virginia Terhune. *From Kitchen to Garret*. New York: Sturgis & Walton's Young Farmer's Practical Library, 1910.

Westermarck, Edward. *The History of Human Marriage*. 3 vols. New York: Macmillan, 1889.

Wood, Grace, and Emily Burbank. *The Art of Interior Decoration*. New York: Dodd, Mead & Co., 1916.

Woolson, Abba Gould, *Woman in American Society*. Boston: Roberts Bros., 1873.

Wright, Henry C. *The Empire of Mother over the Character and Destiny of the Race*. Boston: B. Marsch, 1870.

Wright, Julia McNair. *The Complete Home; an Encyclopaedia of Domestic Life and Affairs*. Philadelphia, Chicago, etc.: J. C. McCurdy, 1879.

———. *Practical Life; or, Ways and Means for Developing Character and Resources*. Philadelphia and Chicago: J. C. McCurdy, 1881.

INDEX